Gift of the Estate of
Robert (1938-2013)
and Gay Zieger (1938-2013)
October 2013

D1571910

Florida's Working-Class Past

Working in the Americas

UNIVERSITY PRESS OF FLORIDA

Florida A&M University, Tallahassee
Florida Atlantic University, Boca Raton
Florida Gulf Coast University, Ft. Myers
Florida International University, Miami
Florida State University, Tallahassee
New College of Florida, Sarasota
University of Central Florida, Orlando
University of Florida, Gainesville
University of North Florida, Jacksonville
University of South Florida, Tampa
University of West Florida, Pensacola

WORKING IN THE AMERICAS

Edited by Richard Greenwald, Drew University, and Timothy Minchin, LaTrobe University

Working in the Americas is devoted to publishing important works in labor history and working-class studies in the Americas. This series seeks work that uses traditional as well as innovative, interdisciplinary, or transnational approaches. Its focus is the Americas and the lives of its workers.

Florida's Working Class Past: Current Perspectives on Labor, Race, and Gender from Spanish Florida to the New Immigration, edited by Robert Cassanello and Melanie Shell-Weiss (2009)

The New Economy and the Modern South, by Michael Dennis (2009)

Film Noir, American Workers, and Post-War Hollywood, by Dennis Broe (2009)

Americanization in the States: Immigrant Social Welfare Policy, Citizenship, and National Identity in the United States, 1908-1929, by Christina A. Ziegler-McPherson (2009)

Black Labor Migration in Caribbean Guatemala, 1882-1923, by Frederick Douglass Opie (2009)

Heritage University Library
3240 Fort Road
Toppenish, WA 98948

Florida's Working-Class Past

Current Perspectives on Labor, Race, and Gender from Spanish Florida to the New Immigration

EDITED BY

ROBERT CASSANELLO AND MELANIE SHELL-WEISS

Foreword by Richard Greenwald and Timothy Minchin

University Press of Florida
Gainesville/Tallahassee/Tampa/Boca Raton
Pensacola/Orlando/Miami/Jacksonville/Ft. Myers/Sarasota

UNIVERSITY OF
SOUTH FLORIDA

Copyright 2009 by Robert Cassanello and Melanie Shell-Weiss
Printed in the United States of America. This book is printed on Glatfelter
Natures Book, a paper certified under the standards of the Forestry Steward-
ship Council (FSC). It is a recycled stock that contains 30 percent post-
consumer waste and is acid-free.

All rights reserved

13   12   11   10   09   08   6   5   4   3   2   1

Florida's working-class past : current perspectives on labor, race, and gender
from Spanish Florida to the new immigration / edited by Robert Cassanello
and Melanie Shell-Weiss ; foreword by Richard Greenwald and Timothy
Minchin.
p. cm. — (Working in the Americas)
ISBN 978-0-8130-3283-2 (alk. paper)
1. Labor—Florida—History. I. Cassanello, Robert. II. Shell-Weiss, Melanie.
HD8083.F63F467 2008
331.109759—dc22
2008025022

The University Press of Florida is the scholarly publishing agency for the
State University System of Florida, comprising Florida A&M University,
Florida Atlantic University, Florida Gulf Coast University, Florida Interna-
tional University, Florida State University, New College of Florida, Univer-
sity of Central Florida, University of Florida, University of North Florida,
University of South Florida, and University of West Florida.

University Press of Florida
15 Northwest 15th Street
Gainesville, FL 32611–2079
http://www.upf.com

For our parents
Keith and Jeanne, Richard and Marie

Contents

Acronyms

AFL	American Federation of Labor
AIFLD	American Institute for Free Labor Development
BITU	Bustamente Industrial Trade Union
CIO	Congress of Industrial Organizations
CIW	Coalition of Immokalee Workers
CMIU	Cigar Makers' International Union
CPUSA	Communist Party of the United States of America
FBI	Federal Bureau of Investigation
FEPC	U.S. Fair Employment Practices Committee
FSA	Farm Security Administration
FSFL	Florida State Federation of Labor
HERE	Hotel Employees and Restaurant Employees International Union
HUAC	House Un-American Activities Committee
IBT	International Brotherhood of Teamsters
ILA	International Longshoremen's Association
ILGWU	International Ladies' Garment Workers' Union
IUMSWA	Industrial Union of Marine and Shipbuilding Workers of America
LIUNA	Laborers' International Union of North America
MCCS	Miami War Camp Community Service
MST	*Movimento dos Trabalhadores Rurais Sim Terra* (Landless Workers' Movement)
NLRB	National Labor Relations Board
NWLB	National War Labor Board
PNP	People's National Party

SEIU	Service Employees International Union
SFA	Student Farmworker Alliance
STCU	Service Trades Council Union of Orlando
TWU	Transport Workers Union of America
UFCW	United Food and Commercial Workers
UM	University of Miami
UNITE	Union of Needletrades, Industrial, and Textile Employees
UCAPAWA	United Cannery, Agricultural, Packing, and Allied Workers of America
UCW	United Citrus Workers
WFA	War Food Administration

Foreword

As the inaugural volume in the Working in the Americas series, *Florida's Working-Class Past* demonstrates the vibrancy of the field of labor and working-class history. Spanning nearly four centuries, this book offers an opportunity to think regionally, extending beyond the borders of the nation-state and highlighting how states and nations change across time. Less a final word than an invitation to future scholars, it promises to stimulate new interest in Florida's working classes and showcases the type of questions that are revitalizing labor history today.

Labor history has influenced the study of the United States' past since the days in the early twentieth century when economist John R. Commons and the Wisconsin School produced institutional studies of unions. In the early 1960s, "new" labor historians, such as Herbert Gutman, David Montgomery, and Alice Kessler-Harris among others, challenged the Wisconsin School's narrow focus on labor unions and labor relations. These historians saw class through the broader lens of community, race, gender, and the shop-floor struggles of ordinary workers. Their influence informed a generation of historians who wrote brilliant case studies. As a result of their work, we know more about small places such as Troy, New York, and small New England towns in the age of industrialization, women labor organizers, and shop-floor struggles in the railroad and other industries. The force of these histories was their accumulated effect, the layering of case studies building a mountain of evidence for the importance and difficult meaning of class in the United States.

Meanwhile, parallel developments were stimulating interest in labor history across the Americas. Where earlier scholarship had focused primarily on elites, peasants, and the middle class, by 1980 a growing number of historians began studying urban workers and quickly moved labor into the mainstream of Latin American historiography. For the most part, however, this literature developed in isolation from studies being written in the United States and Europe. Even as historians expanded their focus beyond institutions to more broadly explore how culture, politics, ethnicity, and gendered experience transform the lives of the working classes through the next decade, as late as the 1990s most historians working on either end of the hemisphere continued to produce work that used the nation-state as the logical unit of analysis.

Today this is changing. Calls to internationalize how we think about history and the emergence of new fields like borderlands and comparative studies have important implications for historical understandings of class formation and class identity. As a methodology that informs the histories of gender, race, social space, consumerism, and social/economic/public policy, labor history has infiltrated the larger study of national and international histories. Many who do labor history now identify primarily as historians of other subfields. Great labor history is still being done but often as urban history or as some such other field. It is our hope that this series will recapture exciting work in labor history and working-class studies, showcasing innovative, interdisciplinary, and transnational studies that are reinvigorating how we think about working-class history across the Americas.

The series and this first volume recognize the importance of race, gender, and place on the study of work and workers in this state where empires met, underscoring "the international and national developments that have shaped, and been shaped by, the lives of working men and women" (1). In short, this volume reminds us that class still matters.

Richard Greenwald
Timothy Minchin

Acknowledgments

The editors would like to thank all of the contributors to this collection for their work in bringing this book to publication. All have been diligent, professional, and outstanding with every contact. We would also like to thank the Southern Labor Studies Conference. It was at the biennial conferences in Miami (2002) and Birmingham (2004) where many of these authors first met and presented the work that is part of this collection. Very special thanks are due to Alex Lichtenstein and Colin J. Davis, who organized those conferences. Without the support of the fine folks at the University Press of Florida, who believed in the project and were excited about it from day one, this project simply would not have been possible.

David R. Roediger and Steven A. Reich improved the quality of the manuscript immeasurably with their insightful comments and suggestions. We would also like to thank Connie L. Lester, Daniel S. Murphree, Kenneth W. Goings, and Eric Arnesen, who read selected chapters and supplied constructive criticism where needed. Thanks, too, to Cornell University Press, Stephanie Munson, and Cindy Hahamovitch for allowing us to republish "'In America Life Is Given Away': Jamaican Farmworkers and the Making of Agricultural Immigration Policy."

Our greatest debt is owed to our families, most especially our partners, Carlos and Kathleen. Their unflagging support and good humor are a constant source of strength. Without them, this project may have been possible, but it would not have been nearly as enjoyable.

Introduction

The Promise of Florida's Labor History

ROBERT CASSANELLO AND MELANIE SHELL-WEISS

People have always worked. Whether toiling for survival, for oneself, or under the direction of another, voluntarily, by necessity, or by force, labor is a fundamental part of the human experience. As such, it touches upon just about every aspect of community life and throws hierarchies of power into stark relief. Viewed from the perspective of the Florida peninsula, at the southernmost tip of what now is the United States, the essays in this collection explore the history of labor in the United States and Caribbean, highlighting the ways this gaze provides new insights into shifting race and ethnic relations, gender roles, class definitions, and human migration from the Spanish colonial period through the present day. As such, Florida provides a unique window onto the transformation of American labor over the past four centuries, underscoring the international and national developments that have shaped, and been shaped by, the lives of working men and women.

While a growing interest in transnational ties, international migration, gender, race, and ethnic relations has recently stimulated a renewed interest in labor and working-class history, this was not always the case. Neither typically "southern" nor "northern," scholars have struggled with where to classify Florida's highly mobile population. Florida was the place where empires met, Spanish, English, and French. It did not become a state until 1845, nearly three-quarters of a century after the American Revolution. Except for two decades leading up to that time, Florida was under Spanish rule. As such, the patterns of labor relations that developed on the peninsula were different from the British legacy that prevailed across much of the rest of the South. Florida was a slave state, like much of the South. But it was also a frontier region, posing challenges to social control and survival, offering a greater degree of freedom at some times and extreme brutality at others. Like its southern neighbors, Florida industrialized late. Unlike in many northern cities, European laborers played a relatively minor part. Yet it is these same differences that throw the prevailing assumptions of U.S. history and historiography into stark relief, posing new questions and contributing new insights.

In 1925, Thomas Frederick Davis penned one of the first histories of Florida. Like many of the state's residents at that time, Davis was not a native son. Born in Chatham, Virginia, in 1877, Davis was the child of a prominent lawyer who moved his family to Gainesville in 1886 and later served as mayor of the city. Davis grew up in Gainesville and attended the East Florida Seminary. Later he made his career working for the National Weather Bureau in a range of locations from Galveston, Texas, to Curaçao in the West Indies. In 1902, Davis returned to Florida and worked in Jacksonville, where he became especially interested in the state's history, writing first about its climate and later about its people. His third book, *The History of Jacksonville and Vicinity, 1513 to 1924*, was intended to be one of the first comprehensive, single-volume histories of the state of Florida.

While this may have seemed an unlikely professional transition, viewed from the perspective of Florida it is perhaps less surprising. The environment has always shaped Florida's history in important ways. Hurricanes provide but one example. The tropical climate that prevails across the lower portion of the peninsula is another, inspiring all manner of agricultural venture from citrus to sugar, prompting historical comparisons between patterns of forced labor and capitalist development between this mainland U.S. region and its Caribbean neighbors. Geography also frames Florida's history in important ways. Seventeenth-century Florida served as a "buffer zone," separating Spain's colonies to the south from French and British holdings to the north. For these reasons, too, Davis's own experiences working in the West Indies as well as on the U.S. mainland prepared him to explore the history of the region's people.

That history was published at a critical time. By 1925, Florida had begun to slip loose from its agricultural moorings and was slowly becoming a more urbanized, industrial state. Davis's book celebrated this tremendous transition, describing a Florida that began with a glorious colonial experiment and now greeted the modern age like other metropolises across the United States. To illustrate his point, Davis highlighted an 1880 labor uprising in one of Jacksonville's mills, beginning with the company's black workers. "On June 23, 1880, a labor disturbance broke out at Alsop and Clark's mill on East Bay Street near Hogans [*sic*] Creek, among the negro hands who demanded shorter hours of work," Davis wrote. "That night five extra policemen were sworn in and sent to the mill to protect property from firebugs, and on the 25th two more were added. On the 26th Joe Nelson, a negro policeman, was killed by Ben Byrd, one of the negro strikers, and the situation assumed a serious aspect."[1] Davis then cataloged all of the major organizing efforts across the city through 1922, including the city's formal and informal labor actions.

To be sure, Davis was no friend to organized labor. His intent was not to write a labor history. Nor was he particularly empathetic to the indignities experienced by many within Florida's most vulnerable communities. Reconstruction was, in his view, "a distracting influence" that for a time waylaid the state from its modernizing mission. Working-class men and women were more often described as "swindlers," "bunco men," "riff-raff," or "rioters" than as disciplined but disadvantaged folk, worthy of respect and hungry for a better quality of life. But Davis's approach did make clear just how aware Floridians of his day were of the important role played by the workers around them. Davis's work also portrayed a different type of workforce than other published labor histories produced by his contemporaries. For example, economist Richard T. Ely's widely read tome on *The Labor Movement in America*, published in 1886, the same year as the Haymarket Square incident in Chicago, devoted only a single paragraph to black workers. Ely was active in labor circles and felt a special burden to recognize the contributions of those with whom he worked and the political milieu around him. Still, Ely's view of American workers was limited to those in organized labor unions, and he prioritized the experience of workers in urban, industrial settings. In Davis's work, a whole range of citizens were present—from the founders of the city's first chapter of B'nai B'rith, to black churches, social organizations, and strikers, to female wage earners, West Indians, Cubans, Europeans immigrants, Native Americans, and native-born white southerners alike.[2]

John R. Commons's four-volume history of American labor followed a similar course as Ely's, even though it was published over two decades later. Commons's discussion of African American labor was limited to slave labor. At no point were blacks viewed as being part of the mainstream nineteenth-century labor movement.[3] Still Commons, and others who emerged as part of the Wisconsin School of Labor History, pioneered with work on the political economy of workers and corporations, formal negotiations, labor organizing, and union leadership. Despite a special interest in the colonial chapter of urban labor history, Commons also neglected Florida workers in this massive undertaking.[4] Jacksonville was mentioned solely as the site of a wage agreement negotiated by coal miners who gathered there from across the nation in 1924.[5] Not until his later collaborations with Ulrich B. Phillips did Florida come to warrant much of a mention in Commons's studies of slavery or indentured labor in the colonial period. When it did, the volume of documents describing runaway slaves, conditions on Florida's colonial plantations, and the importation of slaves from West Africa and indentured servants from Europe made clear just how extensive and relatively unexplored this history remained.[6]

Unknowingly, then, Davis demonstrated the central role that black workers and black officials played in the denouement of Reconstruction. African American workers organized themselves. Black officials sometimes pitted themselves against black workers. In many respects the mill strikes paralleled events like the acclaimed Homestead Strike at Carnegie Steel of 1892, which was well known to students of the labor movement by 1925; only the race of the principals was different. This difference mattered a great deal, however, for it was also over this time that segregation became increasingly formalized, shaping the lives of workers both inside and outside their workplaces in ways large and small.

Women also played an interesting role in Davis's account. Pointing to the strikes at Southern Bell telephone, Davis described how "the loyal girls in a body turned upon their tormentors, and the people in that locality . . . witnessed the most spectacular exhibition of scratching and hair-pulling ever staged in Jacksonville" when they went out on strike on September 11, 1919.[7] Not until some decades later were women's roles in the labor movement written into the broader historical literature, despite their long-standing presence among the nation's wage workers.

Davis's story also prioritized the movement of people into and out of Florida in a way seldom seen in other works of its day. Calling Jacksonville "the gateway to Florida," Davis centralized the importance of transportation networks both into and out of the city, and the state's desire to draw in tourists, laborers, and immigrants alike, many of whom only remained for a season before leaving the state for other locales, then returned again the following year. In this respect, too, Davis's work embodied the promise and potential of the history of Florida workers and the opportunity to bring these stories into the mainstream of labor and working-class history in America, whatever the myriad limitations of his account.

Labor History in the Postwar Period

Several generations passed before this promise could be fulfilled. William Watson Davis (no relation to Thomas Frederick), a student of William A. Dunning's School of Reconstruction at Columbia University, explored the development of labor negotiations among African Americans, the Freedman's Bureau, and white landowners through the lens of white paternalism.[8] This novel contribution to Reconstruction history set the course for a new focus of analysis that would also not see a response for another half-century. Meanwhile, through the mid-twentieth century, few histories of Florida mentioned labor or the working classes. Labor history, for the most part, centered on the upper midwestern and northeastern steel belt. Those studies that did venture further afield geographically, framed by an interest in populism, agricultural labor, or textiles, seldom mentioned Florida.

Then in the 1960s two landmark bodies of work shifted the types of questions that had predominated across the field. The first was the emergence of the postwar British Marxists. Studies like E. P. Thompson's *The Making of the English Working Class* (1963) emphasized the role of the common British worker as opposed to a narrower concentration on unions and institutional histories. This had a profound effect on scholars working on both sides of the Atlantic.[9] The second was the rise of New Left history. These scholars rejected the "consensus" approach favored by an earlier generation. Consensus historians argued that the history of America was essentially a homogeneous one, and they sought to carry out what historian John Higham famously characterized as "a massive grading operation to smooth over America's social convulsions."[10] To be fair, not all consensus histories were wholly uncritical. Political historians like Richard Hofstadter, for example, while often associated with this school of thought, did not see U.S. history unfolding across an even playing field.[11] Yet to New Left historians even these more critical works evidenced moral neutrality. It was the rejection of this morally neutral stance that set New Left historians apart from earlier generations of scholars and recast American history in more complex ways.

The result was a watershed moment. Herbert Gutman, David Montgomery, Melvyn Dubofsky, and David Brody were among those who marked this new generation of scholars. Long a stepchild of American history, as David Brody noted in 1971, it was in this period that labor history clearly came of age.[12] Influenced by the limitations of the institutional approach to labor history, the need to understand the experience of immigrant workers, managerial control, worker protest, and welfare capitalism, these studies left a lasting mark that continued to inspire historians through the late twentieth century and beyond.

Still, the flowering of the new labor historiography did not produce much new work about labor in Florida. But as scholars took a new interest in history on the margins, the voice of the working class did gain greater prominence in other fields. Joe Martin Richardson was among the first to gain attention by researching the role of the Freedman's Bureau in the state. Examining the labor question over Reconstruction and rejecting the paternalism that framed earlier studies, Richardson chronicled the lives of African Americans in Florida and their transition from slavery to freedom.[13]

Other historians studied workers in more general terms, studying class interests and conflict as Florida industrialized. But few showed interest in the perspective of laborers themselves.[14] J. Wayne Flynt explored the role of radicalism within the labor movement, focusing on how those political ideas shaped a generation of unions and union leadership.[15] Jerrell H. Shofner published a series of articles in the early 1970s cataloging the earliest labor organizing and activities by African Americans in late nineteenth century Florida.[16] At a time when other new labor historians were simply questioning the role of black Americans in the national labor movement and drawing criticism from civil rights activists like Herbert Hill, who served as labor director for the National Association for the Advancement of Colored People, for their failure to acknowledge the deep racial divisions among the working classes, these works proved pioneering in their day.[17]

No area of Florida's labor history received more attention over this time than the cigar makers of Ybor. Like historians working on other groups or industries, those working on cigar makers concentrated on the nature of labor organizing within the immigrant community that grew up in and around Ybor in the late nineteenth and early twentieth centuries. Durward Long explored how cigar makers fit into the larger context of the American labor movement, looking at how workers organized and demanded recognition through protest and demands for closed shops.[18] Compared to the relatively short-lived African American unions that scholars like Flynt and Shofner rescued from obscurity, those founded by Italian and Cuban cigar workers lasted well into the twentieth century. But Long did little to integrate their experience within the larger context of activism across the state or in Latin communities elsewhere in the U.S. North or West. This treatment of Tampa's workers as exceptional left a long legacy emulated by later historians as well.

Others like John C. Appel and Louis A. Pérez Jr. looked to a much greater extent at how these immigrant workers created a sense of community away from their native lands, emphasizing the ties that bound workers and activists across national borders. Appel went as far as to argue in one 1956 journal article that Cuban workers in Tampa inspired the American Federation of Labor to support Cuban independence and to help organize workers on the island as well as on the mainland.[19] Pérez, a Cuban American himself, represented another new voice with American labor history. Writing about the international world in which Cuban migrants lived and moved, he broke new ground with his work on the *lectores* (readers) hired by cigar makers to help them pass the hours spent on the shop floor by listening to novels, plays, and political tracts.[20] Like a growing number of works written about western Mexican and Japanese agricultural laborers and Chinese railroad workers, these studies went a long way toward expanding scholarly interest in the working experiences of non-European immigrants. They also helped to challenge earlier studies of American labor that ended with the borders of the contiguous United States.

In these respects, the studies produced about Tampa and Ybor broke important ground. Nationwide, the leading proponents of the new labor history remained interested in the place of white men in working America, both foreign and native-born. Florida scholars, by contrast, took an early interest in people of color. They also questioned the professed benevolence of whites in and out of the labor movement toward people of color, in much the same way that new labor historians tended to champion the rights of the groups and institutions they studied.

The "New" New Labor History: Race, Class, and Gender in the Late Twentieth Century

In the last two decades of the twentieth century, labor historiography moved well beyond the new labor history to explore the lives of workers in ever more complex ways. Race and gender emerged as two dominant paradigms used by historians to reexamine the lives of American workers. David R. Roediger and Eric Arnesen both addressed the role of race in the labor movement, albeit from different perspectives.[21] Roediger's *Wages of Whiteness* examined how white workers used racial policies to enforce discrimination in the workplace and privileged white workers over black. Arneson analyzed the efforts and obstacles faced by black workers in creating their own unions.

Women's historians like Susan Porter Benson, Mary Jo Buhle, Jacquelyn Dowd Hall, Thomas Dublin, Lisa Fine, Nancy Gabin, Nancy Hewitt, Alice Kessler-Harris, Ruth Milkman, Stephen H. Norwood, and Christine Stansell all looked at ways that gender, particularly femininity, functioned in the workplace.[22] Their work challenged prevailing understandings introduced by the new labor historians by depicting the labor movement warts and all. Whereas white workers were largely the heroes of the new labor history, this generation of scholars emphasized the ways that white workers enacted policies and measures that kept women and people of color from truly integrating into the labor movement. By the early 1990s, calls to centralize and critically examine women and work expanded to include calls for gendered analyses of men's role as well. By the turn of the twenty-first century, a growing number of works demonstrated the importance of sexuality in framing labor and working lives, too.[23]

With this shift, debates about the future of the field proliferated. Some scholars decried the "cacophony of prescriptions for how the field should move."[24] Where they heard cacophony, other scholars heard jazz, pushing for a move away from synthetic narratives toward a multiplicity of perspectives.[25] Many also saw this shift toward identities and culture as a way to bridge divides with other relatively new fields, including African American history, Mexican American history, Asian American history, and gender history.

Regional studies proved one way to frame such cross-field and cross-disciplinary endeavors. This was especially clear within Southern history, which itself enjoyed something of a revival over this period thanks to a growing interest in deindustrialization and sunbelt migrations that were so much a feature of twentieth-century life. Interest in Florida's labor history also proliferated. In 1989, under the leadership of Margaret Gibbons Wilson, a group of scholars working on labor in Florida held a symposium devoted to the subject.[26] Wilson's *Floridians at Work: Yesterday and Today* also was published that year and proved a critical next step in the development of labor studies across the state.[27]

Scholars who had pioneered within this latest generation of labor historians also turned their gaze to Florida. George E. Pozzetta and Gary R. Mormino were the first to comprehensively examine the lives of Ybor's cigar makers.[28] Their book, *The Immigrant World of Ybor City*, showed clearly how the workplace, benevolent societies, and unions featured centrally in the lives of Italians, Cubans, Afro-Cubans, and Spanish laborers across the city. Nancy Hewitt built on their studies with a path-breaking article looking at the ways gender, and masculinity in particular, further shaped patterns of organizing among Latin workers in the late nineteenth and early twentieth centuries.[29]

Robert H. Zieger, whose book *American Workers, American Unions, 1920–1985* (1986) breathed new life into histories of organized labor by integrating that history into the broader streams of U.S. historiography, edited two pioneering collections of new work on southern labor, *Organized Labor in the Twentieth-Century South* (1991) and *Southern Labor in Transition* (1997). They remain some of the best sources for scholarship on Florida's labor history, including chapters by Gilbert Gall on the state's "right to work" legislation, Cindy Hahamovitch on how nonunionized black farmworkers used federal intervention to bargain collectively in the 1930s and 1940s, Alex Lichtenstein on Communists, race, and the Transport Workers Union in Miami, James Sullivan on the 1968 Florida teachers' strike, and Mark Wilkens on masculinity and Tampa firefighters' efforts to exclude women. Bruce Nissen and Guillermo Grenier's studies of the contemporary labor movement in Florida are also notable. The state's transforming population, burgeoning service and tourist economies, and prominent role in national politics and elections made it an especially attractive location for scholars to ask new questions about how race, ethnicity, gender, and deindustrialization had transformed the lives of working Americans during the twentieth century.

For the most part, this work followed two distinct paths. One group of historians built on the perspective of new labor historians. They focused on union histories, organizing, institutional bureaucracies, and statewide labor policies. The second group explored class-based organizing as but one in a host of ways that workers identified themselves, inspired by fields such as slavery, unpaid and domestic labor, and the working histories of professionals within the informal sector.

These paths mirrored larger discussions taking place at the national level. Brian Kelly, Tera W. Hunter, Dana Frank, Eileen Boris, and Venus Green built upon the work of Roediger, Arnesen, and Kessler-Harris and merged their analyses of race with gender in order to learn the ways those identities shaped class-consciousness within the labor movement.[30] A new range of working-class histories that integrated ethnic and class studies with analyses of urban space and international migration rejuvenated the field as well.[31] These new directions prompted the founding of the Labor and Working Class History Association in 1998, a scholarly society geared to bridge both labor history and working-class studies. Although interest in labor history appeared to wane for a time, by the late 1990s it seemed that the field was enjoying something of a renaissance, generating an increasing scope and variety of work across periods, fields, and geographic domains.

Immigration from Europe, the Caribbean, and Latin America and migration to Florida by African Americans and native-born whites from elsewhere in the United States proved an especially fruitful focus of this latest generation of Florida historians. Whereas Ybor first attracted the attention of labor historians, after 1980 a growing number of scholars looked to Miami, which emerged as one of the nation's best-known minority/majority cities.[32] Their models of ethnic unions and mutual aid societies, built on earlier scholarship on Tampa, became such an important way to understand how ethnic workers formed communities that they quickly became a point of reference for new works on labor elsewhere in the United States.[33]

As labor and working-class historians expanded their inquiries from formal labor unions and strikes to include the lives of workers, a number of recent studies focused on slavery. Positioned as a challenge to Julia Floyd Smith's plantation histories, these works gave voice to Florida's enslaved African Americans, as earlier work by Shofner and Richardson had done for the Reconstruction era.[34] Larry Rivers's work on Madison County in the antebellum period directly challenged Smith's paternalistic and indifferent view of slave life and offered a window into the public and private lives of the bonded African Americans. Recent work by Jane G. Landers on blacks in Colonial Spanish Florida demonstrated the ways that enslaved and free African Americans interacted with a wider world and deepened the historical gaze on labor and Florida, too. Edward E. Baptist's *Creating an Old South* also examined the working lives of slaves in Florida's plantation belt, paying particular attention to the multiplicity of their experiences.[35]

But each group of scholars also faced important challenges and limitations. Critics frequently pointed to Florida's exceptionalism, questioning just where the state fit in relation to other southern or northern places. Social scientists countered these criticisms by arguing that Florida was simply a harbinger of national changes to come, positioning the Miami metropolis, for example, as "the city of the future." Historians, concerned not about the future but the past, faced hard questions about their works' generalizability. The result was a greater emphasis on state and local histories rather than on integrating Florida studies into larger national and regional frameworks.

Like American labor history more generally, Florida's labor history remains one of the most diverse and dynamic fields of scholarly inquiry. Recently published works like Paul Ortiz's highly acclaimed *Emancipa-*

tion Betrayed: The Hidden History of Black Organizing and White Violence in Florida from Reconstruction to the Bloody Election of 1920 (2006) and Timothy Minchin's works on the mid- to late twentieth-century southern paper industry address the place of labor, race, and civil rights after the height of the civil rights movement within the context of the transforming Southern workplace. They provide just two examples of what the promise of Florida's labor history may hold.[36] Increasing interest in transnationalism, internationally comparative history, frontiers, and borderlands make Florida an ideal climate for new scholarship as well. Nor has the project to more fully incorporate women, gender, race, and ethnicity into labor studies been completed. A great deal of history remains as yet unwritten and undiscovered.

The purpose of this collection is not to provide a comprehensive overview of Florida labor history but to showcase a sampling of how scholars today are approaching these questions. The essays in this volume span more than four centuries of history, utilize a range of English and non-English sources, and blend a variety of disciplinary approaches. They represent work by young and experienced scholars alike.[37] Taken together they provide an overview of the types of questions and themes that unite current scholars of Florida's labor and the working-class past. While by no means exhaustive, this collection aims to provide a bird's-eye view of the state of the field and to highlight the rich ground for future explorations that Florida provides.

Notes

1. Thomas Frederick Davis, *History of Jacksonville, Florida, and Vicinity, 1513 to 1924* (St. Augustine, Fla.: Press of the Record Company, 1925; reprint, Gainesville: University Press of Florida, 1964), 162.

2. On quotes from Davis, see T. Davis, *History of Jacksonville*, 149 ("distracting influences"), 159–204 ("swindlers," "bunco men," "riff-raff," etc.). See also Richard T. Ely, *The Labor Movement in America* (New York: Thomas Y. Crowell, 1886), 83.

3. John R. Commons, David J. Saposs, Helen L. Sumner, E. B. Mittelman, H. E. Hoagland, John B. Andrews, and Selig Perlman, *History of Labour in the United States*, 4 vols. (New York: Macmillan, 1918; reprint, New York: Augustus M. Kelley, 1966).

4. Ibid., 1:1–87.

5. Ibid., 1:562–63. For more on the Jacksonville Agreement, consult Edmond M. Beame, "The Jacksonville Agreement: Quest for Stability in Coal," *Industrial and Labor Relations Review* 8 (January 1955): 195–203.

6. John R. Commons, Ulrich B. Phillips, Eugene A. Gilmore, Helen L. Sumner, and John B. Andrews, eds., *A Documentary History of American Industrial Society* (Cleve-

land: Arthur H. Clark, 1910; reprint, New York: Russell and Russell, 1958), 1:84, 87, 348–52.

7. T. Davis, *The History of Jacksonville*, 276.

8. William Watson Davis, *The Civil War and Reconstruction in Florida* (New York: Longmans, Green, 1913; reprint, Gainesville: University Press of Florida, 1964), 340–41, 594–97; William A. Dunning, *Reconstruction, Political and Economic, 1865–1877* (New York: Harper and Brothers, 1907; reprint, New York: Harper and Row, 1962), 46.

9. Herbert G. Gutman, *Work, Culture, and Society in Industrializing America* (New York: Vintage Books, 1977), 11.

10. John Higham, "The Cult of American Consensus," *Commentary* 27 (February 1959): 94; John Higham, "Beyond Consensus: The Historian as Moral Critic," *American Historical Review* 67 (April 1962): 618, 620.

11. See Richard Hofstadter, *The American Political Tradition and the Men Who Made It* (New York: A. Knopf, 1948). Other prominent historians whose work on American capitalism garnered critical responses from New Labor Historians included Daniel Boorstin, Louis Hartz, and David Potter. See Daniel Boorstin, *The Genius of American Politics* (Chicago: University of Chicago Press, 1953); Louis Hartz, *The Liberal Tradition in America* (New York: Harcourt and Brace, 1955); David Potter, *People of Plenty: Economic Abundance and the American Character* (Chicago: University of Chicago Press, 1954).

12. David Brody, *Workers in Industrial America: Essays on the Twentieth-Century Struggle* (New York: Oxford University Press, 1980). See also Melvyn Dubofsky, *We Shall Be All: A History of the Industrial Workers of the World* (Chicago: Quadrangle Books, 1969); David Montgomery, *Beyond Equality: Labor and the Radical Republicans, 1862–1872* (New York: Knopf, 1967). The impact of Brody's work has been especially long-lived. See "Symposium on David Brody, Steelworkers in America: The Nonunion Era, and the Beginnings of the 'New Labor History,'" *Labor History* 34 (Summer 1993): 457–69.

13. Joe Martin Richardson, *The Negro in the Reconstruction of Florida, 1865–1877* (Tallahassee: Florida State University Press, 1965); Joe Martin Richardson, "The Freedmen's Bureau and Negro Labor in Florida," *Florida Historical Quarterly* 39 (Fall 1960): 176–84.

14. Arch Fredric Blakey, *The Florida Phosphate Industry: A History of the Development and Use of a Vital Mineral* (Cambridge: Harvard University Press, 1973), 61–75; Edward K. Eckert, "Contract Labor in Florida during Reconstruction," *Florida Historical Quarterly* 47 (Summer 1968): 34–50; Richard J. Amundson, "Henry S. Sanford and Labor Problems in the Florida Orange Industry," *Florida Historical Quarterly* 43 (Winter 1965): 229–43.

15. Wayne Flynt, "Pensacola Labor Problems and Political Radicalism, 1908," *Florida Historical Quarterly* 43 (Spring 1965): 315–32; Wayne Flynt, "Florida Labor and Political Radicalism, 1919–1920," *Labor History* 9 (Winter 1968): 73–90.

16. Jerrell H. Shofner, "The Pensacola Workingman's Association: A Militant Negro Labor Union during Reconstruction," *Labor History* 13 (Fall 1972): 555–59; Jerrell H. Shofner, "The Labor League of Jacksonville: A Negro Union and White Strikebreakers,"

Florida Historical Quarterly 50 (Winter 1972): 278–82; Jerrell H. Shofner, "Militant Negro Laborers in Reconstruction Florida," *Journal of Southern History* 39 (Summer 1973): 397–408; Jerrell H. Shofner, "Negro Laborers and the Forest Industries in Reconstruction Florida," *Journal of Forest History* 19 (Fall 1975): 180–91.

17. Hill served as labor director for the NAACP from 1951 until 1977 when he left to join the Afro-American Studies Department and the Industrial Relations Program at the University of Wisconsin, Madison. For Hill's critique of midcentury labor unions, see Herbert Hill, "Myth-making as Labor History: Herbert Gutman and the United Mine Workers of America," *International Journal of Politics, Culture, and Society* 2 (1988): 132–200.

18. Durward Long, "'La Resistencia': Tampa's Immigrant Labor Union," *Labor History* 6 (Summer 1965): 193–213; Durward Long, "The Open-Closed Shop Battle in Tampa's Cigar Industry, 1919–1921," *Florida Historical Quarterly* 47 (Fall 1968): 101–21; Durward Long, "Labor Relations in the Tampa Cigar Industry, 1885–1911," *Labor History* 12 (Fall 1971): 551–59.

19. John C. Appel, "The Unionization of Florida Cigarmakers and the Coming of the War with Spain," *Hispanic American Historical Review* 36 (Winter 1956): 38–49.

20. Louis A. Pérez Jr., "Reminiscences of a Lector: Cuban Cigar Workers in Tampa," *Florida Historical Quarterly* 53 (Spring 1975): 443–49.

21. David R. Roediger, *The Wages of Whiteness: Race and the Making of the American Working Class* (New York: Verso, 1991); Eric Arnesen, *Waterfront Workers of New Orleans: Race, Class, and Politics, 1863–1923* (New York: Oxford University Press, 1991).

22. Susan Porter Benson, *Counter Cultures: Saleswomen, Managers, and Customers in American Department Stores, 1890–1940* (Urbana: University of Illinois Press, 1986); Mary Jo Buhle, *Women and American Socialism, 1870–1920* (Urbana: University of Illinois Press, 1983); Thomas Dublin, *Women at Work: The Transformation of Work and Community in Lowell, Massachusetts, 1826–1860* (New York: Columbia University Press, 1979); Lisa Fine, *The Souls of the Skyscrapers: Female Clerical Workers in Chicago, 1870–1930* (Philadelphia: Temple University Press, 1990); Jacquelyn Dowd Hall et al., *Like a Family: The Making of a Southern Cotton Mill World* (Chapel Hill: University of North Carolina Press, 1987); Alice Kessler-Harris, *Women Have Always Worked: A Historical Overview* (Old Westbury, N.Y.: Feminist Press, 1981); Nancy Gabin, *Feminism in the Labor Movement: Women and the United Auto Workers, 1935–1975* (Ithaca, N.Y.: Cornell University Press, 1990); Ruth Milkman, *Gender at Work: The Dynamics of Job Segregation by Sex during World War II* (Urbana: University of Illinois Press, 1987); J. Carroll Moody and Alice Kessler-Harris, eds., *Perspectives on American Labor History: The Problems of Synthesis* (DeKalb: Northern Illinois University Press, 1989); Stephen H. Norwood, *Labor's Flaming Youth: Telephone Operators and Worker Militancy, 1878–1923* (Urbana: University of Illinois Press, 1990); Christine Stansell, *City of Women: Sex and Class in New York, 1789–1860* (New York: Knopf, 1986).

23. Ava Baron, ed., *Work Engendered: Toward a New History of American Labor* (Ithaca, N.Y.: Cornell University Press, 1991); Eileen Boris, "From Gender to Racialized Gender: Laboring Bodies That Matter," *International Labor and Working-Class History* 63 (2002): 9–13; Kathleen A. Brown and Elizabeth Faue, "Revolutionary Desire: Rede-

fining the Politics of Sexuality among American Radicals, 1919–1945," in *Sexual Borderlands: Essays in the History of Sexuality*, ed. Sharon Ullman and Kathleen Kennedy (Columbus: Ohio State University, 2003); Elizabeth Faue, *Community of Suffering and Struggle: Women, Men, and the Labor Movement in Minneapolis, 1915–1945* (Chapel Hill: University of North Carolina Press, 1991); Donna Gabaccia, *From the Other Side: Women, Gender, and Immigrant Life in the United States, 1820–1990* (Bloomington: Indiana University Press, 1994).

24. David Brody, "Reconciling the Old Labor History and the New," *Pacific Historical Review* 62 (February 1993): 2.

25. Evelyn Brooks Higginbotham, "African American Women's History and the Metalanguage of Race," *Signs* 17 (1992): 251–74.

26. Margaret Gibbons Wilson, ed., *Florida's Labor History Symposium (November 18, 1989): Proceedings*, 2 vols. (Miami: Florida International University, Center for Labor Research and Studies, 1991).

27. Margaret Gibbons Wilson, *Floridians at Work: Yesterday and Today* (Atlanta: Mercer University Press, 1989).

28. George E. Pozzetta, "A *Padrone* Looks at Florida: Labor Recruiting and the Florida East Coast Railway," *Florida Historical Quarterly* 54 (Summer 1975): 74–84, Gary R. Mormino and George E. Pozzetta, *The Immigrant World of Ybor City: Italians and Their Latin Neighbors in Tampa, 1885–1985* (Urbana: University of Illinois Press, 1987); Gary R. Mormino and George E. Pozzetta, "'The Reader Lights the Candle': Cuban and Florida Cigar Workers' Oral Tradition," *Labor's Heritage* 5 (Winter 1993): 4–27; Gary R. Mormino, and George E. Pozzetta, "Immigrant Women in Tampa: The Italian Experience, 1890–1930," *Florida Historical Quarterly* 61 (Winter 1983): 296–312; Gary R. Mormino, "Tampa and the New Urban South: The Weight Strike of 1899," *Florida Historical Quarterly* 60 (Winter 1982): 337–56.

29. Nancy Hewitt, "'The Voice of Virile Male Labor': Militancy, Community Solidarity, and Gender Identity among Tampa's Latin Workers, 1880–1921," in *Work Engendered: Toward a New History of American Labor*, ed. Ava Baron (Ithaca, N.Y.: Cornell University Press, 1991), 142–67. See also Nancy Hewitt, *Southern Discomfort: Women's Activism in Tampa, Florida, 1880–1920s* (Urbana: University of Illinois Press, 2001).

30. Brian Kelly, *Race, Class, and Power in the Alabama Coalfields, 1908–21* (Urbana: University of Illinois Press, 2001); Tera W. Hunter, *To 'Joy My Freedom: Southern Black Women's Lives and Labors after the Civil War* (Cambridge: Harvard University Press, 1997); Dana Frank, "White Working-Class Women and the Race Question," *International Labor and Working-Class History* 54 (Fall 1998): 80–102; Boris, "From Gender to Racialized Gender"; Venus Green, *Race on the Line: Gender, Labor, and Technology in the Bell System, 1880–1980* (Durham, N.C.: Duke University Press, 2001).

31. Lizabeth Cohen, *Making a New Deal: Industrial Workers in Chicago, 1919–1939* (New York: Cambridge University Press, 1990); Elizabeth Faue, ed., "Special Issue: The Working Classes and Public Space," *Social Science History* 24 (Spring 2000); Allen J. Scott, *Metropolis: From the Division of Labor to Urban Form* (Berkeley: University of California Press, 1988).

32. Gerald E. Poyo, "The Impact of Cuban and Spanish Workers on Labor Organiz-

ing in Florida, 1870–1900," *Journal of American Ethnic History* 5 (Spring 1986): 46–63; Andy Banks and Guillermo Grenier, "Apartheid in Miami: Transit Workers Challenge the System," *Labor Research Review* 10 (1987): 46–60; Howard Johnson, "Bahamian Labor Migration to Florida in the Late Nineteenth and Early Twentieth Centuries," *International Migration Review* 22 (Winter 1988): 84–103; Robert N. Lauriault, "From Can't to Can't: The North Florida Turpentine Camp, 1900–1950," *Florida Historical Quarterly* 67 (Winter 1989): 310–28; David Card, "The Impact of the Mariel Boatlift on the Miami Labor Market," *Industrial and Labor Relations Review* 43 (Spring 1990): 245–57; Guillermo J. Grenier, "Ethnic Solidarity and the Cuban-American Labor Movement in Dade County," *Cuban Studies* 20 (1990): 29–48; Alex Stepick, "The Haitian Informal Sector in Miami," *City & Society* 5 (Winter 1991): 10–22; Charles H. Wood and Terry L. McCoy, "Migration Remittances and Development: A Study of Caribbean Cane Cutters in Florida," *International Migration Review* 19 (Spring 1985): 251–77; Bruce Nissen and Guillermo Grenier, "Local Union Relations with Immigrants: The Case of South Florida," *Labor Studies Journal* 26 (Spring 2001): 76–97.

33. The impact of immigration from elsewhere in the Western Hemisphere to southern cities over the past two decades has particularly inspired many new scholars to reexamine labor and race in the twentieth-century South. See, for example, Leon Fink, *The Maya of Morganton: Work and Community in the Nuevo New South* (Chapel Hill: University of North Carolina Press, 2003).

34. Julia Floyd Smith, "Slave Trading in Antebellum Florida," *Florida Historical Quarterly* 50 (Winter 1972): 252–61; Julia Floyd Smith, "Cotton and the Factorage System in Antebellum Florida," *Florida Historical Quarterly* 49 (Summer 1970): 36–48; Julia Floyd Smith, *Slavery and Plantation Growth in Antebellum Florida, 1821–1860* (Gainesville: University Press of Florida, 1973); Larry Eugene Rivers, "Madison County, Florida, 1830 to 1860: A Case Study in Land, Labor, and Prosperity," *Journal of Negro History* 78 (Fall 1993): 233–44; Christopher E. Linsin, "Skilled Labor in Florida: 1850–1860," *Florida Historical Quarterly* 75 (Fall 1996): 183–96.

35. Selected works include Jane G. Landers, "Transforming Bondsmen into Vassals: Arming the Slaves in Colonial Spanish America," in *Arming Slaves in World History*, ed. Philip Morgan and Christopher Brown (New Haven: Yale University Press, 2006), 120–45; Jane G. Landers, "Africans and Indians on the Spanish Southeastern Frontier," *Black and Red: African-Native Relations in Colonial Latin America*, ed. Matthew Restall (Albuquerque: University of New Mexico Press, 2005), 53–80; Jane G. Landers, "Social Control on Spain's Contested Florida Frontier," in *Choice, Persuasion, and Coercion: Social Control on Spain's North American Frontiers*, ed. Jesús F. de la Teja and Ross Frank (Albuquerque: University of New Mexico Press, 2005), 27–48; Edward E. Baptist, *Creating an Old South: Middle Florida's Plantation Frontier before the Civil War* (Chapel Hill: University of North Carolina Press, 2002), 61–89, 191–218.

36. Paul Ortiz, *Emancipation Betrayed: The Hidden History of Black Organizing and White Violence in Florida from Reconstruction to the Bloody Election of 1920* (Berkeley: University of California Press, 2005); Timothy J. Minchin, *The Color of Work: The Struggle for Civil Rights in the Southern Paper Industry, 1945–1980* (Chapel Hill: University of North Carolina Press, 2001); Timothy J. Minchin, *Fighting against the Odds: A History*

of Southern Labor since World War II (Gainesville: University Press of Florida, 2006); Timothy J. Minchin, "'There Were Two Jobs in St. Joe Paper Company, a Black Job and a White Job': The Struggle for Civil Rights in a North Florida Paper Mill Community, 1938–1990," *Florida Historical Quarterly* 78 (Winter 2000): 331–59.

37. A sampling of related published works by the authors in this collection includes Edward E. Baptist, *Creating an Old South: Middle Florida's Plantation Frontier before the Civil War* (Chapel Hill: University of North Carolina Press, 2002); Robert Cassanello, "Violence, Racial Etiquette, and African American Working-Class Infrapolitics in Jacksonville during World War I," *Florida Historical Quarterly* 82 (Spring 2003): 155–69; Thomas A. Castillo, "Miami's Hidden Labor History," *Florida Historical Quarterly* 82 (Spring 2004): 438–67; Cindy Hahamovitch, *The Fruits of Their Labor: Atlantic Coast Farmworkers and the Making of Migrant Poverty, 1870–1945* (Chapel Hill: University of North Carolina Press, 1997); Alex Lichtenstein, "Putting Labor's House in Order: The Transport Workers Union and Labor Anti-Communism in Miami during the 1940s," *Labor History* 39 (Winter 1998): 7–23; Alex Lichtenstein, *Twice the Work of Free Labor: The Political Economy of Convict Labor in the New South* (New York: Verso, 1996); Alex Lichtenstein, "In the Shade of the Lenin Oak: 'Colonel' Raymond Robins, Senator Claude Pepper, and the Cold War," *American Communist History* 3 (December 2004): 185–214; Alex Lichtenstein, *Trouble in Paradise: Labor Radicalism, Race Relations, and Anticommunism in Florida, 1940–1960* (Ithaca, N.Y.: Cornell University Press, forthcoming); Melanie Shell-Weiss, "Coming North to the South: Migration, Labor, and City Building in Twentieth-Century Miami," *Florida Historical Quarterly* 84 (Summer 2005): 79–99; Melanie Shell-Weiss, *Coming to Miami: A Social History* (Gainesville: University Press of Florida, 2009); Brent R. Weisman, "The Origins of the Seminole Plantation System and Its Role in Florida's Colonial Economy," *Colonial Plantations and Economy of Florida* (Gainesville: University Press of Florida, 2000); Brent R. Weisman, *Like Beads on a String: A Cultural History of the Seminole Indians in North Peninsular Florida* (Tuscaloosa: University of Alabama Press, 1989).

1

St. Augustine's Stomach

Corn and Indian Tribute Labor in Spanish Florida

TAMARA SPIKE

In 1659, in a letter to the king, Florida governor Alonso de Aránguiz y Cortés described the relationship between Florida's Indian population and the presidio of St. Augustine. The labor of the Indians, and that of the Apalachee in particular, he said, was absolutely necessary for the well-being and continued existence of the colony. For decades, Florida's Indians had been traveling to St. Augustine to sow and reap a field of corn that fed, among others, the city's infantry unit. The colony also bought surplus corn from Apalachee and other mission provinces to supplement the corn raised locally. This corn and the Indian labor that produced it were so critical to St. Augustine, he concluded, that if it "were ever lacking, we would have to depopulate this presidio."[1]

Aránguiz y Cortés's dire predictions of the complete failure of the colony without the labor of Indians may seem exaggerated. Yet in actuality, it was something of an understatement. Spanish Florida relied on Indians for service, construction, and the defense of the colony itself. Indians fed the presidio and also supplied service to many Spanish households and all of the religious missions. Indians constructed many of Florida's public works, including defensive structures like the Castillo de San Marcos, St. Augustine's fort, and the San Marcos blockhouse. Residents of the Florida missions built all of the buildings found at each of the *doctrinas*. Missions that lay close to the city, like mission Nombre de Díos, provided an early-warning system of terrestrial attacks. In times of crisis, the governor called out the Indian militia to reinforce Florida's infantry. Indians ran the many ferries across the rivers on Florida's Camino Real, the road running from St. Augustine to Apalachee. In short, Spanish Florida could not have functioned, or even existed, without Indian laborers.

In monetary terms, Florida was a failure. The colony never managed to produce a profit for the Crown. Instead, it relied on a yearly stipend, the *situado*, to support its continued existence. Florida was, however, extremely important strategically. Located at the periphery of the Spanish empire, Florida provided a buffer zone between the rich holdings of the more southerly Spanish empire and intruding European holdings to the north. The Spanish Crown had no choice but to maintain the struggling colony. A constant stream of letters flowed from St. Augustine to Spain, complaining of poverty, harsh conditions, and impending starvation in the settlement. Certainly some of the complaints were exaggerated, crafted to leverage as many resources as possible from the Crown. But much of it was true. Spanish Florida existed on the edge in more ways than just its geographic location. Spanish residents at St. Augustine, the primary settlement of the colony, could not even reliably feed themselves. Instead, St. Augustine relied on corn grown by Florida's Indian population. This chapter examines this most important facet of the relationship of labor between Florida's Indian and Spanish residents: the production of food.

The Tribute Labor System

Spanish demands for the labor of Florida's Indians, especially their demand for foodstuffs, capitalized on a prehistoric system that exempted the highest strata of society from doing manual labor. Among the Timucua, members of the White Deer clan were of the highest social rank. Tribal leaders, or *holatas*, later called *caciques* by the Spanish, were derived from this lineage.[2] Caciques and their advisors, or *principales*, were provided for through the tribute labor of lower classes that performed agricultural work to support them.

The tribute labor system was based around the cultivation of agricultural fields called *sabanas*, which were held for the village as a whole by the lineage of the cacique. The cacique granted the right of use of a sabana to individual matrilineages. Each lineage worked enough land to provide for its extended family. In return for the use of this land, the commoners of the village worked several sabanas for high-ranking individuals of the village. Sabanas were worked for the head cacique and his lineage, for the shamans of the village, and for other minor principales and public officials, all of whom were exempted from manual labor themselves.[3]

In addition to the tribute labor in the sabanas, physical tribute items, most often in the form of food, were also paid to the cacique. Commoners brought the cacique and other important residents of the village a share of what they gathered, hunted, and fished.[4] Bishop Gabriel Díaz Vara Calderón recorded the wide disparity in the diets of different social classes of the Timucua during his 1674 *visita* to Florida. The basic diet of the mission Indians, he observed, consisted of *gacha*, a stew made with maize, ashes, squash, and kidney beans. Díaz noted that the more well-to-do Indians supplemented their diets with fish and game.[5] A 1681 tribute list for the Mocama province includes bear fat, deerskins, acorns, and palmetto berries.[6] Tribute labor in the sabanas produced corn, beans, and squash. But tribute in the form of food—gifts from hunting and gathering—rounded out the diet and supplied the remaining dietary needs of the caciques and other high-status individuals.

Items from the hunt were also included in tribute. The hide of the first deer killed was given to the village shaman, who blessed the arrows used. Fray Alonso de Jesús observed that many of the skins of the animals were given to the principal cacique and other lesser caciques as gifts by their subjects in "recognition of the sovereignty and majesty of their superior" and in payment for land use. Bishop Díaz Vara Calderón also stated that many of the skins were taken by the principal cacique after the hunt as part of his rightful share of the proceeds of the hunt. During the mission era, these forms of tribute not only continued but were also extended under the Spanish to include additional demands, making the tribute burdens heavier than ever before.[7]

The earliest Spanish demands for Indian labor fit in quite well with pre-contact labor patterns. As missions were set up, the friars were incorporated into village hierarchies. Like the caciques, friars received tribute labor as the low-ranking matrilineages worked a sabana on his behalf. A second field was planted for the mission church. Food grown in this field supported the Indians who served in the church offices of *fiscal* and *sacristan*. Funds from the sale of surplus corn from this field went to beautify and ornament the mission.[8]

In some cases, other Spaniards also directly benefited from the sabana system. When Spanish soldiers were garrisoned at some Florida missions, additional fields were planted. Unlike the labor that went toward supporting the friars and mission, which mirrored the traditional labor tribute system almost exactly, Florida Indians who worked in the fields on the soldiers' behalf were paid a small wage. Each person who participated in the harvest received four hoes as payment. Florida Indians also seem to have given soldiers many items at no cost whatsoever. Most revolved around food in one form or another: deer meat, shellfish, firewood, cassina leaves for the tea called "black drink," as well as ceramic vessels of many kinds that were used to prepare meals. Unlike the tribute paid to the caciques and friars, a reciprocal gift, often of trade items such as cloth or tools, was usually expected in return for these items. The difference in this relationship between Indians and friars, and Indians and soldiers, notes anthropologist John Worth, is telling. Although friars and soldiers each received much the same labor and goods from Indian laborers, friars were incorporated into native society, effectively becoming part of a so-called Republic of Indians. Soldiers remained on the outside, representatives of the Republic of Spaniards.[9]

Other Spaniards who lived in the missions, most of them high-status individuals, also expected Indians to feed them and prepare their food. A 1699 letter to the king from Don Patrício, cacique of Ivitachuo, and Don Andrés, cacique of San Luis, states that Juana Caterina, wife of deputy Diego Florencia, "caused the village to furnish six Indian women for the grinding [of corn] every day without payment for their work." Juana Caterina also demanded that a pitcher of milk be delivered to her house each day and that fish be brought on Friday. One week when the fish were not delivered, she humiliated the cacique by slapping him twice across the face.[10]

From the earliest days of the missions, demands for tribute in corn came from St. Augustine, which was already having trouble feeding itself. Beginning in 1595, the Spanish governor imposed a head tax on the missions of Guale that required every married male Indian to pay one *arroba*, or about 25 pounds, of corn. By 1681, this tribute payment was extended to missions in other provinces as well. Together they brought some 12,000 to 13,000 pounds of corn into St. Augustine each year.[11] Still, obtaining a regular and reliable supply of food for the presidio remained difficult. Letters complaining about the insufficiency of rations granted to the soldiers by the crown, the inability of the small situado to pay salaries so that the residents of Florida could feed their families, and the scarcity of Spanish foods like wine and flour began flowing back to Spain on a regular basis, even in the earliest days of the colony.[12] Spaniards were left to rely almost entirely on Florida's Indians for their food.

By 1600, direct tribute in the form of corn was replaced by a labor draft, a more indirect form of tribute. In response to a 1597 rebellion in the province of Guale, Florida *factor* Alonso de las Alas noted that Governor Gonzalo Méndes de Canço had obliged "some of the most important caciques of that province [to] come to this presidio with other Indians, and they have helped to cultivate the fields of the people of this presidio." This practice quickly spread to include all Florida mission provinces and proved to be much more effective in supplying St. Augustine with food; it was ultimately far cheaper to feed and house the Indian laborers than to ship food into St. Augustine. Bringing workers into St. Augustine also greatly increased local agricultural productivity, which previously had been negligible because the surrounding Indian populations had been so severely depopulated. Under the new system, the corn crop increased tremendously.[13]

The new labor draft system supplied about three hundred workers annually to St. Augustine. About fifty came from the province of Guale, fifty from Timucua, and two hundred from the more populous province of Apalachee. The numbers of workers appear to have varied from year to year, judging from internal population figures supplied by the Franciscans. All laborers were required to be unmarried men. Each village had to supply a certain number of laborers for the Crown. Timucuan labor practices also dictated that all of the men who served in the labor draft were of lower-status lineages.

Workers were expected to arrive in St. Augustine by March, in time for the spring planting. Laborers from Apalachee province were dismissed at the end of June after four months of service. Those from Timucua and Guale remained until the end of September. As John Worth has observed, if one calculates the total man-hours worked, despite the different lengths of service, the total labor required of these workers ensures that they all put in roughly the same amount of work. Nevertheless, the labor draft was certainly disproportionally taxing for the smaller provinces, since they had fewer numbers of men to spare. For the workers who had to remain away from home for the much longer period of time, the personal and social costs were also certainly much greater.[14]

In return for the labor of their people, Florida's caciques expected gifts. Typically these were given at the beginning of the term of a new governor. When the new governor arrived in Florida, the caciques journeyed to St. Augustine to reaffirm their loyalty to the Crown. Some came "with the news" of the provinces and to economically support the *repartimiento* (tribute) workers who fell sick during their labor in St. Augustine.[15] In return they were given gifts recognizing the importance of their people's labor to the Crown. Over time, a fund that became known as the *gastos de indios*, or the Indian fund, developed as a permanent part of the yearly situado sent to Florida and was used to purchase goods for gifting. Brightly colored cloth was a favorite of the caciques.[16] Other items included tools and flour. By 1615, so much money was being spent on the Indian fund that the Crown imposed a maximum yearly spending limit of 1,500 *ducados*, a limit that remained in place until the Spanish evacuation of Florida in 1763 but was routinely exceeded nonetheless.[17]

Even after the labor draft was implemented, however, food shortages in St. Augustine continued. One particularly dire example was penned by Pablo de Hita Salazar upon his arrival as the new governor of Florida. In a report sent to the king, Salazar noted that the need for food in St. Augustine was so great that "families were obliged to go into the woods and hunt for roots to keep themselves from starvation."[18] The labor draft improved the amount of food available in the royal warehouse, but it was still not able to fill it. To supplement the corn from the repartimiento labor, soldiers planted and raised corn in their own fields. In a letter sent to Governor Reyes y Borjas of Florida in February 1670, the king rebuked him for making the soldiers cut timber, unload ships, and perform other tasks that did not fall within their line of duty, thereby "taking them from their labor of planting corn, the principal subsistence for themselves and their families, causing them to lose their crops and suffer hunger."[19]

In fact, the Spanish government of Florida not only demanded that Florida Indians work fields of corn for the presidio each year, but also required them to bring any surplus corn from the missions as well as from Florida Indians who did not live within the mission system. This practice began as early as 1595. Documentation from the seventeenth century shows that of the Florida mission provinces, the Apalachee, which was the most populous, was also the most important source of surplus corn for the presidio.[20]

From the perspective of the mission friars, missions benefited from the sale of surplus corn as well. Frequently, proceeds from selling corn were used to buy ornaments for their churches. In one letter from 1681, Franciscan friars noted that the harvest of the sabanas "remedies the lack of ornaments and necessary things for divine worship." Franciscans were also able to sell their surplus corn in exchange for other religious goods obtained through the situado.[21] Securing the proper ornaments and keeping a good supply of the objects necessary for performing the sacraments was a great concern to the Florida Franciscans, one that too often proved impossible. During his 1542 *visita* to the province, Bishop Juan de las Cabezas Altimirano noted that the Florida missions and their surrounding native communities were both so poor that they were unable to supply the wax needed for confirmations, making it necessary for him to supply it himself.[22] The distance between missions was also so great that it was difficult for friars to transport the sacramental ornaments from place to place, making the need for these objects at individual missions even greater.[23] Although the friars were supposed to be paid out of the situado, funds often went unpaid. These shortfalls resulted in letters to the Crown, requesting back pay so that friars could purchase the "things necessary to the Divine Cult."[24] A comparison of the inventory of church ornaments from Florida in 1681 with an inventory of the ornaments from the province of Apalachee in 1704 shows that Apalachee missions owned a wide variety of ornaments and vestments over this period.[25]

Ritual Practices and the Developing Labor System

Unlike the province of Apalachee, Timucua was never a great source of surplus corn. But the province provided an even more valuable resource: it served as the primary conduit through which Indian repartimiento labor and surplus corn traveled.[26] Examining how contact with the Franciscans reshaped long-standing ritual practices, then, is critical to understanding the tribute labor system that followed. Timucua was one of the first areas to be missionized by the Spanish. It appears that decades before the first Franciscan friars were sent to Apalachee in 1633, the Franciscans of the Timucua province were making a concerted effort to secure a surplus of corn on their missions. These efforts are highlighted in the 1613 Timucua confessional for first fruits rituals and food taboos, where supplying surplus corn emerges as one of the most prevalent, if unlikely, themes. The preoccupation of this confessional with food is most unusual. Confessionals drawn from other provinces all over the hemisphere during this same period show no such comparable concern with food or food rituals. Rather, when questions about food in other provinces did arise, they tended to focus on questions about eating meat during Lent or not fasting on holy days, not on tribute payments. The Timucua confessional is most unusual in this regard.[27]

The many different ceremonies that commemorated the first food products of the year are documented in the 1613 confessional. There appear to have been first fruit ceremonies and rituals for every kind of food production in the Timucua subsistence system, including agricultural, hunting, fishing, and gathering rituals. The first fruits of gathered foods were not eaten. The first fish caught in a trap was released and placed nearby in order to ensure that more fish would come. The first maize from a new clearing was also not eaten but reserved for these commemorations. Social status determined what sort of ritual Timucuans performed, with the responsibility for commemorating first fruits falling exclusively to caciques and shamans, who could be either men or women.[28] Commoners were also asked questions about food in the 1613 confessional. But for their part, questions were limited mostly to food taboos rather than ritual. While we do not know how often these first fruits ceremonies were performed, it seems likely they took place at the moment they were gathered or shortly thereafter.

The most prevalent treatment of first fruits among the Timucua seems to have been to sacrifice them in some way to unknown deities or powers. Frequently, prayers were offered over them. Still, of all the first fruits rituals we know existed, only one is documented in any detail. French cartographer Jacques Le Moyne described an annual ceremony during which the skin of a large stag was stuffed with "the choicest roots" and decorated with garlands of fruits. Music played as the stag was carried in a procession to a large, open spot. The stag was mounted in a high tree with its head facing the sunrise. The chief and shaman offered prayers to the sun to ensure a bounteous year. After the ceremony was completed, the stag remained hanging in the tree for the rest of the year.[29] So at least some of the first fruits were offered in honor of the sun, identified by the French as one of the two principal Timucuan deities. This would fit a greater southeastern pattern of sun worship.[30]

This ritual was probably the primary harvest ceremony of the Timucua. But other smaller offerings were given throughout the year, even every day. Again, first fruits seemed to play an especially central role. Shamans were given first fruits as payment for services. The first acorns and fruits of the year were dried and subsequently not eaten.[31] In the hunt and in the fields, animals or plants that were deemed valuable to the community were also celebrated in ceremonies that emulated the stag ceremony, but on a smaller scale. While the first fruits of the stag ceremony were sacrificed to the sun god, smaller first fruits rituals could have been devoted to the sun as well, given to a small idol or other depiction of the god on earth. Humans also served as representatives of these gods on earth. Some scholars have posited that the head caciques probably claimed special ties with the sun god and were likely the ultimate religious authority. Thus when workers rendered tribute to the caciques they not only honored them as high-status individuals and paid them for use of the sabanas of the village but they were also worshipping the sun god through his earthly representative. Similar practices have been recorded elsewhere across the Southeast and testify to the importance of these rituals to Timucuan life as well as demonstrate how European rulers used these traditional practices to extract labor from native Floridians in various forms. For Florida's Franciscans, these rituals were a special source of strife as Spanish needs, Catholic doctrine, and Timucuan culture came into conflict with one other. In the eyes of the Franciscans, consecrating the first fruits to Timucuan deities violated the First Commandment, "Thou shall have no other gods before me." The friar who founded the head village in the Timucuan province burned twelve images at the main village, and six more at the satellite villages, in an attempt to wipe out these idolatrous practices. But the friars also saw these food rituals as "wasteful." They would have much preferred to see this food go directly to the presidio.[32]

The sheer volume of questions expressed in the confessionals about food production and the rituals associated with it shows the extent of these concerns. Franciscans began "saving" food by extirpating these rituals, and they probably set these goods aside as surplus for trade with St. Augustine. Although the province of Timucua did not routinely ship surplus corn to the presidio, on occasion there was enough of a surplus to sell.[33] Given the steadily declining population, and hence the declining labor force of the province of Timucua, it seems likely that the occasional surplus they did sell came from food—especially corn—that Franciscans had "rescued" from first fruits rituals and in the observance of food taboos.[34]

The friars also worried about food left unconsumed because of food taboos. It was Timucuan custom not to eat corn from a dead relative's field or from a field that had been struck by lightning.[35] The Franciscans saw these practices as wasteful and would have preferred to see the uneaten corn be sold or traded to St. Augustine. Because lightning was often linked with worship of a sky or sun god, many Franciscans also saw the food taboos as another violation of the First Commandment.[36] If this practice were eliminated, the Franciscans argued, more money could be generated for the missions to purchase church vestments and other necessities, thus putting it to a far "better" use. Although the Timucua were not as successful in producing a surplus of corn to sell to the presidio as Apalachee and Guale, it appears that the friars of Timucua made a concerted effort to participate in the trade for the benefit of their missions.

St. Augustine's Stomach: An Insatiable Demand for Food

Even after the fields of St. Augustine were planted with crops and the city bought the yearly surplus from the missions, St. Augustine still faced a food deficit. In some years, it was critical. Royal *cedulas* remitted food to Florida from other parts of the Spanish empire, like Vera Cruz.[37] Although Florida was officially limited to exclusively trading with Spain and her colonies, at times Florida's governor was forced to trade with unapproved sources, like Dutch merchant ships, in order to obtain flour, corn, and other food-stuffs.[38]

Alternate plans beyond using the labor of Florida Indians were also suggested in an effort to make up for the shortfall of food in Florida. One of the most prevalent strategies was to encourage immigration by importing families to farm. A 1744 cedula provided Florida with fifty families from the Canary Islands every year. These families were to comprise no fewer than five people. They also had to commit to remaining in Florida for at least one year or until they had "taken the fruit of the earth" by producing a harvest.[39] A previous plan called for importing Indian farmers from the Mexican region of Tlaxcala to be settled in Apalachee province.[40] Royal officials of Florida also struggled to import Indian families of master weavers from the Yucatan in an effort to teach Florida Indians to weave, thereby creating a saleable item that could be traded for food.[41] All of these plans became snarled in red tape, however, and not one got off the ground. Instead, the labor of Florida Indians remained the primary source of food for the Spanish on the peninsula.

But St. Augustine's seemingly insatiable demand for corn is a story that was preserved not only in documents but also in bodies. St. Augustine's hunger produced great changes in the diet and in the physical well-being of mission Indians, as evidenced by bioarchaeological analysis. The Timucuan diet changed considerably in the years after missionization, becoming more geographically uniform and much more reliant on corn as a staple food. The nutritional quality of the diet of the Florida Indians declined. This reflected the "civilizing" influence of the missions, which taught native Floridians that foods that were grown were superior to foods that were gathered. The implications of a diet heavily reliant on maize as a major source of calories included increased cavities, growth arrest, and incomplete iron absorption.[42]

The extent to which normal growth patterns were disrupted is especially evident in the Florida population. High rates of enamel hypoplasia are one indication. This condition is seen in the teeth of individuals who have suffered stress episodes (often associated with hunger and malnutrition) during the period of tooth development in childhood. Iron deficiencies from a corn-rich diet are also present in the skeletal record in the high incidence of *cribra orbitalia,* bony lesions in the top of the eye sockets.[43]

Other indicators of the bodily stress caused by the mission environment are more directly linked to the repartimiento system of labor. During the mission period, the bodies of Florida Indians showed that the population had become more sedentary, reflecting a more static work environment. Overall, the skeletal populations of Florida mission Indians appeared more Euroamerican than did their precontact counterparts, a reflection of these changing work habits. Finally, a subset of males displayed skeletal evidence of frequent long-distance travel and heavy work, such as osteoarthritis. This probably was a result of participating in the repartimiento labor draft.[44]

Food and food production stood at the center of Florida's Indian tribute labor system. St. Augustine's constant food shortages and its unending appetite for Indian corn dictated the focus of repartimiento labor and demanded trade for the surplus corn of the missions. Florida Franciscans in the populous provinces of Apalachee and Guale took advantage of this need and sold excess corn in order to beautify and ornament the mission churches. The Franciscans of the depopulated Timucuan province were unable to harness the labor to plant and grow a large amount of surplus corn. Instead, the friars concentrated their efforts on eliminating the "wasted" food, including corn, of the first fruits rituals. Although this strategy did not yield as much of a profit as full-scale corn production, the Timucuan missions were able to sell occasional surplus to the presidio.

Throughout this period, the central role played by Indian laborers is clear. Timucuans, Apalachees, and Guales provided the agricultural labor that ensured the continued existence of the colony. The economic demands that Franciscans and other Spaniards placed on Florida's Indian population sparked rebellions, wrought social, cultural, and religious changes, and added to the increasing Indian mortality rate through malnutrition. Spanish Florida, the first conceptualization of "Florida," eked out an existence largely through Indian labor, sweat, tears, and lives. Far from being a shining jewel in the crown of the Spanish empire, Florida was instead just trying to get by.

*   *   *

I wish to thank Robinson Herrera, Rochelle Marrinan, Claudia Rivas Jiménez, Sarah Franklin, and Monica Hardin for their feedback on this chapter.

Notes

1. John E. Worth, *Timucuan Chiefdoms of Spanish Florida*, vol. 1, *Assimilation* (Gainesville: University Press of Florida, 1998), 150.

2. Francisco Pareja, ed., *Cathecismo en Lengua Castellana y Timucuana: El qual se contiene lo que se les puede ensenar a los adultos que an de ser baptizados*, Religioso de la Orden de Seraphico P.S. Francisco, Guardian del Convento de la Purissima Concepción de Nuestra Señora de S. Augustin, y Padre de la Custodia de Santa Elena de Florida (México: En la Impreta de la Viuda de Pedro Ballo, 1612), 51–52.

3. Gabriel Díaz Vara Calderón, *A 17th Century Letter of Gabriel Díaz Vara Calderón, Bishop of Cuba, Describing the Indians and Indian Missions of Florida*, trans. Lucy L. Wenhold, Smithsonian Miscellaneous Collections, vol. 95, no. 16 (Washington, D.C.: Smithsonian Institution, 1936); J. Worth, *Timucuan Chiefdoms*, 162–67.

4. Francisco Pareja, *Confessionario en Lengua Castellana, y Timuquana Con algunos Consejos para Animar al Penitente. Y asi Mismo Van Declarados Algunos Effectos y Prerrogariuas deste Sancto Sacramento de la Confession. Todo muy util y Provechoso, asi para que los Padres Confessores Sepan Instruyr al Penitente como para que ellos Aprendan á Saberse Confessar* (México: Emprenta de la Vidua de Diego López Daualos, 1613), Manuscript 2401B, Smithsonian Institution National Anthropological Archives, Smithsonian Institute, Washington, D.C., folio 184.

5. G. Díaz Vara Calderón, *17th Century Letter*, 12.

6. J. Worth, *Timucuan Chiefdoms*, 165.

7. F. Pareja, *Confessionario*, 128, 184; J. Worth, *Timucuan Chiefdoms*, 165; G. Díaz Vara Calderón, *17th Century Letter*, 13.

8. Amy Turner Bushnell, *Situado and Sabana: Spain's Support System for the Presidio and Mission Provinces of Florida*, American Museum of Natural History, Anthropological Papers, no. 74 (Athens: University of Georgia Press, 1994), 111; J. Worth, *Timucuan Chiefdoms*, 168–69; Diego Quiroga y Losada to the king, April 16, 1692, John Bannerman Stetson Collection (hereafter cited as SC), P. K. Yonge Library of Florida History, University of Florida, Gainesville (hereafter cited as UF).

9. J. Worth, *Timucuan Chiefdoms*, 169–70.

10. Letter of Don Patrício, Cacique of Ivitachuco, and Don Andrés, Cacique of San Luis, to the king, February 12, 1699, SC. Also translated in Mark F. Boyd, Hale G. Smith, and John W. Griffin, *Here They Once Stood: The Tragic End of the Apalachee Missions* (Gainesville: University Press of Florida, 1951; reprint, 1999), 24–26.

11. J. Worth, *Timucuan Chiefdoms*, 127–28.

12. On soldiers' rations, see Francisco Redondo Villegas to the king, April 18 1600, SC; Diego de Gamboa, "Investigation made in Madrid by licenciate Gamboa on matters concerning Florida," February 4, 1573, Jeanette Thurber Connor Collection (hereafter cited as JTCC), Library of Congress, Washington, D.C. (hereafter cited as LOC). For letters regarding salaries, see Diego de Velasco to the king, St. Augustine, August 1575, JTCC, LOC; Baltasar de Castillo Y Ahedo, Visitador to Florida to the king, February 12, 1577, JTCC, LOC. On the scarcity of Spanish foodstuffs, see Pedro Menéndez Marqués to the king, Santa Elena, October 21, 1577, JTCC, LOC.

13. J. Worth, *Timucuan Chiefdoms*, 128–29, 187–89.

14. J. Worth, *Timucuan Chiefdoms*, 190–91.

15. Cedula to the Governor of Florida, December 24, 1680, Archivo General de la Nación (hereafter cited as AGN), Reales Cedulas Originales 18, exp. 84; J. Worth, *Timucuan Chiefdoms*, 133.

16. Juan Giménez Montalvo to Jose de Veitia Linage, September 29, 1680, SC, UF.

17. "Cedula relativo a la guarnición, situado, y agasajos a los indios," July 20, 1733, AGN, Reales Cedulas Originales 52, exp. 30; J. Worth, *Timucuan Chiefdoms*, 135–37.

18. Governor Pablo de Hita Salazar to the king, St. Augustine, June 15, 1675, SC, UF.

19. "Royal cedula to governor Reyes y Borjas," Madrid, Spain, February 26, 1670, SC, UF.

20. J. Worth, *Timucuan Chiefdoms*, 128, 177–84. See esp. table 12.1.

21. A. Bushnell, *Situado and Sabana*, 111.

22. "Relación of Fray Juan de las Cabezas Altimirano," Florida Miscellaneous Manuscripts Collection, Box 86, Folio 1, UF.

23. Fray Francisco de Marón to Don Fray Antonio Díaz de Salsedo, Obispo de Cuba, January 23, 1597, Woodbury Lowery Collection, box 4, LOC.

24. Letter of the Franciscans to the king, March 13, 1669, AGN, General de Parte 12, exp 405.

25. John H. Hann, "Church Furnishings, Sacred Vessels, and Ornaments Held by the Missions of Florida: Translation of Two Inventories," *Florida Archaeology*, vol. 2 (1986), 147–64.

26. J. Worth, *Timucuan Chiefdoms*, 177–78.

27. Jose Señan O.F.M., *The Ventureño Confessional of Jose Señan, O.F.M.*, ed. Madison F. Beeler, University of California Publications in Linguistics, vol. 47 (Berkeley: University of California Press, 1967), 25–26, 33–34; Buckingham Smith, *Grammar of the Pima or Nevume, a Language of Sonora, from a Manuscript of the XVIII Century* (New York: Cramoisy Press, 1862), 12; Pedro Marban, *Catechismo en Lengua Espanola y Moxa* (Vaduz: Cabildo, 1975), 112. The fourth confessional consulted in the course of this study was Bartolome de Alva, *A Guide to Confession Large and Small in the Mexican Language, 1634*, ed. Barry D. Sell and John Frederick Schwaller, with Lu Ann Hozma (Norman: University of Oklahoma Press, 1999).

28. F. Pareja, *Confessionario*, 124–25, 128–29, 132, 150, 184–85, 207.

29. Charles E. Bennett, *Laudonière and Fort Caroline: History and Documents* (Gainesville: University Press of Florida, 1964), 72.

30. John R. Swanton, *The Indians of the Southeastern United States*, Smithsonian Institution Bureau of American Ethnology, Bulletin, vol. 137 (Washington, D.C.: Government Printing Office, 1946), 761; John H. Hann, *A History of the Timucua Indians and Missions* (Gainesville: University Press of Florida, 1996), 114–15.

31. F. Pareja, *Confessionario*, 125, 128–29, 132, 207.

32. J. Hann, *History of the Timucua*, 115.

33. J. Worth, *Timucuan Chiefdoms*, 178–79.

34. F. Pareja, *Confessionario*, 124, 129, 132, 184.

35. Ibid., 126, 124.

36. John H. Hann, *Apalachee: Land between the Rivers* (Gainesville: University Press of Florida, 1998), 79. There is a great deal of evidence to suggest that this practice was related to sun god worship. Apalachee, neighbors of the Timucua, worshipped a god of lightning. Each group shared similar practices that indicate the Timucua may also have shared a common lightning deity. It is also possible that the Timucuan custom of not eating corn from a field struck by lightning comes from a belief that a lightning, sky, or sun god had marked that field and its produce for its own. Similarly, eating corn from a dead man's field might have angered a deity associated with death and dying.

37. Cedula to the Justicia Mayor of Los Angeles, April 4, 1669, AGN, General de Parte 12, exp. 416; *Cedula* to the governor of Florida, May 2, 1591, AGN, Reales Cedulas Originales 4, exp 445.

38. Don Juan Florencia to the king, October 5, 1696, AGN, General de Parte 17, exp 214; Governor Juan Marques Cabrera to the king, October 8, 1683, March 20, 1686, and May 30, 1681, SC, UF.

39. Cedula to the governor of Florida, February 23, 1744, AGN, Reales Cedulas Originales 64, exp. 21.

40. Cedula to the governor of Florida, November 22, 1704, AGN, Reales Cedulas Originales 32, exp. 67.

41. Letter of Governor Quiroga y Losada to the king, August 10, 1689, SC, UF.

42. Clark Spencer Larsen, Dale L. Hutchinson, Margaret J. Schoeninger, and Lynette Norr, "Food and Stable Isotopes in La Florida: Diet and Nutrition before and after Contact," *Bioarchaeology of Spanish Florida: The Impact of Colonialism*, ed. Clark Spencer Larsen (Gainesville: University Press of Florida, 2001), 22–51, 74–75.

43. Clark Spencer Larsen, "On the Frontier of Contact: Mission Bioarchaeology in La Florida," in *The Spanish Missions of La Florida*, ed. Bonnie G. McEwan (Gainesville: University Press of Florida, 1993), 322–56.

44. Ibid., 342–47; Christopher B. Ruff and Clark Spencer Larsen, "Reconstructing Behavior in Spanish Florida: The Biomechanical Evidence," *Bioarchaeology of Spanish Florida*, 113–45.

2

The Slave Labor Camps of Antebellum Florida and the Pushing System

EDWARD E. BAPTIST

A few years ago, Peter Wood, a prominent historian of colonial North America, warned scholars of slavery in the United States that they should stop using the word *plantation* to describe the places where white people forced enslaved Africans to produce staple commodities. Saturated as it is with centuries of paternalistic propaganda that depicted enslavement as a kindly and natural relationship between inferior and superior, that old-fashioned term trapped historians in a cycle of argument about the wrong images and the wrong issues. Instead, Wood argued, a more appropriate name would be *slave labor camp*.[1] For pre–Civil War Florida, Wood's proposed label illuminates much that has been hidden by the long shadows of the word *plantation*. After all, the purpose of the properties whose names—whether attached to carefully preserved old houses or to the streets and cul-de-sacs of new developments—still dot the landscape around Tallahassee and other north Florida towns was labor and what laborers driven by force and fear could make. The word *camp* also captures the impermanence that characterized most of the pre–Civil War period for enslaved people moved by force to Florida. During booms spurred by new land, easy credit, and high prices for commodity crops like cotton and sugar, white men and women raced bondpeople south. Separating, driving, and buying human beings, they thrust enslaved people together in their camps. In the fields they extracted great quantities of toil from the enslaved through a new set of constraints sometimes called "the pushing system" by its victims. Enslavers made great profits for a time. But when commodity prices fell or other problems occurred, more moves were the inevitable result. Only late in the antebellum era did hard-charging entrepreneurs put significant effort into repackaging themselves as paternalist planters, conservative stewards of land and human property. Only then did "plantations" seem like perennials instead of annuals.

This essay focuses on the experience of enslaved African and African American laborers who lived in Florida between 1821 and 1861, particularly within the territory known as "Middle Florida." These counties around Tallahassee were the main region of commodity production before the Civil War. As elsewhere in the wider "Old Southwest," the cotton and sugar belt that spread in two generations from Florida and west Georgia all the way out to central Texas, the early nineteenth century was a time in which American whites created innovative methods for making the bodies of enslaved people into factors of production. Whites on the "plantation" frontier deployed new kinds of force and constraint, extracted greater and greater speeds of labor, and developed new institutions for converting human reproduction into wealth. Across this wide swath of land, human property became the precursor for whites' wild dreams of wealth. Florida, after its acquisition by the United States in 1821, was no different. Yet Southern whites would not have been so eager to occupy the peninsula territory if the institution of human bondage had not already been well established in the laws and customs laid down by Florida's particular history, one that included centuries of Spanish and British occupation.

During the first two centuries of the Spanish presence in Florida, while slavery existed in both fact and law, the colonizers did not import large numbers of Africans. A settlement of free blacks, including many who had escaped from South Carolina and Georgia, did appear outside of St. Augustine.[2] When Florida changed hands in 1763, at the end of the Seven Years' War, much of the African and multiracial population settled around St. Augustine decamped for still-Spanish Cuba.[3] The British entrepreneurs who took the place of Spanish officials were eager to turn the new colony onto the path of large-scale commercial agriculture. Some of them were, in fact, South Carolina planters. These men not only wanted to participate in reaping the gains of this new frontier but they were also eager to close off the southern escape valve that Florida represented for slaves.[4] The colony adopted a version of the South Carolina slave code as law. Government policy thus committed East Florida to entrepreneurial development by means of enslaved labor.

Most prominent of the numerous enterprises launched by white investors in the years leading up to the American Revolution were the slave labor camps that sprang up near the St. John's River. Many of them grew indigo. And the enslaved people who worked in them came from two main sources. Some, like the 180 who slaved on the land of South Carolina emigrant John Moultrie, were brought from the colonies just to the north. Among them were both "country-born Negroes," who had lived all their lives in American slavery, and "seasoned Negroes," who had been born in Africa but had already become more or less accustomed to the labor and diseases of New World slavery. By 1765, Henry Laurens of Charleston and John Graham of Savannah, American merchants prominent in the African slave trade, were also shipping boatloads of enslaved people bought on the African coast to St. Augustine Richard Oswald, a London-based merchant who acquired 20,000 acres along the Halifax and Tomoka rivers, was one of a company of entrepreneurs who owned the Bance Island "factory," or slave trading fort, off the coast of present-day Sierra Leone. His ship captains delivered several hundred Africans to East Florida over the ensuing decade, many of them to "Mount Oswald," the labor camp established on his land.

By 1776, at least fifteen other camps operated north of present-day Daytona Beach, in the "Mosquito District" near Mount Oswald. Like the ones along the St. Johns River, most produced indigo, lumber, and "naval stores" like tar and turpentine. Other enterprises stretched along the lower St. Johns River. Yet British control in East Florida was always a tenuous proposition. Enslaved people soon outnumbered free, raising the possibility of rebellion. Few whites would stay in the colony. And many proprietors, like Oswald, lived on the other side of the Atlantic. Henry Laurens, acting as Oswald's business agent, sent a Mr. Hewie to Mount Oswald to serve as overseer in 1766. Laurens warned Oswald that, in a slave labor camp far from other sources of white authority, if Hewie attempted to exert "the arbitrary power of an Overseer" without caution, the slaves would "perhaps be sometimes tempted to knock him in the head." Soon reports began coming back from East Florida about men placed in irons and arbitrary punishments. Then came the news that Laurens's prediction had come true. Near the end of his first year, the African people at Mount Oswald had risen up against Hewie and drowned him.[5]

Oswald's representatives continued to experiment with both overseers and crops. Indigo showed some promise, and the population of Mount Oswald grew. From 110 in 1765, by 1780 they had increased through purchase and natural growth to 240. Yet like the colony as a whole, Mount Oswald never fulfilled its British owner's dreams of profit.[6]

The beginning of the American Revolution brought a new influx of population to East Florida. Twelve thousand new arrivals came. Close to two-thirds were enslaved Africans, brought by their Loyalist owners, who escaped to St. Augustine as refugees from the wartorn Carolinas and other colonies. Raiding patriots and privateers soon pursued. Their attacks destroyed much of the physical capital of the colony—houses and sheds, indigo vats, and stored crops. The treaties that ended the war brought another change of flags, as Britain returned East Florida to Spanish control in 1784. Many white Floridians, whether refugees or longer-settled entrepreneurs, left for other points in the British Empire. Some of the departing British entrepreneurs took their slaves with them while others were able to sell land, equipment, and enslaved human beings to whites who planned to stay.[7]

Between 1784 and 1800, the colony's growth slowed. Although slavery remained the main source of labor in East Florida, the manumission rate was relatively high, as was typical of Spanish colonies. But in the first decade of the nineteenth century, both the population of the region and exports of the products of slave labor began to increase rapidly. American whites began settling in the colony in growing numbers. Many were slave owners chasing a dream of Caribbean-style sugar wealth. Wave after wave of new and naïve American whites drove enslaved and, later, nominally free African laborers to grow and harvest sugar cane. They hopped from the eastern coast, to Leon County, to the Tampa Bay area, until the crop at last found a home in the drained areas of the Everglades. Cotton, which had become a mainstay of the burgeoning British textile industry, also left its mark in the history of enslaved labor in Florida. In East Florida, enslaved people had been working in the cotton fields of labor camps like those of Francis Fatio since at least 1793. In October 1800, he reported that his captives had picked over three tons of cotton and that his son-in-law, George Fleming, had "four Negroes at the gins." Fatio wrote, "I hope by next week all his picked cotton will be ginned and baled and ready to be sent with ours; he will have 33 good bales and some left over."[8] As the short-staple cotton revolution just across the Georgia border gained velocity, additional southern enslavers and their captives moved into the region.

Florida's sandy soil and lengthy growing season also allowed the production of Sea Island cotton, a variety produced along the South Carolina coast. This plant produced a long, silky fiber that was easier to separate from its seeds. It was used for specialty cloths and often sold for several times more per pound than the short-staple variety. Slave trader Zephaniah Kingsley transported captive laborers from Africa in his own ship, then drove them to plant long-staple cotton at his Laurel Grove plantation in what is today Jacksonville. In early 1812, his warehouse contained 60 bales, or so he claimed after English-speaking "Patriots" who hoped to use the confusion of the War of 1812 to seize Florida for the United States burned the warehouse to the ground. Kingsley's 20,000 pounds of cotton would have sold

for 50 cents a pound and represented a year's labor by several dozen enslaved people.[9] Kingsley was one of many local cotton planters. He was also
not the only slave trader who transported captives across the Atlantic to
Florida. Thomas Fitch and his partner, Benjamin Chaires, a North Carolinian who eventually moved to Middle Florida, imported dozens of Africans
for Chaires's cotton fields in the East. After the 1807 ban imposed by Congress on the international slave trade, East Florida became a major landing
point for vessels carrying enslaved Africans to North America. Smuggling
was especially rampant around Fernandina and Amelia Island, given their
close proximity to the Georgia border.[10]

The last decade of the second Spanish era saw an increase in the enslaved population of Florida and in the number of slave labor camps in the
northeastern quarter of the colony. But the transformations that followed
the peninsula's transition to American territorial status between 1818 and
1821 were even greater in scope. The transition itself, sparked by Andrew
Jackson's 1818 invasion of the colony to ostensibly stop Seminole raids into
South Georgia, fulfilled a long-standing dream of both American expan-
sionists and many Anglo-American settlers already living in the colony. It
touched off a "Florida fever" of interest among whites, both in the South
and elsewhere, who hoped to move to the territory and take advantage of
the opportunities that they believed Florida's subtropical location would
offer to them. Most of this interest took the form of plans to establish "plantations" or to market the kinds of commodities that one grew in such a
climate. Planners both in and out of the federal government believed with
acting governor William Worthington that Florida would become "an
important Southern slaveholding state—producing as its staples, cotton,
sugar, rice, and fruit." Gang labor by African Americans transported from
the Chesapeake and other older states was the primary method that these
planners assumed they would use to make such goods. For the next four
decades, the migration of wealthy white men, the forcible transportation of
enslaved African Americans, and the nonplanter whites who also wanted
a piece of the opportunities characteristic of a Southern slaveholding state
shaped both the conditions of labor in Florida and the political economy
that emerged from them.[11]

The district soon known as "Middle Florida" became the geographical
area where migrating whites who sought to profit from slave labor focused
their interest. In 1822, a few villages of Miccosukee Seminoles and Apalachicola Creeks occupied the area between the Suwannee River to the east and
the settlements around Pensacola in the west. With the exception of a small

trading post at St. Marks, few if any whites lived in this vast stretch of land. Most of the African Americans living there were either runaways or "Black Seminoles."[12] While some whites hoped to make the Indians "into cultivators of the soil assisted by their slaves," the 1823 Treaty of Moultrie Creek— "in large measure a treaty of imposition," as one of the commissioners who signed it admitted to his superiors—was intended to force the remaining Seminoles into the center of the peninsula.[13] The treaty cleared most of the remaining Florida Indians from the rich soil thought to exist between and along the Suwannee and Apalachicola rivers. Rumors of thick forests of oak, rich river bottomlands, and productive fields long tended by the women of the Seminoles spread as Andrew Jackson's troops returned to their old states and told of what they had seen.[14] By 1825, planners had laid out Tallahassee on the site of an old Native American village, and the territorial seat of government had shifted to the log cabin village that quickly sprang up in the "old fields" cleared more than a century earlier by Indian men and women. Between 1824 and 1830, as surveyors laid out the rectangular lines of townships and sections, settlers staked out their claims and tried to raise the money to purchase them. In the first wave marched poor whites from Georgia and the Carolina low country. Right behind them came the big planners and dreamers: planters and would-be planters from the Chesapeake, Carolinas, and elsewhere.[15]

Seen from above, in time-lapse photography, the woods and savannahs of Middle Florida—or for that matter, the areas of Alachua county or the St. John's River region that were also being settled in the late 1820s—would have appeared to bubble, receding in isolated circles and squares as enslaved people cleared the fields. Over the next year, those open spaces turned brown and red as plows turned up the soil, then green and white with cane or cotton, or first green and then golden with corn. Production of crops and the export of cotton also seemed to swell and grow with impersonal momentum. But down on the ground the process was far more complex, and not just because every tree felled and every row plowed represented minutes or hours of tiring hand labor. Between 1824 and the late 1830s, the labor of enslaved migrants brought south by whites to till the soil of the river bottoms and oak forests created a cotton-growing district between the Suwannee River and the Apalachicola valley. Their labor was highly profitable to their enslavers, and it more than repaid whites' efforts to obtain black folk, drive them south, and extract endless work from their bodies. In order to achieve these profits, migrant slave-drivers first had to create systems of supplying labor. Then they attempted to impose a new, more systematic process of toil upon the already exploitative framework of American slavery.

Labor recruitment was always crucial to frontier cotton and sugar dreams. Here, of course, "recruitment" is a term more abstract than specifically descriptive. Enslaved people did not come voluntarily, attracted by high wages or complex opportunities. Enslaved people came to Florida with migrating owners, with slave traders who planned to sell them to already resident enslavers, and by methods that combined elements of both. The streams of forced migration never dried up, even if they slowed at some points, and rushed forward in cataracts at others. Enslavers also continually tinkered with their labor forces, adding and subtracting human beings. They sold, bought, and sold again parents, children, spouses, siblings, cousins, uncles, aunts, friends, and neighbors. Whites did these things to black people before they left for Florida, on the way there, and after they got there, all in order to produce what they hoped would be a more effective labor machine. This work in Florida's slave labor camps always took place within the context of forced migration and all the continual disruptions that process entailed.

Most of the enslaved people brought to Florida between 1821 and the 1840s came from the Chesapeake states—Virginia and Maryland—and from the Carolinas, especially North Carolina. In part, this was because of the large number of wealthy whites from those states who sought to exploit the "peculiar benefits of Middle Florida." Within five years of Tallahassee's founding, enslavers established slave labor camps in a wide arc to the north and northeast of Tallahassee. Many came from the Upper South, like the Wirts from Maryland, Thomas Brown from northern Virginia, or from the Virginia Piedmont, like Thomas Jefferson's grandson Francis Eppes and his Randolph relatives, and Richmond's Parkhill and Gamble brothers. In the fall of 1827, Thomas Brown marched to Florida with a "cavalcade—140 odd negroes," as he later recalled to his daughter. Day after day the slaves walked, adults and children alike, while the white men of Brown's family rode on horseback and the white women traveled in a coach. Night after night they camped by the road. After two months the party reached Tallahassee. They arrived exhausted. So too did the slaves marched to Florida by the Randolphs in 1829. By their journey's end, their clothes had worn out. Noted Randolph, "Jordan . . . was literally naked . . . all [were] much thinner than when we left home."[16]

These long marches had already begun with separation. This remained an essential part of the new labor system imposed in the cotton fields and sugar experiments that came to form in Florida enslavers' labor camps. To create a still more ruthlessly efficient and extractive system than had prevailed in the older states, white men from the Chesapeake and Carolinas believed they needed a labor force as young, and often as male, as possible. They were convinced that young laborers possessed the best combination of strength, endurance, and adaptability to new kinds of work. Young women, some would-be planters believed, would be too burdensome in this new country. While these same planters may not have had serious qualms about putting axe or plow handles into the hands of women, they still preferred men for cutting, clearing, and plowing. By attempting to engineer lives by the blueprints of their beliefs about ideal labor, enslavers reshaped, tore, and broke lives at both ends of their journey. In the Upper South, two centuries of enslavement had produced kinship networks and marriage bonds that spun out like fragile spider webs across Maryland, Virginia, and the Carolinas. Almost every enslaver who moved his captives south to Florida owned at least several people whose spouses, parents, or other relatives and loved ones lived under the rule of other whites. Moving to Florida sometimes severed these relationships forever. William Stephens' "owner" moved him from Lenoir County in eastern North Carolina to Florida in the 1830s, separating him from a wife and their nine children. Other enslavers tried, at least to some extent, to keep families together. Preparing to move south in 1827, Thomas Brown wrote to his brother, Richard. As silent partner in Thomas's move, Richard planned to send some of his enslaved people south, no doubt for a share of the proceeds his brother hoped to make from new crops on new lands. But both he and Thomas were willing to exempt Richard's slaves Meredith and Sam from the move, if they could sell them to the Virginia men who owned Meredith and Sam's wives "for a fair price in money."[17]

For Meredith and Sam, the Browns made an effort, even if profitability was still their goal. In other cases they made no effort whatsoever. Thomas noted casually that when he moved from Northern Virginia to Florida, he left some "old Negroes" behind. One of these was a man named Jack Paine. Years later, Charley Paine still remembered how his father had remained in Virginia when Brown took Charley, his mother Delia, and five other children to Florida.[18] Other slave owners who moved bond people to the cotton and sugar frontiers became two-plantation planters. They established one labor camp in the Southwest for making money, but did not bother to sell the old homeplace in the Southeast. The young people they owned went south and west to clear and plant, while the aging relatives of those same laborers remained on older properties that would become, for the enslavers, places of respite and relaxation away from Florida's hot and fever-ridden summers. Around 1830, Hardy Croom left a woman named Cherry on his North Carolina land with the others whom he deemed too old to adapt to the new climate and more brutal pace of Florida. Cherry was all of 40 or so at the time. Croom moved her children, William Kenyon and Martin Clark, both almost teenagers, to his new Gadsden County labor camp.[19]

The outcomes of enslavers' decisions were soon evident in the distorted demography of frontier labor forces. In 1830, Benjamin Chaires's slave camp in Leon County imprisoned 213 human beings. Of them, 127 were male and 86 were female. Only one was over 55 years of age. The majority was between 10 and 36 years old. What was true of Chaires's "Verdura" labor camp was true in general of the new counties into which enslavers deployed armies of disproportionately young and male laborers in the 1820s and 1830s. Samuel Parkhill of Leon County, a migrant from Richmond, claimed 21 slaves, 17 of whom were male and all of whom were younger than 36. Jackson County's Peter Gautier, Sr., owned 71 men and women, 50 of whom were younger than 24. In these counties as a whole, 55 percent of Leon County slaves and 58 percent in Jackson County were between 10 and 36 years of age. This was in sharp contrast to the counties from which many planter and slave migrants to Florida hailed. In Virginia's Essex and North Carolina's Halifax Counties, for example, 45 and 46 percent, respectively, fell into that same age category.[20]

Enslavers' decisions, made in the attempt to create particular kinds of labor forces, created the truncated communities and distorted population patterns of Florida slave camps. The decision to leave older or younger family members behind was a significant one for every person who, like William Kenyon or Martin Clark, would never see their mother again. But in numerical terms, the practice that most distorted patterns of age and gender was the domestic slave trade. Although Amelia Island, St. Augustine, and other Florida ports had been termini of the Middle Passage from Africa during the last years of the Spanish era, early territorial legislature not only accepted the federal ban on the international slave trade but also prohibited the domestic trade in human beings from other states.[21] Yet from the beginning, frontier entrepreneurs honored this law more in the breach than strict obedience; slave traders began to arrive in Tallahassee and other new towns of the cotton and sugar belt. These ranged from the large gang of 44 slaves whose imminent arrival from Virginia was announced by the *Tallahassee*

Floridian and Advocate in 1829, to the small number of people whom North Carolina trader Isaac Jarratt might try to deal in Quincy if he could not unload them to buyers in his usual Alabama selling territory.[22] By the second half of the 1830s, the local boom driven by high cotton prices and ready credit—ultimately supplied by European investors, but delivered via the mechanism of the Union Bank of Florida—brought numerous slave traders and their coffles of captives to Tallahassee and other Florida towns.[23]

The business of selling flesh, blood, and anticipated labor had many patterns. Not all of those who traveled to buy and sell were full-time slave traders, despite the later reluctance of would-be paternalist "planters" to admit their own role in this much-criticized aspect of the peculiar institution.[24] French-born Achille Murat, the grand-nephew of Napoleon Bonaparte, wrote in his account of life in Florida that the typical migrant "planter, having returned home" to the Upper South, typically "sold his lands and house, and added to the number of his negroes."[25] In October 1834, Murat himself prepared to go "in quest of negroes" in Maryland and Virginia, where he planned to invest from "$10 to $12,000 in negroes." The older slave states, where people sold for prices cheaper than those asked by traders at the southern end of the trail, were the place to find bargains. Murat decided to "try first in the Baltimore market." But he also asked friends who had migrated from Virginia to write to their correspondents in the Old Dominion in order to "hear of some person either willing or compelled to part with their gang."[26]

The difference between being moved by a "planter" versus a "slave trader" often did not amount to much. Indeed, many enslaved people either could not tell the difference or did not think it worth emphasizing. In each case they lost family and friends, sometimes all of them. At the end of the trail, they had heard, new struggles awaited all in common. Moses Roper, enslaved in Florida during the 1830s, exemplified these disorienting processes of removal from family and community and conversion into a factor of cotton production. Born in North Carolina, Roper was sold repeatedly to cotton planters and slave traders during his teenage years. They moved him from North to South Carolina, then to Georgia, back to North Carolina, then to South Carolina again. Thoroughly bewildered and battered after tortures designed to break him to the work of cotton hoeing and picking, and marked as trouble by frequent runaway attempts, at an auction Roper ended up being auctioned off to Robert Beveridge. This Scotsman, an entrepreneur and developer of Jackson County, Florida, took him down to Apalachicola. Roper, who by this point had changed owners about a dozen times, worked for a while as Beveridge's valet, thereby avoiding the fields for a time. The enslaved man's fortunes turned for the bad again, however. In about 1834, Beveridge went broke. He then sold Roper to a cotton planter named Register. This man, rumored to work slaves to death, prepared to carry Roper to his new clearings along the Georgia-Florida border. Having already labored in the raw cotton fields of pushing upstart planters in the Carolinas and Georgia, Roper did not think he could endure it again: "I did not care if I lived or died. . . . I procured a quart bottle of whiskey, for the purpose of so intoxicating myself, that I might be able, either to plunge myself into the river, or so to enrage my master, that he might dispatch me forthwith."[27]

Roper feared what he already knew. Enslavers disrupted and divided kinship networks and families because on the frontier they planned to make enslaved people work harder than ever. After having done the work of walking themselves to Florida, bondspeople then had to clear forests and erect dwellings for their owners and themselves. This was hard work with the axe and saw in the first months after arrival, and represented the major work of enslaved labor forces moved by migrant planters. William C. Wirt, manager of a large tract in Jefferson County owned collectively by the Wirt family of Maryland, wrote in early December 1835 that he hoped to get 100 acres cleared by planting time in March. Eager to push hard, migrant enslavers sometimes also hired poor whites to work alongside the slaves. Next, slaves were shifted to breaking the soil—red clay in much of Middle Florida, heavy black dirt in the river bottoms, and lighter, sandier soil in other parts of the state—with heavy plows that constantly bounced off of buried roots. Behind the plowmen came women with hoes to break up the furrows in cotton or cornfields, or to help dig shallow trenches for those planters wanting to try their hands at the much-desired sugar cane. Only after that step were slaves able to plant cotton and corn or lay sections of seed cane.[28]

This was only the beginning. In the early spring, the labor forces, already under continual transformation by the multiples means of movement, endured their first initiation into the work that frontier entrepreneurs hoped would create boundless wealth. Roper knew something about this toil from firsthand experience. Others had only heard rumors, but these were fearful enough. Of course, those transported from the Upper South by enslavers like Thomas Brown had worked and worked brutally hard regimens of forced labor in the tobacco and grain fields of their old states. Because cotton and sugar cane were new crops, however, most captive migrants now had to learn new kinds of work.

In Florida, climate and other conditions imposed some changes on the system of cultivating and harvesting sugar. Still, migrant planters looked to experts from the Caribbean who came to the Tallahassee region to teach those who, like Francis Eppes, hoped to "begin life anew as a sugar planter."[29] In the Florida panhandle, would-be magnates were eager to play what white Jamaican migrant and sugar expert Farquhar McRae told them was "the higher game," ready to grasp at the wealth and prestige of the West Indies nabobs who had dominated whole sectors of the British economy in the eighteenth century.

Yet this was easier dreamed than done. Whether on the islands or on the mainland, sugar required a demanding series of labors and processes. After clearing the fields, enslaved workers had to plow deeply, then lay doubled rows of seed cane. Slaves working with hoes then covered the furrows with dirt. In a few weeks, the first sprouts began to emerge. Then enslaved laborers spent much of the summer cultivating and recultivating the rows with the hoe or perhaps, if the rows had been spaced widely, with the more labor-saving plow.

Sugar cane had to be processed quickly after harvest in order to extract the maximum amount of juice. Workers had to chop down cane, take it to the mill, and grind it. Mills in the Brazilian and Caribbean harvest season usually ran all day and all night. Workers toiled double shifts in the field and in the sugarhouse. Then technicians carefully boiled the juice in a series of kettles, progressively refining the cane syrup until they could separate it into molasses and sugar.[30]

A few white migrants to Florida, like Moses Levy, already knew how the higher game was played. Before establishing a sugar plantation at "Pilgrimage" in Alachua County, Levy had planted and processed the crop in Puerto Rico and Cuba.[31] Others eagerly hired the expertise of men recommended by McRae. They bought the requisite supplies, hurriedly imported by merchants like the Armistead brothers of Apalachicola, who in the late 1820s sold sugar kettles to enslavers throughout the Apalachicola valley. They bought slaves and invested large sums of money to build sugarhouses; Brown reportedly sank $20,000 in his.[32]

Ironically, the process of sugar production itself was in the midst of a series of momentous technical breakthroughs. These allowed entrepreneurs in Cuba to handle much larger quantities of cane and made it possible to grow sugar on vast new areas of land in the interior of the island. Railroads helped open up access to those new labor camps. Florida planters were entering the higher game just a few years too soon to take advantage of these newly available efficiencies. They also faced a real difficulty in adopting sugar cane as a commodity crop, one that they would eventually have to admit. In the Caribbean and Brazil, where sugar cane had become the most profitable and celebrated crop in the early modern world, this heat-loving plant grew for 14 or months before harvest. In Middle Florida in particular, the available time was truncated by the very real possibility of a frost in late December or January.[33]

Yet in both sugar and cotton fields, what enslaved migrants confronted was far more than plants that were new to them and more than standards of cultivation and harvesting driven by the biology of the crop plant itself. They confronted slavery, reloaded. When Daniel Wiggins, a Baltimore mechanic whom federal judge Thomas Randall hired to transport ten enslaved people south, accomplished his task by arriving with the captives in Jefferson County in late 1838, he started to look around for work. Wiggins considered himself something of an inventor. Eventually he turned his attention to improving cotton screws, the machines used to press ginned clean cotton into bales. Before that, however, for a day or so Wiggins tried to come up with a scheme for getting more labor out of the enslaved. Yet as he watched the six women and one boy—Matilda, Sophia, Mary, Hester, Marth, Frida, and Willy—whom he had brought down to Randall, going through the process of introduction to rudiments of cotton labor, he changed his mind. He saw that it was because of the soil, the climate, and most of all because of the innovative ways by which white men made enslaved African Americans work with great intensity at unpleasant and repetitive tasks. "The labour of colored people is high [in value]—say 300 to 600 dollars per year." On Randall's slave labor camp, a few dozen men and women had already cleared 300 acres, and annually raised and harvested 100 to 150 bales of cotton.[34]

Nor was Wiggins, a semi-independent white artisan who was willing to exploit black bodies for his own living, the only one who observed the innovative exploitations of the slave labor system on Florida's cotton and sugar frontier. What Wiggins could only see from the outside was experienced inside the machine as a constant and exhausting roar, a life parceled into six or more days a week of incessant fatigue, pain, and fear. Working by torchlight, hungry from a long day's toil with only a noon-time break for food, old and weary before his time, a man in a field near Tallahassee paused to speak with a white traveler in early 1835. "Men grow mighty <u>pushing</u> when they are trying to get rich," he said.[35] Cotton prices were high, and he had been pushed to this Florida field sometime in the previous few years so that white people could squeeze the maximum amount of wealth from his hands. They not only pushed him from one place to another. They also pushed him every minute of every day.

The particular contours of this pushing system were a relatively new development. During the 1820s and 1830s, white men like Thomas Randall implemented major changes in the process of labor, making work in the fields of Florida cotton and sugar camps different in both degree and kind from that which most enslaved migrants had left behind. Like other southwestern slavery entrepreneurs, Florida planters implemented a system of gang labor. Gang labor itself was not new, though it was to some enslaved migrants. But this kind drove people to work in new, more regulated ways than the kinds of gang work that had existed in Virginia, for instance. Florida enslavers adopted the process of "pushing" as their major emphasis. In the process, they created the high value of which Wiggins spoke.

"Pushing" had multiple dimensions, but several components of this new system were usually present and helped make it "certain [that] a man may make five dollars here as easy as he can make two in Virginia." These included driving a higher percentage of the population of any slave labor camp into the fields, longer working hours, more monotonous work, regulating movement, measuring output, a constant increase in minimum production, and harsh—sometimes shockingly violent—torture to compel ever more rapid work.[36]

One must remember, of course, that the labor of captives in the Chesapeake and Carolina slave camps was also difficult and exploitative. Those states, and the colonies that preceded them, grew from the unpaid sweat and stolen blood of hundreds of thousands of Africans. From 1619 to the early nineteenth century, unknown numbers had died in the fields—shot, knifed, beaten, whipped, dead from heatstroke, heart attack, or sorrow. Unknown numbers died of exhaustion in the evenings as well: too early, too young, worn out, broken by disease, slipping off to Guinea or the heavens one night in their cabins. They left uncounted numbers behind to mourn, or—what might be worse—they left none, especially if they came recently from Africa. The lives taken mounted up by the hundreds of thousands. So did the days of work stolen, spent by force, not producing by choice or consent to support one's self and loved ones. These were billions of days squeezed into tobacco hogsheads and rice barrels—days that from the perspective of those who experienced them faded up into the sky like the smoke of new grounds in Virginia, evaporated like the drops of sweat that fell for two centuries on broad, green tobacco leaves in Maryland. A trillion long, unpaid hours had steamed into the air like the rank odor of rotting indigo in South Carolina, had dripped into the cold red clay of North Carolina, until masters could distill them and "drink them up," to borrow the phrase coined by enslaved people who watched prodigal whites finance their own pleasures by selling young men and women to slave dealers. So no one should lightly make the claim that work in the new fields of the planters' frontier was even harsher than the labor that two centuries of captivity had extracted from its victims.

Yet it was harsher. Simply put, "pushing" men used force and system in Florida and other new territories and states to increase the exploitation of the enslaved to new heights. And everyone, from the enslaver to the white observer to the enslaved, understood that increase. When enslaved people went to bed at night, a higher percentage of them than on Virginia properties knew that they would have to work in the fields in the morning. Economists might call this process one of increasing labor force participation in income-generating activities.

For the enslaved, this began with the selective purchase and/or movement of young adults and older children, with all the disruptions that entailed. But it did not end there. Like sugar, but in contrast to grain crops like wheat that had begun to supplement tobacco as the main source of export earnings in the Chesapeake from the 1780s onward, cotton required nearly year-round, intensive labor.[37] On Florida labor camps like Jefferson County's "Chemonie," enslaved African Americans started plowing the soil in February and planted seed by March. Once the cotton sprouted, they hoed the crop three or more times to kill weeds and hill up the rows. By July it was sometimes tall enough to shade out the weeds, and they could turn to working on the corn crop. By August they were getting the baskets ready, and in the middle of that month, the enslaved people at Chemonie were usually picking. Harvesting and ginning the cotton could last until January, when the crop cycle was almost ready to start again.[38]

Although sugar and cotton required nearly year-round labor, a period of four or more months out of the year strained the resources of labor camps and those who toiled in them to the breaking point. The bottleneck in the cotton labor process was picking. Even with the help of the gin to process the raw cotton into clean, an enslaved man or woman could plow and cultivate more acres than he or she could pick. The addition of women to the ranks of the plow gang was one of the expedients of the frontier that increased the amount of labor performed.[39] So during the picking season, enslavers in Florida pressed almost every slave they owned, and often others whom they hired, into the fields to gather cotton. Newly transported captives often found that the more years they had swung a scythe in wheat or primed and picked tobacco, the more difficulty they experienced as they tried to adapt the motions of their fingers and hands. The new task took repetitive, dexterous, machinelike small-motor motion, not strength or complex skills. The difficulty of learning to pick, plus the fact that the labor did not take great strength, made it efficient to purchase older boys and girls. They learned quickly. Compared to enslaved children elsewhere, they also began to make money for the buyer immediately. "The great advantage of a cotton country over ours is this," wrote a Virginia visitor to Tallahassee in 1837, "every description of negroes over nine years of age will count $300 in the crop, whereas with us they are worth nothing as hands."[40] Although enslavers certainly preferred young men for the work of clearing thickly forested land, frontier entrepreneurs soon discovered that women, children, and unskilled men were more relatively valuable to the cotton planter than ever before, so long as they could all be made to work at gathering the cotton crop for long, hard, repetitive hours.

Enslaved people in the Chesapeake and Carolinas often toiled from dawn to dusk, but after transport to Florida they worked more hours still. Long years after slavery ended, they and whites alike remembered that labor began before dawn, typically when an overseer or driver blew the horn. They gathered their clothes, perhaps a little food for breakfast, perhaps a dinner pail for the noontime meal, and rushed out to the fields.[41] "Excepting the ploughboys," wrote one visitor to Middle Florida during the hectic cotton boom of the 1830s, "who must feed and rest their horses, they do not leave the field till dark in the evening." Enslaved people told him that they began "before we can well tell the cotton from the grass," and worked all day until they could not distinguish the two again. Then they had to go back to their huts or, in the first days after migration, to go build their huts in the first place. They still needed to gather firewood, build fences, tend food crops by the light of fires on scaffolds, or do other tasks for their owners. "We didn't have to work nights in Virginia," they told him, "but folks are mighty pushing about here." When at last the work was done, long after sunset, few hours remained before the horn would blow to signal another day in the fields.[42]

For some, lengthened work hours emerged as a result of shifting from the "task" to the "gang" labor system. Especially in the rice and long-staple cotton-growing districts along the coasts of South Carolina and Georgia, enslaved workers often had to complete a daily quota of labor called a "task." A task was the amount of some particular kind of labor—ditching, plowing, hoeing, picking, and so on—that an enslaver could demand a worker complete in the course of a day. This work could vary, depending on the custom of the plantation and on the strength and skill of the slaves. A South Carolina enslaver for whom Moses Roper worked before his forced migration to Florida required his teenage laborers to "hoe three quarters of an acre of cotton a day." One of Roper's companions, a "young lad . . . brought up as a domestic slave . . . was not able to accomplish the task assigned to him." Over the course of the next three days, his owner flogged the young man until he died. Yet in some slave labor camps in lowcountry South Carolina, for instance, many adults could actually complete their task by midafternoon. This gave them time to help others or to raise food crops so that their families could eat more than the bare minimum supplied by scanty rations of rice, corn, or salted meat.[43]

Prevalent in the Chesapeake and much of the Carolina backcountry, however, was the system in which a group or gang worked together across a field, often each with their own row to hoe or pick. Usually they worked under the supervision of a white overseer, although evidence also suggests that in the small and sometimes separated fields of the tobacco country, they might labor away from immediate supervision of whites. Enslaved people in a gang also had to toil not until their piece of labor was complete but until the owner, overseer, or driver said that they could stop. When enslavers from the Chesapeake moved to the southwestern cotton states, it seems they brought the gang system with them. In some areas of Alabama and other states, enslavers from South Carolina who had initially conducted many aspects of cotton cultivation and harvesting using task labor soon adopted the more collective and heavily supervised gang system from their neighbors.[44]

In order to extort labor from groups of people who received no reward for their work and had to toil for a given period of time, owners who resorted to the gang labor system used the threat of violence. They also had to supervise their enslaved people, either directly or through an agent, in order to know when and upon whom to deploy force. In a much-reprinted Benjamin Latrobe drawing illustrating late eighteenth-century tobacco cultivation in the Chesapeake, a white overseer or owner stands carelessly on a stump, smoking and holding his stick. He watches as several black women hoe tobacco plants. In the Florida cotton fields, enslavers adopted a different mode of supervision. Here, owners or overseers often did not rest, but followed up workers who were plowing, planting, hoeing, or picking. In many cases, they demanded that enslaved workers keep up with a "leader," often the woman or man who was the fastest picker or handiest with the hoe. "In the leader of the hoers the principal calculation is speed," wrote a traveler. The overseer, owner, or enslaved "driver" could walk behind the "leader" to make sure she or he did not slow down. In this way, a pushing man could drive a whole line of workers across the field like an agricultural machine.[45]

People did not like being driven in the pushing way. Every time the overseer got behind Margaret Nickerson's sister, Lytie Holly, with his whip in hand, "she'd get behind them. And when they would beat her she wouldn't holler and just take it and go on."[46] To beat down who would not "just take it," or to punish those deemed to be working too slowly, white men in the fields usually carried a weapon. Usually the first weapon used on those who argued or supposedly worked too slowly was a whip, and not just an ordinary one. Travelers to, and survivors of, the new cotton states reported that they witnessed whites wielding a new kind of lash that was much longer than those they had seen even in Virginia. This one had a heavily weighted handle and could inflict horrible gashes in the skin of its victims.[47] The plain purpose of the whip was to cow opposition in the field and to force people to find ways to keep up the pace urged on them by whites. Often the system worked.

Sometimes, however, it produced direct resistance. In April 1849, Leon County overseer Christopher Bryant attempted to whip an enslaved woman who was hilling up cotton. When the lash came down on her, she turned and lifted her heavy hoe. She swung it once, knocking him down, and then kept chopping until Bryant was dead. Enslaved people in the area around Tallahassee would privately celebrate this incident, retelling it for years to come. For this reason, many overseers and owners went about armed with more than a whip. Many also considered it necessary to whip many or all of the enslaved adults on a labor camp at least once, in order to drive out of them the belief that they could resist. "I have driven mine into complete subordination," said one enslaver to another within the hearing of a Northern traveler in the 1830s. "When I first bought them they were discontented . . . but I soon whipped that out of them, and now they work."[48]

Other kinds of resistance were less direct. Thousands of slaves ran away from Florida fields at one time or another. In October 1850, a Jackson County overseer wrote, "The negroes can't pick to suit some of my neighbors and the woods is full of runaway Negroes." October was in the middle of the long season of cotton-picking. Every year, all across the cotton South, the number of runaways peaked during the months stretching from the middle of August to the middle of January, because then exploitation was at its most direct.[49]

The same was true in Florida's sugar camps, because all the ripe cane had to be cut and processed in the late fall and early winter, before frost could ruin the crop. "It is not uncommon for hands, in hurrying times, besides working all day, to labor half the night. This is usually the case on sugar plantations, during the sugar-boiling season" when enslaved people had to work a second shift in the sugar house, wrote an Ohioan visiting Middle Florida in the early 1830s. "Said Mr. ____ to me," he continued, "'I work my niggers in hurrying time till 11 or 12 o'clock at night, and have them up by four in the morning.'" Enslavers were at their most "pushing" during this time of the year. Yet some Florida sugar and cotton entrepreneurs did issue instructions like the ones sent by Hardy Croom in July 1837 to the agent in charge of his plantation: "I wish you to begin to pick out cotton early, at least with the women and boys by the 20th August, or as soon as they can get half tasks."[50]

Task labor in the old-state sense offered the enslaved benefits, such as being able to supervise one's own work. Croom's use of "half task," however, probably referred to a kind of measurement that was not only fully compatible with closely supervised gang labor but also "pushed" work in the cotton fields of Florida to ever more intense levels. During the picking season, the "task" was, in many slave labor camps, a minimum number of pounds that the man, woman, or child had to gather. All day long they picked, stuffing cotton in their sack, emptying sacks into the baskets at the ends of the rows, trying to keep up with the leader. At the end of the day, they put their baskets on wagons or carried them on their heads. The cotton had to go to the gin. But first, the overseer or owner weighed each person's picking and noted the number. Each enslaved person had to meet a certain minimum, and that minimum was the "task" to which Croom and others referred.[51]

"Some planters give tasks which can be finished before night, but I know of none such," wrote a Northerner who visited Tallahassee and St. Augustine in 1835. In any case, as long as the overseer had not called a halt, they had to continue. Even "if by extraordinary exertion they finish [their minimum task] before dark, it is increased the next day." The higher total became the "task." "You ain't done nothin'," one formerly enslaved African American remembered a white Florida enslaver saying after weighing the totals, even though <u>she</u> had exceeded the minimum. The next day she would have to do more. By continual measurement and increase of the "task," the cotton entrepreneur kept his captives at the ever-harder task of pushing themselves, for "the slave is whipped if he does not finish [the new task]."[52]

Among enslaved people in the Upper South, enslavers in the cotton and sugar regions had a reputation for the infliction of tortures more extreme than those common in the older slave states. Violence as part of the minute-to-minute pushing that took place in the field was bad enough, but the tortures inflicted at the end of the day were more dangerous. Sometimes they were diabolical in their premeditation and bizarre depravity. When weighed cotton came up short at the gin stand or when jobs were not complete, enslavers had all day to think about and prepare their attacks. Considering that white Southerners were wont to claim that enslaved human beings were both property and people, such violence could also seem counterproductive. Supposedly, both the strange humanitarianism of the law and the claim of self-interest served as impediments to assaults that might impede the ability of the slave to labor, much less destroy the wealth of the owner by killing the victim. Yet those who survived forced migration often concurred with white travelers who claimed that enslavers, pushing hard for the kind of wealth promised by the cotton and sugar boom animating Florida in the 1830s, behaved as if they had lost their minds. William Ladd, who for a while lived in the Mosquito District along Indian River, reported the words of an overseer employed by a fellow slave owner: "This man told me that he would rather whip a negro than sit down to the best dinner." Nor was this behavior reserved for employees. Owners themselves beat their "property" until people could not work for weeks, maimed the hands of "hands," invented bizarre tortures, drove them to suicide, and burned them to death at times. Another one of Ladd's neighbors, a man named Hutchinson, ruined one young girl for labor by holding her hand in a fire, and he supposedly killed a newly purchased African slave by beating him into unconsciousness, then piling brush on him and setting it afire.[53]

The threat of extraordinary and apparently uncontrolled violence was a key part of a method that produced results. Sometimes these results may have been accidental, an outgrowth of the psychological deformities that led white men and women to inflict torture in the first place. But torture had too many instrumental uses for us to conclude that its contribution to the success of the pushing system was unintentional. "Does Mary keep up with the rest?" asked one slave owner of another. "No, she doesn't often finish the task alone, she has to get Sam to help her out after he has done his, to save her a whipping. There's no other way but to be severe with them."

Sam helped Mary, and thus we see that sometimes the enslaved were able to modify the stark demand that every man, woman, and child focus every fiber of their being on meeting an individual rather than a collective target. Yet more important to the enslaver was that the profit accrued by toil went in the pockets of Sam and Mary's "owner." Driving, weighing, tasking, and torture all enabled the pushing men to produce intense labor from the disrupted and divided people whom they had brought to Florida. The threat of torture for those who did not finish their work, or meet the total production demanded, was an intrinsic part of the pushing system.[54]

Enslavers understood that the practices of overwork, violent torture, and often underfeeding carried potential costs as well as yielding benefits. One Virginia planter who visited Tallahassee and was trying to decide whether or not he should move, wrote: "I have endeavored to find out the real profits of cotton-planting—and, so far as I can form an opinion, it ranges between 300 and 400 dollars, although many persons make more, they are real negro-killers."[55] Many persons made more, indeed. Day by day and year by year, enslavers ratcheted up the demands of the picking "task." In the early 1820s, many enslavers still considered themselves lucky if they could extract 100 pounds a day from the labor of an excellent cotton picker. Over the next 20 to 30 years, improvements in the yield of the cotton plant, plus the gradual effects of pushing, drove the required daily weight upward. By 1854, D. N. Moxley, overseer at the El Destino slave labor camp, reported: "Boy Jack and di has runaway. for picking from 85 to 95 [pounds] I maid prince give them both about 30 [lashes] apeas yesterday." Not long afterwards, the overseer of the Chemonie camp (owned by the same Georgia-based absentee planter) reported that the men and women he drove were picking high weights: "Marier 242 lbs., biner 240 lbs., Martha 210 lbs. . . . . I averaged today 170 lbs. of Cotton a peace."[56]

Despite the notable success of the pushing system in expanding the exploitative character of slavery, the failures of enslavers' projects also reshaped labor in Florida fields. The first was the failure of sugar in the first half of the 1830s. Despite several mild winters that initially lulled migrant planters into complacency, Northern Florida was not the Caribbean. During most Decembers, hard frosts struck at least once or twice. Sugar growers tried to harvest the cane before the freeze, to cover frozen cane, and other expedients, but all to little or no avail. During the early 1830s, cold spells destroyed multiple cane crops. Middle Florida enslavers suffered huge financial losses. Several went bankrupt like Thomas Brown, whose failure forced him to sell at least 50 slaves. Others, like the Gambles and the

Parkhills, switched to cotton. Still, some enslaved men and women continued to toil in fields of sugar cane to the west of Tallahassee. In about 1834, when Moses Roper ran away from the man who bought him from Robert Beveridge, he could still find a hiding place on the edge of Jacob Robinson's Jackson County sugarcane field. Yet by the 1840s, sugarcane was no longer grown as a cash crop in Middle Florida. While the climate from the Alachua County area southwards was better suited for cane, the outbreak of the Second Seminole War in 1834 caused most of the planters of that district to flee. Even many of the slave labor camps along the St. Johns River came under attack over the next eight years.[57]

The failure of the climate around Tallahassee to fulfill the hopes of the would-be sugar magnates who had moved to that district meant more movement and disruption for many slaves. The success of cotton, on the other hand, ultimately led to an even greater failure. Still wider magnitudes of loss and separation followed in economic panic's ragged train. From 1833 onward, rising world cotton prices spread a fever of migration of would-be planters into regions like Middle Florida and drove the interstate slave trade to new heights. Land purchases and slave purchases cost money, especially as demand pushed the price of each commodity higher. But southwestern whites found huge new sources of credit. Historians have traditionally credited President Andrew Jackson's 1832 veto of the renewal of the charter of the Second Bank of the United States and his 1834 decision to spread federal deposits out among various state "pet banks," a causal role in unleashing the sustained overexpansion of credit that characterized the mid-1830s. Still, most of the credit that helped expand the U.S. economy in the 1830s came not from the federal government but from overseas investors in Britain, the Netherlands, and Germany. Much of that credit flowed not through the "pet banks" but through various Southern "planter" banks, chartered by legislatures which sold bonds backed by their respective states or territories. European houses like Barings or Hope and Company bought millions of dollars of Florida bonds from the Union Bank of Florida, which the territorial legislature chartered in 1833. Lending money received from the sale of bonds to planters who mortgaged their land and slaves, sometimes for wildly inflated values of two or three times their worth, the Union Bank threw gasoline on the hot coals of the cotton economy. Enslavers could now buy more slaves, buy, clear, and plant more land, and produce vastly greater quantities of cotton.[58]

The interstate slave trade expanded rapidly in these years, and so, with the slight lag needed to "season" people and clear land, did the production of cotton. In 1826, Florida had produced an estimated total of 5,200 bales of cotton, much of it from the older areas near the northeastern coast of the peninsula. By 1833, the territory exported about 39,200 bales. In the next year the total ballooned to 52,200. As prices rose through 1836, the area around Tallahassee boiled into a frenzy, heated by men seeking the real profits of cotton-planting. "Cotton! Cotton! Cotton! is all the saying in the South now—everyone is going for cotton. It is the theme of nearly all the conversations now a days [sic]," or so wrote a young Maryland man re-creating himself as a Florida planter. "Even the Ladies talk learnedly upon the subject," he added. "If you see a knot of Planters engaged in earnest conversation, without even approaching, you may [know] the topic of their discourse. Get within earshot of them, and, I will guranty, that the first word that you will hear will be <u>cotton</u>."[59] In 1833, the United States produced 931,000 bales of cotton. In 1837, it produced 1,428,000. This 50 percent increase in four years suggests that Florida might have easily produced 75,000 bales by 1837. Yet there were signs of weakness. From 1833 through 1835, cotton prices rose much faster than inflation. By early 1837, the price of a pound of cotton at Liverpool had already started to fall. All the financing of the forced movement of enslaved people and all their stolen toil in clearing, planting, and harvesting fields had worked too well. The market was glutted.[60]

The Bank of England was the ultimate guarantor of the system of international finance. When it grew nervous over reports of soft demand in Liverpool and called in loans made to the big commercial houses like Barings in late 1836, the resulting panic eventually swept thousands of slaves out of Florida fields. By the spring of 1837, commercial houses around the Atlantic basin, unable to meet their obligations, pressed on their debtors. So did the southern banks, and often the debtors were the same enslavers who had gone deeply into the red to subsidize the opening of the pushing system on a large scale in Alabama, Mississippi, Louisiana, and Florida. Their response was to push harder, to make enslaved people make more cotton. But the results only further depressed the price of cotton, their main source of revenue. The worthless paper money issued by the Union Bank of Florida and other such institutions destabilized the economy even more.

By the winter of 1839–40, Florida's economy was in chaos. Thousands of debt suits piled up. The territory defaulted on the bonds that ultimately backed the Union Bank's loans and enslavers put the enslaved under the hammer of the auctioneer once again. The lives and labors of those who toiled in the fields of slave camps, already shaped by the constant disruption of forced migration in, now would acquire the imprints left by forced migration out. By 1847, of the 40 enslaved people brought from Virginia to the El Destino labor camp by William Nuttall, only 15 remained. Another 15 of the young original population had died, suggesting the impact of frontier disease and overwork. Most of the rest had been sold to meet Nuttall's debts to the Union Bank.[61]

After slavery ended, Leon County's Sancho Thomas remembered that his brother Starling "was carried to New Orleans." Others, like Richard Gadsden's siblings, Thankful and Thomas, also ended up in the domestic slave market. Still others went further west with enslavers who dragged their human property with them, often as they themselves escaped from unpayable debts. Daphne Williams, born in Florida in the early 1830s, remembered that when she was about 10 years old her owners moved her and all their bond people out to Texas.[62] Meanwhile, back in Florida, the combined effects of debt, bankruptcy and failure, planter flight, and Seminole raids shrank the territory covered by fields of cotton and cane. Some enslavers shifted toward food crops. In such cases what whites perceived as hard times were actually not necessarily so bad for enslaved people; for a time they did less brutal work with more certainty of full bellies. In the 1840s, as later during the Civil War, whites also forced some black laborers to make import-replacing products like cloth from local cotton or shoes from local hides.[63]

Other enslavers who stayed searched for alternative cash crops. Tobacco became more prominent than ever. Gadsden County was one of the leading areas for the cultivation of the old Chesapeake sot-weed in new soil. Though other clashes with the peninsula's natives would follow, with the end of the Second Seminole War, whites felt that they could relaunch the settlement of the peninsula itself. Soon enslavers tried to embed sugar plantations along the shore of Tampa Bay and south into Manatee County. Robert Gamble, son and nephew of failed Middle Florida sugar entrepreneurs' would-be bank magnates, moved to the shores of the Manatee River to try again. By the early 1850s, the approximately 150 human beings he claimed as his property, many of whom he had recently purchased, had cleared 320 acres and built a vast sugar labor camp. Behind Gamble's imposing mansion of coquina rock hummed two steam engines, one for the mill and the other to run the sugar-refining equipment. Gamble claimed that his system of production would yield between 2,000 and 3,000 pounds of sugar to the acre. The many forced laborers working under him had to toil hard to keep the mighty steam engines fed night and day during the harvest.

Yet even in the warmer weather of the southern half of Florida, sugar never fulfilled the hopes once held by 1820s migrants. Gamble was one of a few willing to risk their human property that close to the remaining Seminole bands of the Everglades. Few investors were willing to sink their money into a state that had already burned so many of their class. And the returns were never as good as they hoped. When sugar prices plummeted in the mid-1850s, Gamble had to surrender his mansion, land, works, and enslaved laborers to his principal creditor. In 1856, he left the area and returned to Tallahassee. The 150 people who lived and worked around the Gamble mansion continued to toil there in the years to come.[64]

As the 1840s turned into the 1850s, however, world cotton prices rose again and the Middle Florida economy reinflated. Enslavers responded by expanding their fields and their slaveholdings. Although the opening of immense new sectors of Texas to cotton development not only made slave prices climb again but drew off potential migrants to other southwestern states, some southeastern enslavers continued moving to Florida. North Carolinian Robert W. Williams, for instance, who become one of the largest slave owners in the Florida by 1860, moved to Leon County in the 1850s. Others, many of them from South Carolina, moved to eastern Florida during the decade. They settled as far south as the Miami River.[65]

Of course, not everything was easy for enslavers in the 1850s. They faced increasing national opposition in the form of a vocal abolitionist movement and the increasing reluctance of some northern whites to accede to the steadily shriller demands of southern pro-slavery politicians for pledges of security for the system of human captivity. Locked into a debate with the North over the morality of slavery, enslavers cranked up a propaganda noise machine devoted to the proposition that slavery was paternalistic and kind. Defenders of the South argued what would eventually become de rigueur for historians of the peculiar institution. They explicitly contrasted slave labor with free wage labor, arguing that in the latter, the "employer" had responsibility for seeing that the employee did not starve or endure a destitute old age. But this did not mean that enslavers provided either sufficient food or good living conditions for those whose labor they owned. Nor did it mean, as some claimed, that the ownership of slaves was unprofitable, a sort of sacrifice made by the master on the behalf of allegedly improvident Africans who needed supervision. It only meant that those who, after the defeats of the Civil War, wanted to justify the cause of those who had ordered the shooting to start would repeat this late-coming set of claims.[66]

Enslavers were still economic modernizers who pushed for new efficiency in their particular sector of the economy. They tried new fertilizers and new machinery. They tested new kinds of cotton. They also launched a massive campaign to convince neutrals in the debate over slavery that they were actually caring traditionalists who, like Northerners anxious at the changes that industrialization had wrought, abhorred the decline of old-fashioned communities. But even these actions look modern and familiar when viewed alongside contemporary public relations/mass deception campaigns, like those familiar to anyone who has studied the late twentieth-century comprehensive offensive against unions in the United States.

From the perspective of the enslaved, the turn to paternalism in the last decades of slavery made no real difference. Margaret Nickerson, enslaved in Leon County, remembered that in the 1850s her owner, William Carr, "fed us, but he did not care what and where, just so you made that money." He was still pushing, even "when you made five and six bales of cotton, [he] said 'You ain't done nothing.'"[67] While slavery had already been established in Florida law and history by 1821, the processes introduced as the territory became part of the wave of forced migration and planter entrepreneurship was in many ways fundamentally new. The slavery that emerged on the frontiers of cotton and sugar production in the nineteenth century was more closely supervised than ever. It was more efficient at extracting large quantities of labor from human bodies and minds than its eighteenth-century predecessor. The "pushing system" implemented by the first generation of cotton enslavers in Florida and elsewhere took a terrible toll on enslaved laborers. This was evident not just in the fields, but in the homes and families of those whose children and other relatives were in effect re-monetized by the domestic slave trade and related forms of forced migration that emerged in the nineteenth-century South.

When the Civil War came, all that was disrupted. Many enslavers turned their labor toward the war effort. Cattle raised in Florida fed Robert E. Lee's Army of Northern Virginia. Panhandle slave owners discovered that salt evaporated by slave labor on the Gulf Coast brought high prices because it could be used to preserve meat for the army. But like cattle-driving in the palmetto scrub, small-scale salt extraction on the beach opened hitherto rare opportunities for the enslaved. Union ships were just off the shore, blockading the coast. When they sent boats ashore, many slaves were "captured." As the war went on and the Union occupied more and more Florida ports, slaves increasingly freed themselves by going to the blue lines. After President Lincoln removed the ban on black enlistment, many joined and eventually fought against former masters. Everywhere that the blue army advanced, slavery dissolved. By the time Union general Edwin McCook arrived in Tallahassee on May 20, 1865, to announce the end to the war and to legal slave labor in Florida, most of the state's labor camps no longer functioned. The question of what would replace them remained open.

Notes

1. Peter H. Wood, "Slave Labor Camps in Early America: Overcoming Denial and Discovering the Gulag," *Inequality in Early America*, ed. Carla Gardina Pestana and Sharon V. Salinger (Hanover, N.H.: University Press of New England, 1999), 222–38.

2. For slavery in the first Spanish period, see Jane Landers, *Black Society in Spanish Florida* (Urbana: University of Illinois Press, 1999).

3. Jane Landers, "African-American Community Traditions in Florida," *African American Heritage of Florida*, ed. David Colburn and Jane Landers (Gainesville: University Press of Florida, 1985), 25.

4. Daniel L. Schafer, "'Yellow Silk Ferret Tied Round Their Wrists': African Americans in British East Florida, 1763–1784," *African-American Heritage*, 71–103; David Hancock, *Citizens of the World: London Merchants and the Integration of the British American Community* (London: Cambridge University Press, 1995); Bernard Bailyn, *Voyagers to the West: A Passage in the Peopling of America on the Eve of the American Revolution* (New York: Knopf, 1986).

5. D. Schafer, "African Americans in British East Florida," 76–81; Thomas W. Taylor, "'Settling a Colony over a Bottle of Claret': Richard Oswald and the British Settlement of East Florida," MA thesis, University of North Carolina, Greensboro, 1984, 34–36.

6. Taylor, "Settling a Colony," 46.

7. J. Leitch Wright Jr., *Florida in the American Revolution* (Gainesville: University Presses of Florida, 1975).

8. Joyce E. Chaplin, *An Anxious Pursuit: Agricultural Innovation and Modernity in the Lower South, 1730–1815* (Chapel Hill: University of North Carolina Press, 1993); Joyce E. Chaplin, "Creating a Cotton South in South Carolina and Georgia, 1760–1815," *Journal of Southern History* 57 (April 1991): 171–200; Adam Rothman, *Slave Country: American Expansion and the Origins of the Deep South* (Cambridge, Mass.: Harvard University Press, 2005); Francis Philip Fatio to Mrs. Fatio, October 18, 1800, from William Scott Willis, "A Swiss Settler in East Florida: A Letter of Francis Philip Fatio," *Florida Historical Quarterly* 64 (October 1985): 174–88, quote 183.

9. Daniel L. Schafer, "Zephaniah Kingsley's Laurel Grove Plantation, 1803–1813," in *Colonial Plantations and Economy in Florida*, ed. Jane Landers (Gainesville: University Press of Florida, 2000), 98–120, cotton totals from 113. For Florida's Patriot War, see Rembert Patrick, *Florida Fiasco: Rampant Rebels on the Georgia-Florida Border* (Athens: University of Georgia Press, 1954); William S. Coker and Susan R. Parker, "The

Second Spanish Period in the Two Floridas," *The New History of Florida*, ed. Michael Gannon (Gainesville: University Press of Florida, 1996), 152–66.

10. Benjamin Chaires to Thomas Fitch, July 27, 1820, folder 11, Thomas Fitch Papers, Florida State Archives (hereafter cited as FLSA); D. Schafer, "Kingsley's Laurel Grove Plantation," 101; James G. Cusick, "Spanish East Florida in the Atlantic Economy of the Late Eighteenth Century," *Colonial Plantations*, 168–88, esp. 178.

11. Acting Governor Worthington to John Quincy Adams, January 8, 1822, *The Territorial Papers of the United States*, vol. 22, ed. Clarence Edwin Carter and John Porter Bloom (Buffalo, N.Y.: William S. Hein, 2006), 329–30.

12. Andrew Ellicott, *The Journal of Andrew Ellicott, Late Commissioner on Behalf of the United States* (Philadelphia: Budd and Bartram, 1803); Charles Vignoles, *Observations upon the Floridas* (New York: Bliss and White, 1823).

13. "Cultivators" from John R. Bell to Thomas Metcalfe, 1822, *Territorial Papers*, 22:463–65; "In large measure," James Gadsden to Secretary of War John C. Calhoun, September 29, 1823, *Territorial Papers*, 22:752.

14. "East Florida, from the Carolina Courier," *Carolina Centinel*, February 10, 1821.

15. John Lee Williams, "Sketches of West Florida, No. XII," *Pensacola Gazette and West Florida Advertiser*, August 27, 1825; Edward E. Baptist, "Creating an Old South: The Plantation Frontier in Jackson and Leon Counties, Florida, 1821–1860," PhD diss., University of Pennsylvania, 1997, 66–101; John C. Upchurch, "Middle Florida: An Historical Geography of the Area between the Apalachicola and Suwannee Rivers," PhD diss., University of Tennessee, 1971.

16. "Cavalcade" from Douglass Memoirs, vol. 19, Special Collections, Robert Strozier Library, Florida State University, Tallahassee (hereafter cited as FSU); Harriet E. Randolph to Mrs. Thomas E. Randolph, May 23, 1829, and Lucy Beverly Randolph, September 8, 1829, folder 3, Randolph Family Papers, FLSA.

17. William Stephens, application no. 634, *Register of Signatures of Depositors in Branches of the Freedmen's Savings and Trust Company, 1865–1874. Tallahassee, Fla., August 25, 1866–June 15, 1874*, National Archives Microfilm Series, M816, roll 5 (hereafter cited as RSD); Thomas Brown to Richard T. Brown, November 4, 1827, Thomas Brown Letter, Mss 2 B1853a, Virginia Historical Society, Richmond (hereafter cited as VHS).

18. Thomas Brown Memoir, Ambler-Brown Papers, Special Collections, Perkins Library, Duke University (hereafter cited as PLDU); Charley Paine, O.A. no. 263, RSD. For networks of community and kinship, see Herbert Gutman, *The Black Family in Slavery and Freedom, 1750–1925* (New York: Vintage Press, 1976); Allan Kulikoff, *Tobacco and Slaves: The Development of Southern Cultures in the Chesapeake, 1680–1800* (Chapel Hill: University of North Carolina Press, 1986); Brenda Stevenson, *Life in Black and White: Family and Community in the Slave South* (New York: Oxford University Press, 1996); Philip D. Morgan, *Slave Counterpoint: Black Culture in the Eighteenth-Century Chesapeake and Lowcountry* (Chapel Hill: University of North Carolina Press, 1998); Stephanie M. H. Camp, *Closer to Freedom: Enslaved Women and Everyday Resistance in the Plantation South* (Chapel Hill: University of North Carolina Press, 2004).

19. William Kenyon, O.A. no. 391, RSD; Hardy Bryan Croom to B. Croom, June

Heritage University Library
3240 Fort Road
Toppenish, WA 98948

20, 1833, Croom Papers, Southern Historical Collection, Wilson Library, University of North Carolina at Chapel Hill (hereafter cited as SHC); William Warren Rogers and Erica R. Clark, *The Croom Family and Goodwood Plantation: Land, Litigation, and Southern Lives* (Athens: University of Georgia Press, 1999), 10, 39; Martin Goldsborough to Paul C. Cameron, June 2, 1851, folder 1089, Cameron Family Papers, SHC; Edward E. Baptist, "The Migration of Planters to Antebellum Florida: Kinship and Power," *Journal of Southern History* 62 (August 1996): 527–54.

20. *U.S. Census of Population: 1830* for Virginia, North Carolina, Essex and Halifax counties, respectively. See also Edward E. Baptist, *Creating an Old South: Middle Florida's Plantation Frontier before the Civil War* (Chapel Hill: University of North Carolina Press, 2002), 70; Stephen F. Miller, "Plantation Labor Organization and Slave Life on the Cotton Frontier: The Alabama-Mississippi Black Belt, 1815–1840," *Cultivation and Culture: Labor and the Shaping of Slave Life in the Americas*, ed. Ira Berlin and Philip D. Morgan (Charlottesville: University of Virginia Press, 1993), 157.

21. *Compilation of the Public Acts of the Legislative Council of the Territory of Florida Passed prior to 1840*, comp. John P. Duval (Tallahassee: State of Florida, 1839), 216; *Pensacola Floridian*, April 19, 1823.

22. *Tallahassee Floridian and Advocate*, December 22, 1829; Isaac Jarratt to Harriet Cash Jarratt, March 6, 1837, Jarratt-Puryear Papers, PLDU.

23. *Tallahassee Floridian*, February 9 and December 20, 1838.

24. Defenders of the Old South both before and after emancipation argued that there were paternalist planters and brutally greedy slave traders (conveniently, often Yankees), and that the two were distinct and mutually hostile. See, for instance, Daniel R. Hundley, *Social Relations in Our Southern States* (New York: H. B. Price, 1860). Others ignored the role of slave traders and trading entirely: Eugene D. Genovese, *Roll, Jordan, Roll: The World the Slaves Made* (New York: Pantheon Press, 1974). But more recently historians have shown that traders were usually planters, and many planters did quite a lot of slave trading. See especially Michael Tadman, *Speculators and Slaves: Masters, Traders, and Slaves in the Old South* (Madison: University of Wisconsin Press, 1996); Walter Johnson, *Soul by Soul: Life inside the Antebellum Slave Market* (Cambridge: Harvard University Press, 1999); Robert H. Gudmestad, *A Troublesome Commerce: The Transformation of the Interstate Slave Trade* (Baton Rouge: Louisiana State University Press, 2003); Edward E. Baptist, "'Cuffy,' 'Fancy Maids,' and 'One-Eyed Men': Rape, Commodification, and the Domestic Slave Trade in the United States," *American Historical Review* 106 (2001): 1619–50. The exception to this recent trend is Steven Deyle, who returns to the distinction between the two. See Deyle, *Carry Me Back: The Domestic Slave Trade in American Life* (New York: Oxford University Press, 2005).

25. Achille Murat, *The United States of America* (London: E. Wilson, 1833), 64.

26. Quotes from Achille Murat to John G. Gamble, October 1, 1834, 459–61, and Achille Murat to Thomas Botts, October 4, 1834, 461, Lipona Letter Book 1, Murat Papers, film 2657 (original in Bibliothèque National, Paris), FSU.

27. Moses Roper, *Narrative of My Escape from Slavery* (London, 1837; reprint, New York: Dover Press, 2003), 1–30, quote from 29.

28. William C. Wirt to Dabney Wirt, December 10, 1835, folder 5, Wirt Papers,

SHC; S. Miller, "Plantation Labor Organization." For legal cases, see *James F. Trottie vs. Wright and Triplett*, 1826, case file 6, Law Case Files, Leon County Courthouse, Tallahassee (hereafter cited as LCC); *Cary Bronaugh vs. W. D. Dandridge*, 1826, case file 17, LCC; *John Addison vs. A. W. Crews*, 1826, case file 8, LCC.

29. *Tallahassee Floridian and Advocate*, December 15, 1827; Mary Eppes to Mrs. Thomas Jefferson Randolph, April 1, 1827, folder 3, Randolph Family Papers, FLSA; Brown Memoir, folder 1, Ambler-Brown Family Papers, PLDU; H. B. Croom to Bryan Croom, June 5 and July 12, 1831, Croom Papers, SHC; Plantation Journal, folder 2, Gamble Family Papers, FSU; Thomas Eppes to Nicholas Trist, June 7, 1828, folder 43, N. P. Trist Papers, SHC; Farquhar McRae, "Of the Agriculture of Florida: The Importance and Value of the Sugar Crop," *Farmer's Register* 4 (April 12, 1836): 85–88; *American Farmer*, December 19, 1828, 211–12; J. P. Duval, "Sugar," *Baltimore Patriot*, December 23, 1828.

30. On sugar processing, see Lewis Cecil Gray, *History of Agriculture in the Southern United States to 1860*, vol. 2 (Washington, D.C.: Carnegie Institution, 1933), 740–51; Sidney Mintz, *Sweetness and Power: The Place of Sugar in Modern History* (New York: Viking Press, 1985); Stuart Schwartz, *Sugar Plantations in the Formation of Brazilian Society: Bahia, 1550–1835* (New York: Cambridge University Press, 1985).

31. Chris S. Monaco, *Moses Levy of Florida: Jewish Utopian and Antebellum Reformer* (Baton Rouge: Louisiana State University Press, 2005).

32. On sugar kettles, see Armistead Account Book, FLSA, 200, 219, 286; Brown Memoir, folder 1, Ambler-Brown Papers, PLDU, 72–74; Frances E. Brown Douglass Memoir, FSU.

33. On the opening of Cuba via the new mechanical, managerial, geographic, and other efficiencies, see Dale Tomich, *Through the Prism of Slavery: Labor, Capital, and World Economy* (Lanham, Mass.: Rowman and Littlefield, 2004).

34. Wiggins Diary, vol. 2, November 5 and 12, 1838, FSA.

35. "*From the Ohio Atlas*. Slavery in Florida. No. 1," in *The Narrative of Amos Dresser, with Stone's Letters from Natchez, an Obituary Notice of the Writer, and Two Letters from Tallahassee, Relating to the Treatment of Slaves* (New York: American Anti-Slavery Society, 1836), 37.

36. Quote from P. A. Bolling to Edmund Hubard, February 24, 1837, folder 72, Hubard Family Papers, SHC. Although the greater intensity of labor on the plantation frontier was a truism in the writings of both black and white abolitionists and appears to have been held as a certainty by enslaved people who either experienced or feared forced migration, I believe it is fair to say that later twentieth-century scholars of slave labor in the antebellum United States have not focused systematic attention on this issue. See Robert W. Fogel and Stanley L. Engerman, eds., *Without Consent or Contract: The Rise and Fall of American Slavery* (New York: Norton, 1992).

37. The shift from tobacco to grain is well documented by scholars of the Chesapeake region. See Paul G. E. Clemens, *The Atlantic Economy and Colonial Maryland's Eastern Shore: From Tobacco to Grain* (Ithaca, N.Y.: Cornell University Press, 1980); P. Morgan, *Slave Counterpoint*.

38. "Chemonie Journal, 1856," *Florida Plantation Records from the Papers of George Noble Jones*, ed. Ulrich B. Phillips and James D. Glunt (St. Louis: n.p., 1927), 443–509.

39. See "Mary Biddle," *The American Slave: A Composite Autobiography*, vol. 17, *Florida Narratives*, ed. George P. Rawick (Portsmouth, N.H.: Greenwood Press, 1972), 33.

40. Quote from P. A. Bolling to Edmund Hubard, February 24, 1837, folder 72, Hubard Family Papers, SHC. For the difficulties of learning how to pick cotton, see Charles Ball, *Fifty Years in Chains* (Indianapolis: Dayton and Asher, 1859), 184–87; Solomon Northup, *Twelve Years a Slave* (Auburn, Tex.: Derby and Miller, 1853), 134; Mary Ker to Isaac Baker, November 19, 1820, Ker Family Papers, SHC.

41. "Douglas Dorsey," *American Slave*, 17:96; "Louis Napoleon," *American Slave*, 17:243; Larry Eugene Rivers, *Slavery in Florida: Territorial Days to Emancipation* (Gainesville: University Press of Florida, 2000), 65–84.

42. Quotes from "Slavery in Florida. No. 1," *Narrative of Amos Dresser*, Samuel J. May Anti-Slavery Collection, Cornell University Library, 37–38. For night work by scaffold fires, see "Mary Biddle," 33.

43. Peter A. Coclanis, "How the Lowcountry Was Taken to Task," *Slavery, Secession, and Southern History*, ed. Robert Louis Paquette and Louis A. Ferleger (Charlottesville: University of Virginia Press, 2000), 59–80; Philip D. Morgan, "Task and Gang Systems: The Organization of Labor on New World Plantations," *Work and Labor in Early America*, ed. Stephen Innes (Chapel Hill: University of North Carolina Press, 1985); M. Roper, *Narrative*, 9.

44. S. Miller, "Plantation Labor Organization," 163–64.

45. *Narrative of Amos Dresser*, 19.

46. "Margaret Nickerson," *American Slave*, 17:253.

47. See William Newnham Blane, *Excursion through the United States and Canada during the Years 1822–1823, by an English Gentleman* (London: Baldwin, Cradock, and Joy, 1824), 67, 161; C. Ball, *Fifty Years*, 67, 161; Louis Hughes, *Thirty Years a Slave: From Bondage to Freedom: The Institution of Slavery as Seen on the Plantation and in the Home of the Planter* (Milwaukee: South Side Printing, 1897), 15–24, 46; William Anderson, *Life and Narrative of William Anderson* (Chicago: Daily Tribune Press, 1857), 17.

48. On the Bryant killing, see *Tallahassee Floridian*, April 7, 1849. Remembered by "Irene Coates," *American Slave*, 17:76. Learned by a man who had been enslaved in Mississippi but who did not come to Florida until after freedom: "Prophet Kemp," *American Slave*, 17:185. "I have driven," from "Slavery in Florida. No. 2," *Narrative of Amos Dresser*, 40.

49. W. W. Boykin to George Gray, October 16, 1850, folder 14, George Gray Papers, SHC.

50. Philemon Bliss, "It is not uncommon," *American Slavery as It Is: Testimony of a Thousand Witnesses*, ed. Theodore D. Weld (New York: Anti-Slavery Society, 1839); Hardy B. Croom to Henry Gaskins, July 30, 1837, no. 44, 26, Hardy B. Croom Papers, SHC.

51. *American Slave*, 17:329.

52. "Some planters," "If by," and "The slave is" from "Slavery in Florida. No. 1," *Narrative of Amos Dresser*, 37. See also "Work until sundown" and "You ain't done," *American Slave*, 17:96, 250–51.

53. *American Slave*, 17:336–37. See also Ladd from T. Weld, ed., *American Slavery as It Is*, 86.

54. "Mary and Sam" from "Slavery in Florida. No. 2," *Narrative of Amos Dresser*, 40.

55. "I have endeavored" from P. A. Bolling to Edmund Hubard, February 24, 1837, folder 72, Hubard Family Papers, SHC.

56. D. N. Moxley to George Noble Jones, September 8, 1854, *Florida Plantation Records*, 97; John Evans to George Noble Jones, Autumn 1854, *Florida Plantation Records*, 95–96. For the impact of new strains of cotton on cotton picking, see John Hebron Moore, *Agriculture in Antebellum Mississippi* (New York: Bookman Associates, 1958), 27–36, 145–60; "Historical and Statistical Collections of Louisiana," *De Bow's Review* 12 (June 1852): 632–33.

57. Mary Gamble to Emma Breckinridge, December 2, 1833, section 1, Thomas Family Papers, Mss1 T3685, VHS; Frances E. Brown Douglass Memoir, FSU; December 29, 1833, vol. 6, Henry Harrington Memoir, SHC; Sarah Atkinson, "The Migration of Wiley Brooks of Williamsville, N.C., to Florida," typescript, 1909, FSU; *Niles National Register*, June 15, 1833.

58. E. Baptist, *Creating an Old South*, 111–14. Many histories of banking in the 1830s and in the slave South have followed Bray Hammond, *Banks and Politics in America from the Revolution to the Civil War* (Princeton, N.J.: Princeton University Press, 1957) in laying the blame for speculation followed by economic panic at the doorstep of Jackson's uneducated policies. See Stanley Engerman, "A Note on the Economic Consequences of the Second Bank of the United States," *Journal of Political Economy* 78 (July/August 1970): 725–29. More econometrically inclined interpretations, such as Peter Temin's *The Jacksonian Economy* (New York: Norton, 1969), rejected Hammond's argument and looked to flows of specie in the world economy as primary causes of massive inflation between 1833 and 1837 and of the crash that followed. Most of these accounts have studiously ignored the role of the banks in financing the vast forced southwestward migration of enslaved laborers and the role of those enslaved people in growing the cotton that provoked both boom and bust. Prime examples include George D. Green, *Finance and Economic Development in the Old South: Louisiana Banking, 1804–1961* (Palo Alto, Calif.: Stanford University Press, 1972); Larry Schweikart, *Banking in the American South from the Age of Jackson to Reconstruction* (Baton Rouge: Louisiana State University Press, 1987). See also Richard H. Kilbourne Jr., *Debt, Investment, Slaves: Credit Relations in East Feliciana Parish, 1825–1885* (Tuscaloosa: University of Alabama Press, 1995); Lance E. Davis and Robert J. Cull, *International Capital Markets and American Economic Growth, 1820–1914* (London: Cambridge University Press, 1994); Peter L. Rousseau, "Jacksonian Monetary Policy, Specie Flows, and the Panic of 1837," *Journal of Economic History* 62 (June 2002): 457–88. By contrast, some earlier accounts openly acknowledged what planters did with the millions of dollars in loans, even if they persisted in identifying slave purchases as "short-term" investments,

as compared to the railroads and canals built with similar monies in the North. See Leland H. Jenks, *The Migration of British Capital to 1875* (New York: Knopf, 1927), 65–98; L. Gray, *History of Agriculture*, 2:898–901.

59. "Cotton! Cotton!" from William C. Wirt to Dabney C. Wirt, December 10, 1835, folder 5, Wirt Papers, SHC. Cotton totals from Levi Woodbury, "Cultivation, Manufacture, and Foreign Trade of Cotton: Letter from the Secretary of the Treasury," *House Documents*, 24th Cong., 1st sess. (1836), doc. no. 146: 13, bales averaging 383 pounds each.

60. Statistics from *Historical Statistics of the United States*, series E 96–100, E 101–12, K 298–306 (Washington, D.C.: Government Printing Office, 1957). The index of commodity prices reflects those in New Orleans. Bales of cotton are those averaging 383 pounds each.

61. "List of Negroes Sent to Florida, March 1st, 1828," in "Documents Relating to El Destino and Chemonie Plantations," part 1, ed. Kathryn Abbey, *Florida Historical Quarterly* 7 (January 1929): 206–7. See also "Documents Relating to El Destino and Chemonie Plantation," part 2, ed. Kathryn Abbey, *Florida Historical Quarterly* 7 (April 1929): 291–329; U. Phillips and J. Glunt, *Florida Plantation Records*, 329–38, 439–42, 511–71.

62. Sancho Thomas, application no. 316, and Richard Gadsden, application no. 354, Freedman's Bank Records; "Daphne Williams," *The American Slave: A Composite Autobiography*, vol. 10: *Texas Narratives*, supplement, series 2, ed. George P. Rawick (Portsmouth, N.H.: Greenwood Press, 1972), 4076–86.

63. "Patience Campbell," *American Slave*, 17:59; L. Rivers, *Slavery in Florida*, 34–46.

64. Michael Schene, "Sugar along the Manatee: Major Robert Gamble, Jr. and the Development of Gamble Plantation," *Tequesta* 41 (1981): 69–81.

65. Marvin Dunn, *Black Miami in the Twentieth Century* (Gainesville: University Press of Florida, 1997), 27–30; Clifton Paisley, *The Red Hills of Florida, 1528–1865* (Tuscaloosa: University of Alabama Press, 1989).

66. For a more extensive version of this argument as it pertains to Florida, see E. Baptist, *Creating an Old South*; William R. Taylor, *Cavalier and Yankee: The Old South and American National Character* (New York: HarperCollins, 1969). For the evidence that shows that whites in the cotton South were the wealthiest class of people in the United States and perhaps in the world—hardly likely if their institution was an unprofitable renunciation of materialisms—see James L. Huston, *Calculating the Value of Union: Slavery, Property Rights, and the Economic Origins of the Civil War* (Chapel Hill: University of North Carolina Press, 1990). See David W. Blight, *Race and Reunion: The Civil War in American Memory* (Cambridge, Mass.: Belknap Press of Harvard University, 2001) for the best account of how the political argument for the white South's righteousness developed into popular (whites') and professional assumptions about slavery and history.

67. Margaret Nickerson interview in *American Slave*, 17:250–51.

3

Labor and Survival among the Black Seminoles of Florida

BRENT R. WEISMAN

On March 30, 1836, the first of General Abraham Eustis's 1,400 troops slogged across a wet prairie and pushed up to the top of a low rise into the town of Pilaklikaha. Weary after days of wading through the watery wilderness of central Florida, the men had to have been relieved to find the settlement abandoned. When the rest of the soldiers arrived, and with practiced precision, Pilaklikaha was put to the torch.[1] As the bark-roofed, board-walled cabins quickly turned to flames, some of the soldiers shot glances inside to the rooms and darkened corners (see fig. 3.1). One noted seeing a type of stick that was used in the Indian ball game, a flute, and a turtle shell rattle filled with palmetto seeds.[2] Archaeologists now tell us that many other things were left in the cabins and around the village for the soldiers to see, the mundane material of everyday life, so ordinary as to not be worth mentioning but so important for our understanding of the world in which the people of Pilaklikaha lived. "Small things forgotten" is how the archaeologist James Deetz famously characterized these objects of everyday life, and at Pilaklikaha they included locally made pottery bowls and jars, imported English plates and saucers, white clay smoking pipes, and heavy dark green wine or ale bottles.[3] For the archaeologist, objects often contain more questions than answers, but these artifacts tell us one thing for sure. The U.S. Army may have had difficulty in coming to Pilaklikaha, but Pilaklikaha had not been cut off from the outside world. Who were these people who once lived among the "many ponds" of central Florida? And how were they able to get the goods then available in the trade economy of the early nineteenth century?

Eustis's army was the left wing of General Winfield Scott's grand but flawed design to choke the Seminole Indian resistance in the early months of the Second Seminole War. The plan called for three columns of soldiers to converge in a pincers movement on the Seminole stronghold in the so-

Figure 3.1. T. F. Gray and James, "Burning of Town Pilak-li-ka-ha by Gen. Eustis," 1837. No. 8 in set of eight "Views of Florida" in *Lithographs of Events in the Seminole War in Florida in 1835*. Lithograph, hand-colored. Published courtesy of the Library of Congress, Washington, D.C.

called Cove of the Withlacoochee, a trackless, 100-square-mile swamp across the Withlacoochee River, near Lake Tsala Apopka, just west of Pilaklikaha. Pilaklikaha was squarely in the path of the left wing and was a key target in the offensive. In sending Eustis to Pilaklikaha, Scott was pitting one Abraham against another, for Pilaklikaha was also known as "Abraham's Town," after its most distinguished resident, a strapping middle-aged former slave of African descent.[4] Abraham was a Black Seminole. To modern historians, Abraham, his people, and hundreds of others like them were "freedom seekers" who fled the slavery of the American South and deliberately forged symbiotic alliances with the more numerous and established Seminole Indians.[5] To the Seminoles, Abraham and his people were property, not to be given up without financial compensation and worth fighting to keep. To the Americans in Georgia and other southern states, Abraham's people were a threat to national security, poised to pour across the border under cover of darkness or to filter up through the swamps to pillage at will (see fig. 3.2).

Before Americans took control in 1821, the Spaniards who ruled Florida had yet another perspective. To them, men and women who fled slavery were potential citizens and able allies who were worth arming and supporting for their value in protecting St. Augustine's back door. Black Seminoles were also considered vital contributors to the colonial economy.[6] To the

Negro Abraham

Figure 3.2. N. Orr, "Abraham, runaway slave, a Negro interpreter who lived with the Seminoles," 1858. As published in Joshua Reed Giddings, *The Exiles of Florida* (Columbus, Ohio: Follett, Foster, and Company, 1858). Engraving. Published courtesy of the Library of Congress, Washington, D.C.

U.S. government after 1821, they were to be counted, watched, placed on a map, identified, and separated from the other Seminoles at all costs. To be a Black Seminole meant living in multiple worlds simultaneously. The central features of Black Seminole life were ambiguity and insecurity. Who was identified as a Black Seminole depended on who was asking, and conditions affecting their liberty could change with the wind and were often outside of their control. Survival depended on Black Seminoles' ability to meet new opportunities with flexible responses, to develop and use specialized skills, therefore becoming indispensable. It also required an intense pragmatism deeply grounded in the will to live. Black Seminoles' use of labor as a means of meeting the challenge of survival cannot be separated from the issue of how they defined what they did as capital, in the sense of controlling something that could be used to underwrite other gains. Labor must thus include knowledge work as well as the physical energy demanded by a particular task. For Black Seminoles, knowledge became an important calling card and was used with great effectiveness by Abraham and his associates to demonstrate their indispensability in a turbulent, uncertain world.

If labor in the modern world is looked upon as a decision-making process in which an individual chooses how to define his efforts to achieve a perceived gain, then we can begin to see how the Black Seminoles divided up their time and effort in the face of certain constraints. We can also see how their own historical traditions conditioned the range of their response. I use the term *modern world* deliberately because the Black Seminoles were very much a part of the global commercial economy that by the late eighteenth century had undeniably engulfed Florida.[7] In the most direct sense, the dominant Black Seminole way of life was a variant of the southern plantation system.[8] The key relationship was not between Anglo American landowners and African-derived slaves, but between Native American agricultural society and the groups of people who had freed themselves from bondage. Theirs was a largely voluntary association rather than coerced labor. Although some were captured in Seminole raids on Florida plantations, for the most part the Black Seminoles came to the Seminoles on their own terms. The Seminoles, of course, operated from their own model of the relationship, one based on identifying themselves as being similar to southern plantation owners, as well as reflecting their long exposure to commercial and mercantile economies in Georgia and Alabama.

The relationship between Seminoles and Black Seminoles was one of negotiated autonomy, with a sliding scale of control over labor and production. In this sense, it is difficult to understand why the Seminoles felt that they owned Black Seminoles. But they did so when they were forced to think of them as real property. This did not mean that the Seminoles wanted to exert control over the Black Seminoles, manage them daily, or keep them close by, as would have been the case in the Anglo American system. Rather, this meant that the Black Seminoles were largely free to go about their business: farming, herding, hunting, and, in time of war, going off on raiding parties or to the battlefield. The questions one might ask, or the assumptions one might have, about how Seminoles and Black Seminoles related to one another are thus different from those generated by the southern plantation model. Were there issues of social inequality? How did the Seminoles and Black Seminoles relate to each other socially and culturally? What specific historical traditions and expectations did both groups bring to the relationship? Ultimately, how did Black Seminoles define their own labor, and how did their perceptions of work and labor map out as strategies of survival? To begin to answer these questions, we first must have some understanding of who the Black Seminoles and Seminoles were and where they came from.

History and Cultural Origins of the Black Seminoles

Nomenclature is a serious issue that deserves discussion. The term *Black Seminole* was created and used by contemporary historians to describe the specific group of people of African origin who became associated with the Florida Seminoles in the late eighteenth and early nineteenth centuries.[9] "Black Seminole" was a descriptive term, focused on a small subset of "blacks" in the Southeast, the rest of whom were slaves or were free as a result of various circumstances. The term *Black Muscogulge* also was introduced by scholars and refers to African peoples who were associated with Creek Indians or other native groups throughout the region.[10] Eighteenth- and nineteenth-century documents, however, referred to all persons of African descent as "Negroes" and then described the status of these individuals in the context of their relationship with whites. Historians who coined and used the terms *Black Seminole* and *Black Muscogulge* stopped short of implying that they were essentially Seminoles or Muscogulges who happened to be black. Rather, most scholars believed these individuals were blacks who were uniquely associated with Seminoles or Creeks.

For the most part, the term *Black Seminole* was relatively uncontroversial until more recent years when it became increasingly laden with political meaning. Much of the current controversy stems from the issue of tribal standing. Pointing to the fact that Black Seminoles were not fully integrated into the clan system, some historians have argued that Black Seminoles should not be entitled to standing through the federal recognition process. This has proved to be a flashpoint between the living descendants of the Black Seminoles and the political leadership of the Seminole and Miccosukee tribes in Florida and the Seminole Nation in Oklahoma. Seminole interests argue that the Black Seminoles are not culturally Seminole; Black Seminoles, federally unrecognized but historically distinct, hold that they are. The history of litigation on this issue, now being played out in federal courts, will certainly provide new inspirations for scholarship. For their part, anthropologists have introduced the term *maroon* into the literature, noting that it shares a root with *Seminole* in the Spanish word *cimmarone* meaning "runaway" or "wild one," and emphasizing the autonomous, freedom-seeking qualities of these blacks rather than the particular nature of their relationship with the Seminoles or other native peoples.[11] *Maroon* can apply to a wider range of groups than those traditionally defined as Black Seminoles, like those communities in the remote swamps of the American Southeast or mountain hideaways in the Caribbean or South America who were largely isolated and functionally independent. Describing the Black Seminoles as "maroons" locates them within a larger spectrum of experience in the Americas, as a specific population of African descent who saw themselves as able to achieve their goal of independence by associating with the Seminoles.[12] This does bring a different perspective to the flow of power in the relationship and, however awkward, does have merit.

In light of these recent sensitivities, to continue to use the term *Black Seminole*, as I will do here, requires some justification. I use it for the following reasons. First, it is a recognizable term and is widely present in the literature. Because the usage narrows the scope to that smaller group of all the African peoples in the hemisphere that became associated with the Seminoles, the reader will know what group of blacks is being described. The story of the Black Seminoles also need not be written from the Seminole point of view, and their believed dominance in the relationship need not be perpetuated by scholarly practice. Finally, there is a small but significant body of historical literature by people who describe themselves as "Black Seminoles." So to at least some of the people whose ancestors are the subjects of study, the term does have meaning and is an accepted ethnonym.[13] For these reasons I continue to use the term *Black Seminole* here.

Black Seminoles' origins as slaves have been widely described.[14] The first runaway slaves came into Florida when the peninsula was a Spanish colony but the rest of the Atlantic seaboard was under British rule. Always tense, the relationship between the two colonial powers was strained even further by Spanish overtures toward southern slaves to seek their freedom in Florida. As citizens of the Spanish crown, slaves could find a new life in Florida if they accepted Christianity. This was required of all new Spanish citizens. They also had to agree to serve a term in the Spanish militia. The nucleus of this movement formed at the famous Gracia Real de Santa Teresa de Mose, commonly known as Fort Mose, the site of which is now a designated National Historic Landmark owned and managed by the Florida Park Service. Located on a marsh island north of St. Augustine, Fort Mose formed a first line of defense against Georgia-based British attacks on the Spanish capital at St. Augustine.[15] The archaeology of Fort Mose indicates that life in this frontier outpost was self-sufficient. Residents relied on hunting and fishing in the tidal estuary and maritime environment to feed themselves.[16] Founded in 1738, the fort was attacked and burned on several occasions, until it was finally abandoned in 1763 when Britain gained control of Florida. Most of the Mose residents moved to Cuba along with the Spanish Floridians. But some decided to stay on. The presence of these blacks in British Florida presented an in-the-flesh reminder to those still living in slavery that freedom might still be possible just across the border.

By the eve of the American Revolution in 1775, trickles of runaways had been wending their way through the Florida wilderness, skirting Seminole towns, exploring what life with the Seminoles might be like. By the Revolution's close in 1782, the relationship between black and Seminole was well on its way to being worked out. William Bartram observed Yamassee Indian slaves among the Seminoles. But he did not record seeing any blacks when he visited Cowkeeper's town on the Alachua Prairie in 1774. In the same area by 1793, however, Cowkeeper's nephew and successor, King Payne, owned at least 20 blacks as slaves.[17] A modern descendant of Black Seminoles also places her own family roots in a group of Gullah runaways who fled a coastal Georgia cotton plantation seeking the protection of King Payne.[18]

For escaped slaves, safety and shelter were powerful needs. Protection certainly has been one of the most historically persistent reasons given for why blacks sought out the Seminoles. From the Seminole point of view, it was paid for by tribute, extracted in agricultural produce or livestock.[19] Slavery, meaning the condition in which one person had absolute control over the labor of other people, was the closest equivalent this kind of relationship had in the conceptual framework of the time. That those enslaved people could also be property was, of course, a concept known to both blacks and to the Seminoles, as the wealthiest of the Creeks had also become slave owners and operated plantations in Georgia and Alabama. By the 1790s, and almost certainly earlier, the relationship between blacks and Seminoles that would later be described by Americans in Florida after 1821 and would help precipitate the Second Seminole War was largely cemented. During the last several decades of the eighteenth century, the cultural identity of "Black Seminole" emerged and took full form. Thus by 1836, when Abraham's village was ransacked by blue-jacketed men led by the other Abraham, the Black Seminoles had existed for close to 50 years.

By the 1820s, most Black Seminoles lived in towns across a broad arc in west central Florida, anchored on the northwest by the wetlands of Lake Tsala Apopka, the Withlacoochee River, and Lake Panasoffkee, bowing out to the east to include the hammock-pond-prairie region of Pilaklikaha, then swinging back to the southwest, skirting the vast Green Swamp, and tailing out around the margins of Tampa Bay to the Manatee River on the south.[20] Most Black Seminoles arrived in central Florida after fleeing attacks by the Georgia and Tennessee militias on the Alachua Seminole region of north central Florida between 1811 and 1814 and Andrew Jackson's strikes against the Miccosukee and Suwannee settlements during his 1818 invasion of Spanish Florida. Their move accompanied a similar relocation by their Seminole owners. Settling across the landscape, Black Seminoles

established themselves on hammocks or high ground so that both agricultural soils and pastureland were accessible.

Horatio Dexter was one of very few outsiders to visit a functioning Black
Seminole village in peacetime. In 1822, at the request of Governor William
P. DuVal, he set off west across the peninsula from his base at Volusia on the
St. Johns River, to spread the word among the Seminoles of upcoming treaty
negotiations to be held at Moultrie Creek, south of St. Augustine. The ap-
proach to Pilaklikaha, Dexter wrote, "appears like islands." He continued:

> The hammocks are very numerous and contain from 20 to 300 acres
> each, all of which are surrounded by Savannahs, which afford cover-
> age [and] sufficient range for innumeral cattle. These savannahs run
> in a S.E. direction. At this settlement there are about 100 negroes
> belonging to Micanopy. Their families of different ages and sex and
> their lands sufficient for a population of 2000 persons. There is not
> to exceed 120 acres planted thereon. The principal crop is rice and
> ground nuts. I have no doubt the corn planted at this place will yield
> ten bushels to the acre. The rice, indeed everything they plant here is
> equal to any I have seen in Florida.[21]

Navigable waterways were also within easy reach of Black Seminole settlements. For most of the year, with the exception of times of extreme drought,
Black Seminoles traveled by canoe from town to town on a network of
streams, creeks, and rivers. Largely concealed from view while moving back
and forth, they could transport produce, meat, or skins in bulk quantities.
These same corridors also provided a quick means of escape in the event of
a threat. At one end of Jumper Creek, for instance, was Pilaklikaha. At the
other end was Boggy Island on the east bank of the Withlacoochee River,
where blacks "mostly concealed themselves in time of war," according to
one military diarist writing in 1837.[22]

A system of trails and roads also connected Black Seminole towns to
Seminole villages and to the outside world. It was likely, however, that the
traveler could only gain passage to a Black Seminole town after first check-
ing in at the main Seminole town, as Dexter had done by going through
Micanopy's Okahumpka on his way to Pilaklikaha. This system maintained
the Seminoles' position as middlemen in the economic exchange between
Black Seminoles and the commercial interests of the outside world. It also
shielded the numerically few Black Seminoles from predation by slave
catchers and other hostile or retaliatory actions from a variety of groups for
whom the Black Seminoles were lucrative and ready-made targets. When

traveler William Simmons visited a Black Seminole town in 1823, he observed:

> We at length arrived at a small Indian town, where we found only one family, the rest having gone out hunting. We here got directions to the Negro settlement, which we reached at about 11 o'clock at night. The Negroes said they were apprized of our approach by the crowing of fowls; which we had also noticed, as being unusual at that hour.
>
> At the house of Cudjoe, one of the principal characters of the place, I took up my lodging for the night, on a bunk by the fire-side. The smoke, however, and the conversation of the Negroes, who sat up till a late hour, prevented me from getting much rest.
>
> These people were in the greatest poverty, and had nothing to offer me; having, not long before, fled from a settlement further west, and left their crop ungathered, from an apprehension of being seized by the Cowetas, who had recently carried off a body of Negroes residing near the Suwaney.
>
> There was, also, a general impression among them, that the Americans would seize upon all the Negro property of the Indians; and the latter were also induced to believe, by designing persons, that the Americans would rob and treat them with every degree of injustice and oppression.[23]

To live outside of this system was to risk great peril, as these descriptions of Black Seminole life make clear.

In looking at issues of Black Seminole labor, we can start by comparing the working relationships of blacks as Black Seminoles to what most had known previously as slaves. To some extent, we can look to the many variations of the slave experience as setting up the diversity and range of the Black Seminole experience. Abraham, for example, had not been a field slave but the personal servant of a well-to-do Pensacola physician.[24] This gave him unique access to the dominantly white world and provided crucial opportunities for building his intellectual capital. Other Black Seminoles at Pilaklikaha clearly had strong agricultural backgrounds, productively cultivating what were often thin and either poorly or excessively drained soils. They coaxed yields of rice, corn, beans, peanuts, and melons from these plots. Their knowledge of animal husbandry could have come from their slave past or may have been picked up from their Seminole masters. In any event, practically everything that slaves did in their many roles and various forms of servitude, Black Seminoles also did. There were, of course, far fewer Black Seminoles than there were plantation slaves, but the tech-nological world of the Black Seminoles was a microcosm of the larger slave experience and built upon its base.

Equality and Inequalities: The Relationship between Seminoles and Black Seminoles

Their social world was even more complex, as the underlying assumptions of equality or inequality that structured the relationships among Black Seminoles and Seminoles make clear. Many Seminoles had been long ex-posed to colonial and American conceptions of slavery. As Creeks, they had themselves either descended from slave-owning families or known of other Creek Indians who owned slaves. To be wealthy and powerful in the colonial Southeast meant that you made your living as a merchant or plan-tation owner and that you possessed slaves. This held true for European Americans and Native Americans alike; the history of the Creek Nation is inseparable from the interests of wealthy and powerful Creeks like Al-exander McGillivray, William McIntosh, and William Weatherford, slave owners all.[25] So the precedent was there. Seminoles modeled their view of slavery after what they knew of the Creek version, which had been heavily influenced by the plantation model.

Slaves provided the labor necessary to produce goods that had economic value. Their role was central to making a profit. But slaves themselves were also capital and had intrinsic value for sale or exchange. Wealthy Creeks used slaves much as their colonial or American counterparts did. But there was also an out, a path toward freedom, and the suggestion that there were other forces at work besides completely accepting the idea that slaves were fixed and inalienable pieces of property. During his travels through Creek country in the 1770s, naturalist William Bartram was hosted by a Creek plantation owner named Bosten. For breakfast, Bartram was served "ex-cellent coffee" by "young negro slaves." At work on Bosten's 100 planted and fenced acres were 15 other Negroes, "several of which were married to Indians." But, as Bartram noted, they were only "slaves till they marry," after which they became "Indians or free citizens."[26]

These observations strongly indicate the late eighteenth-century survival of a post-European contact response by native groups to the circumstances of extreme depopulation. Native Americans set up social rules for fusing previously distinct groups together into one new community. In the pro-cess, survivors of previous populations had to be able to join together, and groups who had suffered moderate declines had to be able to bring in others, providing some means for them to become members of the society. Sometimes this was accomplished by raiding, with captives as the booty. Captives were then put to work at menial or dangerous tasks in their new home. European observers frequently described this as a form of slavery, albeit different from their own.[27] The understanding that natives themselves had a form of slavery quite apart from, and distinctly earlier than, its use in colonial America thus entered into the literature and, to some extent, commonly held knowledge about the nature of native life.

Archaeologists have attempted to push the origins of aboriginal slavery further back into the mists of prehistory. Typically, they also have tried to place it within the context of warfare and raiding or within prestige and status systems.[28] However unintended, the combined effects of archaeological and historical scholarship, and the popular views of native society in the eighteenth and nineteenth centuries, legitimized the existence of slavery as a natural condition of all human "races," making the American Indian in particular something less than noble. But this view was also oversimplified. In the Creek system, the concept of slavery melded control over someone else's actions and the loss of certain rights by that person, with the English-based view of slaves as real, immutable property with worth that could be pegged to market value. The system carried forward by the early Seminoles thus had its origins both in the aboriginal past and their exposure to colonial forms of slavery. Those forms present on the plantations of the Southeast and adopted by the Creeks were especially important models.

To the Seminoles of the late eighteenth century, blacks who came to them looked like slaves. They were then recognized as someone's lost property and thus not the social equals of truly autonomous individuals. So, to the extent that Black Seminoles were viewed as property, Seminoles did not view them as equals. Nevertheless, in their own daily definition and through their own eyes, the Seminoles saw their control over blacks to be entirely conditional and situational. In the view of Seminoles, blacks were free-ranging, like their cattle, and could be gathered up and used when needed but were fine to be left alone. In this way, the Seminoles carried forward the Creek concept that slavery was not an absolute condition or an intrinsic property of a certain group of people, but could change and be renegotiated over time.

Because the Black Seminoles lived a largely autonomous existence from the Seminoles and experienced a great deal of freedom, they could be nearly equal to the Seminoles in the course of day-to-day life. The most adept among the Black Seminoles rose to positions as advisors or "sense-bearers." Abraham, for example, was Micanopy's sense-bearer. The option of social mobility also created a certain tension between Seminoles and Black Seminoles because it helped elevate the Black Seminole above a purely subordinate status. Yet there were also limits to this mobility. Evidence for intermarriage between Seminoles and Black Seminoles, like that described by Bartram for the slaves of the Creeks, is scant. If intermarriage was practiced commonly in the late 1700s through the early 1800s, it had become rare by the time of the Second Seminole War. Some evidence has been produced that the famed war leader Osceola had a black wife.[29] There are also scattered references to Seminole-black intermarriage in the late nineteenth century. In almost every case, these unions involved descendants of Black Seminoles who had escaped deportation during the Second and Third Seminole Wars. But the specific mention of these unions indicates that marriages between blacks and Seminoles fell outside the norm and were increasing viewed with disapproval by the rest of the Seminoles. This historical trend also suggests that marriage as a route to freedom, as practiced in Creek Country, never truly took hold in Florida.

What did take hold was something that looked and felt like freedom. Slave owners of the American South recognized it, too, and regarded these apparently free former slaves with fear and terror. "This, you may be assured, is a Negro, not an Indian war," wrote General Thomas Jesup not long after the onset of the Second Seminole War, "and if it be not speedily put down, the south will feel the effects of it on their slave population before the end of the next season."[30]

Labor, Control, Survival

Black Seminoles possessed two basic resources that were in particular demand by the outside world. The first was the energy of physical labor. The second was knowledge. Black Seminoles used each as capital, and each played a critical role in their survival. Knowledge, in particular, was used as leverage in their relationships with the Seminoles and, when necessary, with the military sent to Florida to dislodge the Seminoles.

The Black Seminoles knew about the larger world and how it worked. They had seen inside the white world to an extent beyond the experience of most Seminoles. This knowledge became a highly valued commodity and existed in two domains. The first was technological knowledge: how to do work, how to plant and harvest rice, how to husband livestock, how to smith metal, and how to build things. Seminoles also knew how to do many of these things and performed some of these tasks as well. But Black Seminoles' firsthand training in agriculturally productive and efficient labor practices set them apart and gave them special expertise in what it took to squeeze out a living from the land. To some degree, then, the plantation experience provided opportunities for apprenticeships that served Black Seminoles well when they became the masters of their own efforts. Indeed, in the years leading to the Second Seminole War, several outside observers remarked upon the lushness and bounty of Black Seminole fields compared with that of their Seminole neighbors, singling out the fullness of their corn cribs for particular praise.[31] These same observers were impressed by the industriousness of Black Seminoles and their generally high standard of living. One of Andrew Jackson's men wrote in 1818 that the houses of the Black Seminoles along the Suwannee River were larger and better framed than those of Bowlegs's Seminoles nearby.[32] Although Black Seminole towns did not completely mimic the spatial layout of a plantation and were not compact, gridded settlements, it does seem that the arable lands were divided into large, single-crop tracts, arranged around the residential areas.

We can also ask whether Black Seminole men and women equally shared this technological knowledge and the labor that went with it. In other words, was sex-based division of labor a significant reality of Black Seminole life? And if so, to what extent did the division of labor in Black Seminole society reflect plantation, Creek-Seminole, or African influences? Although the historical references and archaeological records are limited in what they tell us about the sexual division of labor, some broad contours do emerge. The message from all sources seems to be consistent: There was a strong division of labor among Black Seminoles based on sex. Women worked the fields, planting, cultivating, harvesting. In the words of Horatio Dexter, who wrote about Pilaklikaha in 1823: "Most of the labor is performed by the women, the men are indulged in following the habits of their women and pass most of their time in idleness, occasionally hunting at Pilaklikaha."[33] Women also prepared and served the food and generally minded hearth and home. In all of these activities, they were very much like their Native American counterparts. And like their Native American counterparts, Black Seminole men largely interacted with the outside world and served as conduits of exchange for the flow of goods. These goods then moved into a domestic economy controlled by women and were made possible by their productivity. But they passed through male hands on their way in. We know of other activities in the male domain such as hunting and going to war. We do not know who was in charge of the cattle and hogs, although in Seminole society, managing animals fell largely into the domain of male labor, whereas processing hides may have been women's work. We cannot be sure what taxonomy of activity guided the allocation of Black Seminole effort, dividing tasks into men's versus women's work. But we can be sure that among Black Seminoles, one's sex played a central role in determining the work one performed.

Because men had far greater access to the larger world than women, they played a much larger role in the second domain of knowledge that centered on knowing how the world at large worked and what it took to successfully navigate the extremely complex channels of social, political, and economic interaction and information flow. To be a player in the early nineteenth-century world of the Black Seminole meant melding a cosmopolitan grasp of one's position in the widely spun web of the larger society with the ability to leverage one's strengths to strategic advantage. Certainly all of the Black Seminoles known to us by name from historical accounts had this cosmopolitan quality. Abraham, Cudjoe, John Horse, and John Caesar were all big names. But there were others: Primus, Sampson, and Tom, to mention a few. All had one thing in common: they knew what was important to the Seminole and to the white man, they knew what both wanted, and they knew that they had something to offer each group.

Many Black Seminole men, even those not as distinguished as Abraham, were fluent in English as well as various Indian languages. They achieved status by serving as interpreters and translators in relations between the Seminoles and governmental, military, and trade interests. On occasion Black Seminole men also assumed diplomatic importance by shuttling the finer points of negotiation back and forth between the two sides. Abraham was particularly noted for this ability. He accompanied Micanopy on a visit to Washington, D.C., in 1825. Ten years later, Abraham saw service as a battlefield diplomat on the Seminole side in General Gaines's failed offensive in the Cove of the Withlacoochee. Abraham was granted his freedom by Micanopy as reward for his service. He was also given a wife, a black woman who had been the wife or mistress of the late Bowlegs.[34] The muster rolls of Black Seminoles deported to Indian Territory show several instances where Black Seminoles were owned by other Black Seminoles, men and women alike, suggesting that this reward practice may have been common and applied to Black Seminoles of both sexes.[35]

Multilingualism also became an asset when Black Seminoles were captured by troops in the Second Seminole War. It enabled them to serve as guides to the location of Seminole villages. Although undoubtedly coerced, and in some cases leading unsuspecting troops on the proverbial wild goose chase, Black Seminole men took this role as guides as an opportunity not just to survive but to win their freedom.[36] Here they traded on both their language abilities and on their detailed knowledge of the lay of the land, something the military chronically lacked throughout the course of the war. Just as they had in their dealings with government officials and traders throughout the prewar years, Black Seminoles again acted as agents of information on the margins of contact.

Evolving Responses in the Emerging Capitalist Economy

By the late 1700s, many Seminoles had adopted a variant of the plantation system. They were producing for external markets, using a labor force that was, at least in part, controlled and situationally viewed as property. In the Alachua area, this transformation occurred as leadership passed from Cowkeeper to Payne, and almost certainly prevailed from the 1790s through the dispersal of the Alachua towns south to Okahumpka and Pilaklikaha after 1812.[37] Archaeological and historical descriptions of Paynestown, Opauney's Town, and other settlements indicate that these communities physically resembled the plantations of the lower Southeast and looked distinctly different from the squareground towns of Bartram's day. In the words of Dexter, who visited Opauney's Town over this period: "Two miles east of his [Opauney's] residence you come to his field on which the Negro houses are built. This field is planted with corn and rice and attended in the same manner one would expect in Plantations under the direction of white people."[38] Dexter further noted that Opauney "held about 20 slaves who perform the same labor that is generally expected on plantations in Florida." Seminoles sold corn, rice, and cattle to colonial governments in St. Augustine. At the same time that sugar, rice, and indigo produced in plantations along the St. Johns River were competing in international markets, the Seminole plantations helped to feed the colony.

But archaeology indicates that there is more to the story. At Pilaklikaha, the Black Seminole site that is best known archaeologically, thousands of artifacts have been unearthed in recent excavations.[39] Broken pieces of English-made ceramics in transfer print or shell edged patterns, fragments of heavy, dark green glass wine bottles, broken pipe stems from white kaolin pipes, and shards of brushed-surface earthenwares made by the Seminoles are all commonly found—an assemblage of material indistinguishable from that of a Seminole site of the early nineteenth century. These findings suggest that Black Seminoles had access to the same sorts of goods as the Seminoles and acquired them with much the same frequency. Clearly, Black Seminoles were not going to St. Augustine or to the trading houses to get them. Nor is it likely that traders frequently came to them, particularly given the increasingly hostile environment leading up to and including the early years of American control. If measured strictly by artifacts, the Black Seminoles were indistinguishable from Seminoles. Of course, the slaves at many plantations also ended up with many of the same consumer goods as their owners and overseers, as hand-me-downs or salvaged items. With the exception of the architectural footprint that distinguishes a Great House from the slave cabin, they too might be thought of as materially indistinct from their owners.[40] Historical sources are not sufficiently precise for us to know if this same kind of process was operating between Seminoles and Black Seminoles. But the archaeological record does tell us that Seminoles and Black Seminoles interacted in some regular way and that some type of exchange took place through which the Black Seminoles received their transfer print plates and bottled wine.

The presence of traditional Seminole pottery in its traditional style and forms suggests that the interaction also had other dimensions. This pottery is Seminole in every visible way and is not a type of "colonoware" as described on the lowcountry plantations of South Carolina and Georgia.[41] In this context, colonoware is defined as slave-manufactured, low-fired earthenware that is vernacular to the setting and evinces in some way an African influence. To the best of our present knowledge, the pottery found at Black Seminole sites in Florida is not this, but is instead Seminole Indian pottery with a long native pedigree in southeastern North America. Seminole pottery was typically made in jar, bowl, and open "casuela" forms. It was used for cooking, serving, and storing food. Several distinct decorative styles were used on the rims of jars, such as fingernail pinching, and pinched or punctuated appliqué, clay strips. Although historical accounts of Seminole pottery-making are extremely rare and do not specifically mention women as the potters, references to women potters in other southeastern groups in the historic period suggest that women predominated among Seminole potters as well.[42]

But how did these pots get into Black Seminole villages? Anthropology offers several explanations. One theory is that Seminole women lived in Black Seminole villages as marriage partners and in a family setting with Black Seminole men. This is a standard anthropological model. But in the matrilineal kinship system of the Seminoles, it also meant that children born from the union of Seminole women and Black Seminole men became members of a Seminole clan and therefore fully integrated into Seminole society. Yet except in rare cases, this seems not to have been the case.

A second possibility is that the pots simply moved in as exchange items, changing hands from Seminole women to Black Seminole women the same way that English tableware and wine ended up in these same locations. This is economically feasible. But it is not wholly satisfactory in addressing the social reality that structured the relationship between blacks and Seminoles. To get to the nature of this relationship, it is essential to explore what it meant for Black Seminole women to have and to use these traditional Seminole pieces. In other words, in what social context did it make sense to have traditional Seminole pottery in a Black Seminole setting? Here the comparative methods of ethnohistory, while certainly fallible, can help to flesh out this relationship. In 1930, a government agent by the name of Roy Nash described his own encounter with Black Seminole life. Although not entirely free of the biases of his day, Nash provides some observations that are relevant to our concerns. He wrote:

> In MacCauley's day [1880s] there were still three negro women living as Seminole wives, relics of slavery days, and seven mixed bloods, all Indian-Negro crosses. At one time the Seminoles possessed a considerable number of slaves; all the Negro blood in the tribe traces back to that fact. The males of the superior economic order never have difficulty in finding mates among the females of an inferior economic group; the Indian-Negro crosses were invariably Indian men who mated with Negro women, never vice versa. No Indian woman, so far as I can learn, ever accepted a Negro male as the father of her children.[43]

We know, or at least suspect, from the historical record that Osceola and Bowlegs had Black Seminole wives. If so, their cases might not have been unusual. If Seminole men had Black Seminole wives, and these women continued to live and function as Black Seminoles, would this relationship show up in the archaeological record? Perhaps this is why Seminole Indian pottery is found at Black Seminole sites, indicating that Black Seminole women could live in two worlds just like most Black Seminole men. In one role, Black Seminole women served as wives to Seminole men. To a certain extent they were looked upon as property. But they must also have been recognizably Seminole, because having and using Seminole pottery made them Seminole. In their role as Black Seminoles, however, these women had no place in the Seminole clan system and thus had autonomy in their daily lives, living and working with their fellow Black Seminoles. The labor they performed moved them between the worlds of the Seminole and the Black Seminole, helping to join the interests of these two distinct societies.

By the end of the Second Seminole War in 1842, most of the estimated five hundred or so Black Seminoles were gone from Florida, either dead or deported to Indian Territory.[44] With their removal and demise, this most peculiar institution also disappeared, its curious mix of native and colonial forms of slavery and tributary vassalage fading from view into near obscurity. There is no doubt that the Black Seminoles were a "freedom seeking people" and that they used their labor to secure some measure of power and control in a world that was largely not of their making. As such, the story of Black Seminole labor is far more than a footnote or curiosity in Florida labor history. How Black Seminole men and women defined their labor and used it to survive cannot be separated from who they were as a people.

Notes

1. John Mahon's *History of the Second Seminole War* (Gainesville: University Press of Florida, 1967) is considered the authoritative secondary source on this conflict. He describes Eustis's attack on Pilaklikaha on pages 156–57 and provides several primary citations. For a brief firsthand account of the burning of Pilaklikaha, see M. M. Cohen, *Notices of Florida* (Gainesville: University Presses of Florida, 1964), 174–75.

2. M. M. Cohen observes, "While awaiting the return of the express, I examined the prize captured at Pilaklikaha. Here are a ballstick, and Indian flute, and small gopher shells, or box-turtle, with rattling Indian shot, or palmetto seed: the music of the dance." Although Cohen does not directly attribute these items to the Black Seminoles, we know that is who they expected to find at Pilaklikaha. See M. Cohen, *Notices*, 176.

3. James Deetz, *In Small Things Forgotten: An Archaeology of Early American Life* (New York: Anchor Books/Doubleday, 1996). On objects found at Pilaklikaha, see Terrance Weik, "A Historical Archaeology of Black Seminole Maroons in Florida: Ethnogenesis and Culture Contact at Pilaklikaha," PhD diss., University of Florida, 2002. The archaeological remains of Pilaklikaha lay beneath the sod of a privately owned cow pasture between Bushnell and Center Hill in central Florida.

4. Kenneth W. Porter, "The Negro Abraham," *Florida Historical Quarterly* 25 (July 1946): 1–44. This work is the definitive source on Abraham and identifies the primary documents associated with his life.

5. Recent treatments of the Black Seminoles include Kevin Mulroy, "Seminole Maroons," *Handbook of North American Indians*, vol. 14, *Southeast* (Washington, D.C.: Smithsonian Institution, 2005), 465–77; Kevin Mulroy, *Freedom on the Border* (Lubbock: Texas Tech University Press, 1993); Kenneth Porter, *The Black Seminoles*, ed. Al-

cione Amos and Thomas P. Senter (Gainesville: University Press of Florida, 1996). See also Jane Landers, "Free and Slave," in *The New History of Florida*, ed. Michael Gannon (Gainesville: University Press of Florida, 1996), 167–82; James G. Cusick, *The Other War of 1812: The Patriot War and the American Invasion of Spanish East Florida* (Gainesville: University Press of Florida, 2003), esp. 205, 232, 234, 242, and 299.

6. J. Landers, "Free and Slave."

7. This concept frames Charles Orser's book, *A Historical Archaeology of the Modern World* (New York: Plenum Press, 1996).

8. See Brent R. Weisman, "The Plantation System of the Florida Seminole Indians and Black Seminoles during the Colonial Era," *Colonial Plantations and Economy in Florida*, ed. Jane Landers (Gainesville: University Press of Florida, 2000), 136–49.

9. K. Porter, *The Black Seminoles*.

10. J. Leitch Wright Jr., *Creeks and Seminoles* (Lincoln: University of Nebraska Press, 1986). Wright's work provides solid discussion of this issue in chapter 3. A new approach synthesizing previously unused primary sources is Claudio Saunt, *A New Order of Things: Property, Power, and Transformation of the Creek Indians, 1733–1816* (New York: Cambridge University Press, 1999). See chapter 5 in particular.

11. T. Weik, *A Historical Archaeology*; K. Mulroy, *Freedom on the Border*.

12. Richard Price, ed., *Maroon Societies: Rebel Slave Communities in the Americas*, 2nd ed. (Baltimore: Johns Hopkins University Press, 1979).

13. Belinda G. Quarterman-Noah, *Black Seminoles: The Little-Known Story of the First Seminoles* (privately published, 1995); Alice Fay Lozano and Shirley Boteler Mock, *My Black Seminole Ancestors: Running to Freedom* (Austin: Institute of Texan Culture, University of Texas at Austin Press, n.d.) are examples. See also www.johnhorse.com, a thoroughly researched Web site on this subject.

14. Rebecca Bateman has written an excellent synthesis and literature review pertinent to Black Seminole origins. See Rebecca Bateman, "Naming Patterns in Black Seminole Ethnogenesis," *Ethnohistory* 49 (Spring 2002): 227–57.

15. J. Landers, "Free and Slave."

16. Kathleen Deagan and Darcie MacMahon, *Fort Mose: Colonial America's Black Fortress of Freedom* (Gainesville: University Press of Florida, 1995).

17. See James W. Covington, *The Seminoles of Florida* (Gainesville: University Press of Florida, 1993), 29; J. Cusick, *The Other War*, 214. See also Charles H. Fairbanks, *Ethnohistorical Report on the Florida Indians* (New York: Garland Press, 1974), 246, note with Bell Addition no. 29. William Simmons provides this anecdote about one of Payne's slaves: "Whan, a very intelligent black interpreter, who had been one of the slaves of King Payne, on my questioning him upon this subject, assured me, that his master, as he called him, had always treated him with the utmost humanity and kindness, and often condescended to give him lessons for his conduct, instructing him to adhere to truth and honesty, and endeavor to act well in his course through life." See William Simmons, *Notices of East Florida with an Account of Seminole Nation of Indians by a Recent Traveler in the Province* (Charleston, S.C.: privately printed, 1822; Gainesville: University Press of Florida, 1973), 76–77.

18. A. Lozano and S. Mock, *My Black Seminole Ancestors*.

19. Maj. General George McCall describes tribute as 10 bushels of corn or an agreed upon head of livestock. See George A. McCall, *Letters from the Frontiers* (Philadelphia: J. B. Lippincott, 1868), 166. William Simmons states that the "Negroes" "raised a sufficiency of provisions, both for themselves and their Indian owners." In his words, "[T] hey never furnished the Indians with any surplus produce, for the purposes of trade; but barely made them sufficient provisions for necessary consumption." See W. Simmons, *Notices*, 75–76. I have argued elsewhere that Black Seminole tribute did in fact allow the Seminole to produce an agricultural surplus for trade, even if the food provided by the Black Seminoles was not used for this purpose. See B. Weisman, "The Plantation System."

20. C. Fairbanks, *Ethnohistorical Report*, 245, 248. See map locations of the Bell Addition showing Pe-lac-la-ka-ha, Mulatto Girl's Town, Bucker Woman's Town, and King Heijah's.

21. I cite here and elsewhere in this chapter from a copy in my possession of typescript of the Dexter manuscript from Albert Devane's *Early Florida History*, vol. 2 (Sebring, Fla.: Sebring Historical Society, 1929), on file in the Florida History Collections, Special Collections, P. K. Younge Library, University of Florida, Gainesville. More on Dexter can be found in Mark F. Boyd's "Horatio S. Dexter and Events Leading to the Treaty of Moultrie Creek with the Seminole Indians," *Florida Anthropologist* 11 (1958): 65–95. For a printable version of the primary Dexter narrative in the National Archives, see http://freepages.genealogy.rootsweb.com/~texlance/seminoles/observations.htm.

22. Lt. Henry Prince, *Amidst a Storm of Bullets*, ed. Frank Laumer (Tampa: University of Tampa Press, 1998), 93, entry for April 25, 1837.

23. W. Simmons, *Notices*, 41.

24. K. Porter, "The Negro Abraham," 3–4. See also Charles H. Coe, *Red Patriots: The Story of the Seminoles* (Cincinnati: n.p., 1898; Gainesville: University Press of Florida, 1974), 45–46; G. McCall, *Letters from the Frontiers*, 302.

25. J. Wright, *Creeks and Seminoles*.

26. William Bartram, "Observations on the Creek and Cherokee Indians, 1789," *Transactions of the American Ethnological Society* 3 (1853): 1–81. This article has also been collected in William C. Sturtevant, ed., *A Creek Source Book* (New York: Garland Press, 1987), 37–38.

27. See C. Saunt, *A New Order of Things*; Robbie Ethridge and Charles Hudson, eds., *The Transformation of the Southeastern Indians, 1540–1760* (Jackson: University of Mississippi Press, 2002). For a study set in the American Southwest, see James F. Brooks, *Captives and Cousins: Slavery, Kinship, and Community in the Southwest Borderlands* (Chapel Hill: University of North Carolina Press, 2002). See also J. Wright, *Creeks and Seminoles*, 77–79.

28. The best archaeological studies that address the aboriginal contexts of slavery come from the Northwest Coast. See Kenneth M. Ames and Herbert D. G. Maschner, *Peoples of the Northwest Coast: Their Archaeology and Prehistory* (New York: Thames and Hudson, 1999), chapter 7. Much of the archaeological discussion of social stratification among Mississippian societies in the late prehistoric Southeast also infers the presence of slaves or a slave class as war captives; likewise for late prehistoric Iroquoian

societies in the Northeast. For a useful review and introduction to these areas, see Brian M. Fagan, *Ancient North America: The Archaeology of a Continent*, 4th ed. (New York: Thames and Hudson, 2006).

29. Citing the *American Anti-Slavery Almanac* as the original source, Patricia R. Wickman considers the story that Osceola had a black wife not implausible but insufficiently documented. See Patricia R. Wickman, *Osceola's Legacy* (Tuscaloosa: University of Alabama Press, 1991), 14–15, 21.

30. This much cited quote is from the *American State Papers: Military Affairs*, 7:820–821. The quote, with some discussion of context, is also available at www.john-horse.com/trail.

31. W. Simmons, *Notices*; G. McCall, *Letters from the Frontiers*, 160.

32. Hugh Young, "A Topographical Memoir on East and West Florida," ed. Mark Boyd, *Florida Historical Quarterly* 13 (July 1934): 16–50, 82–104, 129–64.

33. A. Devane, *Early Florida History*.

34. K. Porter, "The Negro Abraham," 11, citing primary sources.

35. The muster rolls of blacks deported from Florida have been transcribed from congressional documents and from National Archives Record Group 75. They were reproduced as appendices A–K in Daniel F. Littlefield Jr., *Africans and Seminoles: From Removal to Emancipation* (Westport, Conn.: Greenwood Press, 1977). Transcribed muster rolls are also available on the Web site of the Seminole Nation of Oklahoma, www.seminolenation-indianterritory.org/negroes_captured_1.htm.

36. See, e.g., the story of the captured Black Seminole named Ansel leading Lt. Henry Prince through the heart of the Seminole stronghold in the Cove of the Withlacoochee in April 1837 in F. Laumer, ed., *Amidst a Storm of Bullets*, 90–94.

37. Brent Richards Weisman, *Like Beads on a String: A Culture History of the Seminole Indians in North Peninsular Florida* (Tuscaloosa: University of Alabama Press, 1989), 77–81.

38. A. Devane, *Early Florida History*.

39. T. Weik, *A Historical Archaeology*.

40. John Solomon Otto's study inspired a multitude of subsequent works continuing up to the present day. The most accessible version is John Solomon Otto, *Cannon's Point Plantation, 1794–1860: Living Conditions and Status Patterns in the Old South* (Orlando, Fla.: Academic Press, 1984). For a different approach see Roderick A. Mc-Donald, *The Economy and Material Culture of Slaves* (Baton Rouge: Louisiana State University Press, 1993).

41. For discussion of colonoware, see Leland Ferguson, *Uncommon Ground: Archaeology and Early African America, 1650–1800* (Washington, D.C.: Smithsonian Institution, 1992). For the first and still most comprehensive discussion of Seminole pottery, see John M. Goggin, "Seminole Pottery," *Prehistoric Pottery of the Eastern United States*, ed. James B. Griffin (Ann Arbor: University of Michigan, Museum of Anthropology, 1953), 200–202; William C. Sturtevant, ed., *A Seminole Source Book* (New York: Garland Press, 1987).

42. J. Goggin, "Seminole Pottery."

43. Roy Nash, "Survey of Seminole Indians in Florida," republished in W. Sturtevant, *A Seminole Source Book.*

44. There are very few population estimates of Black Seminoles prior to the Second Seminole War. Dexter provides a list of "Negroes" belonging to different chiefs totaling 349, not including the 80 "refugee Negroes" he describes as living on the lower Gulf coast. William Simmons indicates a number of 400 without specific citation. Even given the inevitable undercounting, it is unlikely that their number exceeded 500. See W. Simmons, *Notices,* 75.

4

"A Decidedly Mutinous Spirit"

The "Labor Problem" in the Postbellum South as an Exercise of Free Labor

MARK HOWARD LONG

Surely one of the more interesting meetings that occurred in the South during the period of the "intersectional wedding," following the Civil War, was the one between Henry S. Sanford of Connecticut and Joseph W. Tucker of South Carolina that resulted in the founding of Sanford, Florida. Sanford spent the years of the war in Europe as an American diplomat posted in Belgium and was responsible for coordinating much of the Union secret service work on the Continent. Tucker had worked as a secessionist newspaper editor in Missouri and served as a central, if shadowy, figure in the Confederate efforts to sabotage Union boats on the Mississippi River. There were many reasons why these men should have wanted nothing to do with each other after the war. Tucker was an obstinate Confederate who opted to move to the Bahamas for a time rather than pledge an oath of allegiance to the Union he had fought so bitterly. Sanford was a career diplomat and a well-connected Republican who remained active in party politics throughout his life. Yet there on the banks of the St. Johns River near the frontier town of Mellonville, the two found enough common ground to become business partners, frequent correspondents, and founders of a city.[1]

That two men so recently engaged on opposite sides of a bloody civil war found enough accord for their own personal "reconstruction" testifies to the power of the dream of great wealth that drove many men and women to invest in Florida lands. Their shared vision of the "Gospel of Prosperity," in which economic development was seen as the salve to heal sectional wounds, provided an ideological suture that bound former enemies together in their effort to incorporate the southern landscape within the sinews of a heavily capitalized commercial agricultural economy. The form this investment took was significant. Men like Sanford had no intention of living on this new land anymore than he wanted to live in the Belgian Congo, where he also developed a range of financial holdings, including a franchise for transportation and trade on the Upper Congo River. For Sanford, this economy was designed to extract enough wealth to enable him to continue his courtly life in Brussels.[2] Agriculture was thus a colonizing activity that was as much about creating a social and political environment as it was about raising crops. Viewed in this way, agriculture justified cultural practices that consciously differentiated themselves from vernacular traditions of food production and were informed by a science of agronomy and an ideological assumption of progress. Together, this marriage of science and ideology generated a system of control over landscape and labor alike.[3]

In Reconstruction Florida, development was used to justify a wide range of ends. From tourism to large farms and extractive industries, Florida boosters were entirely dependent on cheap labor to achieve these dreams of wealth.[4] Yet the promise of "free labor" that was so central to the Reconstruction period—freedom to move, to choose whether or not to work, and to secure a wage for labor performed—hampered the ability of large developers like Henry Sanford and Joseph Tucker to amass wealth at the speed and on the scale they anticipated. Their experiment with a variety of controlled labor forms and the ultimate recruitment of foreign-born, indentured Swedish laborers sheds light on this critical era and illuminates another chapter in this formative period in American labor history.

"Constant, Unremitting Toil"

By 1870, there was a wealth of competing plans to reorganize South Florida's landscape. Thomas W. Osborne, assistant commissioner of Florida's Freedman's Bureau, advocated using the "open" lands below the 28th parallel as a new territory reserved exclusively for homesteading by freed slaves. Others, like Sanford and Tucker, had much different ideas and dreamed of cultivating a landscape of citrus *latifundia* and a haven for capital investment.[5] Each approach depended upon the exertion of a great deal of physical labor. As Harriet Beecher Stowe, one of Florida's most popular boosters, noted, there were "marshes to be drained, forests to be cut down, palmetto-plains to be grubbed up, and all under the torrid heat of a tropical sun."[6] But it was Tucker and Sanford's vision of transforming this subtropical wilderness into an ordered, fruitful landscape that virtually erased the existing ecosystem and ways of life dependent upon it, and replaced it with a labor-intensive agricultural system.

Who was going to perform this backbreaking labor under Florida's hot sun was an open question, fraught with the white-hot political issues of the day. Many looked to the newly freed African Americans, arguing that they were the "natural laborers" for Florida because they could flourish "physically under a temperature that exposes a white man to disease," not to mention their "docility . . . and perfect subjection to discipline." But such a desirable workforce, however problematic that perception may have been, was not present in this part of Florida. Only forty black male laborers are listed in the Mellonville census of 1870, which included what would become Sanford. This was a far cry from the scores of laborers necessary to fulfill the dream of the region's burgeoning capitalists. Henry Sanford and his managers turned to a racially mixed workforce, importing black workers from other parts of the state and using native white workers wherever they could find them.[7]

The strategy encountered a number of problems. To begin with, there was a deep cultural divide between local whites and their employers, most of whom held their potential workers in disdain. Northerners who flocked to the South after the war were taken aback by the poor whites they encountered. A standard trope in the travel literature generated out of this contact became a lament about the ignorance, backwardness, and crudeness of Florida's "Cracker" population. George M. Barbour, a future Sanford resident, offered what is perhaps the most strident example of this literature. In retelling his encounters with Florida natives, he depicted them as "the genuine, unadulterated 'cracker'—the clay-eating, gaunt, pale, tallowy, leather-skinned sort—stupid, stolid, staring eyes, dead and lusterless; unkempt hair, generally tow-colored; and such a shiftless, slouching manner!" "Simply white savages—or living white mummies would, perhaps, better indicate their dead-alive looks and actions," he wrote. "Who, or what, these 'crackers' are . . . is one among the many unsolved mysteries of this state. Stupid and shiftless, yet sly and vindictive, they are a block in the pathway of civilization, settlement, and enterprise wherever they exist."[8] Even Tucker, a southerner, referred to the local white population as "Mellon-villains."[9] Locals undoubtedly recognized that disdain rather quickly and responded by acting as a "block in the pathway" of developers' schemes. Such complaints became a regular theme in the correspondence between Sanford and his agents in Florida. There was also the uncomfortable fact that Henry Sanford represented the resented Union government and flaunted his class status repeatedly. A career diplomat, Sanford cleaved to an aristocratic way of life, evoking jealousy, one commentator wrote, because he had "the best house, the best furniture, the finest horses and carriage, the best servants, the best table, and perhaps I may say, the most attractive and accomplished wife of any of the United States Representatives at Foreign Courts."[10] Sanford's decision to come to Florida was motivated primarily by his need to supplement his diplomatic income, which came nowhere close to supporting this extravagant lifestyle.

Creating a citrus empire also ran counter to existing social and economic practices across the area.[11] South Florida's deep woods and swamps provided near-perfect cover for squatters and others living on the margins of society. But it also offered a plethora of resources that they could use for themselves or sell and barter to gain access to commercial goods. Hunting, fishing, and gathering local fruits provided the most immediate relief from hunger, but could provide marketable items as well. Locals collected wild vanilla, which was used as filler by the tobacco industry. They appropriated local cypress trees to make rot-resistant shingles, shot and butchered deer to be sold for upwards of 12 cents a pound, and provided fish for local markets. To be sure, the growing number of new residents from elsewhere offered expanded opportunities for trade, and many locals took full advantage. Yet the environmental transformation that the coming of the citrus and tourist industries represented also strained these same resources on which locals depended. When Whitner and Marks, the local firm hired by Sanford to clear and plant his groves, removed all "trespassers," or squatters, from his newly acquired land, hostility toward these new developers grew even keener.[12]

Forced out of these traditional means of survival, some locals turned to waged work in order to survive. But few were willing to rely on this means entirely. Recourse to paid work was occasional or episodic rather than simply seasonal. Given the litany of complaints coming from employers, it is clear that most workers engaged and disengaged from the practice based on their needs at the time. Employers expressed dismay at the lack of consistency displayed by their hands. As one local grower complained, native whites "work one day and play three."[13] Richard Marks, one of the overseers for St. Gertrude, Sanford's first showcase grove, complained that "labor is so unreliable and difficult to obtain as to subject us to many and very grievous trials. We have experimented with the [white] labor of the country to find it utterly worthless. Worse than the Negro . . ."[14]

In May 1870, the very month that Henry Sanford closed on his 12,547-acre tract of land fronting the St. Johns River, Whitner and Marks reported ten black workers operating on one of the tracts. But Sanford's vision of clearing and planting 120 acres of that land required them to "increase our force considerably." They also remarked that the progress the black workers made was "a matter of surprise to the natives [whites]," and they sought to recruit additional black laborers from outside the area. By June, developers of this new city of Sanford had imported black workers from north Florida and were generally encouraged about the labor situation, although they openly worried about their new employees being "contaminated by the worthless white scoundrels who infest" the area. Their fears proved unfounded as the new workers quickly cleared more than 80 acres of land.[15]

The newly arrived workers lived at the grove site itself in "Palmetto-thatched cottages" and, according to Tucker, on an "abundant supply of sulpher water, and substantial rations, with a little *dram* on very hot days, to relieve debility, suffice to give the required stimulants and support for manly labor." The workers seemed to him "cheerful and energetic." He also boasted that they were treated with the right mix of discipline and kindness. Tucker employed a workforce of six black men and two white men to construct a wharf on Lake Monroe, as the wide stretch of the St. Johns River where the town of Sanford was taking shape was called. There, too, Tucker was pleased with his hands' industriousness.[16]

But the peace did not last. In the middle of September 1870, local whites staged a night raid on the African Americans' camp, firing shots into their dwellings and injuring one of the workers. So that their message would not be missed, the attackers left behind a note declaring the whole area around Mellonville to be "a white man's country." Whitner and Marks blamed the raid on the "jealousy and malignity of the low white wretches in the country offering as laborers—unwilling themselves to half work and opposed to the introduction of those who might do better." But Whitner and Marks were not without blame. As Tucker noted, friction between Whitner and Marks and their white employees had sown the seeds of this conflict. Having hired some men to plant trees in the grove on contract, Whitner determined that they were "doing the work badly" and fired them. Thus the attack was prompted by a desire to drive the newly arrived African Americans from the labor market. But it also served as retribution against Whitner and Marks by driving away the labor force on which they relied. Whitner was especially hated by local whites, who saw him as "an unbending and proud man" with an "ill-disguised contempt for men of the class to which these laborers belonged." After additional threats against Whitner, he "went armed for some time."[17]

Attacks against black workers continued in the area. On at least one occasion, white workers killed a black worker for seeking employment at terms below the standard pay for whites. Tucker reported a similar incident in a nearby town in 1877, writing in the *Florida Times-Union* that masked men drove African Americans away by force after "having first ascertained at what price per day" they were working.[18] Tucker's interpretation suggests that Whitner, Marks, and certainly Sanford's interests were also targets. Yet the role of race and racism throughout these attacks is equally clear. Rather than harming the white overseer with connections to the powerful Henry Sanford, disgruntled workers vented their anger on the "colored laborers."[19] As the Great Freeze of 1894–95 pushed the citrus industry even farther south, examples of this behavior proliferated. In Lee County, unknown "wool hat" assailants sent 38 rounds into a house where black workers resided, in an explicit attempt to prevent the establishment of a citrus industry in their county by driving away the labor force that would have made this industrial growth possible.[20]

The response from local employers to these attacks was swift. In September 1870, Whitner and Marks called a meeting of "the law abiding citizens of the community." They agreed to post a guard at the black workers' camp to prevent further attacks. Whitner and Marks meanwhile assured Sanford that they were fully capable of defending themselves and the "camp of laborers in the honest discharge of their duty." The "better men" organized patrols for a night watch. But still no guilty parties were identified. A few weeks later, another group of African Americans working for a different employer were attacked, "prompt[ing] a stampede among the blacks, and work was for a time suspended." In a third attack, Tucker's own employees were fired on at night. This time, his "men ran off."[21]

Tucker took decisive action. He offered a $50 reward for "information to send these rascals to the penitentiary," petitioned to convene a grand jury, and armed his own black workers, instructing them "to return shot for shot—to kill." If the attacks continued, Tucker proclaimed, he would request a squad of mounted cavalry be stationed in the area until "the scoundrels could be caught and hung." Without doubt, the image of a white employer arming his black laborers and instructing them to shoot at white men "to kill" was an uncommon occurrence in the Reconstruction South. But, Tucker argued, the severity of the situation justified such a choice and ultimately proved effective. Noting that his efforts "put a *quietus*" on the events, Tucker wrote, "The colored men are now satisfied all goes smoothly and safely." How satisfied these black workers actually were remains an open question. But the series of events was certainly instructive. Steeped in paternalism, Tucker's defense of "his men" was prompted by his desire to protect his workforce and therefore his bottom line, not on a belief in a larger humanity or race-blindness. Nonetheless, the arming of freedmen and the threat to call for troops suggests just how important these workers were to furthering the development model in play.[22]

As newly arrived immigrants to the area, the freedmen must surely have felt that these attacks challenged the most important and executable freedom African Americans enjoyed in the postwar order: the freedom to move to better their lot or to escape from an onerous situation. Notes like the one proclaiming the area to be "white man's country" only confirmed their fears. Within the context of the racialized labor system then operating in the South, the attack on newly arrived black laborers was geared to undermine a basic principle of free labor: the freedom of movement.[23]

The early defense of freedmen by their white employers also ended all too soon. As violent attacks continued, employers focused not on the danger to freedmen but on the slowing of work they now observed across their entire workforce, black and white alike. Letters emanating from Florida revealed a sharp change in tone regarding freedmen. Whereas a few months earlier, Tucker had written that he believed the "prospect of a speedy accomplishment of our work" was possible, by late 1870 he backed away from such strong support, noting, "My colored labor was far less efficient than I had expected." Whether the violence alone was to blame or whether African American workers had recognized the limitations of hard work for such fickle employers was unclear. But it seemed by year's end that the area's black workers had begun to adopt many of the same practices earlier used by native whites. "These people will not, unless driven by dire necessity, do much work," Tucker fulminated. He later concluded that his black workers "proved unreliable and worthless" and that another of his fellow employers was also "over-run" with labor problems.[24]

Like local whites, African Americans approached their entry into waged labor as a strategic move toward enhancing their overall economic autonomy. It was a temporary measure. For freedmen, "independence was clearly important even though the cost might be a reduced standard of living." Whites in the North and South alike often interpreted this behavior to mean that freedmen would not work without coercion. The "problem" was compounded because freedmen were reluctant to engage in labor that closely replicated that of the slave plantation, especially the type of gang labor system Sanford tried to employ on his land. They understood their independence to be an expression of their fundamental humanity and a hard-won right of emancipation. As historian Alex Lichtenstein has argued, this expression of contractual freedom can best be understood as a financial strategy wherein freedmen earned better wages by working as occasional laborers than by contracting for long periods of time. Rather than entering the wage economy "as permanent sellers of labor-power," in Mellonville and the developing city of Sanford, as elsewhere across the U.S. South, freedmen and white native-born workers alike entered the wage economy only "instrumentally."[25] As such, the pattern of entering and leaving the waged labor market at their own discretion was an indication of rural workers' resistance to proletarianization, as well as to the type of uprooting—both in environmental and social terms—that developers like Tucker and Sanford produced. The litany of complaints about the unwillingness of black workers to submit to the contract terms desired by local growers testifies to this mounting resistance.[26]

Equally frustrated with native white and black workers, developers decided to look elsewhere. Lamenting that the native-born would "work <u>for a time</u> if you work by their side" but would not sign long-term contracts and "often disappoint the employer when he most needs their assistance," Tucker advanced an alternative proposal. In order for Henry Sanford's plans to come to fruition, he concluded, "We must have the <u>Chinese.</u>" These workers would not only labor from sun-to-sun, Rucker argued, but would be willing to "engage for a term of years" without expecting higher wages than either native white or black workers. Tucker advised Sanford to obtain between 15 and 20 Chinese workers. In order to "execute your plans," he wrote, "a great deal of manual labor will be required." Tucker added that he, too, would like to find Chinese laborers to work for him, as would other growers in the area.[27]

This was not the first time that a desire for foreign labor had been expressed by Mellonville and Sanford City developers. Nor were Asian laborers the only alternative. In June 1870, Tucker penned a letter detailing the progress made by his native-born workers, yet he concluded, "Our <u>Fruit Growers Club,</u> by resolution, requested me . . . to correspond with Gen. Sanford, and illicit information as to the practicality of procuring German labor for this community." In November, Whitner also expressed a desire to recruit the foreign-born. "We need good laborers to develop this country," he wrote. "I have been satisfied since 1865 that Chinese laborers will do well in Fla. . . . Will you not be united with us in introducing these laborers?"[28]

The need for foreign workers was a common theme throughout the South in the years following emancipation. A mere six months after the secession of hostilities, a newspaper in Alabama editorialized about the need to replace freedmen with European immigrants. Editorials exploring the strengths and merits of such policies appeared across the South in these years.[29] The ability to import labor from abroad was enabled by the 1864 Act to Encourage Immigration. Alternately known as the Contract Labor Act, this legislation provided federal support for capitalists seeking to import workers on an indentured basis. Typically immigrants signed contracts waiving their wages for the first twelve months of their service, which employers argued would cover the cost of their transportation to the United States. Sometimes they were obligated to work without pay even longer to cover the costs of their room and board. This proved a popular source of European labor recruitment in manufacturing industries across the Northeast. Chinese laborers were imported in large numbers to complete work on the western stretch of the transcontinental railroad. And in agriculture, Scandinavians were recruited to work across the Upper Midwest.[30] To some employers, recruiting Europeans or Asians grew out of beliefs in the biological suitability of specific "races" of people to perform certain tasks. Unlike African Americans or poor native-born whites who, as citizens, would remain even after the term of their contracts had expired, immigrant laborers who were imported solely for the terms of their contracts could be forced to leave at the end of their term of employment. This move to recruit foreign-born workers had a critical economic component as well: immigrant labor, especially contract labor, was intended to provide a countervailing downward pressure on wages by competing with native-born workers in the labor market, pushing the native-born to work harder and more steadily.[31] The case of Mellonville and the town of Sanford also suggests that the attempt to recruit foreign-born workers was a direct response to the unwillingness of freedmen to sign long-term contracts or to engage in gang labor, which they associated with slavery. What employers like Sanford, Tucker, Whitner, Marks, and others wanted most was to create a labor force that was fixed in place and unable to operate on a free basis—that is, one that imitated, albeit in a limited way and on a temporary basis to be sure, the labor system destroyed by emancipation. As the British consul to New Orleans wrote in 1873: "A laborer is a laborer. . . . [W]hether he be French or German, Italian or Norwegian, British or Chinese, he is to be housed, fed, and treated just as the black race used to be."[32]

"A Different Kind of Slavery"

Henry Sanford's search for foreign labor ended in Sweden rather than in China, Germany, or the northeastern United States. By the 1870s, Swedes had already begun moving to the United States in significant numbers. But the vast majority moved to the Midwest or Northeast. Many state governors considered Scandinavians, especially Swedes, to be particularly desirous immigrants, going so far as to argue that they made "ideal citizens."[33] But Sanford didn't want citizens; he wanted a pliable labor force that would work for long hours, cheaply and without complaint. He also faced the problem of convincing immigrants from Europe to move to the South. When foreign workers did arrive, they rarely experienced the benefits of southern hospitality. Instead, as black migrants from elsewhere in the South also experienced in Mellonville and the growing city of Sanford, locals were more likely to view foreign-born workers as a threat to their livelihood and to respond with hostility or violence. For many immigrant workers, this proved a powerful disincentive. In spite of efforts by state governments and area boosters to encourage immigration to the South, the net result on the region was negligible. Elsewhere in the nation, the foreign-born accounted for almost a fifth of the population, but the foreign-born made up 2 percent or less of the population in the South. With the important exception of Texas, between 1860 and 1880, the entire region actually experienced a net loss of the foreign-born population.[34]

For all of these reasons, Sanford turned to the most pliable workforce he could secure and recruited indentured laborers from among the ranks of Sweden's poorest citizens. Although their total numbers were still something of an anomaly across the South, the experiences of these laborers offer some revealing insights into the complexities of establishing a modern agricultural system in the post-Reconstruction South. Their recruitment represented a significant attempt on the part of Henry Sanford, "the founder of the modern Florida citrus industry," to secure an unfree labor force in an era of free labor.

In 1871, Sanford turned to Dr. Wilhelm Henschen, a Swede who was just launching a labor agency for clients in the United States who wanted to recruit European workers. Sanford paid Henschen to supply up to 50 Swedish men who would be willing to work for a year without wages in exchange for the cost of their transportation and basic room and board during their term of employment. Henschen recruited primarily from his home city of Uppsala and obtained the services of a number of craftsmen and artisans, only a few of whom had any experience in agriculture. Although the age of these immigrants is unknown, nearly all were men.[35]

They landed in Florida in late May 1871, under what must have seemed to be particularly inauspicious circumstances. It was the beginning of the long, hot rainy season. The workers' had been told that they were heading to work in a "garden" and that they would have the opportunity to ply their trades in the booming town that bore their sponsor's name. What they found, however, was a sparsely settled "wilderness" that provided almost no opportunity for craft work but demanded a significant amount of unskilled physical labor to create the citrus groves they were then expected to tend. The full extent of the work they were contracted to perform, and the terms and conditions of their daily labors, became apparent to these new immigrants over the next few days.

The Swedish craftsmen were housed in a cramped and hastily constructed dormitory. Most of the men were forced to sleep on the bare floor. Many had no bedding whatsoever. Matters were worsened by the fact that the agent tasked with taking care of the Swedish workers fell gravely ill and ultimately was forced to leave the city of Sanford altogether. Henry Sanford, meanwhile, remained in Brussels, dictating his wishes from afar. So Tucker took the lead in settling these newly arrived Swedish workers into their new environment.

The day after they arrived, Tucker "grouped and classified them, and set them to work and showed them how to do it with [his] own hands." Eventually a work routine was established that was designed to ease the Swedes into work under Florida's hot summer sun. According to Henry DeForest, the manager of Sanford's general store, the Swedes were expected to begin work at 5 a.m. and work until 7:30, at which point they would have an hour for breakfast. After returning to work at 8:30, they were to labor until noon, when they were given two and a half hours for lunch. The final stretch of work lasted from 2:30 p.m. until sunset, approximately 8 p.m. They worked eleven and a half hours, mostly doing arduous physical labor under difficult conditions, as they had been "put . . . in the Grove at grubbing." It is no wonder that DeForest concluded that the Swedes "think the work a little hard." Given that they were "accustomed to indoors work," had never experienced anything like Florida's subtropical climate, and were told to expect a very different set of conditions, their dissatisfaction should have surprised no one.[36]

Henschen visited the Swedes in Sanford a short time later and summoned Tucker to a meeting to hear their grievances. Tucker agreed that their living situation was untenable. He also noted that "some few had worn-out shoes, and no means to get others." The discontent among them was so strong that one of the men had already tried to pawn his watch in an attempt to buy a ticket on a steamer to flee. Tucker assured the men that "Gen. Sanford is a good man," that they would be issued some cloth to stuff with hay for mattresses, and that their concerns would all be addressed.[37]

But when the order was submitted for these materials, DeForest refused to issue them without Henry Sanford's direct approval. As DeForest saw it, Tucker had clearly overstepped his bounds by promising "Shoes, and mattrases [sic] for all those who needed them, and Pillows and Sheets for all." DeForest asserted that none of the immigrants were in need of shoes, but he did advise Sanford that if any of them should need a pair "before the year is out I think it best to let them have them, with the understanding that they work and pay for them when their year has expired," an arrangement he had already made with one of the men for clothing. Tucker reached an even more generous conclusion, suggesting that the shoes simply be provided as a standard issue, because doing so "was a small matter; while the labor of these men for a year is a <u>large matter</u>." Henschen garnered some criticism as well. DeForest reported to Sanford that Henschen had promised his countrymen that "if Mr. Tucker's promises were not kept they were at liberty to leave at any time." DeForest reassured Henry Sanford, however, that he had "not the Slightest fear of them doing" so, as they seem satisfied.[38]

Tucker may well have illuminated a central dynamic that was unfolding in Florida between Sanford's decision to remain in absentia and his newly imported labor force. From Henry Sanford's perspective, the terms of the labor contract seemed fixed well enough. The Swedes would work for one year to cover the costs of transportation and be "treated in a way corresponding to the conditions proposed by Dr. Henschen and approved by General Sanford." But the devil truly was in the details. It is impossible to know who promised what to whom throughout the various negotiations and meetings, with Tucker and Henschen regularly denying DeForest's assertions. But it seems the Swedes also took advantage of the tensions between their various superiors. The fact that the Swedes claimed that Henschen assured them their contracts were voided if Tucker's promises were not kept certainly provides one indication that they were aware of what fissures to exploit.

By July 16, DeForest found that the Swedes were "in very destitute circumstances," despite his reassurances to Henry Sanford just one month earlier. Some of the workers, he wrote, did not even have "sufficient clothing" to perform their jobs.

> Many of them had just one pair of Shoes and some of them none. I have been obliged to furnish some 12 or 15 of them with a pair each with the condition (to which they agreed) to pay for them in Labor at the expiration of their year of Service. I am fearful that a considerable quantity of clothing will have to be furnished them in advance as some of them at present have not even a change; they also want Tobacco upon the same conditions as the Shoes and I have furnished them a little in order to keep them contented but would like advice from yourself as to furnishing the above articles to them in the future.

Nonetheless, DeForest continued, "I can truthfully say the men are contented and are doing much better than we expected, as it is very warm here at present." Living in overcrowded conditions, engaged in strenuous physical labor under a hot sun, surviving on a diet of "principally . . . Flour, Beef and Bacon," which DeForest estimated cost "$3.00 less than is allowed for Negroes rations," and in "destitute circumstances" even by the admission of their employers, it is hard to image that there was a wellspring of contentment in the fields, cookhouse, or bunkhouse among the Swedes.[39]

Already presaged by the attempt of one Swede to flee on a steamer shortly after his arrival, on the morning of July 18, DeForest awoke to discover that three more Swedes had run away during the night, catching a steamer upriver to Jacksonville. His inquiries with the remaining Swedes revealed that the men had learned that they could earn $30 a month in Charleston working in their chosen trades. Feeling they had been "swindled" by Henschen and Henry Sanford, the men had escaped into the night, hoping for better fortunes in South Carolina. The Swedes also claimed that their contracts were violated because they were not allowed to work at their respective crafts and were forced into nothing but unskilled tasks. DeForest was determined to find the three runaways. He obtained warrants for their arrests, tracked them down in Jacksonville, put them under guard, and forcibly returned them to the city of Sanford so they could continue working out their year.[40]

While these workers failed to escape, their attempt to flee was not without consequence. A subtle yet significant shift resulted in the relationship between DeForest and the Swedes who remained. DeForest claimed that he was "astonished" that the three would run, "as these men were apparently satisfied and pleased." Granted, he noted, one of the men had also attempted to escape a month earlier, but he was easily apprehended because he was sick. DeForest also noted that the others "pretend" to be upset with those who ran. But he had "lost confidence in them and [was] fearful more of them may go." While still in Jacksonville, DeForest cautioned Sanford that it was "hard work for them to pay an old debt" and that if his employer had any intention of giving the Swedes land at the end of their terms of service, "it would be well to do so soon as they would be better satisfied if they had something to look forward to in the future." Four days later, DeForest wrote again, this time urging Henry Sanford to clarify whether he was to provide clothing to the Swedes gratuitously or if they should have to contract for longer terms of service in exchange, implying that he felt such benefits should be included as part of their contract. A week later he returned to the subject of the Swedes' diet, which was a bit more involved this time, including "Hominy, Potatoes, Beans, [and] Dried Apples." Carrots, it seems, and not just sticks went a long way toward ensuring that the terms of engagement were fully served.[41] In an effort to effect the day-to-day operations of the creation of Sanford's empire on the ground in Florida, DeForest began to adopt a more conciliatory and pragmatic approach to affairs with the Swedes, conceding ground in the struggle over defining the lived terms of the contracts to the Swedes after they exposed how tenuous their "fixed" status was by picking up and leaving.

A further indication of DeForest's increasing awareness of the Swedes' plight came in his appeal to Sanford at the behest of two of the married men. The workers asked Sanford to pay for their wives' passage to Florida, as the women's circumstances in Sweden had grown quite desperate. But the workers made it clear that they did not "want [their wives] to come over in the same terms" as they had. The Swedes asked instead that the cost of their wives' transportation be considered a loan. DeForest noted that the men were good workers and "to satisfy them I wrote to you." When Sanford failed to respond, DeForest wrote again in August, repeating his missive that both workers were "good men" and advising Sanford to agree with the request.[42] In a clear departure from his earlier, more hard-line approach toward his workers, Henry Sanford appeared to follow DeForest's advice. He authorized DeForest to promise two- to five-acre lots of land to any men who faithfully finished a year of service. This decision represented a significant renegotiation of the terms of the contracts and provided an incentive for the Swedish workers to remain beyond simply "hard work for . . . an old debt."[43] It was not clear, however, if this was indeed enough to convince the Swedes to remain in Sanford's employ. In August, Henry Sanford learned that his experiment with immigrant labor might be failing altogether. In contrast to DeForest's glowing assessments, Joseph Tucker sent Sanford a lengthy note about what he saw as myriad problems with the workers. A few, he wrote, were "capital laborers." But the rest were a bunch of "adventurers," "bad men," or simply confused about the nature of their contracts. Because they were mostly artisans with little or no experience in agricultural labor, Tucker continued, the time required to train them was massive. As a result, Tucker concluded, the Swedes were "less efficient as field laborers than an equal number of natives, white or colored." Another correspondence to Henry Sanford from a different overseer put it even more pointedly. The Swedes, he wrote, "do not earn their grub." It seemed that the goal of achieving a productive, fixed labor force was ever more complicated than Henry Sanford imagined.[44]

More bad news reached Henry Sanford that month as he learned about the damage caused by two hurricanes. Most of the work to construct the city of Sanford had been destroyed. The wharf had been washed away completely. The slaughterhouse had been destroyed. The warehouse had been blown off its supports. The machine shop had been leveled. The orange trees were also damaged, as was the fencing protecting the groves. Tucker's house had been "crushed and shattered" during the "violent and long continued gale." His entire family had been forced to flee into the storm in search of safety. Sanford's store had been split in two. DeForest and others had had to scramble to move it, as the waters of Lake Monroe rose precipitously. The only modicum of hope that had emerged from this event was the performance of the Swedes. Those who could swim worked tirelessly, 12 hours a day for three days, to recover the lumber used for the wharf from the bottom of the lake. DeForest wrote that the "Swedes behaved first rate and if it had not been for them we could not have saved" the lumber.[45]

After a summer of heat, heavy labor, and two hurricanes, one can only imagine that the Swedes must have wondered in what peculiar kind of hell they had landed. Despite their heroism during the hurricane and the promise of five acres of land at the end of their tenure, the Swedes persisted in their efforts to surreptitiously renegotiate the terms of their engagement. Drawing on the tactics common to those who labor, they continued to press what advantages they had. One overseer noted their tendency to "play sick" as a way to control the amount of work they were required to perform. The Swedes also insisted that the schedule created for them as a way to ease them into work under the Florida summer sun be kept throughout the year. Tucker observed that the midafternoon break was a custom "from which no authority has ever been able to make these people deviate." In short, the Swedes were able to use their employers' need for their labor to temper the demands being placed upon them.[46] And unlike in earlier periods when African American and native-born whites tried similar approaches, this time the employers complied.

Another forty new indentured workers soon joined the original contingent of Swedes. They arrived in November 1871. They came to Florida under the same terms as the first group, suggesting that Sanford found enough benefit in the labor of the original group to warrant increasing the size of his indentured workforce. But this time, the Swedes were recruited from the Swedish countryside rather than from the city. They also included a larger number of women, eight out of the total group. "The experience of the city people not having turned out quite satisfactorily," Henschen wrote, he hoped that finding rural workers might make them more pliable.[47] These new workers were also tasked with additional duties and spread across worksites far removed from each other. Sanford used some to replace the remaining native-born workers in the sawmill and to begin the city's main street, Sanford Avenue. Others were used to help rebuild the general store. Some remained in the groves. A few were rented to local employers on a short-term basis. Five of the new men were hired out to a wealthy wine and champagne magnate, Frederick de Bary, who was constructing a vast estate on the far side of Lake Monroe.[48]

Still, a "decidedly mutinous spirit" persisted among the Swedes. On December 11, 1871, nineteen of the earlier Swedish workers signed a petition requesting that Sanford reduce the time they had to work to pay off their transportation. They wrote:

> As we through that much water last summer and that big work in the strong heat of the sun, not, as supposed, in a garden, but so to say in a wilderness, have worn out more of clothes, especial by shoes and shirts, than anybody of us could foresee. . . . [We] have suffered much, not to speak of that strong tempest here and what we suffered then: we altogether wished some abbreviation upon that time—one year—, we have bound ourselves to work here for the expenses of our passing over from Sweden.[49]

No longer were the workers content to use slowdowns, to plan their escape, or to direct their frustrations at their overseers; they began to challenge

Sanford directly. During the Christmas holiday, less than two months after the second group of immigrants had arrived, the Swedes staged a strike. All hands refused to work. The reason they gave was that Henschen had promised they could continue their cultural practices in Florida, and their Swedish Christmas always lasted three days, not one. The Swedes also informed DeForest that they would not be working on New Year's Day, as he had required. To make matters worse, in the first days of 1872, a contingent from the first group of Swedes informed DeForest that they would only work under the terms of their contract until January 19, a full four months short of their obligations. Henry Sanford immediately consulted his lawyer, who informed him that he did not believe that the men could be legally held if they refused to work.[50]

Not to be outdone by the Swedes in Sanford, the men who were rented to de Bary ran away in January, upset over the way they were being treated and what they were being fed. In March 1872, the Sanford Swedes struck again, this time demanding that their rations be improved immediately. DeForest became so concerned about his ability to control these workers that he questioned a plan to send some of them to Jacksonville to paint one of Sanford's buildings for fear that contact with the new arrivals might incite further resistance. "They have us in their hands," DeForest conceded.[51] Against all odds, it seemed the Swedes had turned the tide against their managers.

The Swedes' mutinous spirit grew decidedly worse throughout the spring. On March 28, 1872, three men from the second group ran away. Again they headed up the St. Johns River to Jacksonville. This time the runaways had a specific destination in mind: the house of Peter Anderson, a member of the first group of Swedes who had been released from his contract because of health problems one month earlier. Anderson petitioned Sanford personally, complaining that the heat of the first summer had nearly killed him and that the weather was again "beginning strong warmth, to be sure breaking my health." Understanding all too well the conditions his fellow countrymen and women faced, Anderson was willing to hide those who ran from Sanford and assist them on to Charleston, where they could find safe lodging at a boardinghouse run by a P. Smith. Three more Swedes left in April, as did four of the remaining eight workers being rented by de Bary.[52]

Soon the plight of Henry Sanford's Swedes attracted attention from his political opponents with the Florida Republican Party. They accused Sanford of creating "another kind of slavery" in his developing city. Pointing to what appeared to be an underground railroad, complete with safe houses along the St. Johns River, they evoked damning comparisons with slavery. Henry Sanford's practice of "renting" workers to the highest bidder added weight to that rhetoric. Of course, however brutal and exploitative, the conditions under which Sanford's Swedish workers were living were far from a slave system. There certainly was no racialized hierarchy to determine who was bound and who was not. Swedes were considered "white" by American observers, and their whiteness facilitated Sanford's willingness to bargain with his workers. Further, there is no evidence of significant physical coercion to labor as was common with slaves. This was a decidedly contractual relationship, and in that regard it was a reflection of the faith in "the contract" that so animated the Reconstruction era.[53]

Nonetheless, Sanford's was indeed a backward-looking system in that it was bent toward solving the "problem" of free labor. From an employer's point of view, free labor too often acted, well, free. Free workers could select when and where they cared to labor, with seemingly no regard for the voracious demand for work on the part of southern capitalists. As the response of workers in Sanford clearly shows, human beings resist systems of exploitation designed to bind them to their labors and prevent their movement. Like the black slaves and freedmen before them, Sanford's foreign-born workers likewise resisted attempts to control their labor and their mobility in any way that they could.

"We Can and Should Monopolise This to Florida"

Henry Sanford's biographer, Joseph Fry, observed, as elsewhere in the South, that Sanford's labor experiment proved that "immigrants were neither the answer . . . nor the alternative to blacks as the principal work force." Most southern capitalists ultimately returned to freedmen as their primary labor force.[54] Sanford, however, never gave up on his experiment with foreign labor. The monthly timesheet for May 1876, for example, lists 12 employees at his Belair grove. All but one of the men was Swedish and worked for a monthly wage. The sole worker employed by the day, Henry Gray, was almost certainly not Swedish and was of undetermined race. Gary earned $1.50 a day for "digging." With the exception of the gardener and the overseer, most of the Swedes earned far less, making just over $1 a day for 27 days of work each month.[55]

Swedish labor remained important in Sanford into the 1880s. An advertisement designed to entice investors to Sanford City, written by Henry Sanford's manager in 1881, includes a paragraph touting the benefits of

Swedes as "reliable labor." Swedes, it proclaimed, "will undertake to clear, fence, plant, and keep up under guarantee, orange groves for residents or non-residents." This sturdy and dependable white labor force, the pamphlet assured prospective developers, could be counted on to do any job well.[56] Determined to continue his Florida developments while remaining in Europe, Sanford also created the Florida Land and Colonization Company in 1880 to oversee his interests. Under Sanford's guidance, the company continued to import European laborers, including large numbers of Swedes and Italians. Like the first groups of Swedes who arrived in the early 1870s, these later waves of foreign-born workers also worked in the citrus groves and in related agricultural ventures, and they contributed to the ongoing physical development of the city of Sanford.[57]

But these early 1880s encounters with Swedish labor went no smoother than one decade earlier. One of the immigrants who arrived as part of a group of 60 workers in 1882, Axel Sjoblom, recounted his own miserable experience as an indentured servant in terms eerily reminiscent of what many first arrivals experienced. After only three months in Florida, Sjoblom and his fellow workers organized a general strike for "better feed" in which they all "went off the job." Thirty of the striking immigrants were arrested. Sjoblom was among those hauled off to jail. But still the Swedes refused to return to work until "Gen. Sanford promised better food and Better Treatment." The peace ended, however, when Sjoblom and some others were late for breakfast one Saturday morning, precipitating a confrontation with the overseer of the kitchen. Sjoblom recalled that he stood on the table in the mess hall and proclaimed that he would quit that day. He and two others ran away. Overseers hunted them down and jailed them.[58]

When he was released on Monday, Sjoblom again confronted the overseer and demanded to know whether his four months of completed service rendered had not more than covered the cost of his transportation. The overseer refused to answer him directly. Instead, the overseer reminded the workers that they had all signed a contract for one full year and were now legally bound to finish out that term of service. Sjoblom stayed one more week before he ran away again, determined to find wage work that would not bind him by a contract so clearly exploitative and excessive.[59]

By June 1883 an agent for the Colonization Company who toured the town of Sanford wrote that the Swedes were clearly unprofitable. Their "frequent strikes when some little thing don't suit them and shirking of work when not watched," were a special source of complaint. The agent also noted that only "18 are here out of the 63 sent over—the others have deserted for places where they could get wages, thus defrauding the Co. of their passage money." The desire for wages was certainly a factor inducing them to flee their contracts, as it has been for the first three Swedes to abscond in the night eleven years before, but clearly factors such as their diet, the work regime, and a basic belief that the terms of the contracts lacked simple fairness drove them away as well.[60]

Employers seemed to learn little from these experiences and continued to exploit their laborers, prompting more strikes and desertions. In 1889, Donald Houston, the Scottish manager of Belair, which was by then Sanford's single largest grove, wrote that he was upset with the Swedes for demanding a raise. Given that these workers were no longer even working for monthly wages but were paid the same daily rate as Swedes over one decade earlier, their discontent is not surprising. Houston complained to Sanford that the "Swedes got an idea that you did not want anyone but a Swede to work in Belair and they thought they could get what pay they wanted." He told the workers that although Sanford had been "a great friend of the Swedes by bringing them to America and giving them land and employment to make a home for them which they never could do in Sweden," Sanford was also a great friend of "the Negro of U.S.," and that his record showed that Sanford had "done more for the liberty of the Negro in America than any other man." Just as the threat of importing foreign labor had been used to force more compliance among native-born workers a few decades earlier, now employers like Houston used the threat of returning to native-born black labor to intimidate the Swedes. Noting that he "thought their demand was unreasonable," Houston explained that he would start to recruit only African American laborers to work in Sanford's groves. If claims of Swedes' natural industriousness were used to support their hiring in the first place, Houston now returned to praising the features he believed made African Americans biologically suited to work in Florida. He argued, "The Swedes can't stand heavy hoeing in hot weather like the Negro," the previous two decades of experience notwithstanding. Although Houston admitted that he generally preferred "white labor to black," he was "getting along well with my change of labor and don't care to change back to the Swedes for general work."[61]

Henry Sanford's labor problem had come full circle in eighteen years. Having paid the travel expenses of over one hundred Swedes, moving them from Europe, across the Atlantic, well into the Florida interior, Sanford decided to try to turn this investment to his advantage in a different way. If he could not keep the Swedes at work on his groves for no wages, he reasoned, he could at least use their presence to encourage other Scandinavians to move into the area, thus boosting land sales across the region. In a letter to William MacKinnon, Sanford suggested, "We can and should monopolise this to Florida. My Swedes Colony imported my expense in 1871 has proved a great success made the name of Sanford Grant known and popular in Sweden and Norway, and now this practical, successful demonstration can be made to ensure our sole benefit, and fill our land with Swedish Colonists." He continued, "The success of the Swedes Colony in Sanford Grant . . . is our <u>main reliance</u> for Land Sales." If making money from Swedes' indentured labor proved problematic and less profitable than he had anticipated, Sanford hoped that continued chain migration would at least help him to profit in other ways.[62]

Although the experiment in using exclusively foreign labor was ultimately abandoned in the Sanford groves, it stands as more than a curiosity of the period. Henry Sanford's turn to indentured labor as a tactic to get around the "labor problem" that beset southern capitalists after emancipation was driven by the same desire for a fixed labor force that led to the creation of the convict lease system in Florida and other states. The fantasies of development and the drive to achieve a relatively high level of wealth in a short period of time, coupled with the unwillingness of native laborers, black and white, to allow themselves to be locked into a long-term fixed pattern of labor, created a void that free labor in the state would not or could not fill. By importing bound Swedish labor during the crucial period of early development when the most arduous tasks of clearing and planting made up daily work regimes, Sanford created a "take off" in citrus not unlike that which railroad magnates, mine owners, and steel barons created in the southern Piedmont by using penal labor. Seen in this light, the Swedish workers who were dropped in the middle of a subtropical jungle, rather than in a garden, provided the critical margin of difference necessary to build Sanford's town, clear his lands, and plant his groves, in short, for "progressive" capital accumulation. Their labor must be understood as a necessary link in creating the political economy of the area.[63]

The fact that the benefits of Sanford's experiment in indentured servitude paled in comparison to those reaped by employers of penal laborers elsewhere does not mean that we cannot draw parallels between the two systems. If for no other reason than the marked similarities of the impulse to create a fixed labor force, both systems carved out a space for bound labor at a time when "free labor" was supposed to be on the march across the South. Sanford and his agents in Florida were unable to create a system of labor discipline like the one that emerged for employers of penal labor. That does not mean that his efforts were in vain, however. The fact that Sanford again turned to indentured labor when it came time to plant his second large grove suggests the important role that the labor of the Swedes played in the beginning of the project. No simple counting of Swedish workers or notation of their persistence as a bound labor force accounts for their strategic importance in creating south Florida's citriculture. On the contrary, they played a critical role by filling the "gap" created by native labor's unwillingness to be bent to the dictates of agricultural-led development.[64]

Notes

1. For an account of Sanford's activities in Europe during the war, see Joseph A. Fry, *Henry S. Sanford: Diplomacy and Business in Nineteenth-Century America* (Reno: University of Nevada Press, 1982), 35–65. The evocation of the intersectional wedding was borrowed from David W. Blight, *Race and Reunion: The Civil War in American Memory* (Cambridge, Mass.: Belknap Press of Harvard University, 2001), 4. Sanford and Tucker became partners in the building and operation of a slaughterhouse and a wharf.

2. J. Fry, *Henry S. Sanford*, 84–87, 156–63. For a discussion of "suture" as an ideological practice, see Ernesto Laclau and Chantal Mouffe, *Hegemony and Socialist Strategy: Towards a Radical Democratic Politics* (London: Verso, 1985); Slavoj Zizek, *The Sublime Object of Ideology* (London: Verso, 1989).

3. For an overview of the critical work linking agriculture and colonization, see Frieda Knobloch, *The Culture of Wilderness: Agriculture as Colonization in the American West* (Chapel Hill: University of North Carolina Press, 1996). Some works that explore this theme in a contemporary world context include Vandana Shiva, *The Violence of the Green Revolution: Third World Agriculture, Ecology, and Politics* (London: Zed Press, 1991); Vandana Shiva, *Monocultures of the Mind: Perspectives on Biodiversity and Biotechnology* (London: Zed Press, 1993); Arturo Escobar, *Encountering Development: The Making and Unmaking of the Third World* (Princeton, N.J.: Princeton University Press, 1995); Majid Rahnema and Victoria Bawtree, *The Post-Development Reader* (London: Zed Press, 1997). An insightful critique of the development tradition in western culture reaching as far back as Goethe's *Faust* can be found in Marshall Berman, *All That Is Solid Melts into Air: The Experience of Modernity* (New York: Penguin Press, 1982).

4. Paul Ortiz, *Emancipation Betrayed: The Hidden History of Black Organizing and White Violence in Florida from Reconstruction to the Bloody Election of 1920* (Berkeley: University of California Press, 2005), 12.

5. F. Bruce Rosen, "A Plan to Homestead Freedmen in Florida in 1866," *Florida Historical Quarterly* 43 (April 1965): 379–84; John Beverley, *Subalternity and Representation: Arguments in Cultural Theory* (Durham, N.C.: Duke University Press, 1999), 161.

6. Harriet Beecher Stowe, *Palmetto Leaves* (Gainesville: University Press of Florida, 1999), 279.

7. Like many frontier communities, Mellonville was a predominantly male community where men outnumbered women by roughly two to one. The 1870 Mellonville census lists 480 people in 1870. Of those, 278 (57.9 percent) were male and 202 (42.1 percent) were female. Of the adult population, however, 171 (62.4 percent) were men and 103 (37.6 percent) were women. I use the word "native" here as Andrew Sluyter does, suggesting "not so much . . . any particular ethnicity as an intimate familiarity with a system of production and consumption rooted in the dynamic realities of a particular place—a folk ecology or vernacular ecology, then, that people create over many generations of local tenure or come to share in by learning from those with such tenure." See Andrew Sluyter, *Colonialism and Landscape: Postcolonial Theory and Applications* (Lanham, Md.: Rowman and Littlefield, 2002), 7.

8. Tina Bucuvalas, Peggy A. Bulger, and Stetson Kennedy, *South Florida Folklife* (Jackson: University Press of Mississippi, 1994), 38. See also H. Stowe, *Palmetto Leaves*, 57–58. The association of "clay-eating" with beings not fully human has a long history, much of it associated with Africans, though there was a distinct strain in American fiction that associated the habit with poor rural whites in an effort to undermine the rural populism of Andrew Jackson. See Stewart Lee Allen, *In the Devil's Garden: A Sinful History of Forbidden Food* (New York: Ballantine Press, 2002), 84–85. There is a deep and certainly unintended irony in the invocation of a food way, whether it is an accurate reflection of "Cracker" eating habits or not, to tag the native population as a roadblock to development through which a new set of commercial food ways are to be created.

9. Joseph W. Tucker to Henry S. Sanford (hereafter cited as HSS), September 5, 1871, Sanford Papers in the Sanford Museum (hereafter cited as SP), box 51, folder 11.

10. J. Fry, *Henry S. Sanford*, 2.

11. P. Ortiz, *Emancipation Betrayed*, 31–32; V. Shiva, *Monocultures of the Mind.*

12. *Florida Times Union*, April 1877; Steven Noll, "Steamboats, Cypress, and Tourism: An Ecological History of the Ocklawaha Valley in the Late Nineteenth Century," *Florida Historical Quarterly* 83 (Summer 2004): 20; Sidney Lanier, *Florida: Its Scenery, Climate, and History* (Gainesville: University Press of Florida, 1973), 31–32; Whitner and Marks to HSS, March 31, 1870, SP, 51:15.

13. Thomas Haigh to HSS, April 15, 1871, SP, 48:15. See also E. P. Thompson, "Time, Work-Discipline, and Industrial Capitalism," *Customs in Common* (New York: W. W. Norton, 1991), 352–403; Herbert Gutman, "Work, Culture, and Society in Industrializing America, 1815–1919," in *Work, Culture, and Society in Industrializing America: Essays in American Working-Class and Social History* (New York: Vintage Press, 1977), 3–78.

14. Whitner and Marks to HSS, August 9, 1870, SP, 51:15.

15. Whitner and Marks to HSS, May 25, 1870, June 14, 1870, SP, 51:15.

16. Tucker to HSS, June 5, 1870, SP, 51:11.

17. Whitner and Marks to HSS, September 13, 1870, SP, 51:15; Tucker to HSS, November 9, 1870, SP, 51:11; Unsigned, "Some Account of Belair: Also of the City of Sanford, Florida, with a Brief Sketch of Their Founder" (Sanford, Fla.: n.p., 1889), 45; "A Progressive City: Sanford the City and the Man," *Jacksonville Times-Union*, March 6, 1883.

18. P. Ortiz, *Emancipation Betrayed*, 64; Tucker's account appears in the *Florida Times-Union*, April 22, 1877, with no title.

19. Wilber Cash made this argument decades ago regarding southern whites directing violence against freedmen as a proxy attack against "Yankeedom," an argument recently revisited briefly by David Blight in *Race and Reunion*, 110.

20. "Black Laborers Barred," *Florida Times-Union*, December 9, 1895, 1. See also William Cohen, *At Freedom's Edge: Black Mobility and the Southern White Quest for Racial Control, 1861–1915* (Baton Rouge: Louisiana State University Press, 1991).

21. Whitner and Marks to HSS, September 13, 1870, SP, 51:15; Tucker to HSS, November 9, 1870, SP, 51:9.

22. Tucker to HSS, November 9, 1870, SP, 51:11.

23. W. Cohen, *At Freedom's Edge*, esp. 23–43.

24. Tucker to HSS, July 18, 1870, November 9, 1870, SP, 51:11.

25. Alex Lichtenstein, "Was the Emancipated Slave a Proletarian?" *Reviews in American History* 26 (March 1998): 137–38.

26. These complaints were not limited to agricultural workers. Rural industrial employers also complained about the scarcity and inconsistent pattern of free workers. See Alex Lichtenstein, "Twice the Work of Free Labor? Labor, Punishment, and the Task System in Georgia's Convict Mines," in *Race, Class, and Community in Southern Labor History*, ed. Gary M. Fink and Merl E. Reed (Tuscaloosa: University of Alabama Press, 1994), 147. See also Harold D. Woodman, "Class, Race, Politics, and the Modernization of the Postbellum South," *Journal of Southern History* 63 (February 1997): 21–22; Gerald David Jaynes, *Branches without Roots: Genesis of the Black Working Class in the American South, 1862–1882* (New York: Oxford University Press, 1986), 46; Dernoral Davis, "Hope versus Reality: The Emancipation Era Labor Struggles of Memphis Area Freedmen, 1863–1870," in *Race, Class, and Community*, 97; A. Lichtenstein, "Was the Emancipated Slave a Proletarian?" 132–35.

27. Tucker to HSS, November 9, 1870, SP, 51:11; W. Cohen, *At Freedom's Edge*, 38.

28. Tucker to HSS, June 5, 1870, SP, 51:11; Whitner to HSS, November 1, 1870, SP, 51:15.

29. W. Cohen, *At Freedom's Edge*, 38–39.

30. Vernon M. Briggs, *Immigration and American Unionism* (Ithaca, N.Y.: Cornell University Press, 2001), 33–35.

31. Rowland T. Berthoff, "Southern Attitudes toward Immigration, 1865–1914," *Journal of Southern History* 17 (August 1951): 330–31. Alex Lichtenstein argues, "Southern capitalists unable or unwilling to obtain free labor or convicts frequently turned to peonage or contract immigrant labor to extract maximum labor in minimum time." See Alex Lichtenstein, *Twice the Work of Free Labor: The Political Economy of Convict Labor in the New South* (New York: Verso, 1996), 152.

32. As cited in R. Berthoff, "Southern Attitudes toward Immigration," 331.

33. Vermont was among the states that most actively pursued this recruitment. See Alonzo B. Valentine, *Report of the Commissioner of Agriculture and Manufacturing Interests of the State of Vermont, 1889–1890* (Rutland: State of Vermont, 1890), 15–19. The belief that Swedes made "ideal citizens" and the Vermont experience heavily influenced late federal immigration policy as well. See John M. Lund, "Boundaries of Restriction: Immigration and Vermont Senator William Paul Dillingham," MA thesis, University of Vermont, 1994.

34. R. Berthoff, "Southern Attitudes toward Immigration," 342–45.

35. Irene Scobbie, *Sweden* (New York: Praeger, 1972), 82–83; Franklin D. Scott, *Sweden: The Nation's History* (Carbondale: Southern Illinois University Press, 1988), 366–77; W. A. Henschen to HSS, April 18, 1871, SP, 43:11; J. Fry, *Henry S. Sanford*, x.

36. Tucker to HSS, May 30, 1871, SP, 51:11; DeForest to HSS, June 19, 1870, SP, 46:6.

37. Tucker to Edward Shelton, June 12, 1871, SP, 46:2.

38. DeForest to HSS, June 12, 1871, SP, 47:6; Tucker to Edward N. Shelton, June 12, 1871, SP, 46:2.

39. DeForest to HSS, June 7, July 16, 1871, SP, 47:6.

40. DeForest to HSS, July 19, 23, 1871, SP, 47:6.

41. DeForest to HSS, July 19, 23, 27, August 4, 1871, SP, 47:6. For a discussion of the importance of these power dynamics between employers and employees, see James C. Scott, *Weapons of the Weak: Everyday Forms of Peasant Resistance* (New Haven, Conn.: Yale University Press, 1985).

42. Tucker to HSS, August 14, 1871, SP 51:11; and J. A. MacDonald to HSS, June or August 5, 1871, SP, 51:2.

43. DeForest to HSS, July 23, 1871, SP 47:6.

44. Tucker to HSS, August 14, 1871, SP, 51:11; J. A. MacDonald to HSS, August 5, 1871, SP, 51:2.

45. Tucker to HSS, August 21, 1871, SP, 51:11; DeForest to HSS, August 20, 28, 1871, SP, 47:6.

46. Tucker to HSS, August 14, 1871, SP, 51:11.

47. Henschen to HSS, September 16, 1871, SP, 53:11.

48. Henschen to HSS, November 1, 1871, SP, 55:9.

49. T. Patterson, et. al., *Swedish History*, 12.

50. J. Fry, *Henry S. Sanford*, 101.

51. Petitions from Swedes, SP, 55:7; T. Patterson, et. al., *Swedish History*, 12.

52. Petitions from Swedes, SP, 55:7.

53. J. Fry, *Henry S. Sanford*, 101; Timesheet for Belair grove, May 1876, SP, 45:1.

54. J. Fry, *Henry S. Sanford*, 101.

55. Timesheet for Belair grove, May 1876, SP, 45:1.

56. James E. Ingraham, *The Sanford Grant (Orange Country) Florida*, SP, 56:3.

57. Agent's minutes no. 44, October 23, 1883, SP, 56:5.

58. Journal of Alex Sjoblom, trans. Margaret Wesley, "Swedish Immigration" notebook, Sanford Museum, Sanford, Fla., 5–10.

59. Ibid., 8–12. The role of food, or the lack of good and/or ample food, in precipitating labor revolts among a different set of unfree workers in the postbellum South is mentioned in A. Lichtenstein, "Twice the Work of Free Labor," 146.

60. Report of E. K. Trafford, June 30, 1883, SP, 56:5.

61. Houston to HSS, May 16, 1889, June 28, 1889, SP, 48:13.

62. HSS to William MacKinnon, undated, MacKinnon Papers, file 188, Sanford Museum, "Swedish Immigration" notebook.

63. For a discussion of penal labor in the same context, see A. Lichtenstein, *Twice the Work of Free Labor*, 188. See also Marshall Berman, *All That Is Solid Melts into Air: The Experience of Modernity* (New York: Penguin Books, 1988).

64. A. Lichtenstein, *Twice the Work of Free Labor*, xvii.

5

"We Are White Men and Haven't Got Black Hearts"

Racialized Gender and the Labor Movement in Florida, 1900–1920

ROBERT CASSANELLO

In the summer of 1900, the largest labor unions in Jacksonville, Pensacola, and Key West decided to join forces to create a strong, statewide voice for workers. Called the Florida State Federation of Labor (FSFL), this central organizational body was formed in 1901. Its mission was to hire lobbyists and petition the state legislature on behalf of organized labor.[1] Originally the FSFL wanted to address certain key issues it believed to be important to the movement, such as prohibiting child labor, instituting an eight-hour work-day, strictly regulating convict labor so that it did not drive down wages, and addressing the unsafe and unhealthy working conditions of many factories and work sites. But over the next several years, they added a series of amendments, honing their mission in response to the changing circumstances around them. One of the most striking additions was made in 1902, when the FSFL added this important clause to its constitution: "Equal pay for equal work for both sexes." Coming less than two decades before American women would be granted the right to vote, this remarkable gesture at first glance appeared to be a resounding endorsement of women's central role in Florida's economy and an important step toward pay equity across the sexes. In fact, it was nothing of the kind.

The FSFL prohibited women from attending any of its functions or social activities, including its annual meetings. Women were expected to join separate auxiliaries.[2] They were also kept from fully participating in the decision making of the central body, including the drafting of the FSFL's constitution itself. Less an endorsement of sexual egalitarianism, then, the constitutional clause served a different purpose altogether: cutting women out as a potential source of low-wage workers, placing them in direct competition with men. If women could not be gotten cheaply, these male labor leaders hoped, employers would shy away from hiring them altogether.

The complicated business of ethnic relations also shaped the foundational documents of the state's largest labor organization. Unlike sex, policies surrounding race, racism, and black workers were conspicuously missing from the FSFL's early constitutions. At a time when fears about race mixing were gaining momentum across the South, this too seems remarkable. Many of Florida's earliest continuous labor unions were located in Ybor City, where Cuban-born labor leaders were among the most influential. Rather than challenging the full incorporation of these workers, the FSFL appeared to welcome Cuban members with open arms, allowing Spanish speakers to translate their resolutions and speeches into Spanish, even amending the constitution to allow for future conventions to have Spanish translators. At its 1906 convention, FSFL delegates went one step further, passing a resolution to allow the Cuban Federation of Labor, once it was established, to affiliate formally with the FSFL because they viewed the cause of Cuban workers as central to workers in Florida.[3] Like gender, however, these choices were far more indicative of the complex array of power negotiations that were taking place among Florida's working-class men and women than a blanket endorsement of class-based egalitarianism. African Americans remained marginalized in the FSFL, even though they formed a significant percentage of Florida's workforce.

This chapter explores the intersection of sex, race, and class at this formative period in the history of organized labor in Florida. Rather than a "morality tale" where the characters function either as heroes or as villains, to borrow a phrase from historian Eric Arnesen, scholars must be conscious of the ways that gender, race, and class were embedded in everyday interactions not only with management but also within the labor movement itself.[4] Over this period, Florida's statewide labor movement represented a cross-section of workers and industries and provides a nuanced portrait of workers' lives comparable to other industrial centers throughout North America. Within this movement, workers used a variety of strategies to improve their own socioeconomic conditions, both exploiting and bridging ethnic, racial, and gender differences. By examining the world of Florida workers, we can see that the social environments that workers constructed were a complex web of social categories that point to a mosaic social landscape rather than a movement where unanimous or binary social identities evolved.[5]

Although it was cities like Tampa and Key West that enjoyed some of the longest union traditions in Florida, the organization of the FSFL signaled a period of growing activism in other cities across the state, most notably in Pensacola and Jacksonville. In 1902, Pensacola's streetcar workers launched a series of strikes, prompting Charles H. Bliss to publish a pamphlet entitled "Labor Strikes and Their Effects on Society." Claiming legitimacy as a former Knights of Labor and Populist Party leader, Bliss warned that local streetcar workers were wrong to openly confront corporations through strikes. Instead, he recommended that workers pursue negotiations with management that would help to organize labor cooperatives. By organizing in strikes and demanding recognition for their American Federation of Labor (AFL) affiliated unions, Bliss argued, workers were losing an opportunity to demand contracts that acknowledged they owned their labor as producers and thus were essentially property owners, organizing themselves along the lines of monopolist-capitalists.[6] This depiction had gendered implications as well. To Knights and Populists of Bliss's generation, those who were not producers in their own right were not just lazy but also effeminate.[7] Thugs and other "ungentlemanly" people ran labor trusts, Bliss argued. With the rise of industrialization came affluence, which, in turn, led the privileged class to seek the unmanly pursuit of their own pleasure, ignoring the bottom rungs of society. Left to their own devices, those at the bottom would look to thugs, strikers, and rioters as their natural leaders, and they, in turn, would lead the masses with examples of uncivilized savagery. Bliss was elected mayor of Pensacola in 1905 on the appeal of this platform. His death two years later prevented him from seeing the labor movement in his city take a decidedly different turn from the one he recommended.

Masculinity defined the world of strikers and strikebreakers over this period. Strikebreakers responded to labor actions not only for pay but also to assert their manhood through physical violence in defending their right to work for wages. This fact was not lost on employers who wanted replacement workers who would not be intimidated by protesters.[8] After Pensacola's streetcar workers walked off their jobs, the streetcar company reportedly shipped 85 strikebreakers directly from New York City. They were recruited using advertisements that read, "Wanted—Men for out of town work. Hard manual labor and strong men wanted." When the strikebreakers appeared in Pensacola, one report claimed that someone pushed a "young fellow" into a strikebreaker. In response, the strikebreaker punched the young man, an action that soon drew nearly all of the demonstrators into the melee. This type of uncoordinated violence was exactly what Bliss had warned against; rather than a manly battle between two equals, the action had degenerated into the unmanly act of striking a "young fellow." The strikebreaker was quick to respond. As he told the press, because it was "witnessed by the crowd," the strikebreaker felt he had to explain himself in order to maintain his standing "as a man."[9]

Indeed, it appeared that it was exactly this type of unmanly transgression that mobilized public support against Pensacola's streetcar company in support of the striking workers. Subsequent press reports and state officials alike reported that most Pensacola residents sided with the workers. In 1908, Adjutant General J. Clifford R. Foster of the Florida militia witnessed local police refusing to protect the streetcars and strikebreakers in a show of solidarity with the striking workers. According to Foster, most local politicians hesitated to call the police to break up outbreaks of violence because they feared a public backlash by supporters of the strike. Recognizing that no local help was forthcoming, Mayor Calvin C. Goodwin was forced to cable Florida governor Napoleon Bonaparte Broward, who sent the state militia to guard the streetcar lines and the strikebreakers, a move that was much condemned by local residents.[10]

A groundswell of support surrounded a renewed wave of strikes in 1912, which swept across the city of Jacksonville. In this case, support for striking streetcar workers was led by a group of women who formed the "Citizens' Spirit Committee." They worked to organize carpools so that Jacksonville commuters could maintain a boycott against the streetcars, as called by labor organizers.[11] Refusing to see the situation deteriorate into violence as it had in past years, this time the streetcar company hired security guards from the Pinkerton Detective Agency to escort strikebreakers to the workplace. But again the 1912 strike quickly descended into chaos, ending only with the intervention of Florida governor Albert Waller Gilchrist, who sent the state's militia to Jacksonville to restore order, at the request of the city's mayor. Reporters attacked politicians for being indecisive during the violence, disparaging the mayor, city councilmen, and Jacksonville's police chief as impotent. In the view of Jacksonville's muckraking newspaper, *Dixie*, the Pinkertons were nothing more than "thugs" who lacked any decency and were merely tools of the corporations. Yet, the paper argued, the state's militia deserved greater respect, in no small part because of their sympathy toward Jacksonville's striking workers, manifested in their restrained behavior. Calling the militia a "manly set of soldier boys," the *Dixie* painted the soldiers in sharp contrast to the governor, who called them out, and to the city's civic and business leaders, whom it found utterly lacking gentlemanly traits.[12]

Striking workers in Pensacola and Jacksonville saw their activism as a reassertion of their manhood as well. One of the policies implemented by Pensacola's streetcar owners that brought the most strident objections was a new rule requiring any worker who was suspended without pay to report to the car barns three times daily. The effect of the policy was obvious: it prevented reprimanded workers from seeking other sources of wages, thereby increasing their vulnerability. Alexander Sarra, secretary of the local union, appealed to Pensacola residents for support in overturning these practices, stating, "We [the striking workers] claim the rights of free men to earn what we can during such time or if our circumstances permit to remain in our homes."[13] For these workers, a true man, unlike women or children, controlled his own time and body. The allusion to freedom carried a racial message as well, separating out the special privileges afforded to white men, in contrast to black men, who even in the twentieth century were expected to demonstrate a certain level of obedience in the face of white authority.[14] Chipping away at this right, the streetcar workers argued, reduced them to standing on par with children, wives, or wards. Equally important, by regulating their behavior outside of paid working hours during this time of suspension, employers were looking to expand their control beyond the worksite into the larger public, and even private, spheres.[15]

The same issue lay at the heart of the Jacksonville strike. There, workers asserted that the ability to organize collectively constituted an individual, "manly" right to which they should be entitled. This argument countered management's portrayal of their desire to organize as a form of socialism at best, anarchism at worst. George J. Baldwin, the general manager of the company, received letters of support from employers all over the country for openly combating the "socialist element" in the ranks of labor. J. West Goodwin, president of a printing company in Sedalia, Missouri, for example, lauded Baldwin in a series of letters for helping to defeat the "socialist menace."[16] Most Jacksonville residents, however, did not agree with the management. Local newspaper editorials proclaimed that it was the right of every "man" to organize. Since African Americans were not employed or represented by the streetcar union, but were expected to form separate "colored" unions, presumably this right was limited to white men. One particularly impassioned editorial by Charles E. Jones went on to comment that Jesus of Nazareth trained as a carpenter and would be on the side of labor. Because he spoke out for the meek, Jones argued, Jesus would have come out against capital the same way he did against the money lenders in the temple. "Had his coming been postponed for twenty centuries who doubts that He would be a member of the union?" Jones asked.[17]

After the strike ended, a letter to the *Dixie* editor written by "Dr. J. A. Garrard from Bartow" praised the newspaper's editors, and Jones specifically, for their "defence of the people" and their rights. Garrard also praised Jones because he had not yet "bowed to the knee of Baal."[18] Although management tried to diffuse the class elements of the protest, many residents did not succumb to attacking the strike because they feared an outbreak of socialism and/or anarchism. However much workers tried to counter the management's arguments, then, their portrayal clearly held some sway.

In both the Jacksonville and Pensacola streetcar strikes, race was also central to many workers' grievances and played a central role in how workers saw themselves. G. C. McCain, president of the Pensacola streetcar workers union, delivered an impassioned speech to a supportive audience of local residents. "Ladies and gentlemen, fellow-citizens," he began, "I am here tonight to state that I am proud of the city of Pensacola, and am thankful that it is Pensacola and not the city of Boston. I am thankful that we are white men and haven't got black hearts. I will state that the black as well as white appreciate union principles."[19] McCain's use of the words *white men* was deliberate. Like Sarra, McCain wanted to emphasize not just that these workers were "men" but that they were "white men" and should therefore be entitled to certain privileges not afforded to women or African Americans. For many southern whites, labor policies that undermined the position of white men were important motivators and often united white men and women across lines of class. For streetcar owners to institute a policy that white workers and the broader white public interpreted as "paternalistic" was to cast these workers as somehow less than white, threatening to equate them with black men who, many whites believed, were unable to fully control their passions, their bodies, or their labor. To southerners at this time and in this place, being manly meant being white.[20]

McCain's comparison between Pensacola and Boston was also important. As in many Florida cities at this time, Pensacola's streetcars were not locally owned. In this case, the parent company was based in Boston. To many Florida residents, then, the company was not only an outsider but also a northern one, leading several commentators to go so far as to refer to the owners as "foreign."[21] In 1908, the *Pensacola Journal* reinforced this idea of a foreign invasion, highlighting what they believed to be strikebreakers' immigrant backgrounds along with their northern residency. Gender and ethnicity worked together not only to emphasize the strikebreakers' and management's northern identities but also to refer to them as "white with black hearts," a phrase which harkened back to an earlier generation when it was used to describe white Republicans who allied themselves with black Republicans during the period of Reconstruction.[22] By striking this chord in white collective memory, labor leaders tried to brand management as somehow less than white and therefore as politically and socially illegitimate. In McCain's telling, workers for the streetcars were thus whiter than the northern management.

McCain's assumption that blacks supported their efforts by not joining the strikebreakers is also interesting. During the 1912 strike, Lynn C. Doyle, a reporter for *Dixie*, claimed that some workers who were loyal to the streetcar owners were earning $20 a week while the majority of workers earned only $12 a week, with a penny an hour raise for each year of service. Doyle argued that this income differential created a serious class division so deep that he referred to the $12 a week employees as "less fortunate slaves." A reader from Bronson, Florida, addressing the Jacksonville strike, played up this comparison as well, noting that as workers returned to the city's streetcars, they "must submit to chains and slavery."[23] Like the nineteenth-century workers described by historian David Roediger and others, who compared their plight to that of slaves in order to emphasize the social distance separating them from black workers by virtue of their race, so Florida's early twentieth-century streetcar workers used similar rhetoric to emphasize their own race privilege while highlighting the poor conditions their employers forced upon them.[24]

William E. Terry, the union's chief negotiator and southern organizer for the AFL, pointed out that in Jacksonville, black workers organized into their own unions when white workers could not. Underscoring that his union represented "white labor," Terry underscored that he merely wanted white laborers to have the right to choose their own unions and protect their own interests just like black workers. Ultimately, however, Terry may have overplayed his hand. Shortly after the strike was called, Terry reported that 22 white unions had voted to support a general strike in Jacksonville. He later followed up this claim, noting that representatives from the city's "colored" unions also voiced support for a general strike as a way to force a settlement. But the streetcar company's general manager soon caught Terry in a lie. Despite Terry's claims, only one of Jacksonville's white labor unions voted for a general strike. The position of the city's black unions remained unclear. Convinced that the strike was losing momentum, the management broke off negotiations and turned their attention to other matters.[25]

Although the streetcar strikes of 1908 and 1912 were the largest public labor demonstrations ever seen in Florida prior to World War I, organizing also took other forms. The wives of white union leaders formed a Ladies Auxiliary during the 1914 FSFL Convention to "create a closer and more fraternal feeling between the families of members of the unions" and to "instill the principles of trade unionism in the women relatives of the members." Few of the members of the Ladies Auxiliary worked for wages themselves. Thus they promoted their advocacy for labor from their homes. As historians Dana Frank and Eileen Boris remind us, the home was a working environment, and both male and female labor leaders extended the movement into the home under the direction of wives and mothers.[26] Within the context of these families, white men constructed the principles of unionism in the workplace while white women instilled unionism in the home. Members of the Auxiliary typically held luncheon meetings at the annual convention or in the parlors of their homes. The responsibilities of the Ladies Auxiliary also differed greatly from that of their white male counterparts. The Auxiliary was in charge of organizing the yearly Labor Day "old time basket picnic outing." Not surprisingly, activities at the Labor Day picnic were typically separated by sex. Women engaged in contests that reaffirmed their dominance in the home, judging who was the prettiest, the most popular, and the best pie maker. Sporting events were segregated not only by sex but also by marital status. Married and unmarried women competed separately in the 50- and 100-yard dashes.[27]

Black women in the labor movement were excluded from these activities altogether, as were black men. The FSFL tracked the activities of black unions across the state, and there was no mention of black women's auxiliaries ever being formed during this period. Although black women's clubs served a similar function, they were never granted the status of true auxiliaries, thus underscoring the higher status granted to white women by white male labor leaders who saw them as nurturers and moral leaders but would not grant the same privileges to black women.[28]

Women also played an important role in Florida's labor movement as consumers. Unlike the workplace where men tried to reform wages and standards, labor leaders recognized the primacy of women's roles as consumers and organized them to protest through their purse strings.[29] White women in Florida employed this strategy in the 1910s by bringing attention not only to labor issues but also to the suffrage movement. From its inception, white women and men who supported the Ladies Auxiliary saw it as a way to directly influence the course of day-to-day activities by discouraging women from purchasing non-union label products.[30] Because of women's purchasing power, there were also many male union members who argued that these grounds alone should mandate granting women the right to vote—a right proudly trumpeted by the FSFL's newspaper, *Artisan*, in 1915. It was for this reason, at least in part, that the FSFL endorsed the idea of equal pay for both sexes for equal work in its early constitution, but still insisted on creating a separate space for white women within the movement.[31]

World War I marked a significant change in how the Florida labor movement addressed the place of white women and African Americans within the ranks of the working classes. As a result of the war, the number of industries in Florida boomed along with the number of workers. Women and African Americans made up a significant number of those who were coming to the state to search for economic opportunity. This placed them in direct competition with white male workers for the first time. Whereas before the war, African Americans remained in separate unions and therefore were largely absent from the attentions of the FSFL and white women were treated as benign and affirming to the male labor leadership, after the war the FSFL began to introduce policies they hoped would restrict and control the presence of these groups in the workplace and in the labor movement.

Across the nation, the First World War brought unprecedented numbers of white women into the paid labor force. Florida was no exception. Not only was there a demand for women, black and white, in traditional spheres like domestic service and kindred industries, but women also began to be hired into occupations traditionally reserved for men. Even if these job opportunities were not in the state, Florida's white union men took notice. The Williston Lodge No. 42, a union in Williston, Florida, for example, passed a resolution decrying the use of women in positions of manual labor with the Northern Pacific Railroad, arguing that this type of activity would "demoralize" the home.[32] Men did not have to look far to notice that white women were becoming more important to the wartime labor force. As the *Miami Herald* noted in 1919, "With the growing complexity of the problem of women's employment and the increase in their numbers in industry, it is becoming increasingly important that the state departments of labor should be equipped to enforce laws regulating their employment, as well as to study their needs and observe new conditions."[33]

As women's place in the paid labor force grew and expanded, working-class men came to believe that they had to enforce the strict notion that white women, in particular, were not only essential to the home environment but were ill-equipped for the waged workplace.

This fear of white women in the labor market also forced the FSFL to rethink their mostly symbolic policy of equal pay. During the FSFL Convention of 1917, the organization considered establishing a separate pay scale for women in the state and reducing the number of hours that white women were allowed to work. While white male labor leaders expected the state to strictly define the working environment of women, these same leaders also demanded that white women enter the civic and political sphere "equally" by granting them the franchise. John H. Mackey, the first vice president of the FSFL, noted that many women in Europe were voting by 1917. Since women were found as laborers in the industrial workforce, he argued, "It is a duty that devolves upon all men of this county to place them [white women] upon an equal footing, so far as the ballot is concerned." Although Mackey demanded equality of the ballot for white women, he did not believe white men and women were equal in all other respects. Instead, Mackey hoped that extending suffrage to white women would end the era of corrupt city politics because of what he saw as their inherent moral superiority. "Woman aims for higher things in life, and her very nature is against political trickery," Mackey wrote.[34]

By 1919, when the state legislature debated bills to regulate the wages and working environment of women but still had not passed any legislation, a member of the FSFL admonished them, stating: "Let us hope and trust that our lawmakers, while working for constructive means to safeguard our cattle from tick, our citrus industry from canker, our hogs from cholera, etc., will seriously consider and enact legislation that will limit the hours of female employees."[35] This was not an unusual attitude for the time. Nationally, middle-class women reformers joined many union leaders to promote the *Muller v. Oregon* ruling that a woman, like a child, was a ward of her husband or father first and then of the state. Thus the state was obligated to protect women in the workplace by controlling the hours they could work, the types of jobs they could hold, and the conditions under which they labored. It is clear that by likening white women to cattle and citrus, men in the labor movement believed that the state had an obligation to "protect" white women from the brutality of the workplace. Thus women's bodies were legally defined as not under their own control, but were commodified in the workplace under the direction of the state and white men more generally.

This type of legislation and its justification was not unique to Florida or the United States. Historian Kathleen Canning chronicles similar outcomes in Germany during periods of rapid industrialization. In German factories, mills, and homes, reformers and politicians collaborated to keep women from entering certain sectors of the workforce. Hours, wages, and working conditions in job sectors that employed large numbers of women also were placed under state control. Canning mentions that reformers and labor leaders believed protective legislation would curb the "feminization" of the industrial shop that not only threatened male job security and wages but also disrupted the place of women in the traditional family.[36] Similar to the German example, white women in Florida were in one sense "protected" by this legislation, but the laws also codified their status as second-class workers. The racial specificity of this legislation is equally noteworthy. Because these reformers envisioned only white women as union matriarchs in the home, often ignoring black women's presence in the paid labor force altogether, the gender ideology professed by Florida's white male labor leaders was racialized as well. "Women" became rhetorically synonymous with white women; black women were excluded from this legislation and calls for change altogether.[37]

For labor leaders in Florida, the demographic shift in the paid labor force that accompanied World War I represented a threat to their own Victorian era understandings of gender roles. As Alice Kessler-Harris has observed, by the 1910s, reformers across the United States had begun to demand that women work under a minimum wage. These measures were not necessarily meant to keep pay for women and men unequal, although this is often what happened in practice. Rather, such legislation was intended to guarantee that women would make a wage high enough to support them and their families. Whatever its motivations, however, legislating wages contrasted sharply with the idea of freedom of contract that many labor leaders supported; the ability to negotiate wages was an inherent right of "free, white men" and therefore a staple of their racial and gendered superiority. Advocates for minimum wage legislation also worried that white women would not have the ability, or the moral fortitude, to negotiate wages high enough to support their families and thus would be taken advantage of by their employers. Linking these conditions to the possibility that working women would have to seek out supplemental income through prostitution, reformers argued it was the state's responsibility to strictly regulate women's wages. These are the variety of reasons that influenced labor leaders in Florida to lobby the legislature to enact laws specifically designed to control white women and their wages in the workplace.[38]

Without waiting for protective legislation, women's clubs and social workers in Miami employed a variety of methods to directly diminish the ill effects they believed industrial work would have on white women. A number of women's clubs and relief organizations formed the "Advisory Committee on Girls' Work in Dade County" in 1919. Community leaders used this organization to meet with local working-class women in order to gauge their social and educational needs. One meeting described how M. J. Burkill of the Women's Relief Association offered classes to working women on nursing and how to care for their young children. Although many of these efforts focused on controlling the working and social lives of women, these organizations also emphasized education. Dade's Advisory Committee sponsored numerous meetings and contests to encourage women to "think independently" and to supplement the early education many women lost by entering the paid workforce while still in their teens. Operating as part of the Miami War Camp Community Service (MCCS), the Advisory Committee tended to the needs of a wide range of women, from those working in more "blue-collar" sectors like agriculture and manufacturing, to "white-collar" occupations like salesclerks at several Miami department stores including Burdines and E. B. Douglas and a number of smaller shops. Using monies from the Smith-Hughes Act, which was reserved for agricultural and vocational training, they opened part-time schools for white women workers. As historian Shira Birnbaum has pointed out, coupling homecare training with liberal arts education was also the standard curriculum at Florida State College for Women during this time. Progressive era lawmakers and reformers believed that white women needed a grounding in a classical education, not only to tutor their male children in a variety of topics but also to instruct their African American servants and expose them to the finer points of "civilization" while at work serving the state's white families.[39]

Other MCCS agencies were interested in the social lives of soldiers during the war, concentrating on ways to reduce instances of venereal disease. The MCCS policies initiated toward women were mostly meant to shape young white women into "young ladies," so that they could better entertain returning soldiers in a "wholesome environment." Although the Miami MCCS did engage in these kinds of activities, education predominated.

Throughout the First World War their primary emphasis remained on providing white women with access to education they might not have been afforded before the war.[40]

White- and blue-collar women also proved every bit as willing to strike as their male counterparts. In Jacksonville, white women who worked for the Bell Telephone Company went on strike several times between 1917 through 1919. In a poem featured in the *Artisan* during one of the 1917 strikes, the poet likened the contemporary importance of women in the state's workforce to the familiar Victorian idea that white women served as the moral and emotional compass of the family:

I am Woman
The Mother of man.
The helpmate and comfort of man.
The precursor of progress.
The spur of effort.
I made man to make of the earth a garden.
From me he draws the inspiration to beautify and adorn.
In all his ways and walks am I ever by his side.
His friend, aid and counselor.
In his joys he turns to me for fellowship
In his sorrows he turns to me for strength to bear.
In all things I am his partner
Yet in these days am I broken on the wheel of dividends.
Toured, so that out of my suffering,
Profits may be coined
I am made a wanton
To the same end.
My children are torn from me
So that a few may riot and spend
My mother instinct is used to enslave me
So millionaires may enjoy feasts.
When I grow tired and resent
Then am I maligned and traduced,
The harlot press derides me,
The apologists for tyranny misrepresent me.
I am woman
In my rebellion against greed and power,
I am fighting for man,

For the sons of man—the daughters of man.
Now here and to be.
I, the mother of men,
The helpmate and comfort of man,
His joy and his strength.
I, the woman.[41]

Appealing to the same ideas represented by *Muller v. Oregon*, works like this argued powerfully that white women's experiences in the workplace would not only diminish and retard her natural motherly instincts, but that unchecked corporations would diminish the natural role of women in the home.[42] At a time when more women were securing wages for their work than ever before, women were demonstrating an activist will at least as strong as their male counterparts, and women's labor was seen as essential both to the war effort and to the socioeconomic well-being of the nation. Rather than moving toward an ideology of greater equality, white men and women found themselves more and more at odds.

Two years later, during the 1919 Jacksonville Bell Strike, women's activism took a decidedly different turn. In September, a group of white female workers struck. But a number of their fellow workers remained on the job. The strikers jeered at the remaining workers, calling them "scabs" or worse. Tired of the insults, on the afternoon of September 11, some of the women who remained on the job finally had enough and lunged at the strikers. A physical brawl broke out in the streets below Bell Telephone's offices. Witnesses claimed that insults, fights, and clothing flew until several white men arrived on the scene and broke up the fight. "Members of the male persuasion yesterday afternoon enjoyed the role of peacemakers in separating a little band of telephone girls who walked out last spring and those who took their places," the Jacksonville *Metropolis*.[43] This sharp reversal of gender roles—with women spiraling out of control, requiring men to step in and serve as moral censors—was disturbing to many readers, however glib the press's depiction of the incident may have seemed. Consistently referring to working "girls," in contrast to moral reformers, mothers, and other "ladies," the lack of respect afforded to these uncontrollable, impassioned women is clear, and it underscored their position as wards, mere children not responsible for their actions.

The fact that many of these telephone employees were participating in the paid labor force for the first time in their lives was also used to undermine the strength of their actions. White union men often referred to the striking women as "defenseless girls" who could not protect themselves, even going so far as to argue that they needed the guidance and organizational leadership of white men in the industry to assist them. The single time Jacksonville's mainstream or union press referred to the striking workers as "women" was when they appeared before a judge following a series of arrests. In the face of this paternal authority, and only in this controlled and hierarchical context, did it seem safe to again grant them the status afforded by the term *woman*.[44]

Florida's black women also played a critical role in the state and nation's economy during the war years. But there were no editorials, pieces of legislation, or even fiery speeches directed toward improving their working conditions, wages, or home environments in Jacksonville and Pensacola during this period. That did not mean, however, that black men and women had freedom of contract or even control over their own bodies in the workplace. Rather, policies directed toward them were informal and understood as governed by a separate standard altogether. "Black pay" or "black conditions" existed alongside that for whites, separate and unequal. White labor leaders, reformers, and even management never conceived of black women as having the same innate moral certitude as that of white women. As a result, their place in the working environment did not have to be as closely monitored. Gail Bederman, in her book *Manliness and Civilization*, points to the Victorian idea that gender distinctions existed because whites were seen as a "civilized" race who had developed gender distinctions as they passed further and further away from "savagery." Blacks, however, in the view of many whites, were still "barbarous." Absent the same virtues and inherent moral certitude as white women, Florida's black women were thus denied the same protections as white women.[45]

In 1920, Bessie Paul and Betty Span, both black women from Jacksonville who worked for the Pullman Railroad Company, petitioned the United States Railroad Administration Women's Service over a series of grievances. Both women were officially employed as cleaners, and they were paid a wage commensurate with this work, which the railroad considered semiskilled. Paul, who was a forelady, was paid even more. But as Pullman's labor needs escalated, rather than hire additional workers, the company frequently asked these women to complete additional tasks it considered unskilled, like sewing pillows. During the time they completed this unskilled work, the women were paid a lower wage. Paul and Span argued that since they were semiskilled laborers they should have been paid at their usual rate, irrespective of the tasks they were performing. Unlike most white unions where men and women were organized separately, Florida's black unions organized men and women into the same locals. Thus when Paul and Span petitioned the federal agency, they did so on behalf of black male and female railroad workers alike, making it even more noteworthy that it was black women, not black men, who put forward the complaint to the federal agency. The Railroad Administration responded favorably to the women's complaint and petitioned Pullman's Chicago headquarters on their behalf. Both women received back pay to compensate them for their lost wages while performing these lesser skilled tasks.

In the same complaint, a number of other unionized black women cleaners also asked the Railroad Administration to take action to improve their working conditions on board the trains. Although the company provided separate toilets, equipped with a sandbox, for black men and women, the women complained that their toilets were too close to the male toilets. Again, the Railroad Administration agreed and stepped in to address the complaint. As one official noted, "The toilet is very poorly located near the colored men's and the white men's toilet. The entrance to each is screened."[46] The Railroad Administration recommended that Pullman look into moving the black women's toilet away from the sight of men, since the screen door deprived black women of their privacy.[47] Even though white union leaders, and many white Floridians, refused to recognize black women as "ladies," the federal government, by way of the Railroad Administration, argued the opposite and in these small but significant ways took steps to ensure they were treated as such.

At other times, however, black women and men found themselves at odds. This was particularly true when pay was at issue. On December 26, 1918, 21 black porters who were employed by the Florida East Coast Railway filed a complaint with the United States Department of Labor's Division of Negro Economics. Earlier that year, the Labor Department had warned railway companies that they could no longer force porters—a relatively low paying job reserved almost solely for black men—to perform duties reserved for more highly paid flagmen, brakemen, and conductors. In this case, railroad companies used this technique to punish white workers who threatened to organize or strike. Since flagmen, brakemen, and conductors were almost exclusively white men, the threat that a black, unskilled man could do their job preyed upon racist ideology and proved a powerful means of controlling the working classes. Black men faced threats from white workers if they completed these tasks and from their employers if they did not. White men resented the undermining of the privileged position that their race afforded them.[48] In the interests of preventing riots and the exploitation of workers, the federal government thus declared this practice illegal.

The expanded federal government that was created during the war years also provided a new outlet for black workers, especially on the railroad. Because their industry was viewed as central to the war effort, the federal government was even more likely to intervene. Porters on the Florida East Coast Railroad documented the company's violations of these policies and demanded either back pay for additional duties or formal promotion to the skilled positions with a commensurate increase in pay. But in this case, the Division of Negro Economics eventually refused to support their claims.[49] Arguing that the national need for these workers was so great that they should strive to keep the peace and stay on the job as a civic duty, black men enjoyed little social and economic mobility even as they were offered new job opportunities.[50]

Although the white union press essentially ignored black labor activism altogether, there was one important exception. In the summer of 1916, black workers at Seaboard Air Line in Jacksonville struck for higher wages and better working conditions. Seaboard Air responded by hiring black replacement workers. Within a few months, the Seaboard Line replaced striking workers and actually increased by 13 percent the number of baggage handlers and other unskilled workers they employed.[51] The workers who had walked off their jobs in protest did not take these events idly, but gathered at a northern labor recruiter's office the following day. In response, Jacksonville's sheriff declared that all offices recruiting black laborers had to shut down altogether. Infuriated, African Americans from across the city gathered and continued to demonstrate, protesting the closings and the unfair labor practices at Seaboard. Alarmed at the escalating situation, Jacksonville's Mayor J.E.T. Bowden responded with even more repressive measures, ordering the black protestors arrested for vagrancy.[52]

This particular application of vagrancy laws was also somewhat peculiar to the World War I and immediate postwar period. Earlier versions of the laws never defined vagrancy within the context of gainful employment, but instead included behaviors deemed to be immoral, such as gambling, begging, and prostitution. By 1917, however, in addition to applying to these types of activities, the definition of a vagrant was expanded to include "persons able to work but habitually living upon the earnings of their wives and children."[53] They were also used to discipline unruly or striking workers and to maintain social order and racial codes.

One Miami case illustrates this well. As veterans began returning from

World War I and demand for housing across Miami increased, the city's color line became increasingly contested. Pressure from white residents to control the line separating black and white neighborhoods also increased, resulting in curfews for black residents. Black residents caught outside of the city's black neighborhoods after curfew were subject to arrest and often charged with vagrancy. This appeared to be the case for seven, black women who were arrested in July 1919. As the *Miami Herald* reported: "Seven more dusky vagrants, all females, were rounded up yesterday and sent through the courts. . . . It was alleged that their vagrancy consisted of misconduct on the streets." Noting that all the women pled guilty, the reporter went on to describe how "male friends" had been waiting for the women outside the court. The reporter poked fun at one "dusky belle" who "almost flabbergasted officials by . . . nonchalantly paying her fine and then strolling haughtily out of the building to her waiting automobile, in which, with chin tilted high in the air she was driving away. The life of some 'vags' seems to be something more than the bevo and skittles," the article concluded.[54]

Although it is impossible to know much more about the women, the census identifies their occupations as maids, laundresses, and seamstresses.[55] Given the context in which their arrest occurred, it would seem that perhaps much more was going on. Whether or not these women were actually working as prostitutes, the fact that they were out on the street after curfew in a white neighborhood was enough to convince police, the judge, and white newspaper reporters that these women were prostitutes. Yet one could easily imagine how similar charges could be, and were, leveled at women who participated in demonstrations or sought to exercise their own freedom of movement outside of regulated hours and urban spaces. Breaking these rules not only made women vulnerable to arrest but also cast aspersions on their moral character. Both served as powerful means of control. Civil authorities were granted this control only because it was limited to black women. Had there been any threat, this policy could have been applied equally to white as well as black workers, or to men as well as women. White male workers would certainly have objected to this affront to their manhood. Their silence spoke volumes about the degree to which lines of race and gender had hardened over the war years, securing, at least for a short time, their more privileged position in the hierarchy of racialized gender.

But this trust in the security of white privilege did not last long. As the second major streetcar strike wore on in Jacksonville that same year, labor agents soon extended their northern labor recruitment to black as well as white male replacement workers. Rather than condemn this strategy, Jacksonville's political and business leaders publicly begged the northern black workers to remain in the city because they could pay black men considerably lower wages than white workers would accept. The Florida Labor Council found this action reprehensible. Underscoring that there was already more than enough white labor in Jacksonville to support local businesses, they soundly condemned these efforts by the city's ruling class. In a series of editorials, the *Artisan* blamed white business and political leaders for turning their backs on white labor, pointing to the racial hypocrisy of capitalism. Industry leaders, they argued, were among the most adamant in advocating the segregation of the races on the streetcars. Yet they were more than willing to sit next to black chauffeurs or servants in their private cars. White labor leaders went on to complain that by their willingness to work so cheaply, black workers were the best friends of capitalists, enabling their luxurious lifestyles and helping them to amass their enormous fortunes.

The complexities of Jacksonville's labor situation took an unusual turn in the summer of 1920 when a white labor agent was arrested for trying to contract white labor in the city. He was charged under the city's new vagrancy laws, which had previously been applied only to black residents. Under a headline that read, "Intimidating White Men: Chief of Police Threatening White Men as He Did Negroes," the *Artisan* lambasted Jacksonville's chief of police for using threatening tactics commonly reserved for blacks. Again, the language of freedom and the right of white men to control their bodies took on renewed importance. When the police applied the city's new vagrancy acts to white recruiters and workers, white labor leaders condemned their actions, arguing that because these laws were passed by white voters with the understanding that they would apply only to blacks, this new application of the law constituted a clear attempt to challenge the racial hierarchy, thus making whites equal to blacks.[56]

This debate erupted at a time when many black male workers were also demanding that they be granted the same right to "free labor" as was afforded to white men. Members of the newly formed Florida Uplift Association expressed their expectation that white residents would recognize "the [r]ights [of black men] to labor as free men." In a lengthy letter to the editor of the *Miami Herald* in June 1919, a committee of the organization explained their mission and guiding beliefs. "We believe absolutely . . . Life, liberty and the pursuit of happiness is the constituted right of every man," they wrote. "The common laborer is often abused by white overseers. . . . [A] s free men they are not obliged to suffer such treatment, hence seek other sections."[57] As was the case among white streetcar workers, black workers in other job sectors also believed that they owned their bodies and as "free laborers" should have the right to change jobs, move across job sectors, or leave their workplaces to seek better conditions in "other sections" of the state, region, or country.

In her work on Pullman porters' organization efforts in Chicago over this same period, Beth Tompkins Bates notes that when black men pressed to unionize during and after World War I, they often pointed to elevating their "manhood" rights as a way to achieve equality with white men.[58] Black workers in Florida were equally conscious of their social and legal status as wards of white men and sought to change this. N. B. Young, writing in the *Messenger* in 1923, claimed that everywhere in Florida, "the Negro is a political non-entity . . . in all matters of citizenship a sort of ward [to] his white fellow-citizens [and] self appointed guardians."[59] This view was echoed in other publications as well. One editorial about the conditions of black workers in Miami published in the *New York Age* noted:

> The very fact that the Negro taxpayer in Miami is practically a ward of the white race, should secure for him even more careful consideration than would be accorded an equal . . . that minors and inferiors unable to manage their own affairs and safeguard their own rights are entitled to much greater consideration than those capable of protecting themselves. . . . We wonder if he cannot see the injustice in laws that compel a man who has property worth more than $7,000 and can borrow $5,000 cash, to leave the management of his affairs and the safeguarding of his rights in the hands of the large class of lazy, worthless, loafing, tobacco-chewing crackers that inhabit such a town as Miami.[60]

Juxtaposing the rights granted to working-class whites against the limited control given wealthy African Americans, the writer continued to endorse a class-based hierarchy, but he questioned the validity of a race-based one.

For black men in Florida, equality was directly connected to self-respect. But it was also tied to manhood. In another *New York Age* editorial from 1919, a writer noted, "No colored man can win the good will of the Southern white man except at some expense to his own self respect . . . which debases him more or less in his own estimation; if his estimation of himself is that of a man."[61] Like white men, when black men pressed for better working conditions, higher rates of pay, and greater responsibility they did so not just in response to their place in the racial hierarchy but on a gendered basis as well.

Debates about the equality of white and black men were not limited to the editorial pages of newspapers and magazines, but eventually ended up at the annual convention of the FSFL. During the FSFL Convention of 1920 in St. Augustine, a few delegates convinced two black union members, T. J. Hankerson from the Carpenters Local 1972 and C. E. Todd from the Building Trades Council of Jacksonville, to petition and formally join the meeting. One reason for this initiative was that after the war, the AFL moved to include black workers at their national meetings and symbolically integrated their national conference. Even though these moves produced very little change in the day-to-day working lives of black workers or within individual locals, they were important steps nonetheless and ones that at least some FSFL members hoped to replicate within their ranks. Hankerson's and Todd's arrival caused quite a stir. They were then asked to leave while the delegates debated whether or not to allow them to join the meeting. George M. Hull, representing the Central Trades and Labor Council of Jacksonville, argued that because the AFL recognized no racial distinction among its members, the delegates should be allowed to join the FSFL convention. Others noted that allowing the entrance of black members into the convention would have tremendous benefit for creating a more unified organizing effort across the state. Those who opposed allowing Hankerson and Todd into the meeting countered that by allowing black men to join, the FSFL would be effectively telling these black men that they were equal to whites. Upon further debate, the black delegates were asked to leave. Nonetheless, the men were encouraged to organize on behalf of the labor cause in the state of Florida under the auspices of "interracial unionism."[62] Recognizing the hollowness of this gesture, one black observer later wrote: "The principle of united action for the elevation of labor seemed to have been lost sight of at the fear that the presence of the two colored delegates might in some way bring about 'social equality' as if the Federation was a kind of pink tea party."[63] This blatant comparison between the type of events organized by women through churches and civic organizations spoke volumes, and it sought not just to question the manliness of the white labor delegates but to cast aspersions on their political seriousness as well. Often organized around pink or floral themes, and designed as light social occasions where political talk was abandoned in favor of polite conversation, this reference held a clear double meaning to contemporary readers.[64] What the observer was really saying was that if the FSFL was not going to address equality, it might as well be a polite, effeminate meeting of church women. Pushing his criticism even farther, the observer chastised the FSFL for its "moral weakness" by not protecting the equal rights of the black delegates. By not standing up for equality, he argued, these white male delegates proved they were not really men.

However limited the approach of the FSFL may have been, there were other locals across the state that did embrace a more genuine approach to racial cooperation. Even as the FSFL was debating whether or not to allow black union delegates to attend its annual convention, phosphate workers in Polk and Hillsborough counties were busy organizing into local chapters of the International Union of Mine, Mill, and Smelter Workers (Mine-Mill) and Mulberry Mineral Workers. They met deep resistance from local mine owners who, in an attempt to break the union, proceeded to fire the unions' organizers. Especially frightening to owners was the fact that these locals included black and white workers organized into a single, integrated chapter—something rarely seen elsewhere in the state. At the urging of the national organization, the Florida mine workers decided to have the National War Labor Board (NWLB) arbitrate their cases rather than go out on strike, since the government considered phosphate a war industry material.

As their investigation proceeded, the NWLB conducted numerous interviews with phosphate workers and learned that black and white phosphate workers lived and worked under much different conditions. According to the testimony given to the investigators, black workers and their families lived in squalid conditions with no indoor plumbing. White workers and their families, by contrast, virtually all had a bathroom in their homes. Black workers were also forced to use the camp commissary to purchase food and material they needed, were paid in company script (rather than dollars), and received change from the commissary in aluminum coins that could only be redeemed at the same commissary. Interviewees mentioned that even when black workers received regular paychecks, the commissaries often remained the only place they could cash their checks. Rather than currency that could be used at the place of their choosing, black workers received only credits for use toward future purchases in the commissaries. Commissaries also extended loans to black workers against their future earnings. Unless black workers were given an alternative to these commissaries, the report concluded, they would be forever subject to these policies, which were financially limiting and often punitive.

In arbitration, miners demanded that they be allowed to organize and that the fired workers be reinstated, given a pay raise, granted an eight-hour workday, and made immune from the commissary system.[65] In arguing against the commissary system in particular, the union highlighted that it violated the rights of black workers as "free men." Binding workers to the commissaries for shopping and wage payment, the union argued, forced workers into a system of dependency and restricted their ability to leave the area to shop and spend their earnings. Throughout all of the trials, testimony, and correspondence, union leaders and the NWLB alike always referred to workers as "men." No distinction was made between white and black workers whatsoever.

The fact that the Mine-Mill Union was an independent union and not affiliated with the AFL helped encourage the type of integrated unionism seen among workers in the Polk and Hillsborough mines. But the Mine-Mill Union also created a prickly set of circumstances for laborers in the phosphate mines. First, the Mine-Mill Union attracted the attention of state and local officials who were bent on rooting out alleged radicals. Company owners also used the fear of socialism and anarchism, coupled with flag-waving patriotism, to keep workers from joining the union. But their approach to organization also exposed the wide variety of views that workers had about each other and the hierarchies within their worksites. One union member, T. A. Cason, noted that he was previously with a dispatchers union until they affiliated with the AFL, an organization that, in his view, "went to taking in Tom, Dick, and Harry and the ragtag and bobtail." A white pit foremen, Cason saw the AFL as not being elite enough, chiding them for allowing every sort of white rabble to join its membership. In his view it was far preferable to be in a racially integrated union than to join an organization that let in white men whom he considered "ragtag" and "bobtails." Cason looked for an organization with an intellectual exclusivity. The Mine-Mill Union also created problems for the phosphate companies because they were organizing black workers alongside white workers, thereby making it harder for companies to use race as a weapon to divide workers.

Many workers interviewed by the NWLB raised complaints about a manager named H. M. Mansfield, who was especially hated by the rank and file. Mansfield had hired an African American, whom everyone called "Professor Mays," and purchased a "$500 Ford" for Mays so that he could drive around Ford Meade, visit black workers at home, and convince them to form their own all-black local, thereby leaving the integrated union. Preaching a message of racial uplift and separation, at least seven local leaders, including five pastors, followed Mays on his rounds, promoting a resolution that thanked the mine companies for taking good care of the black population of Polk County. According to local reports, most black workers rejected this movement and refused Mays's call. But whites came out in large numbers to hear Mays and his colleagues defend racial separation.[66] This divide is reminiscent of similar circumstances that Brian Kelly observed in his study of Alabama coalfields over this period, where black working-class organizers rejected black middle-class leaders who promoted similar arguments about racial separatism.[67] In the Florida phosphate mines, black workers enjoyed some solidarity with white workers in addressing racial inequality and more recognition of their manhood from other white workers than black workers enjoyed elsewhere in the state.[68]

Although Tampa workers have been featured prominently in labor histories of Florida, we do not have a sense of how racial and gender ideologies within the state labor movement affected workers in Tampa's more heterogeneous shop floors, where workers lived, moved, and organized in a broadly transnational framework.[69] Like the Mine-Mill Union, workers in the Cigar Makers' International Union (CMIU) criticized the AFL and also adopted a practice of interracial organizing. Cubans, Afro-Cubans, Italians, and Spaniards all played important roles in the Ybor City movement. But this was not always the case. Only by World War I were workers in the cigar factories turning toward a more fully integrated model of unionism, as indicated by a Spanish-language writer, Santiago Castillo. Writing in support of the 1919–20 cigar workers' strike, Castillo observed:

> In 1910 there was a strike that failed Americans, Spaniards, Cubans, Italians, whites and blacks. The history tells that everyone put their hands in the effort and nobody claimed their nationality, and that it was Capital which divided the blacks and whites, making the whites believe that the blacks were breaking the strike, and telling the blacks that the whites despised them and did not consider them their partners. They got whatever amount of money they wanted from the bourgeoisie and the result was what was expected ... by dividing the workers by colors and races, they took every advantage possible. . . . Will the history of division repeat itself in Cuba? It would not be strange if it happened, in spite of the fact that black men know that this is the hobby horse of politicians. . . . Nobody takes care of the black race until they intend to divide us as we see happening at the moment and then, all of them pretend they are defenders of the black race.[70]

As elsewhere in Florida before World War I, workers in Tampa were vulnerable to racial distrust if not full-blown animosity. They also conceived of race differently than other native-born workers, distinguishing between "colors and races" and hinting at a more nuanced racial categorization and hierarchy than prevailed elsewhere in the "one drop rule" South. In the Spanish-language section of Tampa's labor newspaper, "razas de color" was often applied as a plural term that could refer to either Afro-Cubans or other persons of African descent, but was rarely applied to African Americans.[71] Additionally, Castillo indicated that the binary and absolute racial definition not only was, in his view, uniquely American but also had the potential to infect race relations back in Cuba. Clearly, a sense of internationalism influenced this writer's understanding of race, shaping organizing efforts in the cigar factories of Ybor as well as in Cuba.

An African American cigar worker in Ybor made a similar observation about how the international ties of the city's working classes created a more nuanced racial hierarchy. Responding to Castillo's call for international and interracial cooperation, this worker wrote:

> [T]he manufacturers will try to encourage racial and national prejudices, creating a vile conception of colored workmen by presuming that as soon as they will entone [sic] a racial hymn we will follow them like a herd of sheep. Colored workers . . . we must stand by the white workers because their cause is also our cause and if we betray them we will betray ourselves, our children, our families and our race. [T]he manufacturers do not rest one moment, believing that by one way or another they will at last break our union and defeat us—White, Colored, Americans, Cubans, Spaniards and Italians, alike. . . . The manufacturers [will] keep the workers divided . . . until they are forced to treat all of us equally, no matter to what race or nationality we may belong.[72]

Noting several local examples when manufacturers worked to exclude black workers or made claims that black workers were anti-union, this writer saw a broad coalition of the working classes, irrespective of ethnicity, race, or nationality, as integral to the American labor movement itself.

Race did not operate alone in the internationalist world of Ybor; like the rest of the movement in Florida, it operated alongside class and gender. In the pages of the *El Internacional*, words like *man* and *free men* were used as umbrella terms, including both black and white workers and, in some cases, women. In a March 1920 editorial, one worker professed, "The right 'to live like a man' is the enduring principle upon which labor will unite for the common good of all." The writer continued, "Every right-thinking worker recognizes the duty of both the white and black race to enter the industrial field without prejudice or selfishness; to unite against the exploiters and demand a 'square deal.'"[73] Limited neither to whites nor to men, the CMIU adopted a broad use of the ideology of "free labor" to encompass all workers, male and female, irrespective of race or nativity.

This became especially important during the 1919–20 strikes. After the first walkouts in the fall of 1919, cigar manufacturers refused to take back striking workers under any circumstances. For many families this meant as much as a full year without pay, forcing them to rely upon charity in order to feed and clothes themselves and their dependents. Calling the conditions under which workers were forced to labor and the refusal of shop owners to create a closed shop, "industrial serfdom," the CMIU argued that manufacturers' attempts to control these aspects of workers' lives while depriving them of a decent standard of living threatened the gendered social order itself. In the words of one advocate: "No body of men worthy of the name 'men' ever humbly submitted to the damnable use of the blacklist as a punishment for organizational activities." The CMIU targeted the manufacturers' behavior as engendering an unmanly environment for workers, thereby threatening the larger community as well.[74]

The CMIU also took to branding the AFL as an effeminate body, specifically a pink tea party, as did many black critics, especially in Miami. As in Tampa, international developments also played a role. But this time the greatest impact was from the United States' neighbor to the north. As in the United States, Cuban and Spanish cigar workers in Montréal factories were also segregated from white Canadian workers. But in 1920, the AFL demanded an end to Canada's "color line." Publicized in a variety of union papers, the announcement particularly attracted the attention of Tampa's CMIU. In response to some white workers who promoted racial divisions, El Internacional stated, "How dreadful it must be for those who have so vigorously 'worked' the 'race prejudice' propaganda to realize that after all their fatherly warnings and pleadings and predictions of dire disaster to the white workers, their solicitude has been ignored."[75] Chastising the paternalism of white labor leaders who used race to divide working men and women, this writer went on to praise the "true men" and "true leaders" of the labor movement, who espoused "color-blind values," an overt jab at the ardent segregationism of the FSFL that was immediately understood by the paper's readership.

In searching for glimpses into the lives of workers, historians have strived for an all-encompassing theory or single pattern of race and gender relations that prevailed across the nation's working classes. While this work has stimulated serious discussions, it had also led to reductionist approaches to describing the way race and gender have transformed the labor movement. These categories rarely operated separately, as the case of Florida's early twentieth-century workers makes clear. As elsewhere in North America, Florida's labor environment was diverse and complex. Workers in the cigar and phosphate industries held different perspectives on organizing than streetcar workers in Jacksonville and Pensacola. In many cases, the views of the FSFL were divorced from all of these groups. By synthesizing these many examples of worker activism in Florida, however, it becomes clear that if historians want to understand the social environment of working-class people, we must peel away the layers of embedded social categories such as race, class, ethnicity, regionalism, and gender to see exactly how the social labor mosaic was constructed.

*   *   *

Research for this chapter was partially supported by an Extending the Reach: Faculty Research Award from the National Endowment for the Humanities. The author would also like to thank Debora Cordeiro for assistance with the translations of articles from the Tampa newspaper *El Internacional.*

Notes

1. FSFL, "Proceedings of the Convention: 1915," Special Collections, University of Florida, Gainesville (hereafter cited as UFSC).

2. FSFL, "Proceedings of the Convention: 1902," UFSC.

3. FSFL, "Proceedings of the Convention: 1906," UFSC; Gerald E. Poyo, "The Impact of Cuban and Spanish Workers on Labor Organizing in Florida, 1870–1900," *Journal of American Ethnic History* 5 (Winter 1986): 46–63.

4. Eric Arnesen, "Passion and Politics: Race and the Writing of Working-Class History," *Journal of the Historical Society* 6 (September 2006): 323–56. On the embeddedness of these categories in working-class life, see Mark Granovetter, "Economic Action and Social Structure: The Problem of Embeddedness," *American Journal of Sociology* 91 (November 1985): 481–510; Alejandro Portes and Julia Sensenbrenner, "Embeddedness and Immigration: Notes on the Social Determinants of Economic Action," *American Journal of Sociology* 98 (May 1993): 1320–50. On the intersection of race, class, and unionization in Florida and elsewhere in the South over this period, see especially Eric Arnesen, "Following the Color Line of Labor: Black Workers and the Labor Movement before 1930," *Radical History Review* 55 (Winter 1993): 53–87; Brian Kelly, *Race, Class, and Power in the Alabama Coalfields, 1908–21* (Urbana: University of Illinois Press, 2001), 3–16; Daniel Letwin, *The Challenge of Interracial Unionism: Alabama Coal Min-

ers, 1878–1921 (Chapel Hill: University of North Carolina Press, 1998), 188–89; Henry M. McKiven Jr., *Iron and Steel: Class, Race, and Community in Birmingham, Alabama, 1875–1920* (Chapel Hill: University of North Carolina Press, 1995), 1–6; David R. Roediger, *The Wages of Whiteness: Race and the Making of the American Working Class* (New York: Verso, 1991), 167–84.

5. Eileen Boris first described the concept of "racialized gender" that I employ here. See Eileen Boris, "From Gender to Racialized Gender: Laboring Bodies That Matter," *International Labor and Working-Class History* 63 (October 2002): 9–13. See also Ava Baron, "Gender and Labor History: Learning from the Past, Looking to the Future," *Work Engendered: Toward a New History of American Labor*, ed. Ava Baron (Ithaca, N.Y.: Cornell University Press, 1991), 1–37; Christina Burr, *Spreading the Light: Work and Labour Reform in the Late Nineteenth-Century Toronto* (Buffalo, N.Y.: University of Toronto Press, 1999); Dana Frank, "White Working-Class Women and the Race Question," *International Labor and Working-Class History* 54 (Fall 1998): 80–102; Venus Green, *Race on the Line: Gender, Labor, and Technology in the Bell System, 1880–1980* (Durham, N.C.: Duke University Press, 2001), 1–10; Tera W. Hunter, *To 'Joy My Freedom: Southern Black Women's Lives and Labors after the Civil War* (Cambridge: Harvard University Press, 1997), 115–16.

6. Charles H. Bliss, "Leaders to Blame," *Common Sense* 1 (August 1902): 1; Charles H. Bliss, "Labor Strikes and Their Effects on Society," *Bliss' Magazine* 8 (January 1902): iii–iv, 17–19; Leon Fink, "From Autonomy to Abundance: Changing Beliefs about the Free Labor System in Nineteenth-Century America," *Terms of Labor: Slavery, Serfdom, and Free Labor*, ed. Stanley L. Engerman (Palo Alto, Calif.: Stanford University Press, 1999), 116–36.

7. Michael Kimmel, *Manhood in America: A Cultural History* (New York: Free Press, 1996), 106.

8. Stephen H. Norwood, *Strikebreaking and Intimidation: Mercenaries and Masculinity in Twentieth-Century America* (Chapel Hill: University of North Carolina Press, 2002), 1–14.

9. *Pensacola Journal*, April 11, 1908. For a detailed explanation of the 1908 strike, see Wayne Flynt, "Pensacola Labor Problems and Political Radicalism, 1908," *Florida Historical Quarterly* 43 (Spring 1965): 315–32.

10. Adjutant General's Office, "Report of the Adjutant General of the State of Florida, 1908," microfilm, Florida State Archives, Tallahassee, 56–85.

11. *Jacksonville Metropolis*, November 6–8, 1912; *Florida Times Union*, November 6–8, 1912.

12. *Dixie* (Jacksonville), November 16, 1912; "Albert W. Gilchrist for United States Senator, June 1916," Albert W. Gilchrist Papers, Special Collections, Florida State University Libraries, Tallahassee.

13. *Pensacola Journal*, April 7, 1908.

14. Alice Kessler-Harris, *A Woman's Wage: Historical Meanings and Social Consequences* (Lexington: University Press of Kentucky, 1990), 36.

15. L. Fink, "From Autonomy to Abundance," 131–32.

16. J. West Goodwin to George J. Baldwin, May 23 and June 11, 1908, Baldwin Papers,

box 42, Southern Collection, University of North Carolina at Chapel Hill (hereafter cited as BPUNC).

17. *Dixie*, November 16, 1912.

18. Ibid.

19. *Pensacola Journal*, April 11, 1908.

20. M. Kimmel, *Manhood in America*, 106–7.

21. The parent company of Pensacola's streetcars was Stone and Webster, a Boston-based conglomerate. The company's manager, George J. Baldwin, also managed operations in Jacksonville, Tampa, Savannah, Houston, and Columbus. He was born in Savannah, Georgia, and received his college education at the Massachusetts Institute of Technology. It is unclear whether labor leaders did not know that a southerner made these decisions, or whether they simply did not consider him to be "southern" because of his policies or his northern education.

22. *Independent* (New York), May 23, 1895.

23. *Dixie*, November 23, 1912.

24. D. Roediger, *The Wages of Whiteness*, 167–84.

25. *Jacksonville Metropolis*, November 5, 13, 16, 1912; *Florida Times Union*, November 5, 13–14, 1912; George Baldwin to Henry G. Bradlee, November 13, 1912, box 42, BPUNC; George Baldwin to H. H. Hunt, November 13, 1912, box 42, BPUNC; George Baldwin to Boykin Wright, November 14, 1912, box 42, BPUNC; *Artisan* (Jacksonville), February 13, 1915.

26. Dana Frank, *Purchasing Power: Consumer Organizing, Gender, and the Seattle Labor Movement, 1919–1929* (London: University of Cambridge Press, 1994), 55–56; Eileen Boris, "The Home as a Workplace: Deconstructing Dichotomies," *International Review of Social History* 39 (December 1994): 415–28.

27. *Artisan*, September 2, 1915.

28. *Miami Herald*, June 2, 1919. On the separate treatment of black and white women within auxiliaries, see Alice Kessler-Harris, *Out to Work: A History of Wage Earning Women in the United States* (New York: Oxford University Press, 2003), 106; A. Kessler-Harris, *A Woman's Wage*, 47.

29. Susan Levine, "Workers' Wives: Gender, Class, and Consumerism in the 1920s United States," *Gender and History* 3 (April 1991): 45–64.

30. Throughout this period the Ladies Auxiliary changed its name to the "Label League" and then back to the "Ladies Auxiliary."

31. FSFL, "Proceedings of the Convention: 1914," UFSC; FSFL, "Proceedings of the Convention: 1917," UFSC; *Artisan*, May 22, 1915.

32. *Artisan*, June 30 and September 1, 1917, January 11, 1919; FSFL, "Proceedings of the Convention: 1917," UFSC; FSFL, "Proceedings of the Convention: 1921," UFSC.

33. *Miami Herald*, April 3, 1919.

34. FSFL, "Proceedings of the Convention: 1917," UFSC.

35. FSFL, "Proceedings of the Convention: 1919," UFSC.

36. Kathleen Canning, *Languages of Labor and Gender: Female Factory Work in Germany, 1850–1914* (Ithaca, N.Y.: Cornell University Press, 1996), 126–69.

37. E. Boris, "From Gender to Racialized Gender," 9–13.

38. *Artisan*, April 21, 1917; *Muller v. Oregon*, 208 U.S. 412 (1908); A. Kessler-Harris, *A Woman's Wage*, 52–53.

39. *Miami Herald*, March 26, April 4, 1919; National Vocational Education Act (Smith-Hughes), Public Law No. 347, 64th Cong., S. 703; Shira Birnbaum, "Making Southern Belles in Progressive Era Florida: Gender in the Formal and Hidden Curriculum of the Florida Female College," *Frontiers: A Journal of Women Studies* 16 (Spring/Summer 1996): 233.

40. *Miami Herald*, March 26, April 4, 1919; Joseph Lee, "War Camp Community Service," *Annals of the American Academy of Political and Social Science* 79 (September 1918): 189–94.

41. *Artisan*, December 29, 1917. That the poem's author goes unnamed is not unusual for publications of this kind and period.

42. Ibid, *Artisan*, December 15, and 22, 1917; *Florida Times-Union*, September 12–13, 1919; *Metropolis*, September 12–13, 1919.

43. *Metropolis*, September 12, 1919.

44. *Metropolis*, September 12–13, 1919; *Florida Times-Union*, September 12–13, 1919; V. Green, *Race on the Line*, 104.

45. Gail Bederman, *Manliness and Civilization: A Cultural History of Gender and Race in the United States, 1880–1917* (Chicago: University of Chicago Press, 1995), 31–41.

46. Petitions of Women Cleaners to United States Railroad Administration, February 19, 1920, in *Black Workers in the Era of the Great Migration, 1916–1925*, ed. James R. Grossman (Frederick, Md.: University Publications of America, 1985), microfilm, reel 11, frame 671.

47. Petitions of Betty Paul, Betty Span, and Women Cleaners to United States Railroad Administration, February 19, 1920, *Black Workers*, reel 11, frames 664–71. Black women in Jacksonville utilized other venues for highlighting gender inequality, like suffrage campaigns. White women also placed gender issues in the forefront of their labor campaigns. See E. Boris, "From Gender to Racialized Gender," 12.

48. Eric Arnesen, "'Like Banquo's Ghost, It Will Not Down': The Race Question and the American Railroad Brotherhoods, 1880–1920," *American Historical Review* 99 (December 1994): 1601–33.

49. R. E. Stillman to W. S. Carter, December 26, 1918, September 24 and November 10, 1919, *Black Workers*, reel 10, frames 476–508.

50. Eric Arnesen, *Brotherhoods of Color: Black Railroad Workers and the Struggle for Equality* (Cambridge, Mass.: Harvard University Press, 2001), 42–83.

51. *Florida Times-Union*, July 13 and 27, 1916; Railroad Commission of the State of Florida, "Annual Report of the Seaboard Air Line Railway Company," December 31, 1916, Florida State Archives, Tallahassee, 510–511.

52. *Metropolis*, July 29, 1916.

53. City of Jacksonville, Florida, *Ordinances of the City of Jacksonville* (Jacksonville: C. Drew's Book and Job Printing Office, 1868), 10; City of Jacksonville, Florida, *Charter and Ordinances of the City of Jacksonville* (Jacksonville: D. A. Costa Printing and Publishing House, 1889), 58–59; City of Jacksonville, Florida, *Charter and Ordinances of the*

City of Jacksonville 1901 (Jacksonville: City of Jacksonville, 1901), 102–3; City of Jacksonville, Florida, *Charter and Ordinances of the City of Jacksonville 1917* (Jacksonville: City of Jacksonville, 1917), 226.

54. *Miami Herald*, July 25, 1919.

55. On the arrested women's occupations, see *United States Census of Population: 1920*, Florida, Dade County, Precinct 9, Miami City, 12A (Beulah Beverly) and 22B (Mary Annie Brown); *U.S. Census: 1920*, Dade County, Precinct 8, 23A (Maggie Johnson). See also Paul S. George, "Policing Miami's Black Community, 1896–1930," *Florida Historical Quarterly* 57 (April 1979): 434–50.

56. *Artisan*, January 1, February 19, July 22 and 29, August 5, 1916, August 4, 1917.

57. *Miami Herald*, June 2, 1919.

58. Beth Tompkins Bates, *Pullman Porters and the Rise of Protest Politics in Black America, 1925–1945* (Chapel Hill: University of North Carolina, 2001), 28–30.

59. N. B. Young, "These 'Colored' United States: No. VI—Florida: Our Contiguous Foreign State," *Messenger* 5 (November 1923): 896.

60. *New York Age*, September 20, 1917.

61. *New York Age*, July 5, 1919.

62. FSFL, "Proceedings of the Convention: 1920," UFSC.

63. *New York Age*, May 1, 1920.

64. See "A Pink Tea Party," *Ladies' Home Journal and Practical Housekeeping* 2 (November 1885): 2; S. O. Johnson, "Hints upon Etiquette and Good Manners," *Ladies' Home Journal* 3 (July 1886): 11.

65. Cole-Crough interview, Records of the National War Labor Board, Record Group 2 (hereafter cited as NWLB 2), National Archives and Records Administration, College Park, Md. (hereafter cited as NARA); Hancock-Crough interview, NWLB 2, NARA; Crough-Raleigh interview, NWLB 2, NARA; Rowland-Raleigh interview, NWLB 2, NARA; V. Urquhart to National War Labor Board, NWLB 2, NARA; docket nos. 690 and 691a, NWLB 2, NARA; Cason-Crough interview, NWLB 2, NARA; Cason-Raleigh interview, NWLB 2, NARA; B. Rosin to C. C. Martin, March 2, 1917, NWLB 2, NARA.

66. Cason-Crough interview; Cole-Crough interview; Russell-Crough interview; "Welfare of the Colored People," *Fort Meade Leader*, NWLB 2, NARA.

67. B. Kelly, *Race, Class and Power*, 14.

68. The NWLB recommended that the phosphate companies meet the demands of their workers. However, by this time, the war was over, and the companies refused to acknowledge the board or its recommendations. This led to the 1919 phosphate strike, which was one of the most violent to take place over this period. See Arch Fredric Blakey, *The Florida Phosphate Industry: A History of the Development of Use of a Vital Mineral* (Cambridge: Harvard University Press, 1973), 61–75; James Arthur Fisher, "The History of Mulberry and Frontier Florida: A Model for the Teaching of Local History," PhD diss., Middle Tennessee State University, 1974, 209–12.

69. On transnationalizing labor history, see Marcel van der Linden, "Transnationalizing American Labor History," *Journal of American History* 86 (December 1999): 1115–34; Gunther Peck, "In Search of an American Working Class: Nationalist Fictions

in the Making of Western Labor History," *Mitteilungsblatt des Instituts fur Soziale Be-wegungen* 25 (May 2001): 29–45. On Tampa's workers, see Nancy A. Hewitt, *Southern Discomfort: Women's Activism in Tampa, Florida, 1880s–1920s* (Urbana: University of Illinois Press, 2001), 1–20; Gary R. Mormino and George E. Pozzetta, *The Immigrant World of Ybor City: Italians and Their Latin Neighbors in Tampa, 1885–1985* (Urbana: University of Illinois Press, 1987; reprint, Gainesville: University Press of Florida, 1998), 233–59; Susan D. Greenbaum, *More than Black: Afro-Cubans in Tampa* (Gainesville: University Press of Florida, 2002), 1–30.

70. *El Internacional* (Tampa), April 16, 1920.

71. *El Internacional*, January 16, April 16, and May 7, 1920.

72. *El Internacional*, May 7, 1920.

73. *El Internacional*, March 5, 1920.

74. *El Internacional*, March 12, 1920. For more on the Tampa closed shop strike of 1919–21, see Durward Long, "The Open-Closed Shop Battle in Tampa's Cigar Industry, 1919–1921," *Florida Historical Quarterly* 47 (Fall 1968): 101–21.

75. *El Internacional*, June 11, 1920.

6

Chauffeuring in a White Man's Town

Black Service Work, Movement, and Segregation in Early Miami

THOMAS A. CASTILLO

In the early twentieth century, Miami was divided into two cities, one white and one "colored." Blacks lived in several settlements throughout Dade County labeled by whites as "colored towns." The largest, found in present-day Overtown, was known as Colored Town. Divided by residential segregation, Miami was also divided by rigid boundaries in the job market and spatial mobility.[1] Between 1915 and 1919, Miami's white union chauffeurs, seeing the opportunity to use their racial privilege in Miami's growing tourist economy, attempted to monopolize the chauffeur business and prevent blacks from driving in the city. Black protest, combined with tourist complaints against the city's antiblack driving custom, led to a negotiation to extend the color line during this period.

Exploring how the color line applied to driving, particularly the occupation of chauffeuring, highlights the perverse nature of segregation while also demonstrating its limitations. A rereading of newspaper accounts, discovery of untapped newspaper sources such as letters to the editor, reference to national discussions about the chauffeur occupation, and use of city directories and the 1920 and 1930 census manuscripts, yield a more complete picture of race conflict in chauffeuring. Black drivers and community leaders of all ethnic backgrounds turned the chauffeur issue into a moral problem challenging the city's racial etiquette. Blacks used segregation as a progressive policy to achieve race harmony. In not challenging the idea of separateness, blacks in particular forced flexibility of the color line in chauffeuring because of their community's need to move about the city in order to get to jobs and shop in the city's white stores. Pushing for a stopgap to racist tendencies to limit their movement melded well with white employers' need to have blacks working for them. In addition, the ideas of black servility and racial uplift merged neatly as Miami's white business elite sought to protect the viability of the city's tourist economy. As such, the Jim Crow resolution to blacks' right to drive and chauffeur in Miami became the segregation rule until after World War II. In this way the chauffeur debates in Miami serve as another example of how modernizing forces, such as automobile technology, became new focal points for the application of segregation culture.[2]

Few scholars, however, have devoted attention to driving and its place in the history of segregation and African American civil rights. Historian Paul George's recounting of the 1915, 1917, and 1919 conflicts in his dissertation and subsequent articles on Colored Town, brought to light this historical moment. Most recently, Marvin Dunn has restated George's earlier findings with more detail. Neither, however, explored the context from which the struggle between white chauffeurs and Miami's black community emerged, except for general commentary regarding U.S. racial custom. Both highlight the ineffectiveness of the police department to protect black drivers and the racism endemic to the era. But in all these accounts, the story of the chauffeur conflict remains static, devoid of contingency and agency. The city's "leaders," black and white, gain the credit for change, while the workers remain shadowy actors with stereotyped roles.[3]

Rooting the historical analysis in the economic and political context helps clarify the complicated issues of race and class in at least three ways. First, outlining the power wielded by white union chauffeurs points to the role of unionism in keeping the color line in the job market. It also highlights how the scarcity of work opportunities has allowed for the worst discriminatory instincts to flourish. Second, the racial context leads to the larger economic issues defining race and class at the time. What labor concerns shaped the views of white chauffeurs? What economic and political concerns influenced the perspectives of white and black leaders? Finally, black workers' persistent challenge to white chauffeurs' rules and to hard-line segregationists, suggests an active and ongoing tension among workers and between employer and employee over control of the job market. White chauffeurs were eventually unsuccessful in their appeals for a rigid color line not because they were unable to convince other whites about their racial superiority but because, unlike skilled craftsmen, their work fit a culturally hegemonic, servile profile.

Defining the Chauffeur

Miami's incorporation in 1896 coincided with the period characterized by historian Rayford Logan as the nadir of American race relations. Despite the general treatment of African Americans as second-class citizens, 162 blacks voted in the city's incorporation election because their numbers were needed to meet the minimum number of required voters to attain a city charter. Whites depended on black laborers, who mostly worked on construction projects and helped to clear land. In this case, this dependency also extended to the ballot. As the city of Miami grew, institutional forms of segregation and racial custom merged. The subsequent and continuous violations of black civil rights would define the political, economic, and social context of the first half of the next century.[4]

In spite of the limitations of living in a Jim Crow city, blacks continued to migrate to Miami and worked mostly in service occupations. Bahamians made up a large percentage of these migrants. Southern African Americans also moved to Miami, arriving mostly from other parts of Florida and the Deep South states of Alabama, Georgia, North and South Carolina. In 1920, Bahamian immigrants made up 52 percent (4,815) of Miami's black population of 9,270. But by 1925, the number decreased to about 35 percent (7,595 of 22,037), falling to 22 percent (5,152 of 25,166) in 1930. Although Miami's black population increased, it fell in proportion to the city's white population. From a high of 31 percent in 1920, blacks slipped to 23 percent in 1930 (of 110,637), then to 18 percent in 1940 (44,240 of 250,537).[5]

Blacks also found their job opportunities limited in Miami, as they did in the rest of the country. According to the 1930 census, black women worked mostly as laundresses or domestics, and black men worked as laborers, domestic workers, servants, and janitors as well as in other service occupations. Many blacks moved to Miami in pursuit of jobs in the tourist industry and service work in general. While this led to an increase in the permanent population, temporary seasonal growth occurred as well. According to the Works Progress Administration's research on 1930s black Florida, Miami's black population doubled during the winter months, a time when tourism also peaked.[6]

Throughout this time, the exclusion of blacks from jobs that were considered "skilled" is particularly notable. As I have shown in another essay, white men actively sought to exclude black men from skilled jobs in Miami. This practice was most effective in the building trades. The success of such a strategy depended on the degree of control over the occupation that union workers could foster without causing too much of an imbalance in the city's economy. Defining chauffeuring as a skilled job, however, proved difficult. But that did not prevent white chauffeurs from trying. As an occupation, driving had less prestige than the handcrafts in the building industry. Whereas employers relied heavily on building craftsmen for successful completion of construction jobs, chauffeurs never convinced the public that their occupation required as much deference despite the white supremacy discourse they used.[7]

Besides the basic requirement of having to drive an automobile, what defined a chauffeur was not always clear. What did a chauffeur transport? If he moved goods, was he still a chauffeur, or simply a trucker, a driver, a teamster, or a hackman? What if he worked for a particular company to transport goods or a particular family as a domestic chauffeur? Occupational names assigned in the 1920 census for drivers—that is, anyone who earned a fee or wage by transporting people or goods by automobile, truck, or cart—highlight this confusion.[8] The terms *chauffeur, driver,* and *hackman,* for instance, were often unclear in regard to whether people or goods were being transported, particularly when the chauffeur reported that he earned his wages on his own account but did not provide any other information. Was he an independent contractor? Did he solicit tourists to drive them? The terms *chauffeur* and *driver* were used interchangeably through the 1920s, applying to anyone who drove for a living. By the 1940s, however, *chauffeur* took its present occupational designation as being distinct from other drivers, such as teamsters or taxi drivers.[9] In every case these jobs were open exclusively to men.

The 1920 census compilation for occupations did distinguish between domestic chauffeurs and others, although these numbers were not recorded for cities with less than 50,000 residents. But the census did not account for the type of vehicle or what was being transported. Freddie Andrews, the black Miamian whose resistance to the color line in chauffeuring helped lead to its renegotiation, described himself as a "hack driver" who owned a vehicle, but what that meant to the Census compilers was not indicated. Newspaper accounts showed that he did own an automobile (labeled as "car" or "auto" in the manuscript). The 1920 census manuscript rolls, though, demonstrate that blacks succeeded in working as all kinds of drivers. Out of 151 men who labeled themselves as chauffeurs or drivers, blacks constituted 22 percent (33). Out of 41 domestic chauffeurs, blacks made up 39 percent (16). They also dominated in other driving fields that required horses, like carriage drivers (27 of 35), teamsters (35 of 37), and draymen (34 of 35).[10]

Similar problems in accuracy persisted in the 1930 census compilations. While more clarity emerged with the various job designations than the 1920 census schedule, census compilers did not note the finer distinctions between individuals who chauffeured under different arrangements. Bus, transfer, and cab companies were accounted for in the census, for instance. However, a reader would not know from this data how many chauffeurs worked for private families, whether they were white or black and whether they were employed permanently or temporarily. A quick review of the census schedule manuscripts indicates how prevalent black chauffeurs were who worked for private families. The 1930 census listed 428 chauffeurs, truck and tractor drivers (32 percent of 1,342), and 14 owners and managers of truck, transfer, and cab companies (15.2 percent of 92).[11]

The problem of labeling represented more than just a semantic conundrum. Malleability of the labels used to describe this work reflected the newness of driving automobiles as an occupation. It also reflects the racial flexibility this work afforded and the ease of entering into this field. Reduced to its simplest terms, anyone who purchased a car could become a chauffeur for the transport of people. Even with the high cost of purchasing an automobile, entering this profession proved relatively open, though the impact of licensing and insurance laws emerging in the late 1920s created some institutional barriers. This aspect of chauffeuring needs to be studied but does not appear to have hampered the entrance of blacks into this line of work before 1920.[12] At the very least, blacks drove for other blacks. The prevalence of black men serving as domestic chauffeurs in 1930 suggests that they also gained the opportunity to drive whites around town, work that was perhaps seen as an extension of more servile roles.

Whatever employers thought, however, white chauffeurs across the nation identified black and immigrant men as direct competition to their livelihoods. This was particularly clear in the early twentieth century. New York chauffeurs in 1912 complained that Europeans "willing to work for smaller wages than Americans" and "the negro" were lowering wages and reducing the supply of work. "Everybody wants to be a chauffeur," related one white driver, "so, of course, wages have been going down." Black chauffeurs in New York faced sabotage of their vehicles, such as finding mothballs in their gasoline tanks, their ignition systems short-circuited, and their carburetors thrown out of adjustment. White chauffeurs were also right to perceive changes in the racial and ethnic makeup of the available labor pool. Blacks increasingly entered chauffeuring between 1900 and 1910 and continued to do so in the following years. From a national total of 4,639 (10.3 percent) in 1910, blacks made a leap to 38,360 (13.5 percent) in 1920. Pressure from blacks, therefore, increased competition throughout the country.[13]

Expectations of a chauffeur's duties also changed over time and varied with place of employment. Early on, chauffeurs tended to be skilled in mechanics. Unpredictable mechanical breakdowns, along with the lack of infrastructure needed to accommodate such situations, made skilled driver-mechanics necessary. Knowledge of how to fix cars continued to be a useful attribute whether one served as a domestic chauffeur or as a private chauffeur for hire, but technological advances made cars easier to handle, decreasing the need for such specialized knowledge. In addition, with the rise of garage mechanics as a separate and distinct occupation, chauffeurs soon became differentiated by what they drove and who employed them. A domestic chauffeur worked for a private family. Chauffeurs for hire were either independent contractors or hired by a particular company, such as a hotel or garage.[14]

Employers also expected chauffeurs to provide services beyond driving. "People want him not only to be a servant but to know that he is a servant," commented the manager of a garage in New York. The garage man noted that additional chores were also given to the chauffeur, such as washing windows. One writer argued that paying extra for a skilled chauffeur would save money because an employer would not be subject to the exorbitant prices charged in garages. He highlighted that new chauffeurs tended to be young boys "drawn to automobile-driving by the attractiveness of the work and the comparative ease with which automobile-driving is learned," but who lacked "mental balance" and were irresponsible. On the other hand, the writer argued, the "high-priced chauffeur" offered reliability and would not engage in "joyriding," taking the car without permission for either recreational use or using it to supplement one's income by offering taxi service. Garage owners protested being identified as "high-priced" and blamed the chauffeurs for charging commission fees for their patronage.

These debates among employers, chauffeurs, and garage owners defined the "chauffeur problem," which peaked in the first 15 years of the twentieth century. Protests by white chauffeurs suggest that white men resisted wealthy employers' desire to make them act in more servile ways. Racially defined skills and roles played no small role in these discussions. Thus Miami's chauffeur conflict developed in the dynamic context of ongoing labor troubles, racial tension, and debates over the prestige of chauffeuring at a time of rapid change.[15]

The 1915–19 Chauffeur Conflict

On February 28, 1915, a black chauffeur from Palm Beach was run out of Miami for driving for three white women. The *Miami Herald* reported that the black chauffeur had "wagered with a white man that he could come here, drive about the city and 'get away' with it." He "did not realize that a strong sentiment prevails in Miami against colored chauffeurs," the paper reported, and was soon "closely pursued by several cars containing Miami chauffeurs, realizing that unless he vacated the car he would be handled roughly, [he] abandoned the car and beat it afoot for the colored section." The black chauffeur later appeared at the police station to ask for protection. He was put on a train to Palm Beach, while the car remained in Miami for the owner, a Mister Metcalf, to retrieve the next day. The chauffeur was "convinced that while it's healthy to drive autos in Palm Beach, a Negro has no business acting as [a] chauffeur in Miami." The *Metropolis* reported that the black chauffeur owned the vehicle with three other blacks and had come to Miami despite knowing the prejudice existing against black drivers. Instead of criticizing the white chauffeurs, both papers brushed off the incident as the black chauffeurs' failure to respect the boundaries of the color line. Business and labor colluded in maintaining strict segregation rules.[16]

Debate over the chauffeur situation lasted for the next several years, intensifying in the summer of 1915 as a result of the February incident and heightened interest in how segregation in driving would ultimately affect the city's tourist industry. Supporters of Jim Crow legislation first accepted the racial practice of restricting African American chauffeurs from doing business, though some whites did point out that the segregation dialogue bordered on hypocrisy. Disagreement especially centered on the practice of allowing tourists to bring their own black chauffeurs with them when visiting the city.

How many times white chauffeurs prevented blacks from driving in the city is not known. Newspaper reports suggest that it did not occur often, though knowledge of the prejudice against black use of automobiles likely deterred many from purchasing an automobile. The high price of automobiles was another equally important obstacle. Still, the *Miami Metropolis* questioned whether allowing white chauffeurs' threats to shape the city's customs was actually in Miami's best interests. Letters from tourists to the *Metropolis* complaining about the February incident sparked further interest in the topic. In an editorial entitled, "Shall Mob Law Rule Miami," the paper indicated its own stance on the issue: the paper felt it unwise to prevent tourists from bringing their black chauffeurs to the city. Taking a law and order position, while conceding to racial etiquette, the paper's editorial staff suggested that if Miamians agreed to forbid tourists to use their black chauffeurs, then the city needed to inform the tourists of this regulation. If not, then the city of Miami should accommodate these tourists and their chauffeurs, despite the boycott of garages or intimidation from white drivers.

The *Metropolis* did not defend the right of blacks to drive. But it did recognize the damage that the complete elimination of black drivers would have on Miami's tourist industry, its economic engine. "We want the business of these touring parties, and the value of one machine to Miami, with occupants, who are usually liberal persons, means much to the city. . . . It would cost more than could be overcome in the way of hostile publicity." The completion of the Dixie Highway, designed to increase the number of tourists who flooded into the city each winter, would only exacerbate this problem, they argued. Booster ideology led to comparisons with the customs of other southern cities and merged with the racist sentiment common to the era. "In practically every southern city owners of cars have colored chauffeurs," the *Metropolis* reported. "In Atlanta, for instance, a majority of the owned machines are driven by negroes, the same as southern carriages of the Southern gentlemen were driven years ago." This image remained a key strand in the argument for allowing tourists to bring their black chauffeurs with them to Miami.[17]

The leadership role played by the *Metropolis* in Progressive era Miami was not insignificant. Simpson Bobo Dean, part-owner of the newspaper since 1904 and its sole owner from 1914 to 1923, served as a muckraking voice in early Miami. Dean lived a life in newspapers. Born in Alabama, March 21, 1871, Dean began work as a reporter for the *Journal and Tribune* in Knoxville, Tennessee, when he was just 19 years of age. In the 1890s, he moved to Florida. Soon thereafter, he started the *Palm Beach Daily News*. By 1909, Dean had become a strong populist voice against Henry Flagler and the Florida East Coast Railroad. The most famous of his criticisms of Flagler focused on lowering freight rates for growers. When local businessmen petitioned Dean to ease his opposition to Flagler, Dean turned around and published a list of their names in the *Metropolis* on April 1, 1910. Several Miamians wrote letters of support for the paper's position and soon after "the advertisers and subscribers who had dropped their support of the paper through FEC pressure came back. The railroad finally readjusted its rates."[18] The *Miami Metropolis* was also among the city's strongest supporters of Prohibition. As a "dry" paper, the *Metropolis* served as the city's gadfly. Its journalistic style contrasted sharply with the more conservative coverage of city's other newspaper, the *Miami Herald*. Therefore, when wealthy tourists began to complain about their inability to travel with their black chauffeurs, Dean and his paper pushed for a resolution that would be in the best interests of the city, while the *Herald* hesitated, expressing skepticism about whether or not a problem actually existed.

Even more important, the *Metropolis* and *Herald* disagreed about whether or not to publicize the city's race-based chauffeuring regulations. The former believed the Chamber of Commerce, "representing the progressive thought and action of the community," needed to investigate the matter and take a formal stand to protect Miami's tourist industry. The *Herald* did not believe the city had a significant chauffeur problem. Thus they saw no need to publicize the guidelines or for the city's political leaders to take steps to investigate it. The *Herald* continued to refer only vaguely to the ongoing debate, even as a major public forum was convened to address the issue. News of the forum itself was kept extremely brief and relegated to the middle and end of the paper. The *Metropolis*, on the other hand, provided extensive front-page coverage, evoking criticism from the *Herald* that the *Metropolis* was only "creating trouble" for an issue that was "not a burning question."[19] Later, even the *Herald* would be forced to concede that a problem existed. But in the summer of 1915, they continued to offer little coverage of the chauffeur debates while ostensibly deferring to the sensibilities of hard-line segregationists who did not want blacks to drive.

A typical and especially revealing commentary on the reasons why many middle-class and working-class whites opposed allowing black men to work as chauffeurs was offered by George Okell, owner of a Miami garage. In a letter to the *Metropolis*, Okell described the February incident as an exceptional case and the fault of one black driver who was "looking for trouble." According to his retelling, the black driver from Palm Beach had stepped out of his socially accepted place since he knew Miami's racial custom but nonetheless chose to defy it. Arguing on behalf of the white chauffeurs, Okell turned to a discourse focused on standards of living. Miami's white chauffeurs, he wrote, were family men who "organized a union for the mutual protection against low wages and demoralized labor conditions. . . . They realize that when the door is thrown open and the negro chauffeur tolerated that the negro will work for lower wages and under conditions that a white man can not compete."

Floyd McNeil of the chauffeurs union concurred. Moralizing a bit further, McNeil argued that accepting black chauffeurs would be like "asking them to come to the level of the negro, and that is not pleasant." These opponents also criticized the extensive boosterism engaged in by the city's businesses for flooding the local labor market with workers.[20] More than race alone, the class dynamics of the growing chauffeur debate were increasingly plain.

Permeating this discourse was the idea that once one concession was made, complete integration would be the result. In a letter to the *Miami Metropolis*, the carpenter P. L. Ryan argued against allowing blacks to compete with white chauffeurs, stating that no white man wanted competition from blacks. He questioned the racial values of advocates of a more liberal chauffeur policy when he said that some whites "would welcome even Jack Johnson had he a Negro chauffeur." In a hopeful prediction, but one marred with a deep racial hatred, he wrote, "I do not believe there is a man, woman, or child in Miami today that will live long enough to see a Negro chauffeur on the streets of Miami." The *Herald* elaborated on this point, stepping away from its normally more reserved stance. As one 1915 editorial intoned:

> If negro men are to take up the work of chauffeurs it will be followed by garages operated by colored men in the white portion of the city, and the color line once being broken, there will be nothing to prevent other colored business from coming in the white part of the city, and for colored residents to choose any part of the city they desire for their homes. The question resolves itself to this, do we want any change made in the regulation that has prevailed from the beginning?

Such reports were intended to play on the race fears of many among Miami's more vulnerable classes and unite Miami's white community against any change in the racial status quo. Such public confessions that Miami was indeed a white man's town were borrowed from language used by whites throughout the South. Racial hyperbole functioned as a defensive barrier to feared encroachments. Still the Miami Chamber of Commerce refused to take a position on the matter, claiming it had no authority to do so.[21]

More moderate positions accepted racial segregation, but criticized the rigidity of hard-line segregationists for not being more sensitive to the finer sensibilities of the wealthy, an obvious source of increased revenues for the city. C. L. Sheeler, a resident from Buena Vista, a suburb just north of Miami, argued that Miami should imitate Baltimore, "the metropolis of the South," in allowing blacks to drive. Sheeler criticized the white chauffeurs' argument on two counts. First, he argued, employers should have the right to choose their workers; closed shops should not be allowed. And second, he noted, black chauffeurs were willing to work at cheaper rates than many whites and were biologically suited to service. "The negro is a servant, by nature a humble and obedient servant, and a faithful one. I know such in service 20 years," he wrote. Who were these white chauffeurs to challenge the preference for such labor? Some of these employers, Sheeler continued, "have a 'nigger mammy' cooking their dinners, nigger girls serving the guests at the table, and a nigger nurse taking care of their children. . . . Then somebody wants to howl about a black man driving his celebrated Ford car on the streets of Miami, and down Dixie Highway." To individuals like Sheeler, barring black chauffeurs made no economic sense and directly violated not only accepted customs but also the guiding principle of a free market. Sheeler went so far as to suggest that the white chauffeurs who interfered with black chauffeurs' right to ply their trade, or the rights of white or black citizens to hire them, should be arrested.[22]

T. V. Moore, a successful pioneer farmer, highlighted the hypocrisy of garage owners who refused to cater to black patrons. His criticism demonstrated how segregation allowed for interaction between the races in the context of formal economic exchange. Violating this right, Moore argued, created a double standard. While Moore made it clear that he was not a supporter of integration in any form, this, he argued, constituted an issue of basic economic fairness. No difference existed between Miami clerks accepting the money of black patrons and the potential exchange between blacks and garage owners, Moore concluded.

Editors at the *Metropolis* also supported this argument. They found it absurd that complaints would be raised about whites and blacks engaging in the exchange of goods and services when "every store in Miami has in it white men and women who wait on negro customers every day [and] are glad to have the opportunity." The paper also argued that blacks enjoyed mobility throughout the city despite the recent protest. Potential safety concerns as a result of incompetent drivers—another argument used by white chauffeurs to argue against allowing blacks to enter the trade—were also refuted. "Every train arriving in Miami is met at the depot by vehicles, drawn by horses and driven by negroes, and there is no provision that these negro drivers shall not take men, women and children to any part of the city. Nor has there been any complaint that those who use these hacks are not safely driven or that they are subject to any annoyances because of the color of the driver," *Metropolis* editors wrote. According to the city directory, the number of blacks drivers in Miami was also increasing, from 49 in 1913 to 76 in 1915.[23] Driving an automobile, however, remained a problem. At least one black physician, according to Floyd McNeil from the chauffeurs union,

had to ask for permission just to drive his own car.[24] To hard-line segregationists it was all the same: driving, for whatever reason, was a white male
right and one that they did not feel should be extended to black residents.

The chauffeur issue remained a concern through the peak tourist season
in 1915–16, with similar discourse driving the debate. Editors at the *Herald*
continued to insist that the number of black chauffeurs entering the city
was so minuscule that business lost by offending tourists would be insignificant or that most visitors to Miami would comply. The white chauffeurs,
however, decided to hedge their bets and moved to mitigate any negative
associations by offering free service to any white visitors who arrived with
black chauffeurs, thereby adding an incentive for white patrons to accept
their demands of racial exclusion. Still, the first reported example of a black
chauffeur being replaced with a white one that season demonstrated just
how absurd this policy remained. White chauffeurs approached a white
family who had arrived with their black chauffeur and explained the local custom, offering to drive them free of charge if they would consent to
preventing their own chauffeur from taking the wheel as long as they were
in the city of Miami. The white visitors accepted their demands. The black
chauffeur changed "his seat to one of the rear seats and the Miami white
chauffeur climbed and took charge of the car." The tourists were driven
around the city, apparently with the black chauffeur still in the back seat,
where they spent the day shopping. Later, however, the visitors commented
that if they had known of Miami's custom they would never have come.
The white chauffeurs' attempts to control the market hung on a tenuous
line bound to break with the city's continued steady growth and the lack of
prestige associated with their occupation.[25]

Not until blacks actively resisted did black Miamians get the right to
drive automobiles for a living. Freddie Andrews, a 23-year-old native Floridian, attempted to start his own chauffeur service in July 1917. To his dismay, white chauffeurs physically threatened him, forcing Andrews to re-
taliate. He was then arrested. Later that day, the *Metropolis* reported that
Andrews stabbed Randolph Lightburne, a white chauffeur, who Andrews
believed was among his "persecutors." Andrews was eventually sentenced
to pay a $50 fine, the equivalent of two or three weeks' salary, or to serve
60 days in jail. Andrews seems to have paid the fine, since two weeks later
he was arrested a second time for driving a car in one of Miami's white
neighborhoods. *Metropolis* editors continued to defend Andrews, depicting
the white chauffeurs as wrongdoers, noting that they "attempted to make
trouble for the negro" so as to engage in his "persecution."[26]

The black community's response further encouraged editors at the *Metropolis* to actively protest the city's policy of exclusion. On July 14, 1917, the *Metropolis* published an article entitled, "Negroes Not to Use Violence to Gain Privileges." It reported that Miami's Colored Board of Trade did not advocate the use of violence to resolve the chauffeur question, but that they did expect "Negro rights" to be "respected." Resorting to symbols of a peaceful and harmonious community, the Board explicitly "denounced any resort to violence as both imprudent and lawless." Choosing their words carefully so that it was clear they were in no way favoring racial integration, the Board was quoted as saying: "We have no controversy with any individual or body of individuals which call for a resort to violence but we do insist, that negroes as citizens of the commonwealth have certain definite legal and moral rights." Both white and black community leaders believed in maintaining a segregated city so long as basic standards of fairness were maintained.

Members of the Colored Board of Trade appealed to the civility of the community, pointing to the need for "protection of the courts and all law-abiding citizens." Their comments highlighted the desire of black leaders to tap into the sympathies of the white community. "We have faith in the judgment of the best white citizens and we welcome any effort looking forward to a better understanding between the races," they wrote. They then assured white Miami that they had no clandestine plans and encouraged ongoing dialogue, noting that they did "not bar the public from attendance at any of [their] meetings." This shift in the terms of the debate, away from free market exchange to principles of civility, underscored just how much the actions of white chauffeurs threatened peace and harmony across the city. As such, the Colored Board of Trade argued, the policy of excluding black drivers could no longer be accepted as a legitimate, white, working-class strategy or as central to maintaining racial segregation.[27]

On July 16, 1917, racial tensions reached a peak with the bombing of Colored Town's Odd Fellows Hall. The bomb wreaked incredible damage, shattering most of the building's windows, breaking off large chunks of plaster, and cracking its concrete walls. In one place along the front of the building, it knocked out a hole in the structure's façade, leaving it open to the street. The bombers, who writers for the *Metropolis* believed to be white chauffeurs or individuals serving on their behalf, targeted one of the city's most important buildings. Not only was Odd Fellows Hall one of the largest structures in the neighborhood, but it also symbolized the black community's success in establishing a separate state in the "commonwealth" of Miami. For writers at the *Metropolis* and for white community leaders, the Hall also represented the social order and cohesiveness that Miami's biracial society had attained in the roughly two decades since its incorporation. Odd Fellows Hall was a cultural center in Colored Town that served as the meeting room for lodge groups. The Hall also served as a place for entertainment. As local historian Dorothy Jenkins Fields has noted, "[O]n Saturday nights the piano players at Odd Fellows Hall filled the air with music" and blacks engaged in the latest dances. Hence the intentions of the bombers were clear: by hitting Colored Town's largest building and damaging a concrete symbol of the community's independence, they attempted to hurt the black community's sense of accomplishment in a violent demonstration of white might.[28]

Editors at the *Metropolis* tried to ease fears of an impending race riot by reporting that conditions were under control. They blamed a few "white rowdies" for the bombing and noted that ten police officers had been sent to Colored Town to "prevent further disorder." The "fear of negro reprisals and of race riot, which had been generally entertained by leaders of both the whites and negroes" had been "fairly well dissipated," writers for the *Metropolis* claimed. They also urged the Miami community to take action for peace, underscoring that the racial tension present in Miami was the result of criminal activity, not a larger dilemma between the city's black and white communities.[29]

Statements made at town meetings held at the Central School and at a church in Colored Town later that day were also published. The first meeting included white authorities and black leaders alike: a local judge, the chief of police, acting mayor, and members of the Colored Board of Trade. The second meeting included the same attendees and a packed house of blacks that overflowed into the streets. The paper reported that the black community did not "want any trouble" and assured readers that there would be "no trouble if the authorities will control the lawless element among the white population." Black leaders continued to appeal to Miami's "best white citizens," calling for community peace and asking for whites to control those who would perpetuate this kind of violence and harassment. One black pastor went so far as to appeal to white authorities to "exercise the same control over your lawless element that we do over ours." He added, "[W]e have been segregated and do not object, but we want the line guarded and we want to be protected in our rights in our own section."[30]

Miami's black community also tapped into whites' anxiety about maintaining social order by alluding to their willingness to protect themselves if continually threatened. Comparisons between Miami and East St. Louis, where a race riot had broken out just one week before, were also made. There it was black competition for jobs that sparked the riot just two weeks earlier in which 9 whites and about 39 blacks died. Building on the fear that tensions were such that much the same could happen in Miami, some black residents went so far as to note that they had explosives at their disposal and were ready to use them if necessary. But these comments were also tempered by uplifting patriotic discourse.

A deferential tone generally marked communication between blacks and whites at the town meetings, representing a clear understanding by black leaders of how to balance a level of implied threat with a persistent commitment to nationalism and civic duty. When black community leaders met in a church in Colored Town to discuss the bombing with white leaders present, they opened the meeting with black singers performing "America." Given the context, the song was an apt choice. The song's poetic version of liberty ("from every mountainside let freedom ring," for example) evoked a moral call for justice that fit well with Woodrow Wilson's entreaty that the world be made safe for democracy. Blacks had struggled for decades to gain the freedom promised by Reconstruction, if not by the Declaration of Independence. While Wilson's policy of segregation in the federal government made the daily indignities of Jim Crow that much more offensive, a glimmer of hope existed in the patriotic rhetoric of democracy and liberty. Several black leaders, including W.E.B. Du Bois, would call for patriotic support for the war through service. Miami's black community embraced the war effort, as highlighted by the Reverend Jarrel Drake in the meeting. Over 3,000 men registered with the local draft board, and the community did its part to volunteer in the Red Cross and push for Liberty Bonds in the spring and summer of 1917. At some level these black leaders understood the value of performing the song "America." They never challenged a separate world, but they wanted more equality in the division. The context of World War I, meeting in a church, and the threat of a violent race riot sent a powerful message that blacks had a right to drive and that Jim Crow needed to accommodate them.[31]

Black leaders also understood the importance of black labor to the city's economy. They used the threat of emigration to leverage further protection from Miami's white business elite, prompting the city's business leaders to take action to protect Miami's economic prosperity. Local newspapers had been reporting that labor agents from other parts of Florida had begun infiltrating the city, seeking black workers for their own communities. Florida historian Jerrell Shofner has observed that "between 1916 and 1920 about 40,000 blacks left the northern Florida counties," making Miami a prime target for labor agents because of its population growth. On June 9, the *Miami Herald* reported the arrest of C. H. Bryant, a labor agent from Taylor County in northwest Florida. The *Herald* commented that the shortage of unskilled labor in Miami was the result of this recruitment, which was causing black out-migration. Two weeks later, the paper followed up this story remarking, "[T]he negroes of the south are migrating to the north in large numbers, leaving the fields uncultivated and the crops unharvested, and the future an unsolved problem." Dana A. Dorsey, one of Miami's most successful black businessmen, threatened that "if negroes could not be given rights and protection in Miami they have elsewhere, they would leave Miami." Charles Thompson, a black real estate broker, observed that "many of the better class of negroes . . . had already left because of conditions here." This exodus should matter to everyone in the city, they argued: If the better class of blacks left, who would maintain order in Colored Town?[32]

Editors at the *Miami Metropolis* also played up this idea of "respectability." Noting that it was the city's most industrious black residents who opposed the monopoly that white chauffeurs claimed in the city, they again appealed to values of hard work and free market exchange while underscoring the threat of lost business to white prosperity. They also cast aspersions on the city's progressivism, noting, "Miami is probably the only city of any size or importance in the United States where negroes have not been allowed to drive automobiles under any circumstances." Noting that "there was no restriction on the age, condition or qualifications of white chauffeurs" whatsoever and that "until recently, the police court has generally found a reason for fining the negro and discharging the white men when infrequent arrests have been made," writers for the *Metropolis* painted a sharp contrast between black residents' lawfulness and industriousness and white men's unregulated monopoly on driving.[33]

Ultimately, though, it was the argument that granting black men the right to drive in Miami was central to maintaining segregation that held the most sway with many white city leaders. In an editorial published on July 16, 1917, entitled "Wise Heads and Sober Judgment Needed," editors at the *Metropolis* declared that the people of Miami had finally "awakened to a realization of the trouble that they have permitted a bunch of irresponsible white men to stir up for their peaceful city." Reminding readers that the editors had "warned Miami of the probability of trouble" over a year ago, they compared white chauffeurs to hounds and their victims to rabbits and foxes. What were "white rowdies doing in Colored Town at two o'clock in the morning!" they asked. "Why are white men at any hour of the day or night permitted in Colored Town unless they can show legitimate reasons of being there!" Blacks visiting "White Town" at night would be quickly "locked up as suspicious characters." So why were not "the white scum that visit Colored Town all hours of the night put in jail?" "The city, county, and state officials are white men. The courts are presided by white men," writers for the *Metropolis* continued. "The 'justice' that is meted out is all for the White Man, and it is only wonder that negroes of Miami have kept patient as long as they have." The burden of maintaining peace and harmony, then, rested on white community leaders. Only by "securing a common justice for the negro" within the bounds of a racially separate society could there be "progress" in Miami.[34]

These sentiments were taken up by a group of white and black business leaders at a community conference held the following day.[35] The white committee emphasized that by "unwritten law," only white men were allowed to drive automobiles in Miami. "Miami had been built as a white man's town," they noted. As such, the prohibition against black driving was simply "in accord with the prevailing sentiment of the white voters of the city." Nonetheless, they consented that it was "only fair" to blacks to set a more reasonable policy of segregation in driving. The white committee proposed three conditions: (1) blacks would be protected when driving their own cars; (2) blacks would be allowed to drive buses and cars for hire, but only for transporting of other blacks; and (3) "the solicitation of negro patronage by white car and bus drivers" would be discouraged as much as possible. City officials at the conference, including the sheriff, chief of police, the acting mayor, and two councilmen, supported the resolution. Black leaders reluctantly agreed. A week later, a curfew restricting both black and white drivers from working in any city neighborhood after 6:00 p.m. was instituted.[36] It was the first official statement to openly acknowledge the right of both black and white men to earn a living by driving or to place equal restrictions on what could be done in black and white neighborhoods.

With an agreement reached, members of the North Miami Improvement Association increased their calls for the police department to apprehend the bombers of Odd Fellows Hall. Editors at the *Metropolis* seconded this call, noting that they could produce a "long list" of other unsolved crimes. The chief of police eventually resigned, although he denied being pressured by the community's criticism. Still the bombing of Odd Fellows Hall went unsolved. The individuals who caused this destruction and terrorized the community were never found.[37]

In the fall of 1917, the white chauffeurs union finally agreed not to interfere with tourists who came to Miami accompanied by their black chauffeurs. But the peace was relatively short-lived. Two years later, in November 1919, another round of violence and harassment occurred. Again, tourists who came to Miami with their own black drivers were the targets. This time, however, the city took swift action. The Miami Chamber of Commerce passed a resolution condemning the white chauffeurs' actions and called for city authorities to "prosecute anyone intimidating a chauffeur, negro or white, or else, who comes to this city." Tourists needed protection, they argued, for the sake of "upholding law existing in our country." One member compared chauffeurs' actions to closed union shops, claiming that "80 percent of the chauffeurs are under age, boys who have undertaken to run the automobile situation in the City." Another member thought it irrational to drive tourists away from Miami. The mayor supported the Chamber of Commerce's resolution. He asserted a few days later "that if a man comes to Miami . . . he is going to be treated fairly." "I am no 'nigger lover,' was born in Georgia, have no chauffeur myself," he continued. "[B]ut if a man comes down here I am going to see that he gets square treatment."[38]

Coming at the same time that a series of bombings shook cities from Washington, D.C., to Chicago, including one that partially destroyed the home of U.S. Attorney General A. Mitchell Palmer, protests against the social status quo in any form became suspect, and labor unions proved special targets. Although no such actions occurred in Miami, the increasing hostility toward organized labor was clear in the Chamber of Commerce's statements. The chauffeurs union countered that depictions of November confrontation were "a cowardly thrust, clothed in the most cunning and deceptive language . . . meant to deceive the public into the belief that the union men are a lot of unprincipled, coldblooded, heartless rogues [willing] to resort to any mean and ruthless tactic in order to gain a point." Attempting to salvage their image, the union stated that its members were "peaceful, respectable citizens in times of peace and also in times of commercial war." But their pleas fell upon deaf ears. The tide of public opinion had turned squarely against the union members, and they were unable to garner much sympathy.[39]

Fear of labor strikes by Miami's Central Labor Union also loomed large that fall. Still, with peace at a premium, organized labor proved far less willing to force change in the city as elsewhere in the nation. Despite the mass hiring of nonunion men in construction jobs, the Central Labor Union called off a general strike in Miami because they believed it would "be for the best interests of the city of Miami." Only then did they win the support of *Metropolis* editors, who commented that these "fair-dealing Miamians" were "thinking union men [who] are the efficient, dependable workmen that Miami wants to rely upon."[40]

Conclusion

The *Metropolis*'s support of the black community and the white community's concession to them in the 1917 segregation policy are indicative of what was perceived as progress in race relations at the time. The color line had been redrawn to meet the needs of both the black community and the white business leadership. In the process, community leaders, both black and white, pointed to the resolution of the chauffeur conflict as evidence that Miami's drive for economic prosperity and growth was secured in the spirit of compromise. Miami's white leaders, ever cognizant of the prevailing sentiments of their racial and economic class, were acutely aware of the benefits of making the city's black community content—namely, ensuring peace and harmony and maintaining the racial status quo. This concern outweighed demands by white working-class chauffeurs to grant them a monopoly over driving in the city. By conceding to black demands and protecting black men's right to drive, for either personal use or economic gain, they ensured that the lines of segregation in Miami would remain sharp, if somewhat redrawn. Editors at the *Metropolis* played an important role in redrawing that line.

The socially condescending and racist view that blacks belonged in service occupations thus enabled blacks to enter chauffeuring despite continuous violent threats from white drivers.[41] Black worker insistence, as evidenced in their actions, combined with the real economic threat that if black chauffeurs were not allowed to drive, white tourists would stop coming to Miami. However, the debate was not one-sided. Black leaders, including businessmen, professionals, and Protestant pastors, took advantage of the opportunity to insist on racial uplift and the unreasonableness of the Jim Crow rule that some were advocating. Likewise, building craft workers' reluctance to support lesser skilled workers weakened the white drivers' attempts to keep blacks out of driving as a profession, even when it entailed chauffeuring tourists. This in no way should devalue black agency.

Indeed, it is in the opportunities offered within this oppressive social system for economic improvement that one may discover "hidden" transcripts of resistance as well as open attempts by black Miamians to fight for their dignity through economic self-improvement.[42]

These battles were also far from over. Thanks in no small part to continued efforts by Miami's black community, between 1917 and 1923, the city's curfew was slowly extended from six to nine in the evening. While the presence of any curfew at all in this thriving tourist metropolis still surprised some northern visitors, as in much of the South, Miami leaders continued to insist that having clear boundaries offered a better solution to racial conflict than the violence that defined mob rule.[43] Black residents also continued to mount challenges to attempts to control their economic and physical mobility in other ways. By the early 1930s, African Americans controlled 14 bus, transfer, express, and cab companies in Miami. By 1936, the number of black jitneys had jumped to 25. The number of black owned and operated taxicabs grew apace. And while whites continued to periodically challenge the right of black men to be able to drive, Miami's black community continued to fight to preserve this basic economic and social right.[44] For all of these reasons, the chauffeur debates proved a pivotal chapter in Miami's civil rights and labor history, foreshadowing continued controversy about taxicabs and buses and ultimately the attempts to desegregate public transportation itself.[45]

*   *   *

I would like to thank Joe Armenio, Herbert Brewer, Linda Noel, and Jeff Coster for their suggestions as well as Alex Lichtenstein, Alison Isenberg, and Brian Peterson for their input in earlier versions of the essay. I dedicate this chapter in loving memory of my father, Oswaldo Ramon Castillo.

Notes

1. Paul S. George, "Colored Town: Miami's Black Community, 1896–1930," *Florida Historical Quarterly* 56 (April 1978): 435–36, 442; Raymond Mohl, "Black Immigrants: Bahamians in Early Twentieth-Century Miami," *Florida Historical Quarterly* 65 (January 1987): 281; Marvin Dunn, *Black Miami in the Twentieth Century* (Gainesville: University Press of Florida, 1997).

2. Edward Ayers, *The Promise of the New South: Life after Reconstruction* (New York: Oxford University Press, 1992), 132–59, 426–37; Grace Hale, *Making Whiteness: The Culture of Segregation in the South, 1890–1940* (New York: Pantheon, 1998), 85–197;

August Meier and Elliot Rudwick, "The Boycott Movement against Jim Crow Streetcars in the South, 1900–1906," *Journal of American History* 55 (March 1969): 756–75.

3. *Miami Metropolis* (hereafter cited as *MM*), October 4, 1915, 6. See P. George, "Colored Town"; Paul S. George, "Criminal Justice in Miami, 1896–1930," PhD diss., Florida State University, 1975; Paul S. George, "Policing Miami's Black Community, 1896–1930," *Florida Historical Quarterly* 57 (April 1979): 434–50; M. Dunn, *Black Miami*, 94–95.

4. P. George, "Colored Town," 433; Rayford W. Logan, *Betrayal of the Negro: From Rutherford B. Hayes to Woodrow Wilson* (New York: Collier Books, 1965). For a more recent treatment, see Leon F. Litwack, *Trouble in Mind: Black Southerners in the Age of Jim Crow* (New York: Alfred A. Knopf, 1998).

5. R. Mohl, "Black Immigrants," 271–72, 289–90; Nathan Mayo, *Fifth Census of the State of Florida, 1925* (Tallahassee: State of Florida, 1925), 74, 115; U.S. Bureau of the Census, *Negroes in the United States, 1920–1932* (Washington, D.C.: Government Printing Office, 1935), 33; U.S. Bureau of the Census, *15th Census of the United States: 1930*, vol. 3, part 1 (Washington, D.C.: Government Printing Office, 1932), 410; U.S. Bureau of the Census, *16th Census of the United States: 1940*, vol. 2, part 2 (Washington, D.C.: Government Printing Office, 1943), 166.

6. U.S. Bureau of the United States, *15th Census of the United States, 1930, Population*, vol. 4 (Washington, D.C.: Government Printing Office, 1932), 358–61. The winter season lasted between November and April. See also Gary W. McDonough, *The Florida Negro: A Federal Writers' Project Legacy* (Jackson: University of Mississippi Press, 1993), 39–40; Raymond A. Mohl, "Miami: The Ethnic Cauldron," in *Sunbelt Cities: Politics and Growth since World War II*, ed. Richard M. Bernard and Bradley Rice (Austin: University of Texas Press, 1983), 72–75; Raymond A. Mohl, "The Patterns of Race Relations in Miami since the 1920s," in *The African American Heritage of Florida*, ed. David R. Colburn and Jane L. Landers (Gainesville: University Press of Florida, 1995), 340–41.

7. Thomas A. Castillo, "Miami's Hidden Labor History," *Florida Historical Quarterly* 82 (Spring 2004): 438–67.

8. Individuals who transported people or goods by rail or ship were identified separately in the U.S. Census during this period.

9. U.S. Bureau of the Census, Miami Census Manuscript: 1920, reels 215 and 216. I recorded all drivers appearing in the 1920 census. The labels applied were determined by whether these "drivers" drew a wage or were paid on salary and by their place of employment (whether self-employed driving a vehicle for hire or by the name of a particular establishment). The list of categories used to describe drivers included chauffeur/driver (drives car and transports people), driver of jitney buses, domestic chauffeur, hackman and carriage (transport of people not clear), deliveryman, caddying, teamster, drayman, driver (transports of goods), driver of construction materials, drivers of trucks (not clear what they transport). On the challenges of identifying occupations based on driving over this period, see Kevin Borg, "The 'Chauffeur Problem' in the Early Auto Era: Structuration Theory and the Users of Technology," *Technology and Culture* 40, no. 4 (October 1999): 797–832, note 70; Rachel Moskowitz, "When the Drive to Work Lasts All Day: Taxidrivers and Chauffeurs," *Occupational Outlook Quarterly* 37, no. 2 (1993): 32–36. The plethora of union locals for drivers in major cities like Chicago

further indicates the diversity of this sector. See Sterling F. Rigg, "The Chicago Teamsters Unions," *Journal of Political Economy* 34, no. 1 (1926): 13–36.

10. Miami Census Manuscript: 1920, reels 215 and 216.

11. U.S. Bureau of the Census, Miami Census Manuscript: 1930, reels 308–10; *15th Census of the United States*, vol. 4, 359.

12. Julian Street, "The Passing of the Old-School Chauffeur," *Collier's, The National Weekly, Automobile Supplement* (January 1912): 46, 48; Lorenzo J. Greene and Carter G. Woodson, *The Negro Wage Earner* (Washington, D.C.: Association for the Study of Negro Life and History, 1930), 111–12; Gorman Gilbert and Robert E. Samuels, *The Taxicab: An Urban Transportation Survivor* (Chapel Hill: University of North Carolina Press, 1982), 63, 65–66, 95; Paul S. George, "Traffic Control in Early Miami," *Tequesta* 37 (1977): 3–18.

13. J. Street, "The Passing," 46; Jacqueline Jones, *American Work: Four Centuries of Black and White Labor* (New York: W. W. Norton, 1998), 322; L. Greene and C. Woodson, *Negro Wage Earner*, 111–12; K. Borg, "The 'Chauffeur Problem,'" 822; U.S. Bureau of the Census, *13th Census of the United States, 1910*, vol. 4 (Washington D.C.: Government Printing Office, 1914), 414–15; *14th Census of the Population, 1920*, vol. 3 (Washington D.C.: Government Printing Office, 1922), 350–51.

14. K. Borg, "The 'Chauffeur Problem,'" 809–11, 821; J. Street, "The Passing," 46, 48; "The Reform of Chauffeurs," *Literary Digest*, February 10, 1912, 273–74; T. H. Parker, "The Worth of a Good Chauffeur," *Harper's Weekly*, April 6, 1912, 14.

15. J. Street, "The Passing," 46, 48; T. Parker, "The Worth," 14; "A Word for Chauffeurs and Garages," *Literary Digest*, June 8, 1912, 1215–16; K. Borg, "The 'Chauffeur Problem,'" 809–11, 821. The white chauffeur arguments here echo David Montgomery's on worker's control. See David Montgomery, *Worker's Control in America: Studies in the History of Work, Technology, and Labor Struggles* (Cambridge: Cambridge University Press, 1979).

16. *Miami Herald* (hereafter cited as *MH*), February 28, 1915, 5; *MM*, March 1, 1915, 2.

17. *MM*, June 29, 1915, 4. For images of blacks and the shaping of segregation custom and law, see George M. Fredrickson, *The Black Image in the White Mind: The Debate on Afro-American Character and Destiny, 1817–1914* (New York: Harper and Row, 1971); Joel Williamson, *The Crucible of Race: Black White Relations in the American South since Emancipation* (New York: Oxford University Press, 1984); G. Hale, *Making Whiteness*, 85–197; L. Litwack, *Trouble in Mind*.

18. Howard Kleinberg, "History of the *Miami News*, 1896–1987," *Tequesta* 57 (1987): 14–16 (quote found on page 16); Ethan V. Blackman, *Miami and Dade County, Florida: Its Settlement, Progress, and Achievement* (Washington, D.C.: Victor Rainbolt, 1921), 116; *Miami Daily News*, March 24, 1945, 1, 4; *MH*, March 25, 1945, 10-A; Nixon Smiley, *Knights of the Fourth Estate: The Story of the Miami Herald* (Miami: E. A. Seemann, 1974), 27–29; Jeanne Bellamy, "Newspapers of America's Last Frontier," *Tequesta* 7 (1952): 7–10. Dean established the *Weekly Lake Worth News* in 1894. He then began the *Daily Lake Worth News*, later renamed the *Palm Beach Daily News*. See H. Kleinberg, "History of the *Miami News*," 14.

19. *MM*, June 29, 1915, 4; *MM*, June 30, 1915; *MM*, August 3, 1915, 1–2; *MM*, August 4, 1915, 1; *MH*, June 31, 1915, 8; *MH*, August 5, 1915, 8; *MH*, August 8, 1915, 4, 8; *MH*, August 6, 1915, 4.

20. *MM*, June 30, 1915, 2. Okell's letter appeared at the end of the article starting on page 1 entitled, "Should Advise Tourists as to the Feeling in Miami [against Negro Chauffeurs]." For NcNeil's statements, see *MM*, August 5, 1915, 1 and 3. For an excellent study on the context of living wage discourse and linkages to exclusionary discourse, see Lawrence Glickman, *A Living Wage: American Workers and the Making of Consumer Society* (Ithaca, N.Y.: Cornell University Press, 1997).

21. For P. L. Ryan's letter, see *MM*, August 5, 1915, 8. For Ryan's occupation, see Miami Census Manuscript: 1920, reels 215 and 216. See also *MH*, August 6, 1915; L. Litwack, *Trouble in Mind*, 181. For a history of Jack Johnson, see Randy Roberts, *Papa Jack: Jack Johnson and the Era of White Hopes* (New York: Free Press, 1983). On manliness and racial dominance, see Gail Bederman, *Manliness and Civilization: A Cultural History of Gender and Race in the United States, 1880–1917* (Chicago: University of Chicago Press, 1995).

22. *MM*, August 5, 1915, 1, 8. Another letter by Sheeler appeared later in October in which he made a sharper attack on organized labor. "Can we afford to herald abroad the fact that the Chauffeurs unions or any other Unions dictate the policies of conduct of our city affairs?" See *MM*, October 4, 1915, 1; K. Borg, "The 'Chauffeur Problem.'"

23. Although the directory listed only one chauffeur, problems of categorization likely also plagued directory entries.

24. *MM*, August 6, 1915, 1, 3 (Moore and McNeil comments from this report); *MM*, August 7, 1915, 6 (*MM* editorial). For references regarding the perceived competency of blacks, see also *MM*, August 4, 1915, 3; *Miami City Directory*, 1913–15. Not much is written about blacks becoming chauffeurs in the early auto years. A few references point to fluidity being the rule with attempts made by some whites to place restrictions. See John Dittmer, *Black Georgia in the Progressive Era, 1900–1920* (Urbana: University of Illinois Press, 1977), 21; Neil R. McMillen, *Dark Journey: Black Mississippians in the Age of Jim Crow* (Urbana: University of Illinois Press, 1990), 8, 11; L. Litwack, *Trouble in Mind*, 336.

25. On the continued debate, see *MM*, September 9, 1915, 2; *MM*, September 22, 1915, 7; *MM*, September 25, 1915, 1; *MM*, October 4, 1915, 6; *MM*, October 15, 1915, 10; *MM*, November 18, 1915, 2 (first reported chauffeur incident); *MM*, January 4, 1916, 3; *MH*, December 1, 1915, 5. On free service, see *MM*, August 6, 1915, 1, 3; *MH*, August 7, 1915, 4.

26. *MM*, July 9, 1917, 5; *MM*, July 11, 1917, 2; *MM*, July 12, 1917, 1; *MM*, July 23, 1917, 2; *Carpenter*, August 1917. Biographical information on Andrews is drawn from the U.S. Census schedules for 1920, reel 216 and World War I Draft Registration Cards (accessed through Ancestry.com). Andrews had signed up at the local draft board on June 6. There are no extant records recording his view on the war. Earlier in the year, the *MH* reported a tourist accepting Miami's segregation policy without incident. See *MH*, January 14, 1917, 1.

27. *MM*, January 14, 1917, 2.

28. *MM*, July 16, 1917, 1; P. George, "Policing Miami's Black Community," 441; Dorothy J. Fields, "Black Entertainment, 1908–1919," *Update* 2 (December 1974): 11. See also Walter B. Weare, *Black Business in the New South: A Social History of the North Carolina Mutual Life Insurance Company* (Urbana: University of Illinois Press, 1973), for a similar celebration of black uplift in a southern city.

29. *MM*, July 16, 1917, 1; *MM*, July 17, 1917, 2.

30. *MM*, July 16, 1917, 1; *MM*, July 17, 1917, 2. See also *MM*, July 16, 1917, 12.

31. *MM*, July 16, 1917, 12; Elliot Rudwick, *Race Relations at East St. Louis, July 2, 1917* (Carbondale: Southern Illinois University Press, 1964); George B. Tindall, *The Emergence of the New South, 1913–1945* (Baton Rouge: Louisiana State University Press, 1967), 150. On racial uplift as strategy, see Kevin Gaines, *Uplifting the Race: Black Leadership, Politics, and Culture in the Twentieth Century* (Chapel Hill: University of North Carolina Press, 1996); L. Litwack, *Trouble in Mind*. On World War I and African Americans, see Mark Ellis, *Race, War and Surveillance: African Americans and the United States Government* (Bloomington: Indiana University Press, 2001).

32. Jerrell Shofner, "Florida and the Black Migration," *Florida Historical Quarterly* 57 (January 1979): 267. On growing anxiety of black migration, see *MH*, June 9, 1917, 3; *MH*, June 10, 1917, 7; *MH*, June 14, 1917, 8; *MH*, June 15, 1917, 5. Comments by black leaders from *MM*, July 16, 1917, 12.

33. *MM*, July 16, 1917, 1.

34. *MM*, July 16, 1917, 6.

35. Members of the white committee included F. M. Hudson, Dr. James M. Jackson, Frank B Love, J. M. Berecegeay, A. H. Adams, J. I. Conklin, and Frank S. White. Black members included Reverend S. H. Travis, Allan Stokes, R. A. Powers, H. S. Braggs, K. L. Pharr, Reverend J. W. Drake, and Dr. W. B. Sawyer.

36. *MM*, July 17, 1917, 1–2; *MM*, July 23, 1917, 17.

37. *MM*, July 18, 1917, 1; *MM*, July 21, 1917, 6.

38. Miami Chamber of Commerce, *Minutes of the Board of Directors Meetings*, November 3, 1919, 12–13; *MM*, November 6, 1919, 1; *MM*, November 7, 1919, 1.

39. *MM*, November 5, 1919, 3.

40. *MM*, November 8, 1919, 1; *MM*, November 10, 1919, 6.

41. For a discussion of blacks as servile workers, see Beth Thompson Bates, *Pullman Porters and the Rise of Protest Politics in Black America, 1925–1945* (Chapel Hill: University of North Carolina Press, 2001), 17–39; Doug Bristol, "From Outposts to Enclaves: A Social History of Black Barbers, 1750–1915," PhD diss., University of Maryland, 2002; G. Hale, *Making Whiteness*, 85–197; W.E.B. Du Bois, *Darkwater: Voices from Within the Veil* (1921; Millwood, N.Y.: Kraus-Thomson, 1975), 109–21.

42. On hidden transcripts, see Robin D. G. Kelley, *Race Rebels: Culture, Politics, and the Working Class* (New York: Free Press, 1994); Robin D. G. Kelley, "'We Are Not What We Seem': Rethinking Black Working-Class Opposition in the Jim Crow South," *Journal of American History* 80, no. 1 (1993): 75–112; James Scott, *Domination and the Arts of Resistance: Hidden Transcripts* (New Haven: Yale University Press, 1990); Kenneth W. Goings and Gerald L. Smith, "'Unhidden' Transcripts: Memphis and African American Agency, 1862–1920," *Journal of Urban History* 21, no. 3 (1995): 372–94. For an example

of these ideas applied to Florida, see Robert Cassanello, "Violence, Racial Etiquette, and African American Working-Class *Infrapolitics* in Jacksonville during World War I," *Florida Historical Quarterly* 82 (Fall 2003): 155–69.

43. Clara G. Stillman, "Florida: The Desert and the Rose," *Nation* (October 1923), in *These United States: Portraits of America from the 1920s*, ed. Daniel H. Borus (Ithaca, N.Y.: Cornell University Press, 1992), 87–93. On segregation culture, see G. Hale, *Making Whiteness*. The Baltimore *Afro-American* noted in 1926 that "white elements" were against black chauffeurs operating in Miami. See *Afro-American*, July 3, 1926, 14.

44. *15th Census of the United States*, vol. 4, 359; *Miami News*, June 18, 1936, 6; Miami Census Manuscript: 1930, reel 309; *Miami Times*, January 12, 1957, 3; Polly Redford, *Billion-Dollar Sandbar: A Biography of Miami Beach* (New York: E. P. Dutton, 1970), 211, 223–24; G. McDonough, *Florida Negro*, 40; *MH*, June 4, 1936, 1.

45. For a discussion of how black movement into white neighborhoods was limited to service employees at designated times, see Richard Wright's essay, "The Ethics of Jim Crow," in *Uncle Tom's Children* (1936; reprint, New York: Harper Perennial, 1993), 10.

7

"We at Last Are Industrializing the Whole Ding-busted Party"

The Communist Party and Florida Workers in Depression and War

ALEX LICHTENSTEIN

The day after Christmas in 1944, the *Miami Herald* ran a glowing profile of one of South Florida's most energetic young labor organizers. In a city with no prior Congress of Industrial Organizations (CIO) representation, the paper credited Charles Smolikoff, age 28, with building up over a dozen CIO locals with a total membership of 3,000 in less than two years of organizing. Smolikoff was born in New York and relocated to Miami for health reasons in 1939. He had little in his background that would suggest his success as a labor organizer. As the *Herald* reporter joked, "The closest Smolikoff ever came to labor was as a dance instructor at a New Jersey summer resort." His greatest local success had come at the Miami Shipbuilding Company, where he had almost singlehandedly built a local of the Industrial Union of Marine and Shipbuilding Workers of America (IUMSWA) 700 members strong. Centrally located on Flagler Street, Miami's CIO headquarters also oversaw organizations of laundry workers, air transport workers, furniture workers, and tent and awning makers, among others. Smolikoff's resume boasted positions as regional director for IUMSWA, membership on the War Labor Board's regional panel, and state director of the Florida CIO's political arm, the CIO-PAC.[1]

As remarkable as this list of accomplishments may have seemed, Smolikoff's apparent lack of working-class bona fides also made him typical of the new generation of activists who poured into the labor movement in the 1930s, eager to make their mark by helping to build the exciting new industrial unions of the CIO in the country's mass production industries.[2] In doing so, this cadre imagined they could radically transform the economy and politics of the United States. As Murray Kempton remarked two decades after the fact, "To yearn for a place in the labor movement in the 30s was to conceive yourself on the barricades."[3]

A second-generation immigrant, highly literate without having completed his formal education, and eager to use the new tools placed at the disposal of organized labor by the New Deal and wartime state, Smolikoff, like many other CIO activists, had a knack for both recruiting unskilled and unrepresented workers to the new industrial unions and negotiating with powerful employers. In the *Herald*'s profile, Smolikoff appeared proud of his wartime service as a labor organizer able to secure stability in industrial relations and smooth over Florida's seething workplace racial tensions. "There has not been a single CIO strike in Florida, no race trouble of any kind in any CIO union in the state," he pronounced. Along with many of his fellow CIO activists, Smolikoff envisioned the new union movement as an important political presence that could use the war effort to help nudge the flimsily constructed New Deal social democracy in a leftward direction. And, though this fact went unremarked by the *Miami Herald*, like a significant minority of these activists, Charles Smolikoff was a Communist.

The *Miami Herald* profile did casually mention that Smolikoff had at one time written for the *Southern News Almanac*, a "radically New Dealish pro-labor weekly paper" published in Birmingham, Alabama. In fact, it was a Communist Party paper. The *Herald* also listed, without comment, many other activities that would take on a far more sinister cast when revisited by postwar anticommunists in a different climate just four or five years later: the fact that when traveling to Puerto Rico in the late 1930s, "somehow [Smolikoff] never got beyond Miami," his use of "various pen names," the local "discussion groups" he led about "the need to expand the union movement," his apparently independent and unsolicited efforts to proselytize among shipyard workers, his arrests by city police, and his frequent trips to Jacksonville and Tampa. Still, anyone who read the 1944 *Herald* profile might be forgiven for being taken aback less than four years later when Smolikoff hit the local papers again, hailed this time as "a Key Man for the Reds," as a headline in the *Miami Daily News* put it. They might indeed have been surprised to learn that when a subcommittee of the House Un-American Activities Committee (HUAC) descended on Miami in March 1948 to investigate local Communist influence, it determined that Smolikoff was a Communist Party functionary and that the CIO local in Miami he led at the time, the Transport Workers Union (TWU), was under Communist domination. Those same readers might have registered further shock in

1949 when a major exposé in the *Miami Daily News* revealed Miami as the "Center of Latin Red Network" and proclaimed that a Latin American red courier network operated under cover of the TWU.[4]

By the time Miami's multiple red scares had run their course several years later, an assistant state attorney general charged in an overheated 1955 special report that "all within the last ten years, Comrade Smolikoff exerted iron control over an estimated 150 potential saboteurs in Dade County alone while working his way through one labor union after another."[5] This time, however, the onetime state director of the Florida CIO's Industrial Union Council had already been driven from the labor movement by the TWU's and CIO's own internal purges of Communists in the late 1940s. Facing a grand jury indictment for contempt that would have kept him in the Dade County jail for a year, Smolikoff had fled Miami for exile in Mexico in 1954.[6]

Smolikoff's radical political affiliation would not have come as a surprise to the Federal Bureau of Investigation (FBI), however. Their local field office began keeping tabs on him even before 1944. Indeed, shortly after Smolikoff began organizing in Miami in 1942, the FBI used a network of "confidential informants" and a pile of newspaper clippings to investigate him, his activities, and his associates. FBI reports on Communist infiltration within IUM-SWA Locals 32 (Jacksonville) and 59 (Miami) and the Transport Workers Union Local 500 (Miami), all locals Smolikoff helped to organize, constitute one of the most complete narratives of CIO organizing in Florida available today.[7]

A confidential memorandum found in the papers of the 1956 Florida Legislative Investigative Committee (FLIC), presumably prepared by the FBI for the state's anticommunist committee, summarized the basic "known" facts about Smolikoff up to 1947. The FBI believed that Smolikoff had attended New York University "for an unknown period." They also wrote that he had an arrest record and was placed on probation in his late teens, having been "charged with receiving stolen property." Equally suspicious, in their view, Smolikoff had written stories for *ACE* and *Modern Adventure* magazines "under assumed names" and after coming to Miami in 1940 he had first resided with a Cuban Communist, Raul Vidal. Smolikoff "first entered the local labor picture during the Miami laundry strike of November 1942 and kept the Sec. of the Communist Party for the state of Florida cognizant of the progress of this strike." In 1942, Smolikoff began organizing shipyard workers for the CIO. He worked closely and "tirelessly" with Vidal, another Cuban communist named José Carbonell, and black Bahamian trade unionist James Nimmo. By spring 1943, Smolikoff had outmaneuvered the company union at the Miami Shipbuilding Corporation and won CIO representation for workers there. From this initial success, Smolikoff was able to "spread the CIO throughout the state of Florida."[8]

Other sources confirm the basic outline of this sketch. According to Smolikoff's widow, Berthe Small, Smolikoff arrived in Miami in the late 1930s. Though in contrast to the FBI, she recalled that Smolikoff had only an eighth-grade education, Small described him as "the most educated person" she had ever met, "a skilled mathematician" and "a charismatic, gifted public speaker." By the early 1940s, she recalled, Smolikoff had begun to work closely with Nimmo, whom he had encountered at a church meeting, to organize Miami's shipyard workers. In order to avoid arrest, Smolikoff and Small passed out leaflets signed simply "CIO" to the graveyard shift at Miami Shipbuilding, "because that's what he was organizing for." When they had independently accumulated enough signed union cards to call for a National Labor Relations Board (NLRB) election, Smolikoff went to the shipyard workers international and said, "Here's a union, do you want it?" Unwilling to discuss the role of the Communist Party, all Small would say is: "Charles certainly had strong, committed socialist beliefs. . . . Everything he did was focused in that direction."

Smolikoff's gravitation to labor organizing came, she suggested, because he was a "pragmatist" and the "most practical weapon he could think of was the trade union movement, because the war industries were beginning to build up in Florida, and it was a natural." Unlike the "dismal" AFL, the CIO "was open, burgeoning, interested in any kind of organization." Smolikoff asked himself, "How do you organize people? Well, you hand out leaflets, and maybe they'll talk to you." And so they did.[9]

A quarter of a century later, while in exile in Mexico, Smolikoff claimed (with some self-inflation) that his initial IUMSWA organizing work marked the first distribution of CIO literature in Florida. "The work was very dangerous and few wanted to do it, so if a union could get established there it was big for prestige," he told his friend and Cuernavaca neighbor, the radical journalist Cedric Belfrage. In fact, Smolikoff noted, "Red-baiting began early on, but unions were most reluctant to ditch any successful organizer," allowing him room to continue his activities. Because of the danger of arrest or violence or both, Smolikoff insisted, "probably no one but a red w[oul]d have the dedication to take it on and stay with it." Even if Smolikoff somewhat exaggerated his pioneering role, there is little reason to doubt this latter claim.[10]

From early 1943, Smolikoff had been observed by the FBI standing on the corner outside the Miami Shipbuilding Corporation yards almost daily, distributing "hand bills from the CIO" to shipyard workers on their lunch break. Later that year, a "confidential informant" who worked in the shipyard told the FBI that at first "it was believed by some of the workers" that the IUMSWA organizers spearheading the drive "appeared to be a little too radical and possibly on the Communistic side." But "the fears had subsequently been dispelled." The informant admitted, however, that he "had not been attending any of the union meetings and did not know to what extent SMOLIKOFF actually controlled the activities of Local 59." By this time, the Bureau was well aware that Smolikoff was the Communist Party's key man in Miami and that Florida's state secretary of the Communist Party, Alexander Trainor, had been briefing him regularly from Jacksonville on "the procedure that should be taken in organizing the shipyard workers in the Miami area."[11]

By October 1943, the FBI reported that for the Florida Communist Party, "most activity is still infiltration and control of unions." The Bureau regarded the two Miami shipyards Smolikoff organized, as well as the Merrill-Stevens shipyard in Jacksonville, the AFL's Tampa Cigar Workers Union, and the Miami laundry workers, as "controlled by the Communist party," and warned of the efforts to organize workers at Pan American Airways in Miami. "The main activity of District 25 of the Communist Party continues to be infiltration and control of the labor movement in the state of Florida," the FBI concluded.[12] By the end of the year, the FBI reported that "in Miami five shipyards [are] controlled by [the] Communist Party" and that attempts were being made across the state "to recruit Negro members."[13] But the Bureau also grudgingly admitted that Smolikoff's "organizational efforts were considered to be outstanding by the IUMSWA and he is held in high regard by them, particularly by one GALLAGHER [Thomas Gallagher] who is Chief National Organizer of the union," an assessment borne out in IUMSWA correspondence.[14]

Judging from the frequent reports he filed with IUMSWA, Smolikoff showed great energy, aggressiveness, and tenacity as an organizer. Shuttling between Jacksonville and Miami, he worked on contract negotiations, fended off his AFL rivals and the threat of company unions, petitioned government agencies, catered to the needs of black workers fighting employment discrimination, and published dozens of newsletters and leaflets promoting the union's cause and exhorting workers to remain loyal to the

CIO. At the end of 1942, a visiting IUMSWA organizer praised Smolikoff's ongoing organizational work in Miami, and he especially commended his understanding of the "Southern approach, Negro problem, and white workers' angle." Smolikoff, this organizer claimed, "is respected by the negroes and whites alike in Miami."[15] His efforts to build interracial CIO unions appear especially notable. Unable to make inroads in Jacksonville's enormous St. John's Shipyards where the AFL metal and building trades held sway among 10,000 workers, Smolikoff and other CIO organizers set their sights on that city's smaller shipyards. These organizers, black and white radicals, endured frequent beatings in 1942 and 1943 from both AFL members and company stooges, as they sought to build an interracial CIO union at Merrill-Stevens and Gibbs Gas Engine yards in 1942 and 1943.[16] At Merrill-Stevens, where African Americans who were denied entry into many AFL unions made up nearly one-fourth of the company's production workers, IUMSWA Local 32 won an election in July 1943 by a slim margin of 81 votes.[17] AFL metal trades leaders pledged to "move their men out of the yards if they lost the election" to the CIO, the War Manpower Commission reported. But they did not make good on the threat.[18]

As a Communist dedicated to addressing what the Party called the "Negro Question," Smolikoff worked hard to address the grievances of Local 32's black members. By 1944, Merrill-Stevens employed 2,000 workers in Jacksonville, one-fourth of them black, but only 50 black workers were classified above laborers, according to the CIO.[19] Smolikoff repeatedly pressed the U.S. Fair Employment Practices Committee (FEPC) office in Atlanta to investigate discriminatory wages, improper job classifications, and lack of upgrades suffered by black employees at Merrill-Stevens.[20] He also took advantage of the union's access to the National War Labor Board, a federal agency that adjudicated union-management disputes in defense plants during the war, to press these discrimination grievances. In one case, the IUMSWA charged that four separate, semiskilled labor classifications in the yard had been lumped under the rubric of "laborers" and "helpers" by the company and thus paid at rates incommensurate with the actual labor done by black workers. "There seems to be no other [reason] than . . . the workers' color for the company to insist [on] classifying [them] as mere helpers," claimed Local 32 in its complaint to the board.[21] Unlike the FEPC, which depended on moral suasion, the National War Labor Board had the legal power to compel Merrill-Stevens to upgrade its black workers, and they wielded it. Several months after the IUMSWA brought the complaint, the company instated either premium pay or upgrades for over 60 black workers. Smolikoff pursued much the same strategy, with similar success, on behalf of black workers at Miami Shipbuilding Company.[22]

By the end of the war, IUMSWA's regional director, William Smith, reported with pride that in the opinion of "numerous labor, civic and govt. leaders in the state," under Smolikoff's leadership, "one of the best Public Relations jobs that has ever been done by any CIO Union has been done by ours in the State of Florida." Defending Smolikoff against attempts by the IUMSWA's national leadership to remove him in 1946 over his suspected Communist ties, Smith continued: Smolikoff is "loved by the rank and file and officials of our union and other CIO unions. . . . [T]he rank and file of this and other CIO unions in the State will be in revolt if attempts are made to remove him." Noting that he was "convinced that [Smolikoff] is not taking orders from the Party," Smith, who was ready to step down for family reasons, recommended that IUMSWA make Smolikoff regional director in his place.[23]

Meanwhile, well aware that the end of the war would bring severe cutbacks in shipbuilding, Smolikoff also set his sights on building peacetime locals in other area industries, like furniture, and hoped that the continued necessity of boat repair shops in South Florida would help the IUMSWA survive.[24] As early as fall 1943, Smolikoff and another Communist TWU organizer named Jerry Lee, whom Smolikoff knew through the IUMSWA, began distributing a union paper, *Contact*, to workers at Pan American Airlines. They also organized social events and collected enough authorization cards from workers who wished to enroll in the company union that Smolikoff and Lee were able to petition the National Mediation Board for an election.[25] Smolikoff's technique at the airport mirrored what he had used at the shipyards, only now he had his CIO position as a platform. As before, he distributed flyers to airline workers as they left the airport. The FBI's informant noted that the flyers invited workers to attend a meeting at CIO headquarters, where a "member of the regional War Labor Board" would address them. By this time, that member was Smolikoff himself.[26] By 1945, as the war drew to a close, the CIO had successfully organized Local 500 of the TWU, which in March of that year won representation for over 2,000 workers at Pan American Airways, Miami's largest employer.[27] When IUMSWA dismissed Smolikoff over Smith's objections in March 1946 for being "more interested in following [the] party line than IUMSWA-CIO policies," the TWU's national leadership, in which the Communist-oriented

Left remained strong, did not hesitate to hire the skilled organizer to build its most important local outside of New York City.[28]

The Communist Party's success in organizing workers into the CIO during the war can be attributed to Smolikoff's skills as an organizer, his willingness to recruit and represent black workers who were barred from the AFL and eager to join the CIO, and his savvy use of government pressure brought to bear against recalcitrant companies dependent on federal wartime contracts. "The pressure of Washington threats . . . is working out pretty good as far as contract negotiations go," Smolikoff wrote to Tom Gallagher in 1944, noting that this sort of intervention could be used to solidify loyalty to the union.[29] Throughout his CIO work during the war, Smolikoff's ability to address the "Negro Question" rested heavily on his clever use of federal administrative agencies like the FEPC and the National War Labor Board to intervene in shop floor relations on behalf of black workers. Smolikoff's other organizing successes during the war followed much the same pattern. He helped James Nimmo organize Miami's black laundry workers, for example, when he took photographs documenting their essential contribution to war work, allowing them to present their case to the War Labor Board and win representation.[30] The TWU's ability to win a National Mediation Board election at the Miami airport followed from Smolikoff's initial organization of the black porters and cleaners as a separate "class and craft" of workers under the Railway Labor Act, thus giving the CIO a foothold in this crucial South Florida industry.

Smolikoff's union organizing in Florida shipyards relied similarly on government intervention in an essential war industry with an unusual amount of federal oversight of its industrial relations. He used the NLRB to challenge the company union that prevailed at Miami Shipbuilding before the CIO and prepared a similar case against the Dade Dry Dock Company.[31] The IUMSWA organizer who arrived in Miami in 1942 to scout the situation remarked that Smolikoff, whom he described as "a liberal who has worked for a long time with the colored people," "has done a marvelous job of setting up the organizing drive and has prepared our Labor Board case . . . better than I have ever seen one prepared before." Smolikoff also succeeded in securing the intervention of the War Manpower Commission when he sent a telegram complaining of the "slowing down of production" through the labor disputes breaking out at Miami Shipbuilding. In Jacksonville, the commission interceded on behalf of IUMSWA Local 32 when Merrill-Stevens introduced a penalty for lateness and absenteeism, a move that in Smolikoff's view was "needed to build workers' morale as far as Union goes."[32]

Smolikoff received high marks from fellow IUMSWA organizers, who evidently were either unaware of, or chose to ignore, his membership in the Communist Party. He also was a favorite with Communist Party leaders, like Alexander Trainor. Trainor advised Smolikoff on his organizing tasks and praised his progress throughout the 1940s. In 1942, Trainor widely distributed Smolikoff's "mass trade union educational material" and commended "the striking method of presentation," including Smolikoff's "excellent art work heading each leaflet," "the direct approach to concrete working class and trade union problems" based on actual incidents in the workplace, and the "clarity and brevity" in his propaganda work. In Trainor's view, Smolikoff's Miami efforts were exemplary in every respect, organizing "new proletarian workers in shipbuilding" while "increasing the production of ships to the maximum tempo." The fact that Smolikoff himself was not a worker clearly caused some anxiety at a time when the Party hoped to increasingly "proletarianize" its cadre. But Trainor insisted that Smolikoff's example demonstrated the lesson that even "middle-class" comrades can carry educational work "to the workers at the factory gates." "Well, comrade," Trainor wrote in closing his letter, "we at last are industrializing the whole ding-busted Party. Up the state down the state and acrost [sic] the state all are talking trade unions, NLRB, elections, conventions and unity for Victory."[33]

Education about union organizing was a critical step in the Communist Party's efforts and reflected the shift in the Party's own line after June 1941. Between the Nazi-Soviet Pact of August 1939 and its collapse twenty-two months later, the American Communist Party had advocated nonintervention and, abandoning its Popular Front antifascism, had been active in the American peace movement. With Hitler's invasion of the USSR "changing the entire character of the war," as Trainor put it, working to win the war and "open a second front" meant eager cooperation with government agencies and established unions, as well as a corresponding tempering of militancy, indeed, an active role in upholding the unions' wartime no-strike pledge and repressing wildcat strikes. Trainor gave a sharp dressing down to local Communists who attempted to lead a wartime strike among Tampa cigar workers. Even Smolikoff's efforts on behalf of black workers were stimulated by a desire to head off potential work stoppages. As Ellis Rubin's 1955 special report on Communist influence in Florida grudgingly admitted in retrospect, "[N]ot one strike was reported in Florida during World

War II."[34] By beginning with education, the Party hoped to consolidate their "contacts into organizational form."[35]

The Communist Party's ability to build industrial unions from the ground up stemmed from the dramatically changed social conditions of labor in the Sunshine State. Previously, the only large, concentrated groups of workers could be found in the cigar factories of Tampa, in the citrus groves and packinghouses in the "ridge district" counties of central Florida, and on the docks of the state's port cities. During the 1930s, the Party tried its best to organize inside these industries, but to little avail. In the early years of the Depression, the Party pursued its tactic of "dual unionism," trying to build independent unions to challenge the AFL in the ailing citrus and cigar industries. They abandoned this tactic in 1934, opting instead to build influence within the existing AFL unions in these sectors, including among the black members of the International Longshoremen's Association. After 1936, the Florida Communist Party threw most of its efforts into organizing locals among citrus workers of a nationally Communist-led CIO union, the United Cannery, Agricultural, Packing, and Allied Workers of America (UCAPAWA). They had little success in any of these efforts. By 1938, the Federal Writers' Project reported that the CIO had "gained a foothold in several Florida industries." But of the 1,925 workers supposedly organized into the new industrial unions, 1,400 of them belonged to UCAPAWA. This was surely an inflated figure, and as Jerrell Shofner has shown, after the failed strike of 1938, the UCAPAWA retreated from Florida's citrus groves.[36]

Records from the Communist Party of the United States of America (CPUSA) that made their way back to Moscow were preserved in the Russian Comintern archives, and they provide an unparalleled glimpse into the Party's organizational work in Florida during the 1930s.[37] Typically, historians have used this material to weigh in on the contentious question of how much Moscow controlled the Party's activities in other settings. Here, however, I am far more concerned with using the extant Party archives on American Communist Party activities in "District 25" (Florida) to examine how conditions in Florida became more conducive to establishing industrial unions during the war than in the relative merits or flaws of the Party's oscillating approach to trade union work, which has dominated much of the historical literature.[38] The contrast between the Party's dismal failure to organize Florida workers over this period compared to their successful trade union work during the war years is particularly notable. Why, then, did the CPUSA's successes come to Florida nearly a decade later than in other areas? What does their failure to spark successful organizing in Florida during the 1930s tell us about the state of the industrial labor movement in the state during the Depression?

It was certainly not for lack of trying. Smolikoff's predecessor was a man by the name of Isadore Sapphire. What little we know about Sapphire ironically derives from his evasive testimony before HUAC when it visited Miami in March 1948 to investigate Smolikoff's meeting with Elizabeth Gurley Flynn and his activities among the city's transport workers. Smolikoff conveniently absented himself from the city when HUAC came to town. Sapphire, however, endured two uncomfortable sessions in the witness chair. By his own testimony, Sapphire was born in Germany in 1905, emigrated to the United States in 1923, and became a citizen six years later. He was less forthcoming about his former Party membership, first denying it, then vaguely stating that he had belonged to the Communist Party for "maybe three years, two years" but that he "wasn't very active."[39] Sapphire claimed that he stopped going to Party meetings in 1938. Although this latter assertion may be true, internal evidence from the Comintern Records indicates that Sapphire arrived in Florida from Mexico in early 1934 and spent the next several years actively trying to build the state's trade union movement on behalf of the Communist Party. Sapphire's correspondence and reports to Party leaders in New York, under the alias of "Jack Strong," make up the bulk of the material on Florida in the Comintern files. Through these documents, we get an unusually close glimpse of the obstacles facing trade unions in Florida during the 1930s, particularly between 1934 and 1936.[40]

Tampa's cigar workers, concentrated in the dense working-class community of Ybor City, made a natural target for the Communist Party. In 1930, one-fourth of Tampa's jobs were in the cigar factories. Those who worked there, including a majority of Cuban immigrants or their children, had a deep-rooted tradition of labor militancy and political radicalism on which to draw, as well as a long-established AFL union, the Cigar Makers' International Union (CMIU), already in place. Established in the city's plants since 1901, the CMIU had led general strikes of cigar workers in the city in 1911 and 1920, and at its peak in 1923 it had over 11,000 members. Although membership had dropped considerably by the 1930s, the union remained a force to be reckoned with.[41] In the early years of the Depression, in line with the Comintern's ultraradical "Third Period," the Communist Party refused to cooperate with AFL unions, seeking instead to organize its own independent, "revolutionary" unions under the banner of the Trade Union Unity League. In Tampa, this took the form of the Tobacco Workers Industrial Union, which was suppressed violently by local police and vigilantes when it led a strike and series of public protests in Ybor City in November 1931.[42]

When Sapphire arrived in Florida roughly three years later, he immediately encountered a number of obstacles when he tried to organize these same workers under the auspices of the Communist Party. At this point, the Party had shifted its tactics and sought to "carry out the Party line in the opposition work within the AFL" rather than build "dual unions." What at first glance appeared as an advantage—that Ybor cigar workers comprised a concentrated, urban community of ethnic workers in a single industry, with a well-established base in the AFL—proved to be nothing of the kind. Sapphire soon discovered that few of the workers spoke much English. "In Tampa alone of the 12,000 cigar workers," he noted, "75 percent are speaking Spanish only." His initial correspondence with comrades back in New York urged the translation of key pieces of party literature into Spanish, since it was taking up too much of his own time to do so. In order to spark interest among workers with strong national ties and consciousness, Sapphire also asked the Communist Party headquarters in New York to send him some literature on Cuba. One of his contacts assured Sapphire that the Party was still "looking for a good Latin-American friend who could qualify as a leader in the trade union work among the cigar makers." Yet there is no evidence that any progress was made on this front. Indeed, six months later, Sapphire expressed frustration at the Party's inability to follow through on this proposal.[43]

Sapphire also believed that the high concentration of young women in the cigar industry militated against organization.[44] He reported that he had attempted to build a Young Communist League chapter among the women employed in one Tampa factory, but he had found them resistant. "Because of Spanish traditions," Sapphire remarked with frustration, "it is hard to get girls into any organization." Indeed, in a subsequent letter to New York, Sapphire noted the absence of women in the Communist Party in Tampa and complained that "therefore it is hard to find suitable element[s] to take charge of illegal quarters," making his clandestine work and existence precarious in the face of a local "terror campaign" against organizers. Finally, the tight-knit enclave of Cuban cigar workers may in fact have limited the Communist Party's ability to encourage even the most militant of them to build links to other workers. "What is really in our way," Sapphire suggested in July 1934, "is lack of knowledge by the Party members of the experience in other fields of struggle." The insularity of these workers meant that they were unable, or unwilling, to build contacts with the young English-speaking women who worked in the newly mechanized cigar-rolling factories that had begun to displace the hand-rolling plants where the Cubans had traditionally worked, Sapphire claimed.[45]

For example, the enormous Hav-A-Tampa plant, which was both the largest and the most modernized in the city, employed 700 women at its machines. Few of them were Hispanic. None were from Ybor City. Instead, as one interviewee told the Federal Writers' Project, "all their employees are women who come from little towns near Tampa." Sapphire was only able to recruit two workers from within this factory, failing to make enough inroads to establish a functioning "shop nucleus." Unfortunately, Hav-a-Tampa appeared to represent the future of the industry. By 1935, complaining that "the union to date has no contact with these machine cigar workers, many of whom are American," Sapphire warned prophetically: "We cannot talk today about maintaining the union in Tampa unless we will raise sharply the need for launching an organization campaign among the machine made cigar workers." This proved to be an accurate assessment. By the late 1930s, the pressure to obtain efficiency and to compete with cigarette makers impelled many owners of Tampa's factories to abandon the tradition of a high-quality hand-rolled product for machine-made cigars. As a consequence of this mechanization, a large number of cigar workers lost their jobs. By 1939, this amounted to nearly one-third of workers across the industry.[46]

In addition to the problem of language, national and gender barriers, and the impending threat of mechanization, Sapphire remarked that "the ideological level of the Party members [among Tampa's cigar workers] is rather low." By this he did not mean to imply that Cuban workers suffered from a natural conservatism. Rather, he found many of them somewhat hotheaded and thus apparently reluctant to abide by the Party's new desire to cooperate with the AFL.[47] Still, in Sapphire's view, the combination of economic depression, the threat of mechanization, and the apparently moribund craft unionism in the factories created a perfect situation for the Communist Party. "As we stand now," Sapphire wrote to New York in September 1934, "there is every opportunity to take the leadership of the cigar workers in Tampa, but not unless our forces are organized in the AFL union." Six months later, in the wake of a strike, Sapphire reminded Party officials, "Our party members in Tampa were all opposed to the decision of the Party to work in the AFL unions. A tireless struggle was conducted against the radical phrase mongers, who refused to recognize in the AFL the only existing organized union in Tampa at the time." Sapphire felt this "boring from within" strategy had been a success, despite local comrades' resistance to it. Still, a great deal of work remained to be done. Sapphire's confidence that "the workers now see the correctness of our policy" may have been misplaced. He continued to express frustration at local Party members' insistence on forming a "Progressive Association" of unionists inside the cigar factories, fearing that it would drive less militant workers away and squander the Communist Party's growing "prestige among the union rank and file and among the cigar workers generally of Tampa." It would be far better, Sapphire insisted, to continue building the rank and file on union issues rather than to pursue "progressive" political work. If the Party's trade union work took this latter course, he cautioned, "[W]e will soon be isolated from the rest of the union members, and maybe from the whole union." "The excuse for Red Baiting must not be furnished by us," Sapphire concluded, lest the Party return to the isolation and repression that it faced in the early 1930s. Yet local comrades failed to heed his advice. Sapphire soon reported that the Party's ticket in union elections, "made up of 'pure' communists," went down to defeat. "No attempt was even made to secure a United Front ticket," he lamented.[48]

While the loss caught Sapphire off guard, he had recognized the potential weakness of the Tampa section from the start. The inability to organize beyond the tightly knit, Spanish-speaking concentration of cigar workers led Sapphire to look elsewhere for a potential center of gravity among workers, both to the English-speaking industrial enclaves of Jacksonville and, even more significantly, to the citrus belt that dominated Florida's economy in the central part of the state.[49] His experience in the groves could not have been more different from what Sapphire encountered in Ybor City. True, at least citrus workers were native-born English speakers. But here Party organizers confronted a far-flung labor force of seasonal workers who were spread across four rural counties, sharply divided by race. Many citrus workers were migrants, both inter- and intrastate, who spent half the year in central Florida's orange groves and then drifted away, only to return the next season. The structure of the citrus industry and the habits of its owners remained deeply hostile to unionism. At least in Tampa, despite sporadic conflict, many cigar producers had made their peace with the AFL, which had deep roots in the local community. Florida citrus growers, by contrast, were, in the words of Civil Works Administration investigator Lorena Hickok, "mean-spirited, selfish, and . . . about as irresponsible an employer as you can imagine." They refused to cooperate with New Deal government efforts at price control even while they found themselves overwhelmed by falling prices and rising stocks of unsold fruit. As for their workers, the "citrus growers simply turn them off whenever they feel like it after paying them so little that they couldn't possibly get along on it until they get work again." Hickok concluded, "No wonder there is an 'outlaw union' in the citrus belt."[50]

The "outlaw union" was the United Citrus Workers (UCW), the Party's vehicle in the groves affiliated with the Trade Union Unity League. It had served as the Party's primary organizing wing among agricultural workers in an earlier period but now entered its twilight phase. Like Tampa's cigar workers, the UCW's independent and sectarian efforts were notorious. The winter season before Sapphire's arrival, the Civil Works Administration noted that "the inability of the citrus industry to pay living wages and make a profit is due to the bone-headed unwillingness . . . of the industry itself to get together and operate as a unit." Attending an AFL meeting of citrus workers, Owen Lovejoy, a local observer who shared information with the Resettlement Agency, noted that Florida citrus workers "looked like pictures we get from Dickens of colliery and textile workers a century ago." The AFL organizers insisted on the right to "meet the employers for an adjustment of hours and wages." Nevertheless, they "made it clear they had no intention of striking or causing any labor disturbance," Lovejoy remarked approvingly. Not so within the UCW, the citrus belt's other union, which had already called a strike at one corporation—a company managed, not incidentally, by Lovejoy's nephew. Lovejoy claimed that many of the workers wanted to return to work, but "the place is picketed and they are afraid to come in." Noting that many of the strikers were black, he surmised that "they shrink from offending the whites." In Lovejoy's view, the "radical labor group" of the UCW was "closely akin to the Communist group here" and "offer a serious menace to a satisfactory adjustment in the Florida situation," unless the responsible elements in the AFL and the growers with a "considerate attitude toward labor" could be brought together. "Evidently," Lovejoy concluded after attending a meeting of growers with union organizers from both the AFL and the UCW, "there is likely to be a war between them and the conservative A.F. of L. group."[51]

This proved not to be the case. Instead, Sapphire's arrival in late 1934 seemed to herald some discontinuity in organizing citrus workers, perhaps because of the seasonal nature of the work or, equally possible, because of the murder of a citrus organizer, Frank Norman, in Polk County that year. Indeed, a subsequent Party state conference attributed the UCW's organizing failure to "the terror initiated by the KKK and the local authorities, in conjunction with the growers and canners." When Sapphire arrived in central Florida, he found workers far more open to the idea of "an AF of L organization" than a model like that of the UCW. Nevertheless, so far as Sapphire was concerned, it represented a welcome change from the "half-heartedness with which the party members took to carry out the Party line in the opposition work within the AFL," he had encountered in Tampa. The Party continued to hold that "it is up to the revolutionary workers, and above all the communists, in the citrus industry" to take the initiative, organize black and white citrus workers, and seek AFL charters from the ground up.[52] Sapphire believed this could be done within Florida's groves.

By July 1935, District 25 had established a training school for Florida's Party workers. Much of the school's work focused on the important task of organizing the state's citrus workers. The result was a comprehensive document entitled "Our Task in Citrus."[53] Mirroring efforts by the Communist Party to build unions of agricultural workers in California and elsewhere, this period marked a critical recommitment of the Party to organize rural workers rather than focusing primarily on urban industries.[54] Yet the students at District 25's training school also "felt it necessary to point out certain differences" in local conditions that made Florida distinct from other regions in the United States and that they believed should shape local organizing approaches.[55] Both citrus and vegetable crops "required large numbers of workers both in the fields and in processing." But, unlike California, students at District 25's school underscored, "Florida does not concentrate the processing around large cities, nor are the agricultural workers to be found mainly around the few large cities in the State." Producing for a national, rather than a metropolitan, market, isolated from a larger concentration of industry, a congeries of semipermanent residents and migrants "from all over the South," Florida's rural proletariat combined characteristics of California's "factories in the fields" with the southern plantation. Their grievances were many: long unpaid travel time to work, months of seasonal unemployment, poorly paid piece rates, lack of drinking water in the fields, and speed-ups in the packing sheds. Given the isolation of rural field workers, the Party concluded that "organization of the agricultural workers must be through the towns where the packing houses are located." Indeed, the packinghouses were "the key to the citrus situation," organizers believed, because they tended to hire the picking crews rather than subcontracting the process to grove owners.[56]

In theory, these conditions seemed promising for the Party. But in practice, Communist organizers confronted a number of problems that required significant tactical adjustments. First was the question of finding adequate local leadership. By this point, the UCW had completely collapsed. Its fatal flaw was the tendency of "small politicians, lawyers, and salesmen" in the citrus belt, who were "finding their position in the rural business class insecure," to "organize citrus workers for their own personal advancement." The Communist Party hoped to build a rank-and-file leadership from below and "initiate a campaign for legal union organization and affiliation to the federal Union [of agricultural workers] of the A.F. of L." Yet, as Sapphire acknowledged elsewhere, "[W]hatever labor organization ever existed in Fla. has been for years controlled from the top by crooked political graftors [sic]." The state's AFL unions had also traditionally resisted taking in the unskilled workers who predominated in the citrus industry. They also had organized on behalf of Florida resident workers <u>against</u> migratory workers from other states, often excluding workers who had not resided in the state for at least a year. By contrast, the Party argued, "[C]omrades in citrus must work for unity of migratory and non-migratory workers." In an industry characterized by long stretches of seasonal unemployment during the summer months, the Party further recognized that "the struggle of the unemployed workers for greater relief is of the utmost importance to the citrus workers." As a result, Party organizers insisted that they had to "pay the closest attention to organizing the unemployed as part of our work in citrus. It is impossible to separate the two fields of work." Indeed, the Party's larger goal was to affiliate citrus union locals with the Unemployed Councils they had formed elsewhere in the state. Later that season, Sapphire went so far as to suggest that citrus workers, who were increasingly subject to long bouts of unemployment, be brought directly into a federal union of unskilled workers. "[T]his union will serve them the year round," Sapphire noted, while a citrus union "would only serve for the season."[57]

Finally, when the Communist Party entered the citrus belt, they had to directly confront the problem of organizing labor sharply divided along racial lines. Judging from a 1937 Resettlement Administration report, migratory black workers were highly concentrated in Florida's winter vegetable industry, as "from the decaying cotton economy just to the north a great flood of labor flows in with the season." The "muck" farms, or recently drained lands, around Lake Okeechobee were notorious for the presence of "40,000 Georgia niggers" who migrated there to pick tomatoes and celery or to harvest sugar cane in the winter months. Their white counterparts mostly worked in the packing sheds adjacent to the "truck" farms. The same report also suggested that in the citrus industry one could observe "the constant crumbling of racial barriers," as more desperately poor white migrants sought work beyond the confines of the packing sheds. For agricultural workers of both races, they noted, "wage levels remain those which will be accepted by lowest-income farm people for supplementary work."

While precise numbers are difficult to come by, it appears that African Americans made up approximately 12 percent of the labor force in Florida's citrus industry, with most of them concentrated in unskilled subsidiary work, such as loading and driving trucks, or as "handy men about the buildings." Many migratory white workers came to the citrus groves and packinghouses as impoverished and landless day laborers and sharecroppers from Arkansas and Mississippi, a circumstance that, in the Resettlement Administration's view, at least, did not lend itself to friendly relations between blacks and whites. "Improvident, slovenly, and without pride," the investigators wrote, these workers "in desperation, drifted to Florida." Describing these laborers as "poor white trash," they surmised that "while the poor white knows the Negro better now, he hates him worse, and the resentment born of the political and social demoralization of the South during Reconstruction days continues to the present day as bitter race hatred," with these migrants as its carriers.[58]

Faced with this volatile situation, Communist Party organizers proceeded carefully. "In the past struggles of citrus workers," the District School report claimed, "the Negroes have played a militant role." This was despite the fact that African American workers were usually organized into Jim Crow locals "under the complete jurisdiction of the nearest white local," a situation that denied black workers "the right to vote on any action of the union." In line with the Party's somewhat contradictory aims of "the building of unity of the Negro and white workers" and "the struggle for equal rights for the Negro People," Florida organizers proclaimed their commitment to "keep to the forefront the slogan: No discrimination and for equal rights for the Negroes in the union." At the same time, they acknowledged, "[I]t may be necessary to propose at first the formation of Negro locals separate from the white locals," provided that blacks could elect their own officials, vote on union matters, and were guaranteed equal representation on the executive board and on strike committees. "From a fight against jim crow [sic] on the picket line, we will be able to go on to a successful fight for the end of jim crow in the union," they hoped.[59]

Despite repeated attempts, however, the Communist Party's effort to attract black workers met with only limited success. At the end of 1935, local Party leaders sought to build a broad-based constituency for the upcoming inaugural meeting of the National Negro Congress, which could then serve as the main conduit to recruit black workers into Party-oriented trade unions. Not unlike the Party's move to work within the AFL, in February 1936 the National Negro Congress became the Communist Party's vehicle for achieving influence in an emerging New Deal civil rights coalition that included the National Association for the Advancement of Colored People, the National Urban League, black churches and civic organizations, and other "mass organizations."[60]

In a southern state like Florida, voting rights stood as a central issue for African Americans. In order to attract blacks to its program, the Party began agitating around the campaign to abolish Florida's poll tax. Meanwhile, Sapphire reported that "our Negro comrades have to work hard in the churches (the most popular form of organization) and over the heads of the preachers" to urge participation in the establishment of the Negro Congress. Party organizers also hoped to build support for the Congress in Florida's all-black towns, remnants of Reconstruction, where city councils could be encouraged to endorse the new organization, perhaps even sending delegates to its inaugural convention in February 1936. Black Party members were further urged to be the ones to approach the churches, black towns, and other "Negro mass organizations," because whenever whites broached the subject of the National Negro Congress with black groups, Party officials argued, "[T]hey scare them away from it and brand it communist." In an unmistakable sign of this new "Popular Front" approach, Party leaders also cautioned black organizers to avoid the "Scottsboro and Herndon issues." Although in the early 1930s, the Party's active legal defense of the Scottsboro Boys and the work of black, southern Communist organizer Angelo Herndon both served as powerful tools to recruit a black constituency under the "self-determination in the Black Belt" slogan, now Party leaders regarded this sort of agitation as inimical to building a broad "People's Front." The slogan of the day became "Forward to the National Negro Congress!"[61]

There is little evidence, however, that this approach to the Negro question did much to build Party influence among black, nonagricultural workers in Florida, the bulk of whom worked in the state's ports as stevedores. So in April 1935, organizers acknowledged their failure and tried another approach. In October, the Communist Party hit upon the international campaign to defend Ethiopia against its invasion by fascist Italy as a way to mobilize black dockworkers. Special leaflets were distributed urging black dockworkers in Tampa, Miami, and Jacksonville to "take part in the movement for the defense of Ethiopia by refusing to handle war material destined for Italy." Because of the high concentration of black workers in Florida's ports, Florida Party leaders hoped that this action would help in the formation of locals within the International Longshoremen's Association (ILA). "Although we have often raised the question of the ILA," the directive complained, "our accomplishments so far have been practically negligible. Now, by coupling ILA work with Ethiopian defense, we have a good opportunity to succeed [with] both."[62]

If the national question had proved a stumbling block and distraction for the Party with Cuban cigar workers, this attempt to exploit the same sentiments to the Party's advantage met with equally disappointing results among black longshoremen. Separate black locals within the International Longshoremen's Association, an AFL affiliate, had been cropping up in the ports of the Gulf and South Atlantic coasts for decades, from Brownsville, Texas, to Wilmington, North Carolina. A study done by the National Urban League on the eve of the Depression estimated that African Americans, grouped into forty segregated and two racially mixed locals, comprised one-third of the International Longshoremen's Association's 37,000 national members. The proportion was far higher in southern ports, where, as Sterling Spero and Abram Harris reported in 1931, "[T]he great majority of the longshoremen . . . are colored." By 1936, substantial locals of several hundred black longshoremen could be found in Pensacola, Tampa, Miami, and Jacksonville. Still, despite all its cheerleading, the Communist Party wielded very little influence among these workers. Sapphire's most promising contact was in Pensacola, where he discovered that the local's black president, Leon Anton, was "a militant local worker, old in the Labor movement dating back to the days of the Knights of Labor." In Sapphire's view, Anton was "more than just a Progressive in the AFL." Like the longshoremen's leader Harry Bridges on the West Coast, Anton was "participating in a movement on the Gulf Coast to form a Maritime Conference" that would build a left-wing waterfront union to compete with the ILA, a group notorious for the corruption of its national leadership. But the larger locals in Tampa (900 members) and Jacksonville (700 members) remained aloof, as AFL organizers "warned local Negro leaders of ILA to stay away from the Maritime [Conference] as it is a communist scheme." Sapphire was reduced to pleading with national Communist Party leaders to "connect us with the national [Party] fraction of the ILA."[63]

In October 1937, 8,000 African American stevedores shut down nine Gulf and South Atlantic ports for nearly a week, bringing "shipping to a standstill." Altogether, 800 longshoremen in Miami, 1,200 in Tampa, and another 1,500 in Jacksonville struck on October 15, demanding union recognition, a closed shop, an eight-hour day with time-and-a-half for overtime, and a wage increase of ten cents an hour (25 percent). Black workers in these southern ports, who were paid considerably less than the predominantly white longshoremen in the Northeast, wanted to bring their earnings up to par with their white counterparts elsewhere. Because of this demand, the strike had obvious racial overtones. Indeed, when twenty-four black longshoremen were arrested on the second night of the strike in Miami, the police charged them with "being disorderly persons in that they were in 'white' territory after dark." After calling for a "truce" and insisting that "the city is not going to take sides in this strike," Miami's mayor declared his own "opposition to organizing Negroes in Miami." He warned, "It will spread from the docks to truck drivers and all other occupations and the result will be that negroes will be making all sorts of unreasonable demands." After six days, International Longshoremen's Association members agreed to return to work for two weeks while contract negotiations continued. Two weeks later, the longshoremen and the shipping lines came to an agreement that can only be regarded as a victory for the union. They secured demands for recognition, the eight-hour day, overtime pay, and a basic wage increase from 40 to 48 cents an hour, only slightly less than the rank-and-file had requested. "The settlement of the longshoremen's strike," concluded the *Miami Daily News*, "is an example of what can be accomplished when moderate, fair-minded people get together in an honest effort to find peace."[64]

Although the Communist Party's paper of record, the *Daily Worker*, also covered the 1937 longshoremen's strike, the Party itself remained on the sidelines. The *Worker* sought to create the impression that the strike represented a direct rank-and-file challenge by black workers to the "reactionary president of the ILA," Joseph Ryan, and could form the basis of a CIO push to organize southern dockers under the auspices of a Gulf Coast Maritime Federation, as Bridges was doing on the Pacific Coast. In fact, the outcome of the strike suggests something much different: Florida's black longshoremen found a good deal of local power inside the segregated AFL and were reluctant to pursue the interracial alternatives represented by other organizations like the CIO or the Communist Party. As Texas longshore organizer Gilbert Mers remarked in his autobiography, the African American longshoreman was the "aristocrat of black southern labor" and thus appeared reluctant to "step into a situation that he considered would be risking what he already had."[65] By 1943, the National Urban League also reported that

Miami's International Longshoremen's Local 1416, for example, had "a virtual monopoly on longshoremen's work." "This union works under contract with employers and is able to command respect because of the performance of its men on the job and the integrity of its locals in other ports," they wrote. Still, the Urban League observed that Miami's longshoremen's local did not participate in the city's Central Labor Union, "where it understands it could only be represented by a white person." This would certainly seem to indicate the limits of this alliance with the AFL. Nevertheless, it is perhaps not surprising that when he was casting around for CIO allies in Miami during the war, Smolikoff did not look to the black longshoremen, ensconced as they were in the AFL.[66]

For Florida's Communists, the disappointing climax of their struggle to organize citrus workers came a year after the longshoremen's strike, with the November 1938 strike of 600 CIO members in Lake Alfred and Winter Haven, in the heart of the "ridge" district of citrus production. Organized by the Communist-led UCAPAWA, 600 orange and grapefruit pickers, who were employed by six of the district's largest packinghouses, staged a three-week strike over wages and union recognition. The union argued that fruit pickers worked for the packing sheds and thus should receive protection from the NLRB. The citrus growers and packinghouse employers' associations countered that the dispute remained "purely a pickers' strike" and that these workers were not entitled to union rights. Assisted by Ku Klux Klan intimidation, the citrus growers and packers unceremoniously crushed the strike with a lockout, an injunction, and a refusal to recognize the CIO as a legitimate bargaining agent, despite the presence of a federal mediator.[67]

Indeed, as a 1940 study of production and labor in Florida's citrus belt made for the National Youth Administration suggested, "[A]ttempts at organization in the citrus industry have failed almost continually since the inception of the industry in the state." Conceding that by the end of the 1930s both the CIO and the AFL were still "working hard to gain a foothold among the citrus workers," the study concluded that "their progress has been exceedingly slow since it is difficult to get a strong grip on workers because of the seasonal aspect of the work."[68] Every effort on the part of the Communist Party, whether through the "independent" UCW prior to 1934, attempts to work within the AFL, or as a crucial element in the nascent CIO in 1937–38, came up against this unbreakable constraint. The intransigence of most citrus employers only compounded the problem. In the wake of the failed 1938 UCAPAWA strike, the president of the United Growers and Shippers Association of Florida insisted to Congress that because "work is seasonal and must be done when the fruit is mature . . . we are therefore most emphatic that this work should not come under the NLRB or [Wagner] act."[69] By the end of the 1930s, even as the CIO became a powerful presence in plants, factories, mines, and fields across much of the country, neither the Communist Party nor the CIO had managed to build any lasting presence inside Florida's labor movement.

As we have seen, this record of failure changed dramatically during the war years. The development of wartime industries and a far more favorable climate for organizing both black and white workers provided another, even more important, opening for the Communist Party, which, under Smolikoff's tutelage, proved instrumental in building Florida's most powerful CIO unions. Other scholars have attributed the CIO's limited gains in Florida's citrus groves to "the nature of the citrus industry," as well as "regional animosity toward organized labor" and "the extremely depressed conditions of the 1930s." Moreover, Jerrell Shofner's important account of the "abortive effort" of the CIO to organize among Florida citrus workers in 1938 argued that the UCAPAWA's Communist affiliations made "labor leaders . . . much easier to categorize as 'Communists' or 'outside agitators.'"[70] Yet the successful wartime organizing of industrial unions by Charles Smolikoff suggests that this charge did little to thwart the CIO's efforts among shipyard and airline workers during the war, even though the Communist Party could, in fact, genuinely claim to have played a central role in these unions' success. It would not be until the late 1940s, with the advent of the cold war and a newly ultrasectarian phase by the Party, that radical labor organizers operated again in such a climate of hostility and vulnerability to anticommunism as they had in the 1930s. By then, having done their job, the Communists proved expendable to the larger labor movement, which, once self-purged of its "red" taint, secured itself a position as a tolerated, if tamed, part of Florida's political culture.

*   *   *

The author extends his gratitude to Miles Rodriguez of Harvard University for helping him access the microfilm copies of the RGASPI files on District 25 of the CPUSA. He would also like to thank participants in the 2004 Workshop on Real Socialism and the Second World, Centre for Russian and Eastern European Studies, University of Toronto, for their comments. Thanks, as usual, to Lara Kriegel for all her support.

Notes

1. *Miami Herald* (hereafter cited as *MH*), December 26, 1944, 8-B. In its basic outline, this profile was confirmed by my interview with Smolikoff's widow, Berthe Small, New York, December 8, 1995.

2. Robert Bussel, *From Harvard to the Ranks of Labor: Powers Hapgood and the American Working Class* (University Park: Pennsylvania State University Press, 1999); Len De Caux, *Labor Radical: From the Wobblies to CIO, a Personal History* (Boston: Beacon Press, 1970); Anthony P. Dunbar, *Against the Grain: Southern Radicals and Prophets, 1929–1959* (Charlottesville: University of Virginia Press, 1981); Steven Fraser, *Labor Will Rule: Sidney Hillman and the Rise of American Labor* (New York: Free Press, 1991); Gilbert J. Gall, *Pursuing Justice: Lee Pressman, the New Deal, and the CIO* (Albany: State University of New York Press, 1999); Mario T. Garcia, *Memories of Chicano History: The Life and Narrative of Bert Corona* (Berkeley: University of California Press, 1994); Rick Halpern and Roger Horowitz, *Meatpackers: An Oral History of Black Packinghouse Workers and Their Struggle for Racial and Economic Equality* (New York: Twayne, 1996); Dorothy Healey and Maurice Isserman, *Dorothy Healey Remembers: A Life in the Communist Party* (New York: Oxford University Press, 1990); Howard Kester, *Revolt among the Sharecroppers* (1936; reprint, Knoxville: University of Tennessee Press, 1997); Edward Levinson, *Labor on the March* (Ithaca, N.Y.: ILR Press, 1995); Nelson Lichtenstein, *The Most Dangerous Man in Detroit: Walter Reuther and the Fate of American Labor* (New York: Basic Books, 1995); Nell Irvin Painter, *The Narrative of Hosea Hudson: His Life as a Negro Communist in the South* (Cambridge: Harvard University Press, 1979); John A. Salmond, *Miss Lucy of the CIO: The Life and Times of Lucy Randolph Mason, 1882–1959* (Athens: University of Georgia Press, 1988); Junius Irving Scales and Richard Nickson, *Cause at Heart: A Former Communist Remembers* (Athens: University of Georgia Press, 1987); Robert H. Zieger, *The CIO, 1935–1955* (Chapel Hill: University of North Carolina Press, 1995).

3. Murray Kempton, *A Part of Our Time: Some Ruins and Monuments of the 30s* (New York: Simon and Schuster, 1955), 47.

4. *MH*, December 26, 1944, March 5, 1948; *Miami Daily News* (hereafter cited as *MDN*), March 1, 1948, May 9, 1949.

5. Ellis S. Rubin, *Report on Investigation of Subversive Activities in Florida, by the Special Assistant Attorney General, in Cooperation with the American Legion* (Miami: n.p., 1955), 45.

6. For the full story of the purge of Smolikoff from the CIO, see Alex Lichtenstein, "Putting Labor's House in Order: Anticommunism and Miami's Transport Workers' Union, 1945–1949," *Labor History* 39 (Winter 1998): 7–23.

7. "Communist Infiltration of Transport Workers Union of America," December 31, 1943 (100-7319-241), April 4, 1944 (100-7319-251), July 29, 1944 (100-7319-266), December 7, 1944 (100-7319-281), February 7, 1945 (100-7319-287), May 16, 1945 (100-7319-299), Federal Bureau of Investigation Files, released by Freedom of Information Act request (hereafter cited as FBI-FOIA); "Communist Infiltration Industrial Union of Marine and Shipbuilding Workers of America, CIO (Miami Field Division)," November 13, 1943 (100-8284), FBI-FOIA.

8. Memorandum, n.d, Court Cases, *State ex. Rel. Smolikoff v. Kelly*, box 15, folder 17, Florida Legislative Investigative Committee Papers, Florida State Archives, Tallahassee (hereafter cited as FLSA).

9. Author's interview with B. Small.

10. In his scathing account of the Red Scare, Cedric Belfrage devoted only a few pages to the anticommunist campaign that swept Miami in the mid-1950s and drove Smolikoff and Small into a quarter-century of Mexican exile. But in Belfrage's papers can be found a draft of a full chapter that never made it into his published book. The chapter is entitled "High Wind in Miami." Belfrage's extensive notes for this unwritten chapter suggest that Smolikoff provided him with much of the information on Communist Party activity in Florida in a 1969 interview. Belfrage knew Smolikoff from when they both lived in Cuernavaca during the 1960s. See Cedric Belfrage, *The American Inquisition, 1945–1960: A Profile of the McCarthy Era* (Indianapolis: Bobbs-Merrill, 1973), 220–23. See also, Cedric Belfrage Papers, Tamiment Library, New York University, box 7, folder 9; box 6, folders 2–5 (notes of Belfrage interview with Charles Small, c. 1969). On the exile community of American communists in Mexico, see Diana Anhalt, *A Gathering of Fugitives: American Political Expatriates in Mexico, 1948–1965* (Santa Maria, Calif.: Archer Press, 2001).

11. FBI Report 100-9749-29, IUMSWA Locals 32 and 59, Miami, December 29, 1943: 5 and May 12, 1944: 2, FBI-FOIA.

12. FBI Report 100-3-48-46, Communist Party Activities, District 25, Miami Field Division, October 25, 1943.

13. FBI Report 100-3-48-91, December 28, 1943, Communist Party Activities, District 25, Miami Field Division.

14. FBI Report 100-9749-29-3X, February 2, 1945, 2.

15. Alexander Trainor to Charles Smolikoff, June 8, 1942; Miami Report 100-7319-241, December 31, 1943, FBI-FOIA; Charles Smolikoff to Thomas Gallagher, June 9, 1944; "Report: Merrill Stevens—Jacksonville," IUMSWA Papers, McKeldin Library, University of Maryland, College Park (hereafter cited as IUMSWA, UMD); "Election Results, Held June 15th [1944]," series II, subseries 4, box 16, Organizers' Reports, Merrill-Stevens Dry Dock and Repair, IUMSWA, UMD; "Florida Organizer Reports," series II, subseries 4, folder 18, IUMSWA, UMD; "Survey Report of Miami Florida," n.d. (c. December 1942), series VI, subseries 3, box 6, folder: Miami Shipbuilding Corp., IUMSWA, UMD; William Smith to Thomas Gallagher, "Report and Recommendations of Survey of Florida Area," January 28, 1946, series II, subseries 4, box 18, IUMSWA, UMD.

16. Report by Charles Smolikoff, April 22, 1944, and "Report of Beatings in Jacksonville, Fla.," March 13, 1943, "Florida Organizer Reports," series II, subseries 4, folder 18: Florida organizers' reports, IUMSWA, UMD.

17. Charles Smolikoff to Thomas Gallagher, April 10, 1944, series II, subseries 4, box 18, IUMSWA, UMD.

18. "Labor Market Development Report," Jacksonville, July 15, 1943, War Manpower Commission Reports, box 1, folder 26, Florida Industrial Commission records, RG389, FLSA.

19. Clarence Mitchell to Malcolm Ross, July 10, 1944, Field Reports, Region VII, Closed Cases, Merrill-Stevens Dry Dock, roll 84, Fair Employment Practices Committee records, Center for Research Libraries, Chicago (hereafter cited as CRL).

20. Charles Smolikoff to A. Bruce Hunt, July 2, 1944, and August 17, 1944, and A. Bruce Hunt to Harvey Baker, September 28, 1944, FR, Region VII, Closed Cases, Merrill-Stevens Dry Dock, roll 84, FEPC Papers, CRL; A. Bruce Hunt to Will Maslow, "Weekly Report," September 2, 1944, FEPC Papers, CRL.

21. E. C. Holman to Wallace Miller, March 22, 1944, series VI, subseries 4, box 15, Merrill-Stevens Dry Dock and Repair Co., IUMSWA, UMD.

22. Report and Recommendations of Hearings Officer, May 11, 1944, and Directive Order, October 9, 1944, series VI, subseries 4, box 15, Merrill-Stevens Dry Dock and Repair Co., IUMSWA, UMD; Alex Lichtenstein, "Exclusion, Fair Employment, or Interracial Unionism: Race Relations in Florida's Shipyards during World War II," *Labor in the Modern South*, ed. Glen Eskew (Athens: University of Georgia Press, 2001), 135–57.

23. William Smith to Thomas Gallagher, January 28, 1946, series II, subseries 4, box 18, IUMSWA, UMD. William Smith returned to Florida later as the CIO regional director, which strongly suggests he was not a Party member himself.

24. Charles Smolikoff to John Green, July 29, 1944, IUMSWA, UMD; "Furniture Industry (Miami)," November 19, 1944, IUMSWA, UMD; Charles Smolikoff to Thomas Gallagher, May 12, 1945, IUMSWA, UMD.

25. "Communist Infiltration of Transport Workers Union of America," Miami Report 100-7319-241, December 31, 1943, FBI-FOIA.

26. FBI Report 100-3-48-46, October 25, 1943, "Communist Party Activities, District 25, Miami Field Division," 56.

27. Charles Smolikoff to Lucy Mason, May 31, 1945, Lucy Mason Papers, Special Collections Department, Perkins Library, Duke University.

28. Telegram from Ross Blood to Jack Livingstone [*sic*], March 19, 1948, series II, subseries 4, box 12, IUMSWA, UMD; telegram from John Green to Hoke Welch, February 24, 1948, series II, subseries 4, box 12, IUMSWA, UMD; William Smith to Thomas Gallagher, "Report and Recommendations of Survey of Florida Area," January 28, 1946, series II, subseries 4, box 18, IUMSWA, UMD; Charles Smolikoff to Douglas MacMahon, May 8, 1946, Transportation Workers Union of America Records, Local 500, Robert F. Wagner Labor Archives, New York University.

29. Charles Smolikoff to Tom Gallagher, July 5, 1944, series II, subseries 4, box 18, IUMSWA, UMD.

30. Testimony of James Nimmo, U.S. House, Committee on Un-American Activities, *Investigation of Communist Activities in the State of Florida*, part 2, 83rd Cong., 2nd sess. (Washington, D.C.: Government Printing Office, 1955), 7428–30.

31. "Survey Report of Miami, Florida," n.d., series II, subseries 4, box 18, IUMSWA, UMD; William Smith to Thomas Gallagher, April 9, 1943, series II, subseries 4, box 18, IUMSWA, UMD.

32. "Survey Report of Miami, Florida," n.d. (c. December 1942), series VI, subseries 3, box 6, folder: Miami Shipbuilding Corp., IUMSWA, UMD; Charles Smolikoff, "Report on Florida Area for the Week ending April 29 [1944]," series II, subseries 4, box 18, IUMSWA, UMD.

33. FBI Report 100-8794-101, "Communist Infiltration IUMSWA," July 1, 1943, 11–13.

34. On the wartime change of line in Florida, see *MDN*, March, 3, 1948; Alexander

Trainor, "Party Structure and Party Organization," November 14, 1941 in FBI Report 15-100974-42, November 28, 1945, Miami Field Office; FBI Report 100-3-48-46, October 25, 1943, Communist Party Activities, District 25, Miami Field Division; E. Rubin, *Report on Investigation*, 33.

35. Alexander Trainor to Charles Smolikoff, June 8, 1942, published in *MDN*, February 25, 1948.

36. Federal Writers' Project, *The WPA Guide to Florida: The Federal Writers' Project Guide to 1930s Florida* (New York: Pantheon, 1984), 94–98; Jerrell H. Shofner, "Communists, Klansmen, and the CIO in the Florida Citrus Industry," *Florida Historical Quarterly* 71 (1993): 300–309. Shofner notes that neither the AFL nor the CIO made significant gains among citrus workers over this period.

37. Records of the Communist Party of the United States of America, 1919–43, from the Russian State Archive of Socio-Political History (hereafter cited as RGASPI), Fond 515, Opis 1, on microfilm at the Library of Congress and elsewhere. Subsequent citations to Fond 515 will refer to "Delo" (file) and reel number.

38. The historiography of American communism can be divided roughly between those scholars who emphasize the impact of Soviet foreign policy and Comintern directives on Party policy and those who argue that grassroots organizing activities in labor, civil rights, and other areas had a logic and practice of its own, even if shaped from above. For examples of the former school, see Theodore Draper, *American Communism and Soviet Russia: The Formative Period* (New York: Viking, 1960); Irving Howe and Lewis Coser, *The American Communist Party: A Critical History* (Boston: Beacon Press, 1957); Max Kampelman, *The Communist Party vs. the CIO: A Study in Power Politics* (New York: F. A. Praeger, 1957); Harvey Klehr, *The Heyday of American Communism: The Depression Decade* (New York: Basic Books, 1984); Wilson Record, *The Negro and the Communist Party* (Chapel Hill: University of North Carolina Press, 1951). For the latter, see Maurice Isserman, *Which Side Were You On? The American Communist Party during the Second World War* (Middletown, Conn.: Wesleyan University Press, 1982); Roger Keeran, *The Communist Party and the Auto Workers Unions* (Bloomington: Indiana University Press, 1980); Fraser Ottanelli, *The Communist Party of the United States: From the Depression to World War II* (New Brunswick, N.J.: Rutgers University Press, 1991); Steve Rosswurm, ed., *The CIO's Left-Led Unions* (New Brunswick, N.J.: Rutgers University Press, 1992); Mark Solomon, *The Cry Was Unity: Communists and African Americans, 1917–1936* (Jackson: University of Mississippi Press, 1998). For recent summaries of this historiography, see John Earl Haynes, "The Cold War Debate Continues: A Traditionalist View of Historical Writing on Domestic Communism and Anti-Communism," *Journal of Cold War Studies* 2 (Winter 2000): 76–115; Bryan D. Palmer, "Rethinking the Historiography of United States Communism," *American Communist History* 2 (December 2003): 139–73. On black workers and the Communist Party, see Eric Arnesen, "No 'Graver Danger': Black Anticommunism, the Communist Party, and the Race Question," *Labor: Studies in Working-Class History of the Americas* 3 (Winter 2006): 13–52.

39. U.S. House, Committee on Un-American Activities, "Investigation of Communist Activities in Miami, Florida," House Unpublished Hearings Collection, March 3–4, 1948, 80th Cong., 2nd sess., March 4, 84, 87; *MDN*, March 3, 1948.

40. Jack Strong (aka Isadore Sapphire) to "Brown," May 23, 1935, Delo 3990, reel 298, RGASPI.

41. Archer Stuart Campbell, *The Cigar Industry of Tampa, Florida* (Gainesville: Bureau of Economics and Business Research, University of Florida, 1939), 1, 3–6, 48–51, 59; Nancy A. Hewitt, *Southern Discomfort: Women's Activism in Tampa, Florida, 1880s–1920s* (Urbana: University of Illinois Press, 2001); Robert P. Ingalls, *Urban Vigilantes in the New South: Tampa, 1882–1936* (Knoxville: University of Tennessee Press, 1988); Robert P. Ingalls and Louis A. Perez Jr., *Tampa Cigar Workers: A Pictorial History* (Gainesville: University Press of Florida, 2003).

42. H. Klehr, *Heyday of American Communism*, 118–35; Edward P. Johanningsmeier, *Forging American Communism: The Life of William Z. Foster* (Princeton, N.J.: Princeton University Press, 1994). On the Tobacco Workers' Industrial Union, see Robert P. Ingalls, "Radicals and Vigilantes: The 1931 Strike of Tampa Cigar Workers," *Southern Workers and Their Unions, 1880–1975: Selected Papers, the Second Southern Labor History Conference, 1978*, ed. Merl E. Reed, Leslie Hough, and Gary M. Fink (Westport, Conn.: Greenwood Press, 1981); Anita Brenner, *Tampa's Reign of Terror* (New York: International Labor Defense, 1933).

43. Jack Strong to "Brown," June 1 and July 12, 1934, Delo 3674, reel 283, RGASPI; "WEINER" to Jack Strong, July 12, 1934, Delo 3674, reel 283, RGASPI; Jack Strong to "Brown," February 25, 1935, Delo 3990, reel 298, RGASPI.

44. One study found that by the late 1930s, half the workers in the industry were women. See A. Campbell, *Cigar Industry of Tampa*.

45. Jack Strong to "Brown," July 12 and September 24, 1934, Delo 3674, reel 283, RGASPI.

46. A. Campbell, *Cigar Industry of Tampa*, 5, 59; Federal Writers' Project, quoted in R. Ingalls and L. Perez, *Tampa Cigar Workers*, 191–92; Jack Strong to "Brown," July 12, 1934; Jack Strong to "Brown," "Monthly Report of Shop Nuclei," July 14, 1934, Delo 3674, reel 283, RGASPI; Jack Strong to "Brown," October 28, 1935, Delo 3990, reel 298, RGASPI. The Federal Writers' Project study remains the most extensive study undertaken of the Depression Era cigar-making industry to date.

47. Although the Communist Party did not officially abandon dual unionism until early 1935, it seems clear from these internal documents that by mid-1934 local Party members in Tampa encouraged cigar workers to work within the existing AFL union.

48. "Draft Resolution presented to the District Committee at the Third Party State Conference," April 27–28 [1935], Delo 3991, reel 299, RGASPI; Jack Strong to "Brown," October 28 and December 17, 1935, Delo 3990, reel 298, RGASPI.

49. Jack Strong to "Brown," September 24, 1934, Delo 3674, reel 283, RGASPI.

50. Lorena Hickok to Harry Hopkins, January 29, 1934, "Hickok Reports, 1933–34," Harry Hopkins Papers, box 67, Franklin Delano Roosevelt Library, Hyde Park, N.Y. (Thanks to Gary Mormino for this document.)

51. Alan Johnstone to Harry Hopkins, January 16, 1934, with attachment of Owen Lovejoy to Alan Johnstone, January 4, 1934, Hopkins Papers, box 56, Florida Field Reports, Franklin Delano Roosevelt Library, Hyde Park, N.Y.

52. J. Shofner, "Communists, Klansmen," 301; "The KKK vs. the People," March 27, 1936, Delo 437, reel 305, RGASPI; "Draft Resolution"; Jack Strong to "Brown," July 12,

1934, Delo 3674, reel 283, RGASPI; "Brown" to Jack Strong, June 16, 1934, Delo 3674, reel 283, RGASPI; Jack Strong to "Brown," February 25, 1935, Delo 3990, reel 298, RGASPI.

53. J. Shofner's "Communists, Klansmen" is the only historical treatment of Communist Party organizing in Florida during the 1930s. But it focuses solely on failed CIO efforts to organize citrus workers in 1937 and 1938.

54. Donald Henderson, "The Rural Masses and the Work of Our Party," speech delivered at the Meeting of the Central Committee, American Communist Party (May 25–27, 1935), published in the *Communist* 14 (September 1935): 866–80.

55. "Our Task in Citrus," Report of District 25 Training School, July 1935, Delo 3990, reel 298, RGASPI. There is an enormous literature on the organizing drives among agriculture workers in California during the 1930s, many of them led by Communists. See Cletus Daniel, *Bitter Harvest: A History of California Farmworkers* (Ithaca, N.Y.: Cornell University Press, 1981), 141–257; Carey McWilliams, *Factories in the Field: The Story of Migratory Farm Labor in California* (Boston: Little, Brown, 1939), 264–82; Devra Weber, *Dark Sweat, White Gold: California Farm Workers, Cotton, and the New Deal* (Berkeley: University of California Press, 1994), 79–111, 162–99. For good firsthand accounts of the early Communist-led strikes in the San Joaquin and Imperial valleys, see *Hearings on Violations of the Right of Labor to Organize*, part 54: Agricultural Labor in California: 19947–20036, reprinted in Paul S. Taylor, *On the Ground in the 30s* (Salt Lake City: G. M. Smith, 1983); Dorothy Healey, with Maurice Isserman, *Dorothy Healey Remembers: A Life in the American Communist Party* (London: Oxford University Press, 1990), 42–58; Paul S. Taylor and Clark Kerr, "Uprising on the Farms," *Survey Graphic* 24 (January 1935): 19–22, 44.

56. "Our Task in Citrus." Much of this analysis is confirmed in non-Party documents. See Florida Department of Agriculture, *Citrus Industry of Florida* (Tallahassee: State of Florida, 1949), 14, 133; Aubrey Clyde Robinson and Glenore Fisk Horne, "Florida Migratory Workers," Confidential Report to the Administrator, Resettlement Administration, June 1937, box 20, Records of the Resettlement Division, Farmers' Home Administration Records, RG96, National Archives.

57. "Our Task in Citrus"; Jack Strong to "Brown," December 6 and 23, 1935, Delo 3990, reel 298, RGASPI.

58. A. Robinson and G. Horne, "Florida Migratory Workers," 7–8, 10–12, 24; A. R. Mead, *The Citrus Industry and Occupations in Florida* (Tallahassee: National Youth Administration for Florida, 1940), 25.

59. "Our Task in Citrus."

60. M. Solomon, *The Cry Was Unity*, 301–5.

61. Jack Strong to "Brown," October 28, 1935; "Report on the Proceedings and Decisions of the Enlarged District Committee Meeting," December 6, 1935, Delo 3990, reel 298, RGASPI. On the self-determination thesis, see M. Solomon, *The Cry Was Unity*, 301–5.

62. "Draft Resolution"; "Directives on the Struggle in Defense of Ethiopia," October 12, 1935, Delo 3991, reel 299, RGASPI.

63. Sterling Spero and Abram Harris, *The Black Worker: The Negro and the Labor Movement* (New York: Columbia University Press, 1931), 182–96, quote on 186; Ira De A. Reid, *Negro Membership in American Labor Unions* (New York: National Urban

League, 1930), 48–49. On the ILA in the Gulf ports, with a mention of Pensacola and Leon Anton, see Eric Arnesen, "'What's on the Black Worker's Mind?' African-American Workers and the Union Tradition," *Gulf Coast Historical Review* 10 (Fall 1994): 5–18. See also E. Arnesen, "Following the Color Line of Labor," *Radical History Review* 55 (Winter 1993): 53–88, esp. 62–64; Lester Rubin and William Swift, "The Negro in the Longshore Industry," *Negro Employment in the Maritime Industries: A Study of Racial Policies in the Shipbuilding, Longshore, and Offshore Maritime Industries*, ed. Lester Rubin, William Swift, and Herbert R. Northrup (Philadelphia: Industrial Research Unit, Wharton School, University of Pennsylvania, 1974), 112–25; Herbert R. Northrup, "The New Orleans Longshoremen," *Political Science Quarterly* 57 (December 1942): 526–44; Gilbert Mers, *Working the Waterfront: The Ups and Downs of a Rebel Longshoreman* (Austin: University of Texas Press, 1988), chapter 5; Samuel Harper, "Negro Labor in Jacksonville," *Crisis* 49 (January 1942): 11–13; Judge Henderson, "'Negro Labor in Miami," *Crisis* 49 (March 1942): 95; Jack Strong to "Brown," December 17, 1935 and March 3, 1936, Delo 3990, reel 298, RGASPI; *Miami Tribune* (hereafter cited as *MT*), October 16, 1937.

64. *MT*, October 16, 1937, October 17, 1937 (second quote), October 20, 1937 (third quote), October 21, 1937 (first quote), October 22, 1937; *Tampa Tribune*, October 19–21, 1937, November 6, 1937; *MH*, November 6, 1937; *MDN*, November 6, 1937.

65. *Daily Worker*, October 16, 20, 1937; J. Henderson, "Negro Labor in Miami"; G. Mers, *Working the Waterfront*, 147–48; Bruce Nelson, "Class and Race in the Crescent City: The ILWU from San Francisco to New Orleans," *The CIO's Left-Led Unions*, ed. Steve Rosswurm (New Brunswick, N.J.: Rutgers University Press, 1992), 19–45, esp. 41; Bruce Nelson, *Divided We Stand: American Workers and the Struggle for Black Equality* (Princeton, N.J.: Princeton University Press, 2001), 103–8.

66. National Urban League, Department of Research, *A Review of Economic and Cultural Problems in Dade County, Florida, as They Relate to Conditions in the Negro Population* (New York: National Urban League, 1943), 28.

67. J. Shofner, "Communists, Klansmen"; *Tampa Tribune*, November 19–20, 25, 30, 1938, December 1, 1938; *CIO News*, December 5, 1938, January 16, 1939; "Testimony of W. A. Stanford, United Growers and Shippers Association of Florida," Senate Committee on Education and Labor, *National Labor Relations Act and Proposed Amendments*, part 19, 76th Cong., 1st sess. (Washington, D.C.: Government Printing Office, 1939), 3584–86; *WPA Guide to Florida*, 97.

68. A. Mead, *The Citrus Industry*, 122–24.

69. *National Labor Relations Act and Proposed Amendments*, part 19, 76th Cong., 1st sess., 3584–85.

70. J. Shofner, "Communists, Klansmen," 309.

8

"In America Life Is Given Away"

Jamaican Farmworkers and the Making of Agricultural Immigration Policy

CINDY HAHAMOVITCH

Even as the United States extended its economic and political reach across the globe in the twentieth century, its officials exerted an ever-increasing amount of energy in an effort to secure their control over the nation's borders. This was a new function for the nation's bureaucrats and law enforcement officials. The Constitution had given Congress the right to determine which immigrants could become citizens of the United States, a power congressional representatives used in 1790 to limit the right of naturalization to whites only. But all other immigration questions had been left to the individual states, which meant, in practice, that the nation's borders were effectively open for much of the country's history. As in Canada, Argentina, and Australia, immigrants seeking work, land, or asylum in the United States could enter freely and stay permanently. Federal officials only began screening immigrants for infectious diseases late in the nineteenth century, and no one policed the nation's land borders. This laissez-faire immigration policy only began to change in the nineteenth century as Congress first barred the importation of slaves and then, in the latter half of the century, banned employers from contracting workers abroad, prohibited the immigration of prostitutes, and excluded Chinese immigrants. But, with the notable exception of the slave trade ban, these laws had little effect on the scale of immigration to the United States, which increased dramatically over the course of the century. Even the 1885 law banning employers from contracting labor overseas failed to prevent private labor contractors from advancing the fares of foreign workers and then renting them out to the highest bidder.

In contrast, the twentieth-century timeline is dotted with legislative and executive actions designed to limit immigration, such as literacy tests, quota acts, the rejection of Jewish refugees in the Nazi era, the mass expulsions of Mexicans during the Depression, and the creation of border patrols. We could almost say that the nineteenth century was a period during which immigrants (with the significant exception of Asians) were welcomed, while in the twentieth century immigration was discouraged.

Almost, but not quite. The problem with this formulation is that the countless examples of twentieth-century efforts to restrict immigration have rarely been applied to agriculture. While industrial employers lost their ability to hire whom they pleased, the small percentage of agricultural employers who hired migrant laborers continued to demand and get workers from abroad. Industrial employers were starved for labor during the First World War, but only farm employers were allowed to drive to the Mexican and Canadian borders and contract with foreign farmworkers. When unemployment during the Depression inspired the U.S. secretary of labor to order the mass expulsions of Mexicans living in the United States, growers were able to convince local officials to ease up on repatriating farm laborers (except those involved in strikes). Agriculture has long been the exception to the twentieth-century history of federal efforts to restrict immigration, and immigration policy continues to be shaped by the demands of the nation's largest agricultural employers.[1]

Up to the Second World War, federal immigration policy in agriculture was basically permissive. Rules that applied to industry were simply not applied to agriculture. During the Second World War, however, the federal government embraced a much more activist immigration policy. Beginning in 1942, the governments of the United States, Mexico, and the British West Indies agreed to a plan whereby the U.S. government would transport, house, and feed tens of thousands of Caribbean and Mexican farmworkers who would labor in the United States under no-strike, fixed-term contracts. The U.S. government became, in a sense, a *padrone* or crew leader, supplying foreign workers to the owners and managers of the nation's farms. The workers would not be immigrants but temporary labor migrants or agricultural guest workers, required by the terms of their contracts to leave when they were no longer needed.[2]

We could write off this new direction as a wartime anomaly, except that the "Emergency Labor Importation Program" did not end when the war did. Although American legislators renewed restrictive immigration policies in the two decades after the war, they allowed employers of farmworkers to import some 4.5 million Mexican braceros and Caribbean "offshores," as the workers were called. The 1952 McCarren-Walter Act closed the door tightly to permanent immigrants, but section H-2 of the act institutionalized Caribbean farm labor migration (which became known from that year forward as the H-2 program). Likewise, the western Bracero Program brought ten times more workers to western farms in the 1950s than it had a decade earlier.[3]

Why growers were able to play such a major role in shaping immigration policy is an open question. Certainly the effectiveness of the agricultural lobby is a large part of the answer. U.S. agricultural capital became highly concentrated in the years following the war, with a shrinking number of "agribusinesses" dominating markets at home and abroad. At the same time, the nation's biggest agricultural producers became better organized as a group, in no small part because only large producers and associations of producers could obtain guest workers. Farmers' organizations could not promise to deliver votes—the number of Americans living on farms plummeted in the twentieth century—but they could deliver dollars into the campaign coffers of strategically influential politicians. Moreover, although agribusinesses increasingly produced farm products much in the way General Motors produced cars—with machines, engineers, chemicals, and shrinking workforces—they were nonetheless very effective in promulgating the hallowed notion that farming is a "way of life" necessary to the preservation of the American republic. Ironically, the power of the agrarian myth helped undermine what little remained of its reality.[4]

Another part of the answer to the mystery of agricultural exceptionalism, certainly, is that agricultural employers have different needs than other employers. Like industrial employers, agricultural producers have mechanized to a degree unimaginable fifty years ago, but there has always been (at least thus far) a limit to what can be done to crops by machines. And the turn to machines has not eliminated the need for harvest labor in many cases; it has merely reduced the days of work being offered, making farm jobs even less attractive than before. Thus mechanization has both solved and exacerbated agricultural labor shortages. Similarly, while industrial employers can cut costs by moving plants to lower-wage labor markets, farmers seeking to cut costs have to bring lower wage workers to their plants. Agricultural capital can be mobile—agribusinesses were, after all, some of the first multinationals—but once a field is planted here or elsewhere, the workers must come. None of this should be taken to mean that agricultural employers have faced a dearth of labor in the last half-century. Farm employers might have drawn from the enormous numbers of poor people who immigrated to the United States after the liberalization of immigration laws in 1965. But legal permanent immigrants were not nearly as attractive to employers as guest workers were precisely because, as residents, they would have had the freedom to negotiate, to quit before the end of the season, and to protest. And, most importantly, they would not have been susceptible to the threat of deportation.

Had the guest workers programs remained small and had the guest workers always left at the end of their contracts as promised, both programs might have continued with little controversy. Instead, the Bracero Program grew, and many guest workers chose to overstay their official welcome. Public alarm over the Bracero Program's expansion resulted in its cancellation in 1964. But by then West Coast growers were unwilling or unable to wean themselves from foreign labor, and they turned increasingly to undocumented workers. Always much smaller and more isolated from surrounding communities, the H-2 program continued with only occasional bursts of controversy. In both cases, growers' learned dependence on foreign workers resulted in the rapid internationalization of the agricultural labor market and the persistence of migrant poverty. In no part of American life, then, have the effects of state-driven immigration policies been more profoundly felt than in agriculture.[5]

This essay examines the roots of U.S. immigration policies in agriculture by focusing on one group of wartime migrants. Jamaican war workers were not the first to arrive—Bahamians and Mexicans came first—but the Jamaican program, which expanded into the British West Indian program, has operated continuously since its start in 1943. Moreover, the Jamaican experience reveals in stark detail the rapid decline of immigrant farmworkers' condition in the United States. Jamaicans came eagerly to northern farms in the United States, and they were welcomed as war workers. As black men with what sounded to American ears like British accents, who behaved as the equals of whites, the press treated them as curiosities. Though they encountered inadequate conditions in some regions, they demanded respect and by and large got it. Yet, as Jamaicans ventured reluctantly into the Jim Crow South, taking jobs as cotton pickers, vegetable harvesters, and sugarcane cutters, they found themselves to be no better off and more highly regarded than the African American farmworkers who labored alongside them. Which of these norms would prevail would depend to some extent on the struggles of Jamaican migrants themselves, but even more on the intervention of U.S. and Jamaican officials—that is, on the intervention of the state in the affairs of farm labor migration.

The Politics of Labor Scarcity

It would be several years after the outbreak of war in Europe in 1939 before employers of migrant farmworkers had cause to worry about any reduction in their labor supply. After twenty years of agricultural depression, the nation's fields were glutted with labor. In Belle Glade, Florida, the southern source of the East Coast migrant stream, growers could pick from among thousands of black farmworkers who would gather at dawn for the daily "shape-up." With many more people looking for work than there was space to stand upright in the back of growers' trucks, employers enlisted the help of local police to beat off the workers who clung to the outsides of their vehicles.[6]

Although nearly 10 percent of African Americans left the South during the war to take war jobs or enlist in the military, and a similar number shifted within the South from farm to city, many of these wartime migrants abandoned the fields, not because they saw better opportunities beckoning them, but because they had been supplanted by agricultural machinery. Indeed, officials of the Departments of Agriculture and Labor, who were given the responsibility of estimating farm labor needs in early 1941, insisted that, despite pockets of labor scarcity, the overall supply of labor was still more than adequate to meet farm employers' needs.[7] Even after Pearl Harbor, as growers started to predict disaster if their accustomed workforce abandoned them, federal officials pointed out that the growers who complained most vociferously about labor scarcity and spiraling wages were the growers who paid the least. The problem, according to federal officials, was not labor scarcity but a maldistribution of labor, made worse by many growers'—particularly white southern growers'—unwillingness to recruit workers by paying attractive wages.[8]

Federal officials could not address the problem by trying to ensure that farmers paid the minimum wage established by the Fair Labor Standards Act in 1938, because the act had specifically excluded farmworkers from its provisions. The problem of labor maldistribution seemed more tractable. The Farm Security Administration (FSA), which had been created during the Depression to address the most stubborn forms of rural poverty, quickly stepped into the breach, transforming the migrant labor camps it had built to house homeless farmworkers into a labor redistribution system. Rather than encouraging farmworkers to abandon the migrant life for more sedentary work as the labor camps had been designed to do, the FSA shuttled domestic workers from job to job, transferred large groups from areas of surplus to areas of need, and provided them with meals, shelter, and sanitation facilities in Quonset huts and orderly tent camps.[9]

Many small farmers were content with this arrangement—happy to be spared the expense and effort of securing harvest labor themselves—but large growers were often outraged when federal officials stepped in to remove men and women deemed "surplus." Southern growers became particularly angry when African American farmworkers, who made up the vast majority of the eastern migratory workforce, used federal labor camps as bases for impromptu strikes. Excluded also from the National Labor Relations or Wagner Act, fieldworkers did not enjoy the right of collective bargaining, but they could agree among themselves to delay entering the fields as crops ripened on the vine and growers became more open to persuasion. The more American farmworkers demanded higher wages, the louder agricultural employers demanded access to foreign labor.[10]

Federal officials capitulated to growers' demands in June 1942. Secretary of Agriculture Claude R. Wickard left quietly for Mexico City, returning with an agreement that allowed Mexican laborers to work on American farms in the Southwest. To growers' dismay, however, the agreement came with strings attached by Mexican authorities. The FSA would transport the migrants and would use its extensive network of temporary and permanent camps to house them. Growers would have to provide cooking, sleeping, laundry, bathing, and waste disposal facilities to anyone not housed in FSA camps. Growers could charge rent for these conveniences, but they would have to specify the amount before the workers signed their contracts. Even more, farm employers would have to pay a minimum wage of 30 cents an hour or the prevailing wage, whichever was higher. And if a harvest was delayed and contracted workers sat idle, growers would have to pay them three-quarters of the minimum wage for each day they lost. It was an unprecedented agreement, one not at all like the First World War era plan, which had simply allowed growers to pick up farmworkers at the Mexican border and drop them back there at the end of the season. The FSA began supplying farmers with Mexican workers in the fall of 1942, and within a few months, 4,000 laborers from south of the border were working on California and Arizona farms.[11]

Aware that the federal government was supplying West Coast growers with Mexicans, East Coast producers demanded access to foreign workers as well. "Just 48 miles across the Gulf Stream," the Dade County Farm Bureau president testified before a congressional hearing, "are some 18,000 men, willing laborers who want to come to Florida . . . and despite the fact that Mexican labor is permitted to enter this country—we haven't had one Bahamian laborer offered to us." The offer was not long in coming. In February, Edward, Duke of Windsor, then governor of the Bahamas, traveled to Washington and met with President Roosevelt to negotiate an agreement to import unemployed workers from that colony.[12]

Then, in April, Congress passed a remarkable bill that the nation's two most powerful growers' lobbies—the American Farm Bureau Federation and the Associated Farmers—had penned. The new law—Public Law 45—allowed for the expansion of the farm labor supply program, so long as federal funds were *not* used to improve the wages or conditions of *American* farmworkers. American farmworkers would have to stay where they were, unless their local county agricultural extension agent signed a release allowing them to take work elsewhere. The FSA's farm labor supply program would serve large farms or associations of farmers who could contract with foreign farmworkers under the terms negotiated by foreign governments.[13]

Bahamian men and women began departing for Florida almost immediately, and negotiations soon began to extend the migration program to Jamaicans who were available in far greater numbers.[14] Thus just at the point when American farmworkers had gained some power after twenty long years of depression wages, they found themselves thrown into competition with workers imported from abroad.

Just across the Gulf Stream

In 1943, Jamaicans were desperate to find work of any kind. Already devastated by the Great Depression, Jamaica's 1.2 million people had been pushed to the brink of starvation by the outbreak of the Second World War. While the war had recharged the U.S. economy, the dearth of commercial shipping vessels made it difficult for Caribbean exporters to unload their perishable produce. In November 1940, the British government had prohibited the use of scarce ships to transport bananas, the principal cash crop of Jamaica's peasant farmers. Before the banana market collapsed, most Jamaicans had depended for their survival on a combination of wage labor and peasant farming. The coming of war thus forced them to buy goods at inflated wartime prices with nothing but their decreasing earnings from wage labor alone. "We were small farmers," one Jamaican explained to an American reporter, "but we were dumping out bananas because we had no market for them. There is no export now." A Jamaican seaman, who arrived in London in time for the first blitzkrieg after his ship was torpedoed, agreed: "There is no shipping . . . so we had to find other work."[15]

Jamaica's black majority had little hope of redressing its grievances through political channels. Most Jamaicans were excluded from political participation by property qualifications that reduced the electorate to the wealthiest 6 percent of the population—in effect, white Jamaicans and a small number of successful "browns." This tiny electorate chose fewer than half the members of Jamaica's legislative council: the "Electives." The remaining members, the "Officials," were appointed by the governor, who was himself appointed by the British prime minister. Only Officials could serve on the governor's executive council. As elsewhere in the British West Indies, what reform initiatives there were tended to come from above, from the British Parliament or Britain's Colonial Office. Jamaica's Electives saw their job as resisting reform in the interest of their class. This meant that black Jamaicans could usually improve their circumstances only by searching for work elsewhere. But when the Depression dried up the usual offshore work opportunities in Cuba, Panama, and the United States, Jamaican workers dug in at home, organizing trade unions and public protests. Labor rebellions racked the British Caribbean in 1937 and 1938, strengthening reform forces in England and leading, in 1942, to the appointment of Oliver Stanley, a reformer, as secretary of state for the colonies.[16]

As a result of Stanley's pressure from above and popular pressure from below, by 1944 Jamaica had a new constitution that required secret balloting and universal suffrage and that would make five out of ten seats on the executive council elective. This did not constitute an end to colonial rule, but it did represent dramatic change nonetheless. Instead of having to appeal to an elite electorate of just 70,000, Jamaica's "Electives" would soon have to court the favor of 750,000 mostly black voters. Thus with constitutional reforms looming, white and elite "brown" Jamaicans did what they could to ensure their continued hegemony by forming the disingenuously named Democratic Party. It was at this tumultuous moment in Jamaican history that U.S. State Department officials arrived bearing manna from heaven: a labor migration scheme that they predicted would create an estimated 100,000 jobs for Jamaicans in the United States, allowing Jamaican electives to reap political patronage even as they exported the destitute and the discontented.[17]

The legislative council thus approved the participation of Jamaican men (and men only) in the migration program and began distributing tickets in April 1943. Rather than allow officials of Jamaica's Labor Department to give out the tickets by some equitable system, however, the Electives doled them out themselves, assuming (falsely, it turned out) that a ticket holder's gratitude would later translate into a vote. The Electives concentrated their recruitment activities in the countryside where the opposition parties were weakest and trade unionists rare, while at the same time avoiding men already employed on Jamaican plantations. They bypassed Kingston, Jamaica's largest city, entirely. Too anxious to wait for a ticket distributor to come to them, thousands of islanders began sending letters of inquiry to the Jamaican Labor Department and to the United Fruit Company, whose president, Samuel Zemurray, had been asked by U.S. authorities to help screen the Jamaican recruits.[18]

Not everyone in Jamaica was so enthusiastic about the migration scheme. Some planters protested what they saw as competition for their labor supply, and the governor worried about the impact the migrants might have on Jamaican society at the end of their stint in the United States. "What will happen when these highly paid gentlemen return from the States God only knows," he wrote to an official in the Colonial Office in March 1943. The leaders of the socialist People's National Party (PNP) and the Jamaican Labor Party accused the Democrats of denying tickets to their members, and both appealed unsuccessfully for the right to send trade union officials to the United States as the migrants' representatives.[19] Likewise, the secretary of state for the colonies, as well as the workers themselves, worried that the contract offered few guarantees that workers' rights would be protected. Still, the prospect of sending an estimated 100,000 unemployed West Indians to the United States left Stanley with little choice but to approve the scheme.[20]

Ultimately, Stanley set aside all his objections but one: he would not allow West Indian workers to be assigned to farms south of the Mason-Dixon Line for fear that they would be abused. The contract devised by the Colonial Office, the Jamaican government, and the U.S. State Department was otherwise similar to the Mexican deal in most details. The U.S. government would import Jamaican men and would guarantee them at least 30 cents an hour for a ten-hour day. Workers would pay a dollar a day—or a third of their minimum daily earnings—for food, and 50 cents a week to sleep in an FSA bunkhouse or an approved private labor camp. Another dollar a day would be deposited in a Jamaican bank as a compulsory savings program (and to ensure that workers returned home at the end of their contracts). If work was unavailable for any reason, workers were to be paid for at least three-quarters of the period for which they had been contracted (though, unlike the Mexican deal, the Jamaican contract failed to specify how long a period of unemployment would have to last before this benefit took effect— an omission that would be the source of many later grievances). If local wages were higher than the 30 cent minimum wage, the migrants would be entitled to the prevailing wage. On the other hand, workers who refused work for any reason would be subject to deportation.[21]

"Reaching Over": Jamaican Encounters in the Wartime North

News of the migration program and the publication of the contract in the *Daily Gleaner* met with great excitement in Jamaica. "For the past four weeks the question asked by the average man on the street is: Are you going to America?" one observer wrote to the *Gleaner* from May Pen. The men who got hold of the first tickets in North Clarendon were so nervous that they might miss their opportunity to work in the United States that they assembled at the embarkation point a full twenty-four hours before they were scheduled to leave. Even in Maroon Town, where descendants of escaped slaves still lived in isolation from the rest of Jamaican society, a delegation called for the inclusion of two hundred Maroons in the migration scheme and the construction of a road to make it easier for recruiters to get to their mountain community. The PNP's paper, *Public Opinion*, soon began reporting a brisk trade in black market recruitment tickets.[22]

As the first recruits prepared to leave for the United States in May 1943, communities across the island organized alternately jubilant and solemn farewell ceremonies at which workers said special prayers, received pocket editions of the Bible, and feasted on curried goat. Men departing Buff Bay sang a chorus of "We Are All Jolly Good Fellows" before boarding the train that took them to the port at Kingston. Once at sea, however, everything that could go wrong did go wrong. The U.S. troop transport vessel, the SS *Shank*, which had been built to hold 1,800 men, was so overcrowded that the 4,000 recruits aboard had to arrange shifts for meals, water, toilets, and bunks. George Pitt, a machinist from Spanish Town, wrote home to *Public Opinion* that men had to wait in line for hours to eat and were treated like prisoners by the military police who guarded the vessel. On their third day at sea, he and other observers reported, MPs turned a fire hose on the recruits. One man died on the voyage—by his own hand, according to the

Jamaican official who investigated the incident, by accident, according to the U.S. State Department, and at the hands of MPs, according to Jamaicans on the boat. In any case, it was an inauspicious beginning.[23]

Upon their arrival in New Orleans's port, the men were processed and fingerprinted before being sent north by train. Each man left with a pamphlet written by J. Harris, Jamaica's labor adviser, and Herbert MacDonald, who would be the workers' chief liaison to the Jamaican government while the men were in the United States. Although assuring the men that they would be "among a friendly English-speaking people," the brochure warned them to expect habits and customs "somewhat different" from their own. "In the United States the word 'Negro' is not used to offend," the pamphlet explained, "but is used and accepted in the same way as the word 'coloured' in Jamaica." "Respect the 'Star Spangled Banner,'" the brochure admonished, and "try to recognize it whenever it is played . . . remember it is as sacred to Americans as 'God Save the King' is to us." "Try to save all of your surplus money," the pamphlet added in closing. "The more you have, the better off you will be when you go back home."[24]

Jamaican migrants did find Americans friendly and certainly were fascinated with them, though conditions varied enormously from place to place. Rupert Holn wrote from Burlington, New Jersey, that "we have found the Americans a very fine lot. I am feeling very homely and would not mind if stay could be for all times . . . the experience that I have gathered could never be bought in a lifetime in Jamaica." Another recruit wrote his relatives from Bridgeton, Connecticut, that he and the other men on the boat "got over safely and have started to work. We are not in a place where the people are very fine and courteous to the Jamaicans." One man noted that they had been "treated royally" on their voyage from New Orleans to Bridgeton, remarking, hyperbolically, that Uncle Sam provided them beer to drink "every hour of the day." Ernest Pendley and thirty-four others were surprised to find a military band waiting to greet them when they arrived in Randolph, Wisconsin, in May 1943. Pendley and the others were invited to attend various churches the following Sunday and were offered full use of the Randolph Country Club for as long as they were in the area picking the peas that had been planted on the golf course's fairways and greens. C. W. Creightney was amazed to find white locals willing to "come from miles with their cars to take us around and show us a good time." "They were not expecting us to be such fine fellows," he noted, and "we never expected to rub shoulders" with them in restaurants and stores. David Bent wrote a former teacher that his Wisconsin boss was a "gentleman." Samuel Gayle only wished he had come twenty years earlier. "It is just like a honeymoon to me. . . . Please tell them that life is given away in United States."[25]

Other recruits were not nearly as content with the conditions they found on northern farms and in hastily built farm labor camps. George Pitt recalled that after disembarking the "hell-ship" at New Orleans, and taking the long but "pleasant train trip" to Hebrant Camp in New Jersey, he worked over the next few days for three different employers, one of whom never paid him despite his complaints. After a week the FSA moved him to Swedesboro, where the recruits worked overtime (without overtime pay, he noted), and then the work slowed, until there was only enough for fifty of the four hundred men. Food and water supplies dwindled. Fourteen hundred and fifty workers sent to Michigan were without work for a month. While they waited, they lived off food bought on credit from the camp store. Because growers did not begin paying them the three-quarter wages that the Mexican contract would have demanded, some were reduced to demanding relief at police stations. "State of affairs . . . is deplorable and fraught with danger," the Jamaican governor telegraphed to Oliver Stanley. When they were finally put to work the following week, then men complained that they were paid less than prevailing wages and that they were the butt of race prejudice stemming from the recent race riots in Detroit. One hundred and sixty men insisted on returning to Jamaica. Another two hundred arrived in Centerville, Maryland, after an unusually long voyage to Norfolk during which a German submarine chased their ship and the delay caused the food on board to spoil. They arrived in Centerville so hungry that, when they discovered that the camp manager was not prepared for their arrival, "they broke into a neighboring orchard and consumed large quantities of green apples." After two weeks of work, with which "the farmers on the Eastern Shore of Maryland [were] very pleased," the men were quickly relocated when the Colonial Office discovered that Centerville was well south of the Mason-Dixon Line.[26]

With the notable exceptions of Michigan, generally, and Swedesboro, New Jersey, in particular, most new arrivals experienced conditions in northern states that were satisfactory, if not luxurious, and the men were pleased and sometimes moved by the welcome they received from nearby communities. Four hundred Jamaicans working near Manhattan were treated to a tour of the city on Labor Day, which ended with a dinner and a cricket match between the Jamaican farmworkers and West Indian New Yorkers (the New Yorkers won). The Brant Labor Camp, near Buffalo, New York, held a celebration on August 1 to commemorate the abolition of slavery in Jamaica 105 years earlier, an event noted by the press as far away as Fort Wayne, Indiana. "Here they were in a country other than their own," Fort Wayne's *Protestant Voice* reported, "celebrating an event that happened 30 years before American negroes were freed. Their eloquence—the sheer beauty of their words in praising of ancestors who had won freedom for them—was surprising."[27]

Wherever Jamaicans worked in northern states, white Americans seemed similarly struck by the fact that they were black people—but not like black people they had known or read about. The white press, in particular, could not resist comparing the recruits to African Americans, at least implicitly. Arriving at Swedesboro, *Waterbury Republican* reporter Sigrid Arne remarked on the "queer sound" that could be heard coming from a long building that looked like an Army mess tent. "Dominoes," explained the FSA official who was driving. "They play dominoes with a fine fury." Writing for a local population that had been hiring African Americans for sixty years, Arne explained, "The Jamaicans come from a Negro country," a place "without color prejudice." "It's a British colony," he noted, "a fact which lends to amusing situations when the Jersey farmer runs into his first Jamaican. Many of them have clipped, British accents that are quite surprising coming from a Negro field hand. I was talking to one," he continued, "who told me 'we're rather fond of cricket, you know. But we're having extreme difficulty acquiring the gear.' I could have closed my eyes and thought I was in a Park Avenue drawing room."[28]

In a story that found its way to Kingston's *Daily Gleaner*, the Humboldt, Iowa, paper also compared Jamaicans to African Americans. First noting where Jamaica was located, the paper described Humboldt's visitors as "happy men" who sang as they worked. "Sometimes, while they wait to start along the rows, they break into a soft shoe dance. The only language the Jamaicans know is English. However, among themselves they speak in rapid vernacular which no midwesterner ever could follow. But in talk with visitors, some become almost Oxfordian. In physical appearance," the reporter explained, "the Jamaican resembles the American Negro of the deep south. But they have enjoyed generations of equal social rights with white men in Jamaica. . . . There are no Jim Crow laws in Jamaica and some of the men, encountering racial prejudice for the first time in their lives, have been deeply hurt in several instances." "The employers," the paper continued, "are defending Jamaicans loyally." As one farm manager noted to Chief Liaison Herbert MacDonald, "We have had only one serious complaint about one of our boys." The "boy" had earned $23 in one day, blocking beets (loosening the soil around the plant to allow it to grow). "He is a real good boy; but he works too hard," the manager quipped.[29]

While compared by others to African Americans, the Jamaicans compared themselves to white Americans. In an open letter thanking the people of Humboldt City, for example, three Jamaican men wrote: "I suppose you all must have heard about us. We are from a British West Indies Island, a peaceful and law-abiding country as you are in Humboldt City." "I can assure you all that when we get back to our sunny Jamaica homes," the letter ended, "we will always remember America, especially Humboldt City where you have treated us so good that the only difference between us is colour and that's nature's work. . . . Men are judged by their minds." "We are made form the same clay," added Gerald Johnson, a cook from Port Antonio.[30]

When Jamaicans encountered discrimination while working in northern states, they reacted to such affronts openly and sometimes aggressively, with few if any repercussions. For example, Renford Glanville, who came to the United States in 1943 at the age of 19, worked for a year alongside black and white Americans at Seabrook Farms in New Jersey, loading and unloading cartons of asparagus for 50 cents an hour, ten hours a day. The Americans had a union, and the Jamaicans did not—"since we were foreigners and on contract." "Still," he later recalled, "we were treated nicely." On one occasion, however, he and other Jamaicans stopped at a local restaurant on their way home from working in the fields. "We had worked all night, and some of the fellows wanted to get something to eat before we went home. The restaurant people wouldn't serve us. They served all of the other people before us." According to Glanville, the men "kept sitting there," but finally "some of the boys got mad. . . . So they jumped over the counter and started breaking up the dishes, tearing up the place. All for one and one for all, you know." Not knowing what the do, the restaurant staff called John Seabrook, who managed Seabrook Farms. Seabrook, by Glanville's telling, said, "Feed them. You better feed them." "So, that" according to Glanville, "was that."[31]

The fact that Jamaican farmworkers were being treated with more consideration than African American farmworkers was not lost on African American observers. African American reporters presumed a kinship with the Jamaican workers reporting news of the program regularly and protesting cases of mistreatment with vigor. Yet they keenly observed the special treatment accorded Caribbean workers. Roy Wilkins, writing for New York's *Amsterdam News*, noted that when the government brought several thousand Jamaicans here to work as farm laborers, "it was careful to explain that these people were not accustomed to racial discrimination and must be handled accordingly." "But for its own Negroes . . . ," Wilkins complained, "the War Department says not a word." "Fair Wages Should Begin at Home," began a similar editorial in the *Norfolk Journal and Guide*. The author noted that West Indian laborers had been guaranteed a minimum wage of 40 cents per hour and adequate housing, "which is much more than any U.S. Negro farm laborers are assured of making." "A minimum wage has been denied Negro or white farm labor in the United States," the author continued, though "the experiment points up what the farmers can do, and what our government can do when necessity demands that something be done."[32]

Jamaicans Jump Jim Crow: Encounters in the Wartime South

The first few months of the Emergency Farm Labor Importation Program did indeed reveal what governments could do to guarantee farmworkers decent conditions and fair treatment. As long as the Importation Program placed Jamaicans only in the North, and as long as FSA officials and the Jamaican liaisons responded promptly to workers' complaints, the scheme seemed useful to all concerned and at least to some a promising experiment in interracial cooperation. However, U.S. pressure on colonial officials to allow Jamaicans to venture south never relented, and the pressure increased as winter approached. Harvests in the North would soon come to an end, the War Food Administration (WFA) warned, and Jamaicans already in the United States would either have to work in the South or return home. "In avoiding districts like Delaware and Maryland in the Northeast and the 'deep south' where a rigid colour bar exists," as Jamaica's labor adviser put it, Jamaicans would soon run out of crops to harvest. "We tried hard . . . to have numbers of the men sent to California," Harris noted, "but this State is worked almost entirely by Mexicans." The director of the WFA asked for permission to send Jamaicans to Texas to pick cotton, but Harris refused, enforcing the ban on work south of the Mason-Dixon Line, though he checked again with the colonial secretary, just to be sure.[33]

Thus by the time the first Jamaican farm laborers were arriving in the United States in May 1943, the recruitment scheme had already been suspended back home. On May 17, recruitment was postponed for an indefinite period, leaving men who had hoped to go "in a state of despondency." And on June 12 the recruitment staff disbanded. Over the next five months, the colonial secretary held his ground as anxious recruits gathered in Kingston, hoping the migration program would resume.[34]

Meanwhile, Florida growers continued to demand Caribbean workers, estimating, rather vaguely, that their labor supply would be "25 to 85 percent" short during the coming winter harvest season. The "importation of labor from the British West Indies was the only chance of meeting the situation," according to the Florida Vegetable Committee. The staff of the FSA's Office of Labor refuted such claims, citing field reports that suggested an adequate supply of labor. But while FSA officials argued that reports of labor scarcity were "considerably exaggerated," the director of the War Food Administration, the FSA's parent agency, chose to heed Florida growers. Thus U.S. officials added to the pressure on the colonial secretary to allow Jamaicans to work in the South by suspending further recruiting until he relented. [35]

While U.S. officials waited, pressure to resume transporting migrants mounted within Jamaica. The Jamaican press published heartbreaking tales of recruits who had spent what little they had to travel to the port at Kingston, only to discover that the program had been called off. Even the PNP, whose party organ, *Public Opinion*, had kept up a steady barrage of criticism against the program, could not help but notice how important the program was as a relief measure. *Public Opinion* reported that workers still in the United States had sent home remittances in the amount of £20,000 or $100,000 for the month of June alone. Calling for the "fullest and most sincere and earnest provisions" to be made for the workers' protections, the PNP reluctantly endorsed the proposed change in policy. And while the *Daily Gleaner* editorialized about the "real and serious difficulty" of sending Jamaicans to the U.S. South, its editors reasoned that "if the men who volunteer for such a trial are made fully aware . . . of the realities of 'down South' conditions . . . the experiment might end satisfactorily. Perhaps, too, as a racial experiment," the *Gleaner* added, "it may prove instructive, certainly enlightening."[36]

Colonial officials also feared what might happen if Jamaicans faced discrimination or violence in the U.S. South. But because Bahamians were already working in Florida under a separately negotiated contract, and because Barbadians and Puerto Ricans were clamoring to be included in the scheme, they worried that failure to comply with the U.S. demand might mean the loss of the offshore program to other Caribbean workers entirely. Thus, in September 1943, Oliver Stanley reluctantly gave in, and Jamaican and WFA officials drafted a new agreement that allowed Jamaican workers "to proceed south." The conditions of the agreement provided that only those recommended "for character and efficiency" would be allowed to stay in the United States for winter work in Florida. And those who chose to remain would have to be fully informed of the "racial and other conditions prevailing in the Southern States." To start, Jamaicans would only work in Florida, where they would be under the supervision of an expanded staff of Jamaican liaisons.[37]

To smooth their way, Herbert MacDonald, the chief liaison, announced to the Miami press, that Jamaicans were "good workers" "and only those who have made excellent records" would be given contracts for work in Florida." Although the Jamaicans' contract still stipulated that they would suffer no discrimination while at work in the United States, MacDonald announced unilaterally, that "these men *want* to abide by the customs of the South." "They are not arrogant," he assured white readers, "and do not wish to get out of bounds." "If one should enter a restricted place, for example, it will be through a lack of knowledge of Southern customs, and he will leave immediately when he is reminded." So, while northern employers had been advised that they would have to adapt to black workers from Jamaica, and most seemed willing to do so, southern growers were assured that Jamaicans would adapt to them.[38]

Jamaicans began arriving in Florida to cut sugarcane for the U.S. Sugar Corporation on October 7, 1943. To ensure that the first eight hundred Jamaicans shifted south would in fact abide by the customs of the "Jim Crow"—that is, the formally segregated—South, MacDonald insisted that the men agree to what the *Amsterdam News* dubbed the "Jim Crow Creed." MacDonald made it clear that "a distinction is made in Florida with colored people and you must be careful and endeavor to help the position, as by your conduct you will be judged." He continued, "It is well to tell you for the sake of general information that there is a law in many Southern States, including Florida, which makes the offense of rape punishable by death. This, of course, is a very serious offense anywhere, but down there it is viewed even more seriously." "There will be ample opportunity for you to make friends among the colored people," he assured them, "as every city, town and village has its colored section." "You are free to purchase wherever you wish, but there are certain places of amusement, restaurants, and bars where you will not be allowed." MacDonald also noted that the new contract included "a misconduct and indiscipline clause," which gave the U.S. government the right to terminate the contract "if the worker misconducts himself." He exhorted the men to "behave themselves" because there was "a slight possibility that the success of the Florida venture might well influence any future recruitment in Jamaica." Those who refused to behave, he said in conclusion, would be turned over to the Immigration and Naturalization Service for "repatriation."[39]

In fact, the workers who began arriving in Florida from northern states and from Jamaica were not nearly as content to "abide by southern customs" as MacDonald had promised, nor were they at all satisfied with the wages and conditions offered by U.S. Sugar. While the city of Hartford, Connecticut, held farewell ceremonies for Jamaican workers, congratulating them on the work they had done, ninety-three men arrived in Florida incensed at the "Jim Crow Creed" and upset that they were being sent to cut sugarcane. They "refused to get off the buses," MacDonald later reported, and when they did, "they refused to carry their own luggage." When they got to the mess hall, "they scraped their food on the ground and trampled on it" and "abused everyone and everything in sight." The men were quickly shipped off to the Dade City jail to await deportation. Within two weeks the number of Jamaicans sitting in Florida jails had risen to seven hundred. "I must advise caution as they are in an ugly mood," Herbert MacDonald warned Jamaica's Labour Adviser.[40]

Still, many got to work, and Jamaicans harvested 65 percent of Florida's sugarcane in 1944. Those who had agreed to stay in Florida, however, quickly discovered that Bahamians and African Americans were working in nearby vegetable fields, earning three times as much for work that was far less difficult and dangerous. Their complaints went unheeded. One group of men recruited directly from Jamaica for work at U.S. Sugar accused MacDonald of "lying to them and of being in league with the sugar people to keep them in Florida."[41]

The conditions in U.S. Sugar's camps were also far worse than anything the recruits had experienced in places like Humboldt, Harford, and Bridgeton. Upon their return to Jamaica, a group of men complained of abysmal conditions and racist camp officials in Florida. They told of "odorous" drinking water, a plague of mosquitoes, flies, snakes, and deadly insects, and of "sanitary conditions in their living quarters that were absolutely intolerable." Upon entering the U.S. Sugar Corporation barracks at Clewiston, Florida, Stanley Wilson discovered that he was expected to sleep on a bare mattress, without sheets, pillow, or blanket. When he and the other cane cutters protested, the camp superintendent exclaimed, "Pillows . . . you aren't serious! This is the first time in my life that I ever heard niggers slept with pillows, too." To make matters worse, the barracks adjoined a latrine that was in an "unimaginable" state of filth. Because the latrine stood directly across from the mess hall, swarms of flies "trafficked regularly between the food served to the workers and the deposits in the convenience." "Workers made the strongest representations against these conditions," Wilson reported, "but could secure no redress." While in the fields the men were given water to drink that not only smelled rank but "changed the colour of any of the more delicate metals with which it came in contact." If Jamaican workers wanted the same water that white workers drank, they had to pay 35 cents a gallon for it. When they refused to work under these conditions, Wilson and fifty-eight others were loaded onto a truck and taken to jail, where they spent the next three weeks awaiting passage back to Jamaica.[42]

Rather than attempting to redress the conditions in Florida's labor camps, U.S. immigration officials jailed the Jamaicans who complained and then deported them. Detention was not meant as a punishment, though imprisonment certainly had that effect. Its purpose was to keep angry migrants awaiting their return to Jamaica from influencing newly arrived recruits, who had no experience in the United States with which to compare the conditions at U.S. Sugar. In December 1944, the War Food Administration began to deport dissenters without imprisoning them by turning Fort Eustis in Virginia into a repatriation center, which housed only workers awaiting boats back to the Caribbean. That same month, however, the War Manpower Commission shifted almost 2,000 West Indians into war industries, as industrial employers were willing to accept workers who had been blacklisted by the WFA. When news spread at U.S. Sugar that workers facing repatriation in Virginia had been transferred to coveted industrial jobs in New Jersey and Wisconsin, four hundred sugar workers in Florida promptly threatened to strike. Their hope was that they would be transferred to Virginia for repatriation and that, once there, they too could sign up for industrial work. Its plan undone, the WFA closed the Fort Eustis Repatriation Center, and opened one at Camp Murphy, near West Palm Beach, Florida. There men who refused work, or who simply wanted to go back to Jamaica, waited impatiently for transportation, while they spent their savings on food and other necessities.[43]

The guards at Camp Murphy and the problem of securing transportation back to Jamaica remained sources of discontent for the remainder of the war. The *Christian Science Monitor* attributed a riot of 250 workers at Camp Murphy in August 1945 to "the Negroes [sic] unwillingness to return to their comparatively drab former existence after sampling the high wages and luxury goods during their employment in the United States." In fact, it was a fight between Barbadians and Jamaicans as to which group would get to leave first.[44] And while discontent among Jamaicans in northern camps had sent managers scrambling to find cricket equipment and Jamaican-born cooks, the managers of Camp Murphy went scrambling for their guns. A week after the Camp Murphy riot, a white camp employee, Lacey A. Griffin, fired his weapon while chasing a Jamaican who had urinated against a building. Griffin lost his quarry and was taunted by a group of men who dared him to enter their barracks. He went for help, telling Captain R. G. Ray, the camp manager, that he would quit before he took "such talk off of these men any further." Ray, Griffin, and two other camp employees then returned to the barrack armed, yelling at the men to stand up as they entered and beating with billy clubs those who moved too slowly. "If we did not behave ourselves," one worker later quoted Ray as having said that he would "shoot us and throw us in a hole." To make themselves clear, Ray shot his gun toward the floor and Griffin fired his through a window, hitting a man in the leg in another building. The military police sent to replace the camp's hired staff were "well received by the men," according to Herbert MacDonald, but a month later, another worker was shot, this time by the military police brought to maintain order.[45]

Delaware was no better than Florida, according to Nathaniel Allen, whose letter to his mother in Montego Bay caught the eye of an official in the Office of Imperial Censorship. Work was scarce, he complained, and dust plentiful: "No Latrines, no water to bathe, no beds to sleep in, no lights to sleep with and see at nights [sic] and worse than all, no work to do." "What this thing is going to lead up to I don't know," he wrote, "but what I can tell you is that every one is getting panicky." "Mam, you can't imagine," he wrote. "This is a one man's place. Everywhere you look belongs to no one else but him, so then he runs the place and fixes the rates the people must work for. . . . I am not working because working here is only putting money in some one else's pocket."[46]

What Jamaicans were encountering, of course, were the conditions that African Americans had long faced as agricultural workers in the U.S. South. In the Vienna, Maryland, War Food Administration camp, for example, Jamaicans objected to the daily "shape-up," complaining that only those who got in the trucks first got work. Jamaicans also resented having to arrive early in the fields and then wait without pay until the farm manager declared the fields dry enough for picking. Likewise, their organizing attempts brought an immediate, hostile response. When a white camp manager reported James Morrison to the local police as an "agitator," he was arrested and held at the Vienna police station, without so much as a warrant or a hearing. Although he was eventually released, he noted that two other workers had already been deported as "trouble-makers."[47]

How an Experiment Became an Institution

The more Jamaicans soured on the southern "experiment," the more the workers' distaste for working and living conditions seemed to spread northward. And the more dissatisfied they were, the more frustrated they became with Herbert MacDonald, the chief liaison, and he with them. In November 1944, after quickly settling a Wadsworth, Ohio, strike over the phone, MacDonald remarked, "As far as I can see, the only reason these men had for striking was to keep in practice for the day when they return home." Likewise, in March 1945, he reported that a worker had punched a Cleveland camp manager in the face "and got away with it." "I told the Camp manager," MacDonald noted, "that he should have reported this and I would have taken responsibility [for] removing the man. Subsequently another worker abused him shamefully and was removed. The effect of this," MacDonald lamented, was that "the workers are under the impression that it is safer to punch the Camp Manager than to abuse him." "Men write home or go home and say they have never seen me," MacDonald added two months later. "That is their theme song," he complained But he also estimated that it would take him nearly four years to visit every man.[48] MacDonald and the other liaisons on his staff would, of course, have been hard pressed to attend to every grievance made by their far-flung compatriots. However, with U.S. immigration authorities ready to deport importees who contested their wages and treatment, the workers could not redress their grievances themselves. By 1944, in effect, the federal government was serving not just as a crew leader for the nation's largest farms but also as an enforcer of workplace discipline.

Jamaican leaders did try to follow up on the migrants' complaints, but their desire to expand the program outweighed their concerns. While strikes in the United States became more frequent and workers in repatriation camps fought to return home, men and women in Jamaica and elsewhere in the Caribbean were struggling bitterly to get to the United States. In April 1944, "bedlam and minor damage to property" were the result when police used batons to beat back 3,000 people trying to get the 180 available tickets at the Port Maria recruiting station. Even outrage that American doctors were requiring recruits to strip naked on Kingston's open pier for venereal disease examinations failed to put a damper on public enthusiasm for the program. Jamaicans may not have been receiving prevailing wages in the United States, but they were sending more money home than Jamaican off-shore workers had ever sent before, and that fed the program's popularity, no matter how bad the reports from the United States got.[49]

Jamaican officials were reluctant to attack the program, both because of its popularity and because they still stood to gain from it. 1944 brought Jamaica its new constitution, universal suffrage, and, therefore, the first democratic elections in its history. The Jamaican Labour Party, the political wing of the Bustamente Industrial Trade Union (BITU), swept the polls, completely unseating the Democratic Party and winning twenty-two seats to the PNP's five. The Democratic Party's monopoly over the ticket distribution process had failed utterly in keeping white Jamaicans in power. Nonetheless, once ensconced in the new Jamaican House of Representatives, Alexander Bustamente, the BITU's "president for life," happily inherited the tickets and the patronage system that went along with them. In May 1945, four opposition PNP members made a motion on the floor of the Jamaican House of Representatives to condemn the ticket distribution system, arguing that nonelected officials should distribute the tickets. But after a rancorous debate, the motion was defeated by 20 votes to 4, and the migration program and patronage system it spawned became permanent features of Jamaican political life.[50]

Citizens of other Caribbean colonies were also demanding to be included in the migration scheme, but in its first year the program remained restricted to Jamaicans, Bahamians, and Mexicans. U.S. officials were trying to avoid importing Puerto Ricans. "As they are United States citizens," an American diplomat explained in a letter to Oliver Stanley, "they could not be sent back to Puerto Rico against their will." "This cannot, of course, be stated," he added, so the "reason given is lack of shipping facilities." If workers were brought from Barbados or elsewhere, the "falsity of the reason given would be apparent." In the spring of 1944, however, the point became moot, as employers began importing Puerto Ricans on their own. The importation of Barbadians thus began immediately, and once the log-jam broke, the governors of St. Lucia and the British Honduras insisted that their subjects be included as well, citing protests and demonstrations at home.[51]

With workers from many nations scrambling to work in the United States, American growers and officials had little incentive to improve conditions. Those who did not like them could simply leave. In the last year of the war, 38,000 Jamaicans, Barbadians, St. Lucians, and British Hondurans labored in the United States alongside almost 62,000 Mexicans, 5,800 Bahamians, 120,000 prisoners of war, and an undisclosed number of Puerto Ricans. Herbert MacDonald now supervised Jamaicans and the other British West Indians under the rubric of the British West Indies Central Labour Organisation, which had been set up jointly by the various British Caribbean governments (with the exception of the Bahamas).[52]

The end of the war came and went with little change in the "Emergency" Farm Labor Importation Program. Congress moved quickly to expel foreign workers from industrial jobs, but at the urging of farm lobbyists, the agricultural program received an extension. In the year following the war, 39,630 guest workers from the British West Indies worked in nearly 1,500 localities in thirty-six of the forty-eight states, and Jamaicans harvested most of Florida's sugar crop.[53]

Once the war ended, the new secretary of state for the colonies, Fabian socialist Arthur Creech-Jones, demonstrated that he at least was still ambivalent about the migration program. In April 1946, colonial officials insisted on pulling all Jamaican workers out of Florida for the same reason that the government of Mexico tried unsuccessfully to keep its citizens from working in Texas. Both of these state-sponsored strikes against poor working conditions and racist abuse failed, however. Mexican citizens undermined their government's effort by crossing the border illegally and taking whatever work Texas growers had to offer. The government of Barbados took advantage of Jamaica's "strike" against Florida to expand opportunities for its citizens in the United States. The Emergency Farm Labor Importation Program had, in essence, re-created the prewar labor surplus. Only it had created an international shape-up: if one nation's workers failed to climb onto the back of growers' trucks, another nation's workers would.[54]

Jamaicans and the Making of Agricultural Immigration Policy

Could the United States have fashioned a guest worker program or open-border policy that would have allowed foreign farmworkers temporary immigration status without subjecting them to the kind of conditions depicted here? Nothing in this tale precludes such a possibility. The mere presence of Jamaican workers in the United States did not account for the rapid decline in conditions described here. Indeed, Jamaicans raised the bar for other farmworkers when they first arrived in the North. The problem was not so much the fact of a temporary workers program but the combination of a program that put the authority to deport in the hands of growers with labor laws that denied farmworkers the right of collective bargaining. Had the INS insisted that Jamaicans could not be deported simply for protesting violations of their contracts, the last fifty years of agricultural history might have turned out quite differently.

Instead, what began in 1942 as an emergency measure became, in the aftermath of the war, a fixture of modern agriculture. The "jolly good fellows" from Jamaica turned out to be among the vanguard of a great migration, as monumental in scale and impact as any that had come before it. In the decades that followed, the wartime Labor Importation Program mutated into the Bracero Program on the West Coast and the H-2 program in the East, both of which continued to provide growers with temporary harvest labor without permitting the "migrants" to become "immigrants." In the 1950s U.S. growers hired ten times more temporary foreign workers than they had during the Second World War, although the federal government got out of the business of recruiting, transporting, feeding, and housing foreign workers, leaving those aspects of the program to private employers. Growers' associations were allowed to buy FSA labor camps for a dollar apiece, and some remained in use thirty years later. Federal officials continued to set "prevailing wage" standards and deport those who caused trouble. As a section foreman supervising three hundred West Indian sugarcane cutters in Florida explained in 1966: "We bring the Jamaican here under contract. If he violates his contract we can send him home. So we've got leverage over that West Indian that we don't have over American workers. When that offshore comes in here, he's either going to cut cane or get sent home—or if he violates his immigration status and runs away from his employer, the law will get him."[55]

The agricultural guest worker programs came under attack repeatedly over the decades, but campaigns to end the use of braceros in the West and scale back the number of H-2 workers in the East have only resulted in growers' increased use of illegal immigrants. Since penalties against employers who hire undocumented workers have rarely been enforced on farms, the undocumented workforce—which is much bigger than the H-2 workforce—functions as a sort of unofficial guest worker program, only without the housing and prevailing wage guarantees. Both groups can be disciplined by the threat of deportation. On the occasions when Congress has determined to roll back illegal immigration, it has tended to expand the H-2 program. The relationship forged by growers and the state during the Second World War persists; the agricultural exception is alive and well.

* * *

Reprinted Cindy Hahamovitch, "'In America Life Is Given Away': Jamaican Farmworkers and the Making of Agricultural Immigration Policy," from *The Countryside in the Age of the Modern State: Political Histories of Rural America*, ed. Catherine McNicol Stock and Robert D. Johnston. Copyright © 2001 by Cornell University. Used by permission of the publisher, Cornell University Press.

The author would like to thank Raymond B. Craib, Rohan D'Souza, Judith Ewell, Leon Fink, Rhys Isaac, Robert Johnston, Kay Mansfield, Scott R. Nelson, Richard Price, Jim Scott, Michael Simoncelli, Catherine McNicol Stock, the College of William and Mary's Faculty Summer Grant Program, the Breakfast Club, and the Program in Agrarian Studies at Yale University.

Notes

1. On U.S. immigration policy during the First World War, see Camille Guerin-Gonzales, *Mexican Workers and American Dreams: Immigration, Repatriation, and California Farm Labor, 1900–1939* (New Brunswick, N.J.: Rutgers University Press, 1994), 114–16.

2. This argument and those made over the next few pages are made in greater detail in my book, *The Fruits of Their Labor: Atlantic Coast Farmworkers and the Making of Migrant Poverty, 1870–1945* (Chapel Hill: University of North Carolina Press, 1997). See also Wayne D. Rasmussen, *A History of the Emergency Farm Labor Supply Program, 1943–1947*, Agricultural Monograph no. 13 (Washington, D.C.: U.S. Department of Agriculture, Bureau of Agricultural Economics, 1951).

3. The best recent book on the Bracero Program published in English is Kitty Calavita, *Inside the State: The Bracero Program, Immigration, and the INS* (New York: Routledge, 1992). See also Ernest Galarza's classics, *Merchants of Labor: The Mexican Bracero Story: An Account of the Managed Migration of Mexican Farmworkers in California, 1942–1960* (Charlotte, S.C.: McNally and Loftin, 1964) and *Spiders in the House and Workers in the Field* (Notre Dame, Ind.: University of Notre Dame Press, 1976).

4. For example, the Florida Fruit and Vegetable Association grew out of the Fruit and Vegetable Committee of the Florida Farm Bureau, which lobbied vigorously for foreign workers during the Second World War. When Congress granted Florida growers access to Caribbean workers in 1943, the "committee" became an association that could sign the international labor agreement and share imported workers. For an interesting discussion of the power of the sugar lobby, see Nancy Watzman, *The Politics of Sugar* (Washington, D.C.: Center for Responsive Politics, 1995).

5. On the tendency of guest workers to become permanent workers, with or without a state sanction, see Philip L. Martin, *Guestworker Programs: Lessons from Europe*, U.S. Department of Labor, Bureau of International Labor Affairs, Monograph no. 5 (Wash-

ington, D.C.: Government Printing Office, 1980). According to Richard Mines, Susan Gabbard, and Ann Steirman, "A Profile of U.S. Farmworkers: Demographics, Household Composition, Income, and Use of Services," U.S. Department of Labor, Office of the Assistant Secretary for Policy, unpublished report prepared for the Commission on Immigration Reform, April 1997 (in the author's possession), iii, some 70 percent of the agricultural workforce in 1997 was foreign-born.

6. Lawrence E. Will, *Swamp to Sugar Bowl: Pioneer Days in Belle Glade* (St. Petersburg, Fla.: Great Outdoors, n.d.), 189–93; C. Hahamovitch, *The Fruits of Their Labor*, 3–4, 113–37.

7. Memorandum, "The Impact of War and the Defense Program on Agriculture: Report No. II," transmitted by J. A. Fleming, chairman, Subcommittee of Interbureau Coordinating Committee, to the secretary of agriculture, February 17, 1941, cited in W. Rasmussen, *History of the Emergency Farm Labor Supply Program*, 14–15; report of the Interbureau Planning Committee on Farm Labor, "Review of the Farm Labor Situation in 1941," December 31, 1941, National Archives and Records Administration (hereafter cited as NARA), RG 16, Records of the Office of the Secretary of Agriculture, no. 17, General Correspondence of the Office of the Secretary, 1906–1970, subject: Employment, file: "Labor October 4 to" [1941?].

8. In 1941 average hourly wages were 31 cents in the eastern states from New Jersey to Maine. Wages in Delaware, Maryland, and Virginia averaged 22 cents an hour, and in the coastal states from North Carolina to Florida, wages were among the lowest in the nation at 12 cents an hour. Wages climbed slightly between October 1, 1942, and January 1, 1943, but farmworkers still made only 39 percent of what unskilled factory workers earned. See N. Gregory Silvermater's report to Wayne H. Darrow, director, Agricultural Labor Administration, March 20, 1943, NARA, RG 244, FSA correspondence, box 75, file 4-FLT-R36, labor estimates; "Farm Labor Notes," June 20, 1942, NARA, RG 16, general correspondence, employment, 1–4 Farm, May 14–July 15, 1942; C. Hahamovitch, *The Fruits of Their Labor*, 163–66.

9. C. Hahamovitch, *The Fruits of Their Labor*, 151–81.

10. Ibid. See also telegram to Secretary of Agriculture Claude R. Wickard from Mrs. William J. Krome, January 29, 1943, NARA, RG 224, Office of Labor, FSA correspondence, 1943–44, box 75, file 4-FLT-R57; James W. Vann, Vienna, Md., camp manager, monthly report, August 1942, NARA, RG 96, general correspondence, box 16, file RP-M-85-183, monthly reports.

11. W. Rasmussen, *History of the Emergency Farm Labor Supply Program*, 25–29, 200–201; K. Calavita, *Inside the State*, 8–25; Sidney Baldwin, *Poverty and Politics: The Rise and Decline of the Farm Security Administration* (Chapel Hill: University of North Carolina Press, 1968), 346–61.

12. Cindy Hahamovitch, "'Standing Idly By': 'Organized' Farmworkers in Florida during the Second World War," in *Southern Labor in Transition*, ed. Robert Zieger (Knoxville: University of Tennessee Press, 1997), 15–36; Edward, Duke of Windsor, governor of the Bahamas, to Oliver Stanley, secretary of state for the colonies, January 30, 1943, Public Record Office, London, Colonial Office Records (hereafter cited as PRO, CO), 967/126.

13. W. Rasmussen, *History of the Emergency Farm Labor Supply Program*, 42; C. Hahamovitch, *The Fruits of Their Labor*, 173–74; S. Baldwin, *Poverty and Politics*, 394.

14. PRO, CO 318, 448/10, Recruitment of Labor for U.S.

15. The Depression had caused world sugar prices to collapse, which resulted in falling wages on Jamaican plantations and dried up opportunities for some 10,000 Jamaican offshore workers in places like Panama and Cuba, who had been bringing home £125,000 in remittances every year. Ken Post, *Strike the Iron*, vol. 1 (Atlantic Highlands, N.J.: Humanities Press, 1981); Cedric O. J. Matthews, *Labour Policies in the West Indies* (Geneva, Switzerland: International Labour Office, 1952), 52–53, 116; Dawn Marshall, "A History of West Indian Migrations: Overseas Opportunities and 'Safety-Valve' Policies," in *The Caribbean Exodus*, ed. Barry B. Levine (New York: Praeger, 1987), 23–24; *Amsterdam News*, June 5, 1943, 13; Paul Blanshard, *Democracy and Empire in the Caribbean* (New York: Macmillan, 1947), 47, 91; Winston James, *Holding Aloft the Banner of Ethiopia: Caribbean Radicalism in Early Twentieth-Century America* (New York: Verso, 1998).

16. According to census data, in 1943, Jamaica's black population made up 78.1 percent of the population. All nonwhites together accounted for 96 percent of the total population. G. W. Roberts, *The Population of Jamaica* (London: Cambridge University Press, 1957), 64–65; P. Blanshard, *Democracy and Empire*, 79. On the Depression era labor rebellions, see O. Nigel Bollard, *On the March: Labour Rebellions in the British Caribbean, 1934–1939* (Kingston, Jamaica: Ian Randle, 1995) and Ken Post, *Arise Ye Starvelings: The Jamaican Labour Rebellion and Its Aftermath* (The Hague: Martinus Nijhoff, 1978). For a fascinating discussion of Jamaican politics during the war, see Trevor Munroe, *Politics of Constitutional Decolonization: Jamaica, 1944–1962* (reprint ed., Mona: Institute of Social and Economic Research, University of the West Indies, 1983). And for a discussion of changing British attitudes toward colonialism during and after the Second World War, see John Darwin, *Britain and Decolonisation: The Retreat from Empire in the Post-War World* (London: Macmillan, 1988), 3–68.

17. T. Munroe, *Politics of Constitutional Decolonization*, 25–26; P. Blanshard, *Democracy and Empire*, 96; PRO, CO 859, 46/16, 12251/1, Minutes of Meetings, 1943.

18. *Daily Gleaner*, April 8 and December 6, 1943; *Public Opinion*, April 14, 1944. United Fruit had long been recruiting Jamaicans for work on its Latin American plantations, so Zemurray was a sensible choice.

19. Governor of Jamaica to Mr. Beckett, March 26, 1943, PRO, CO 448/10, Recruitment of Labour for U.S.; *Public Opinion*, April 1 and 12, 1943.

20. Telegram from secretary of state for the colonies to Barbados, April 20, 1943, PRO, CO 859, 12261/1/43, Conditions of Employment and International Labour Conventions, West Indies; Anglo-American Caribbean Commission (hereafter cited as AACC) to secretary of state for the colonies, March 20, 1943, PRO, CO 318, 448/10, Recruitment of Labour for U.S.; *Daily Gleaner*, April 1, 1943.

21. Telegram from secretary of state for the colonies to Barbados, April 20, 1943, PRO, CO 859, 12261/1/43, Conditions of Employment and International Labour Conventions, West Indies, AACC to secretary of state for the colonies, March 20, 1943, PRO, CO 318, 448/10, Recruitment of labour for U. S.

22. *Daily Gleaner*, April 30 and May 5–6, 1943.

23. Ibid., May 5 and June 5, 1943; *Public Opinion*, September 25, 1943, 1; AACC to secretary of state for the colonies, May 22, 1943, PRO, CO 318/448/10.

24. PRO, CO 318, 448/10.

25. *Daily Gleaner*, May 29, June 4–7, 1943.

26. *Public Opinion*, September 25, 1943, 1; Sir A. Richard, Jamaica, to secretary of state for the colonies, June 29, 1943, PRO, CO 318, 448/11, Recruitment of Labour for U.S.; Anglo-American Caribbean Commission to secretary of state for the colonies, July 7, 1943, PRO, CO 318, 448/11, Recruitment of Labour for U.S.; *Chicago Bee*, July 11, 1943, 2; report to Mr. Middleton, July 1, 1944, PRO, CO 318/460/1.

27. The Labor Day celebration included a Jamaican-style dinner, during which public officials and members of New York's many West Indian civic organizations welcomed them to the area and the assembled guests sang both the American and British anthems. The dinner and the cricket match were broadcast on Jamaican radio stations. *Amsterdam News*, August 28, 1943, 4 and September 25, 1943, 4-A; *Daily Gleaner*, September 8, 1943, 11. The *Protestant Voice* story was reprinted in the *Daily Gleaner*, September 22, 1943, 4.

28. *Waterbury Republican*, June 27, 1943, 14.

29. *Daily Gleaner*, August 6 and 28, 1943.

30. Ibid., August 6 and September 8, 1943. For more comprehensive studies of West Indians' experience of American race relations, see among others Ira De A. Reid, *The Negro Immigrant* (New York: Columbia University Press, 1939); Lennox Raphael, "West Indians and Afro-Americans," *Freedomways* 4 (Summer 1964), 438–45; Roy S. Bryce-Laporte, "Black Immigrants: The Experience of Invisibility and Inequality," *Journal of Black Studies* 3, no. 1 (1972): 29–56; Philip Kasinitz, *Caribbean New York* (Ithaca, N.Y.: Cornell University Press, 1992); Milton Vickerman, *Crosscurrents: West Indian Immigrants and Race* (New York: Oxford University Press, 1999).

31. Life History 2, in *Looking Back: 11 Life Histories*, comp. Giles R. Wright (Trenton: New Jersey Historical Commission, Department of State, 1986), 18–24.

32. *Amsterdam News*, May 22, 1944 (clipping in NARA, RG 224, box 25, file: Publications 1-1 Negro Press); *Norfolk Journal and Guide*, July 17, 1943.

33. J. Harris, May 21, 1943, and Colonel Bruton, WFA to Taussig, AACC, undated, PRO, CO 318, 418/11, Recruitment of Labour for U.S; *Public Opinion*, May 17, 1943, 1.

34. *Daily Gleaner*, May 17 and 19, 1943.

35. Ibid.

36. *Public Opinion*, July 17, 1943; *Daily Gleaner*, September 22, 1943, 4.

37. *Daily Gleaner*, September 21 and 29, 1943.

38. Emphasis mine. Reprinted in the *Daily Gleaner*, October 4, 1943.

39. *Amsterdam News*, November 6, 1943, 7-B; *Pittsburgh Courier*, October 30, 1943.

40. *Daily Gleaner*, November 6, 1943, 15; *Palm Beach Post*, October 9 and 15–16, 1943, 12; Herbert G. McDonald [sic] to labour adviser, Labour Department, Kingston, Jamaica, Office of Censorship, U.S.A., October 21, 1943, PRO, CO 318/460/1.

41. PRO, CO 318, 460/3; Sir J. Huggins (Governor of Jamaica) to secretary of state for

the colonies, December 4, 1943, PRO, CO 318, 448/11; excerpt of letter from Herbert G. MacDonald to labour adviser, Labour Department, Kingston, Jamaica, Office of Censorship, U.S.A., PRO, CO 318/460/1.

42. *Public Opinion*, June 20, 1944, 1.

43. Report of Herbert MacDonald for December 1944, PRO, CO 318, 460/2.

44. August 28, 1945, clipping in PRO, CO 318, 460/2.

45. Depositions, September 10, 1945, PRO, CO 318, 460/2; chief liaison's report for September 1945, PRO, CO 318, 460/2.

46. PRO, CO 318, 460/1.

47. *Washington Bee*, July 22, 1944, 2.

48. Extract of letter from Edon (?) to Hon. and Rev. Dr. P. G. Veitch, J. P., Legislative Council, Kingston, Jamaica, quoted by Imperial Censorship, Jamaica, July 10, 1944; chief liaison's report for month ending May 31, 1945, June 2, 1945, PRO, CO 318, 460/1 and 2.

49. *Daily Gleaner*, August 28, 1944.

50. The remaining five seats went to independents. *Public Opinion*, December 16, 1944; Munroe, *Politics of Constitutional Decolonisation*, 42.

51. Governor (Sir) Grattan Busche to the Colonial Office, June 29 and July 12, 1943, and decoded telegram from AACC to secretary of state for the colonies, March 11, 1944, PRO, CO 318, 448/10, Recruitment of Labor for U.S.; Sir A. Grimble, Windward Islands, to secretary of state for the colonies, August 30, 1944, PRO, CO 318, 448/11; telegram from AACC to secretary of state for the colonies, March 22, 1945, PRO, CO 318, 460/2.

52. K. A. Butler, acting director of labor, to Nathan Koenig, executive secretary to the secretary of agriculture, 1/24/46, NARA, RG 224, General Correspondence 1946, box 107, POWs.

53. The *Norfolk Journal and Guide* (October 5, 1946) protested the continuation of the program, arguing that farm operators and the federal government were defeating any New Deal for agricultural workers by "continuing a war-inspired importation of foreign laborers when the conditions which made that imperative no longer exist." Protests such as this one were few, and they went unheeded.

54. Annual Report of Chief Liaison, covering April 1, 1945 to March 31, 1946, PRO, CO 318, 460/3.

55. Peter Kramer, *The Offshores: A Study of Foreign Farm Labor in Florida* (St. Petersburg, Fla.: Community Action Fund, 1966), 39. For more on agricultural guest workers in Florida since the Second World War, see Alex Wilkinson, *Big Sugar: Seasons in the Cane Fields of Florida* (New York: Knopf, 1989); Josh DeWind, Tom Seidl, and Janet Shenk, "Caribbean Migration: Contract Labor in U.S. Agriculture," *NACLA Report on the Americas* 2, no. 8 (November/December 1977): 4–37; David Griffith, "Peasants in Reserve: Temporary West Indian Labor in the U.S. Farm Labor Market," *International Migration Review* 20, no. 4 (1986): 875–98; Charles H. Wood and Terry L. McCoy, "Migration, Remittances, and Development: A Study of Caribbean Cane Cutters in Florida," *International Migration Review* 19, no. 2 (1985): 251–77.

9

"I Dreamed I Went to Work"

Expanding Southern Unionism in the Mid-Twentieth-Century
Lingerie Industry

MELANIE SHELL-WEISS

As a magnet for migrants from across the hemisphere, Florida is neither
typically "southern" nor "northern." It is a place where both meet. Florida
provides an ideal framework for exploring how class and trade-based identities were forged and mobilized across lines of state and nation in an early
period of deindustrialization. This chapter focuses on the efforts of the
International Ladies' Garment Workers' Union (ILGWU) to forge a unified labor movement among lingerie workers in Florida and Puerto Rico
between 1949 and 1969. As such, it provides a prelude to the types of new
labor internationalism that have developed over the past few decades across
the Southern Hemisphere.[1]

For manufacturers, Puerto Rico was a kind of testing ground. There they
explored the challenges of offshore production and a non-English-speaking
workforce. Labor leaders viewed the island in much the same way. Florida
and Puerto Rico served as a kind of proving ground and a place where labor organizers tested new approaches and trained new Spanish-speaking
leaders, and where workers expanded the ideology of "American" labor to
encompass both the United States and her southern neighbors.

In the wake of the Spanish-American War, Congress assumed ultimate
power in making laws and shaping trade relations affecting the people of
Puerto Rico. Puerto Ricans were made U.S. citizens with the passage of the
Jones-Shafroth Act in 1917. They were free to move between the island and
mainland. But in other respects, Puerto Ricans were treated as a foreign
people. As the U.S. Supreme Court ruled in a series of decisions on trade
restrictions, Puerto Rico "belongs to but is not part of" the United States.[2]
Neither wholly foreign nor domestic, Puerto Ricans were denied minimum

wage protections, full political representation in the federal government, and sovereign power on the island.

This in-between status changed little over the mid-twentieth century, despite efforts by Puerto Rican nationalists to become a wholly independent nation-state. On July 3, 1950, Congress passed Public Law 600, which created the Commonwealth of Puerto Rico and allowed the nation to establish its own constitutional government. But as the wording of the law itself made clear, "the measure would not change Puerto Rico's fundamental political, social, and economic relationship to the United States."[3] As such, Puerto Rico proved a stepping-stone on the path to globalization. Viewed through the lens of lingerie manufacturing, the challenges, questions, and costs raised by these new production methods and a diversifying labor force are thrown into stark relief.

The Maidenform Empire

In 1949, Maidenform launched a new advertising campaign targeted at the "modern" woman.[4] Using the tagline, "I dreamed . . ." one particularly long-running example featured a woman in a pink bouclé skirt and high heels, perched on the edge of her desk with her head thrown back, phone held to one ear, pencil tucked behind the other. She wore nothing above the waist, except for a brassiere. The heading read, "I dreamed I went to work in only my Maidenform bra" (see figure 9.1). The full-page, color advertisements were printed in *Vogue, Harper's Bazaar, Ladies Home Journal, Mc-Call's, Good Housekeeping*, and *Parents' Magazine*, to name just a few. They greeted visitors to New York City's Carnegie Hall and the Metropolitan Opera, riders on Fifth Avenue buses, and subscribers to publications like the *American Journal of Nursing* and the *American Journal of Obstetrics and Gynecology*. Readers of local newspapers in Akron, Detroit, Buffalo, Houston, Los Angeles, and Miami—to name just a few—all were entreated to gaze upon the "circles that uplift and support, spokes that discreetly emphasize your curves" for "pointed roundness of bosom contour." By 1950, there were few places women—or men—could go where they could avoid the new Maidenform campaign. Published in English, Spanish, Dutch, and French, advertisements published in the full swath of Caribbean nations, South America, Europe, Africa, and Asia ensured that women around the globe were equally aware of Maidenform's new product.[5]

Initially the campaign was slow to take off. Some criticized the ads for being too explicit. But they became enormously popular. Maidenform market

CHANSONETTE* with famous 'circular-spoke' stitching

Notice two patterns of stitching on the cups of this bra? Circles that uplift and support, spokes that discreetly emphasize your curves. This fine detailing shapes your figure naturally—keeps the bra shapely, even after machine-washing. The triangular cut-out between the cups gives you extra "breathing room" as the lower elastic insert expands. In white or black: A, B, C cups. **2.00**

Other styles: Broadcloth: Cotton, Dacron® Polyester " 2.50; Lace, 3.50; with all-elastic back, 3.00; Contour, 3.00; Full-length, 3.50.

*REG. U.S. PAT. OFF. ©1964 BY **Maidenform, Inc.**, makers of bras, girdles, swimwear, and active sportswear.

Figure 9.1. "I dreamed I went to work in my Maidenform bra. . . ," c. 1964. Full color print, orig. 10 × 13. Used by permission of the Smithsonian National Museum of American History.

analyses showed a sales increase of more than 200 percent in stores across the United States and Latin America by the second year of the campaign. The company reprinted the ads for more than twenty years, making it one of the best known advertising slogans in American history and Maidenform the largest producer of lingerie in the world.[6]

By playing to the fantastic, the ads also lightened what was really a structural marvel. As company founder and owner Ida Rosenthal was quick to point out, "A brassiere is a matter of design but also of engineering."[7] Known colloquially as the "bullet" or "torpedo" bra, Maidenform's "Chansonette" was the most rigidly structured undergarment since the Victorian corset. Encasing each breast in a set of spokes, the boning for each cup was held together with rows of reinforced, concentric lock stitching. Elastic and nylon bands were affixed to the cones, holding them together and forming the straps that circled the wearer's shoulders and torso. The bra was often cloaked in layers of silk, satin, or lace. Some were further enhanced with additions of padding designed to enhance a woman's "natural" figure. The result was revolutionary in two senses: it redefined the idealized female form and produced the thoroughly artificial breast shape associated with Hollywood starlets of the period like Lana Turner, Jane Russell, and Marilyn Monroe.[8] Maidenform's creation, and others like it, also ushered in the most labor-intensive garment to be manufactured since the advent of ready-made clothing.

Because of their design, the brassieres were potentially very expensive to produce. The simplest brassiere produced by Maidenform had at least twenty separate pieces, several of them no bigger than a quarter. (See figure 9.2.) Some models had as many as fifty pieces. The design was also very unforgiving to the seamstress. A discrepancy in as few as two or three stitches could affect the fit of the entire bra, making for an unhappy customer and lost business. Making these bras required a tremendous amount of skill, dexterity, and care. Even in an era of postwar prosperity, the modern, middle-class woman who was the target of Maidenform's "I Dream" campaign would only pay so much for her lingerie. Getting the "Chansonette" into every home in the Americas, then, required keeping the cost of manufacturing down while still employing a workforce skilled enough to handle its construction demands.[9]

They found this workforce below the Mason-Dixon Line. By 1950, Maidenform had opened three new plants in Clarksburg, Huntington, and Princeton, West Virginia. "Because the mountainous areas of Virginia and West Virginia had an abundance of intelligent, easily trained, young women eager

March 7, 1944.

W. ROSENTHAL

2,343,476

BRASSIERE

Filed Feb. 25, 1939

2 Sheets—Sheet 1

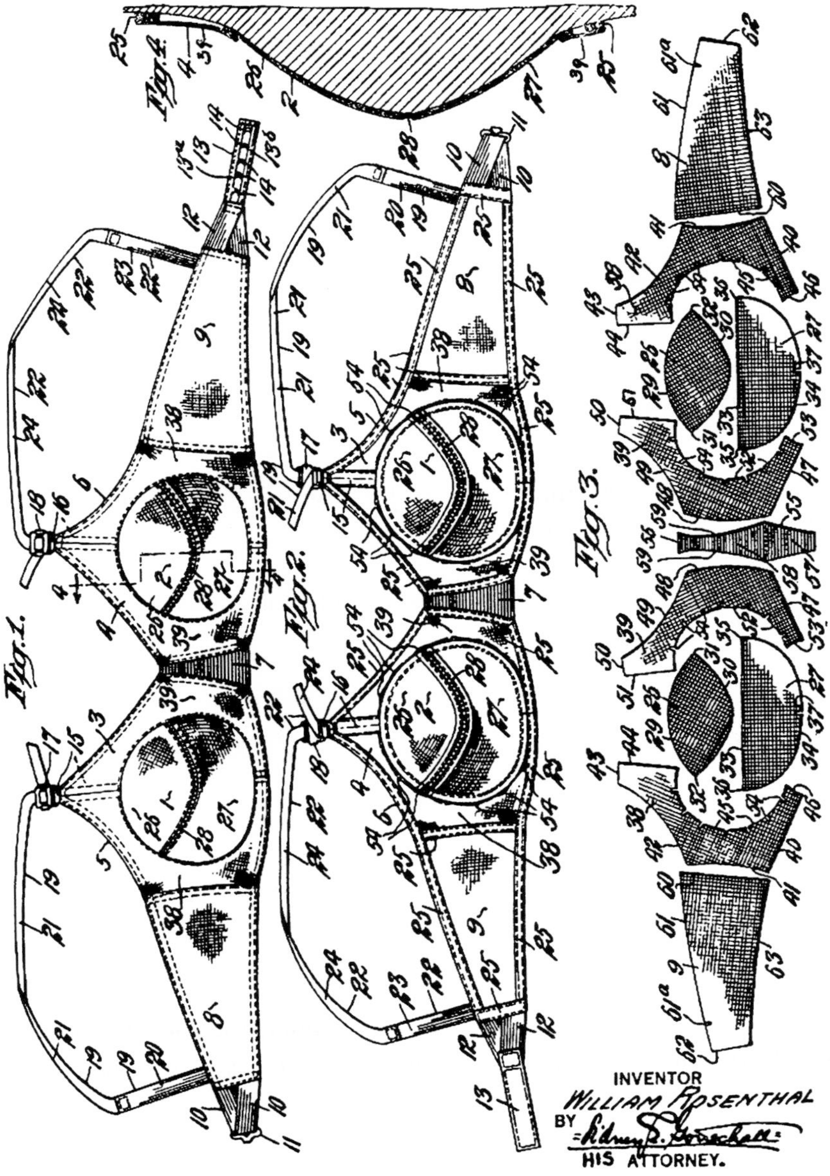

INVENTOR
WILLIAM ROSENTHAL
BY
HIS ATTORNEY.

Figure 9.2. Design Patent, William Rosenthal, "Brassiere," #2,343,47, filed Feb. 25, 1939. Image provided by the United States Patent Office.

for employment, the search narrowed to this part of the country," Maidenform executives explained in a press release, noting that the company
only hired "the highest type of woman available."[10] Other leading brassiere
manufacturers followed suit. Lovable, Exquisite Form, Playtex, Peter Pan,
and Contessa all moved significant portions of their cutting and assembly operations to the Upper South and so-called Sunbelt where lower rates
of hourly pay, piece rates, and transportation costs made their work more
profitable and willing workers were easy to find.[11]

Tax incentives and recruitment on the part of local government further
accelerated this trend, enticing owners farther south, first on the mainland
United States and then beyond. As one industry observer for the *Congress
Weekly* noted in 1954:

> In the days when the textile plants were moving South there was no
> attempt to disguise the major inducement: "Bring your plant down
> South. We have thousands of white, native-born Anglo-Saxon work-
> ers who give a full day's work for a day's pay." Today the approach is
> not so crude. The Southern executive-salesmen who are now bringing
> the garment factories to the South stress the accessibility to transpor-
> tation and water power; the wonderful year-round climate, the four-
> hour air service to New York or Miami, and the proximity to sources
> of the raw materials. . . . And of course, in some states there are more
> tangible concessions, most important of which is the newly enacted
> labor legislation against the closed shop.[12]

While regions bordering the Piedmont, which had been a major center for
textile production since the 1920s, were the first to develop, improved transportation networks soon lessened the importance of geographical proximity and made wages alone even more important. Florida was one of the
sixteen states that passed "right to work" legislation in the early 1950s. The
possibility that the garment trades would create year-round jobs to supplement Florida's seasonal tourist industry proved a powerful incentive.[13] As
communities with significant numbers of Hispanic and Asian immigrants,
cities like Miami and Los Angeles also promised less explosive race relations than elsewhere in the U.S. South. Miami's Chamber of Commerce, for
example, dubbed the city "the playground of nations," claiming that unlike
other U.S. cities, Miami had "practically no poverty, slums, or tenements."[14]
This was patently untrue. But combined with the promise of tax breaks,
cheap and plentiful labor, and a relatively low cost of living, the campaign
was quite successful. By 1951, Miami had more than 251 apparel manufac-

turers, up from less than 10 a decade earlier. Garment manufacturing also became the city's third largest employer.[15]

Even greater financial advantages for corporations were offered by Puerto Rico. Under the island's industrialization campaign, *Operación Manos a la Obra* (Operation Bootstrap), Puerto Rican governor Luis Muñoz Marín enticed manufacturers with promises of tax exemptions for new industries, subsidized factory space, and help with recruitment and training from local government.[16] Island employers were also not subject to the same minimum wage laws as on the mainland. Some companies reported paying as little as 20 cents an hour to skilled seamstresses, compared with the 50 cents or more paid to mainland workers.[17] For labor-intensive industries like brassiere manufacturing, this was an irresistible combination. In 1952, Maidenform added several Puerto Rican plants to its growing roster in Poncé and Mayaguez. Within a few years they opened additional facilities in Juana Díaz, Añasco, and Rincón. To escape accusations of violating its mainland union contracts, and also to reap the benefits of Puerto Rico's tax-exempt status, their offshore operations were separately incorporated. Named Beatrice Needlecraft and Catherine Needlecraft, for Ida and William Rosenthal's daughters, these island branches were family owned just like the rest of the company's operations. Through later acquisitions, they soon operated under the names Puerto Rico Needle Craft, Wilida, May Lingerie, and Juana Díaz Company, Inc.[18]

Hundreds of garment manufacturers moved their operations out of the Northeast, permanently transforming the topography of the American industry. Whereas just a decade earlier New York had been the unequivocal heart of the American garment trade, by 1950 Los Angeles and Miami emerged as new centers for fashion and design and the second and third largest garment-producing cities on the mainland.[19] Puerto Rico was hailed as "the miracle of the Caribbean," a place where "one century of development" had been "achieved in a decade."[20]

International Labor Leadership: Robert Gladnick and the ILGWU

The increasing use of offshore producers worried union officials who were already struggling to secure pay scales and work hours for southern laborers that were comparable to those in the Northeast. Managers at large companies like Maidenform were quick to point out that manufacturers who sent work abroad were "cutting the floor from under the brassiere industry" because they could pay workers a fraction of what they paid on the mainland.[21] If they were going to be able to bring a new generation of lingerie workers and manufacturers into the fold, union leaders knew that their efforts would have to focus on local and international policies alike.

Robert Gladnick emerged as a particular visionary. Like the earlier generation of ILGWU leaders, he was an "American by choice."[22] Born in Eastern Europe, Gladnick emigrated to the United States on his own while still in his late teens. He lived first in New York where his political interests led him to develop close friendships with members of the Communist Party. He became interested in labor organizing. In the 1930s he moved west, accompanied by several friends, to help organize Mexican and Japanese agricultural workers in Washington and Oregon. He then moved to Texas, where he participated in similar campaigns in the state's oil fields. It was an experience that proved critical in that it impressed upon him the particular challenges facing a highly mobile workforce. Gladnick applied these skills to the Seaman's strikes of 1936 and co-founded the National Maritime Union. In 1937, he joined the International Brigade and fought in the Spanish Civil War. In Spain, he learned to speak Spanish fluently, and he attributed that period to his political conversion as well. Gladnick renounced Communism altogether, becoming well known among his fellow soldiers for his outspoken, anti-Communist views, and in 1940, one year before the United States formally entered World War II, Gladnick enlisted in the Canadian army and served until 1946 in Italy, France, Holland, and Germany. This was a battle he felt compelled to fight both as a Jew and as a committed opponent to the pact signed between Nazi Germany and the Soviet Union. After the war, Gladnick returned to the United States and joined the staff of the ILGWU Upper South Department, where he allied himself closely with other avowed anti-Communists like David Dubinsky, who predominated across the union's leadership.[23]

Organizing the workers in Maidenform's West Virginia operations was among Gladnick's first major efforts, and he used his proximity to Washington, D.C., to try to enlist congressional support for wage regulations both offshore and on the mainland. But he quickly became convinced that the "most important" work lay elsewhere if the industry was really to be brought under control.[24] Whereas a generation earlier, seamstresses cursed in Yiddish, Italian, and English at broken needles and tangled bobbins, by 1950 Spanish was fast becoming the lingua franca of industry workers. Puerto Rican and Cuban women, drawn by the promise of higher wages, soon filled more and more of the seats at sewing tables in these plants. By some estimates, more than 40,000 Puerto Ricans relocated to the mainland United

States between 1945 and 1953.[25] While Washington, D.C., held a particular appeal for Gladnick, who wanted to have an active hand in policymaking, he grew increasingly convinced that workers' themselves must be engaged if these efforts were to have long-term results.

Dubinsky shared this conviction, at least in part. As ILGWU president, he scrambled to find enough Spanish-speaking organizers and managers to meet workers' needs. "Runaway" shops, companies that broke their contracts with the union by closing their doors rather than negotiating with workers and relocated south or west, remained one of their greatest challenges. As late as 1950, even in cities like Miami and Los Angeles where the garment industry employed 20 percent of the cities' workers and was more than 40 percent Spanish-speaking, many organizers and managers could not speak directly with the workers.[26] The national origins of these various Hispanic workers created challenges as well. In Los Angeles, virtually all the city's Latina garment workers were Mexican or Mexican-American. In Miami, Puerto Ricans filled the bulk of the city's garment industry jobs, but they were soon joined by a growing number of Cubans and Cuban-Americans, reflecting the women who filled many of these jobs on the shop floors of New York and New Jersey. As more workers began moving to Miami directly from the islands, rather than coming by way of the North, language became a bigger and bigger issue. On numerous occasions Miami's joint locals were forced to cancel meetings because no one was there to translate, and none of the local managers could speak enough Spanish.[27] Citizenship also divided workers, with Puerto Ricans claiming entitlement to preferences in hiring on the basis of their American citizenship, a view not necessarily shared by either employers or Cuban workers.

Union organizers faced similar problems in Puerto Rico. As industrial development increased, the American Federation of Labor (AFL), Puerto Rican Nationalists, and native labor organizations started reaching out to the island's needleworkers. Native organizations like the Boríquan Agricultural Union were among the first to begin organizing efforts at Maidenform's plants and to use a specifically nationalist platform in hopes of mobilizing workers across trade lines. "We have to inform you that the . . . factory manager, a foreigner . . . has given out a leaflet to try to confuse you because it is not convenient to him for you to organize," one appeal to Maidenform's Poncé workers read. "Remember this, fellow workers, to vote against the Union is equivalent to betraying yourself, and more so, to betraying your own family."[28] While these impassioned pleas did much to mobilize emotions across the plants, "yanquí" leaders in the AFL and industry-specific unions like the ILGWU brought the most bureaucratic know-how.[29] Yet they were hampered by an inability to speak the language or an understanding of local cultural practices. In 1953, Dubinsky moved Gladnick out of the Upper South Department and instructed him to apply his energies to the needleworkers in Puerto Rico and Miami.

As the union organizer in Maidenform's West Virginia plants, Gladnick was well known to the Rosenthals and had always enjoyed an "open and cordial relationship" with them.[30] Maidenform went to even greater lengths than other corporations in maintaining good ties with its union representatives, including sending an annual gift of brassieres to all members of the ILGWU's Upper South Division staff and their spouses each Christmas. In what was often a spirited and fun-loving exchange between union and owner, the ILGWU office staff composed poems to Ellis Rosenthal, son of the company's founder and Maidenform assistant general manager, which they sent him along with their sizes. One example from 1952 read:

> There's a Maidenform bra for every type of figur'
> We have them all—small, large, and BIGGER!
> Our cups runneth over from A's until Z's
> We challenge your wares to fill all of theeze [sic].[31]

The outright hostility of these same owners to attempts to unionize their Puerto Rican shops surely came as a surprise.

In April 1953, Beatrice Needlecraft fired one of its Poncé employees, Julia Angleró de Colón. The company claimed she had not met production quotas, but Colón charged that she was fired for trying to organize workers in the plant. She took her case to the National Labor Relations Board (NLRB), which served notice to the company of their investigation in July.[32] Representatives from the AFL and Independent Puerto Rican Needleworkers' Union began making regular appearances at Beatrice and other lingerie manufacturers. By the time Gladnick received his directive from the ILGWU, owners and managers of the island shops had already appealed to the Insular Government for protection and were threatening to relocate their operations farther afield, to the Philippines and Japan, if the unions persisted or met with too much success.[33]

Gladnick arrived in mid-November with little instruction from Dubinsky other than that he was to make a survey of wages and working conditions among the island's 8,000 needleworkers in preparation for a major organizing campaign. One of his first stops was at Beatrice Needlecraft. Although Gladnick was quick to reassure the plant managers that "Dubinsky had told him specifically to leave Maidenform alone," his visit unnerved the management on both the island and the mainland.[34] Reports on Gladnick's actions—how many copies of *Justice*, the ILGWU's newspaper, were distributed at neighboring plants, who talked to him, even where he ate his lunch—were sent to Ellis Rosenthal every few days.[35] Yet Gladnick persisted. Despite an increasing volume and variety of intimidation techniques geared to discourage employees from unionizing in Maidenform and kindred plants, more than twenty shops had signed contracts with ILGWU Local 600 within one year's time. Working in partnership with the AFL and Independent Needle Workers, organized labor also won several important legal victories including reducing the workweek from 40+ hours to 37.5 hours and raising the minimum wage.[36] Although the ILGWU still hoped to bring wages and hours fully in line with the mainland, the gains were an important victory won in a remarkably short time.

Maidenform's efforts to resist unionizing among her Puerto Rican employees, however, were successful. In May 1954, the NLRB found in favor of Beatrice Needlecraft, supporting the management's contention that their employees did not want a union in any of their Puerto Rican shops.[37] Kurt Metzger celebrated the victory from New Jersey with a gift of champagne and a hefty dose of irony, sent air express from Beatrice's lawyer and plant manager in San Juan. "[I'm] paying [this] bet with pleasure," company attorney Hernán Franco wrote to Ellis Rosenthal. "Do you charm all ladies thus?"[38]

Building a Joint Organizing Campaign in Florida and Puerto Rico

In June, Gladnick joined his wife and two young sons in Miami and began actively working with ILGWU international organizer Abraham Plotkin and Miami Joint Council manager Samuel Macy on a major organizing campaign in the city.[39] At first, they put into motion what, by then, was employed as a fairly tried-and-true formula by the ILGWU. Local organizers began meeting with shop owners and talking with employees about wages and working conditions. They would distribute literature, including membership cards, and hold classes and social events designed to appeal to local workers. In Puerto Rico, these included dances, courses in home decorating, movies, and theater productions. In Miami, a city well known for its anti-Communist fervor, union organizers focused on English-language training and citizenship classes. "Language barriers between Spanish-speaking women in Miami's garment industries and employers were being erased today with the inauguration of classes in English for workers," boasted the *Miami Daily News*, a paper that was usually sharply critical of labor unions. "More than thirty women from Cuba, Puerto Rico, and Ecuador turned up last night for their first lesson."[40] Although this was a far cry from the nearly 1,200 Spanish-speaking women who were on the Miami locals' membership rolls, many of whom were recent immigrants and therefore unlikely to speak much English, Gladnick took an optimistic view. "It was heartening to see that many," he told a writer for *Justice*. "It follows the original work of the union in 1900—when it taught English and citizenship to the immigrants in New York and Chicago."[41] After the initial assessment, President Dubinsky made a high-profile trip to the area where he talked with the local press, promised workers higher wages and shorter working hours, and threatened strikes and work stoppages in plants where owners undermined their activities.

But in Miami, these methods met with limited success. In part, organizers grappled with personality conflicts and broken promises from past campaigns. Samuel Macy, who had managed the Miami locals since the late 1940s, was alternately described as a "colorful rebel" who was never a "sheep" to union politics or Communists by those who loved him, and an obstinate, incompetent by those who did not. The union was headquartered in a building whose owner specifically prohibited interracial meetings. They held their annual picnic and other union events in "whites only" venues. The language barrier remained a constant obstacle.[42]

Gladnick broke important ground. As in Puerto Rico, he began by making a series of home visits to workers in Miami's developing Hispanic neighborhoods like Wynwood, and a new area southwest of the city's downtown that later became dubbed "Little Havana." He talked with women workers and their families. He ate dinner and drank coffee with them. And he gradually built up trust and a personal relationship with community leaders in the Puerto Rican Democratic Organization and local social clubs. He also brought on additional Spanish-speaking organizers, both of whom had ties to other trade unions in Miami. By mobilizing seamstresses along with their spouses who worked in carpentry or transportation, Gladnick hoped to make even greater gains across the Miami community and to begin to build a labor movement united across trade, sex, and geography.[43]

Gladnick also drew on his business connections and social networks developed over the past year in Puerto Rico to address issues of concern to workers on the island and the mainland, and emphasized the connections between the two. One of the most dramatic cases the union dealt with over this period concerned the Caribe Employment Agency. Owned and operated by a U.S. citizen named William Campbell, the agency's main office was located in Florida and used newspaper and radio advertisements, run in small island towns and rural communities, to recruit Puerto Ricans to work in a range of Florida agricultural and clothing industry jobs. In exchange for the promise of a job and passage to the mainland, men and women recruited by the agency "signed their lives away," as one investigator later observed. Women recruited to work in Miami's garment factories were locked in a hotel room and escorted to work by armed men. They were not allowed to leave for any reason, and they were frequently used by employers as strikebreakers or to staff night shifts at times when production needs peaked. Men who worked in the state's tomato and citrus fields suffered physical abuse and equally demeaning conditions. Because the employment agency was not physically located in Puerto Rico and they avoided the more carefully controlled steamship lines in favor of airlines or privately chartered flights, Caribe managed to avoid prosecution by the Commonwealth of Puerto Rico. Gladnick was one of the first people contacted by Puerto Rican Department of Labor commissioner Fernando Sierra Berdecia. Together with Abraham Plotkin, members of Miami's ILGWU physically rescued several women from a Miami hotel and ultimately got the agency shut down and the owners prosecuted under both state and federal statutes.[44]

In Miami, Puerto Ricans also faced a host of negative stereotypes from native-born workers and owners. The press frequently portrayed Puerto Rico as a "U.S. poorhouse." Some native-born residents complained that all Puerto Ricans seemed to do was "congregate in groups," "claim not to understand English," and "make obscene remarks at women." These negative perceptions often had dire results. Miami police chief Walter Headley was extremely vocal when it came to his local distrust of Puerto Ricans across the community. As he told the *Miami Herald* in 1957, Puerto Ricans represented "one of the greatest crime threats" to the city." "Crimes of violence recorded for Puerto Ricans are greatly out of proportion to their numbers," he claimed.[45] Despite contradictory reports from juvenile authorities and the Florida State Attorney's office documenting that crimes involving Puerto Ricans were actually much less frequent than for the state's English-speaking population, police harassment of Puerto Ricans in Miami intensified through the 1950s. Those crimes that were committed by Puerto Ricans were largely related to subsistence: stealing inexpensive articles of clothing, basic food staples, and small amounts of cash.

In August 1958, Eladio Reíces, a window washer and father of two, was talking with several friends on the front lawn of his Wynwood home when police pulled up, arrested him and his friends, and took them to jail. "We weren't doing anything but standing around," he told the *Miami Herald*. "That's the way we pass the time back home."[46] The friends collected enough money to hire a Puerto Rican lawyer. Their case was dismissed, and the men were allowed to go free. But confrontations with police did not always end so well. One Sunday evening in April 1960, Margaro Capeles was asleep in his home with three of his children and his newborn baby. His eldest son, Victor, was 19 and worked as a dishwasher at a coffee shop on Miami Beach. As Victor was walking home from his bus stop, two policemen pulled up alongside and began to follow him. Victor was frightened and began to run. When he reached the front door of his home, the officers caught him by the neck and began choking him. Margaro heard the struggle outside and opened his front door. There he saw two men in dark raincoats beating his son. The men were not wearing hats and had no distinguishable markings on their clothing that would identify them as being police officers. Nor did the officers identify themselves when Capeles tried to stop them. Margaro began calling for help and told his 24-year-old daughter, Catalina, to bring him his pants. As he went to get dressed, one of the officers followed Margaro inside and began to beat him and his daughter, dragging them back outside. It was then that Capeles noticed the police car. "I thought the police had just arrived and were coming to help us with these crooks," he recalled. The entire family was arrested. Although they were released the next day, the police refused to apologize and blamed the incident on Victor for "running off" in the first place. "The police have been working hard to keep down crime in the Latin Area," one supervising officer reported. "Sometimes we round up as many as 150 and bring them in."[47] The Capeles family had been living in Miami for over ten years without prior incident.

To counter these negative images and growing hostility toward Hispanics, Gladnick became an outspoken advocate for Latin workers in the local press and community. He was quick to point out that Puerto Ricans "do not lend themselves easily to strike-breaking," and he spoke often about organizing efforts under way on the island.[48] To make his point, Gladnick posed frequently for photos with Hispanic strikers. He and Plotkin also moved Miami's ILGWU headquarters to a location where workers of all races and ethnicities would be welcomed.

Perhaps most remarkable, however, Gladnick negotiated a new model within the ILGWU by alternately managing locals in two separate locations, one offshore and one onshore, and traveling frequently between the two.

From 1953 until 1966, Gladnick divided his time between Florida and Puerto Rican locals, serving as full-time manager of Puerto Rico's Local 600 from 1954 to 1957 and again from 1964 to 1966. The rest of that time, Gladnick managed Miami's Joint Locals 415 and 339. Although this approach met with some resentment from a few native-born members of the mainland local who questioned Gladnick's commitment to them, his approach was generally well received, particularly by Hispanic workers.[49]

This process also allowed Gladnick to deal directly with the challenges of highly mobile capital and a highly mobile workforce. When Florida manufacturers like Joe Feibenbaum of Miami, for example, looked to send specialized embroidery to a shop in San Juan, Gladnick intervened and worked with the Florida ILGWU office to ensure that the type of work he required could be found locally.[50] The union also was better able to intervene in cases of "runaway" shops like Atlantic City Knitting Company, which made underwear, swimsuits, and sportswear. After refusing to pay dues to the Jersey-Philadelphia Joint Board, the company opened up two new plants in South Florida and Puerto Rico, but was quickly chastened by the union, which managed to bring a successful case before the NLRB.[51]

Gladnick's working model was not just about control. Bringing community leaders up through the ranks and integrating workers' own identities, as women, as mothers, and as Latinas, into union drives proved a particular strength. The Miami and Puerto Rican locals collaborated on developing new education and training programs that were less centralized and more community based than earlier ILGWU efforts. As Southeast Regional Director E. T. Kehrer noted in a 1958 letter to President Dubinsky, "My impression is that the more community type approach being used in Puerto Rico would necessarily change a good deal of the approach being used in our own institute."[52] Some of these innovations included greater emphasis on ways that families could better manage their money and how to get the most out of their dollars for food, transportation, house-hunting, medical costs, and even clothing. Workers were encouraged, for example, to employ the same techniques many used in the workplace when selecting their own garments. "Look for reinforcements at points of special stress. . . . [C]heck the weave. . . . Faulty tailoring of [a] suit can result in rippling of lapel edges, seams and coat edges," guidelines distributed at the training institutes reminded workers.[53] Although little information about these efforts has been preserved, Gladnick also worked with the Department of Parks and Recreation in Puerto Rico to establish a workers' theater program, similar to that run by mainland labor colleges in the New Deal era and by anarchists and labor organizers in Cuba and Tampa in the 1920s. Their plays often blended themes of Puerto Rican independence and strength with challenges faced by the working classes.[54] His programs to improve health care for Puerto Rican workers through mobile clinics and partnerships with local caregivers were implemented, in part, in Miami and in Florida. Most of this work focused on care for workers' dependents, both children and the elderly, treating on-the-job injuries and muscular-skeletal stresses, and respiratory ailments. There is no evidence that suggests these clinics were involved in sterilization, although whether or not they would provide contraception to workers who requested it was the subject of some controversy.[55]

The union also played a critical role in labor recruitment. Locals helped to find positions for workers who had lost their jobs because of strikes or retribution by plant owners, as well as assisting those who wanted to move. Workers who migrated to Florida from Puerto Rico often sought employment by contacting the local union office. As skilled seamstresses were almost always in demand, this became a service many union shops relied on to keep their plants at full production. Gladnick's network of personal contacts also helped to facilitate union work in both locations. Organizers like Victoria Iziquerry were among those with whom Gladnick worked in both locations. Others like Emília Rodríguez Maisonet cut their political teeth under Gladnick's management in Puerto Rico, then went on to work as organizers in New York City or elsewhere on the mainland. Employees from union plants in Puerto Rico were also found working in kindred plants on the mainland through the 1960s. Again, Gladnick's role was critical. As the president of Puerto Rican Local 600 lamented after Gladnick returned to manage Miami's locals full time, "It is now that we really know how valuable Mr. Gladnick was to Local 600, and how the members miss him. And we ask ourselves why he was taken away."[56] Gladnick was replaced by a manager who was unable to speak Spanish and had to rely on a translator.

Cross-Ethnic Unionizing

In 1959, the Cuban Revolution transformed the work of labor organizers in Florida's garment industries. Although Miami's newspapers still referred to Puerto Ricans as the city's "fastest growing Latin American group," the number of Cubans soon dwarfed all other newcomers. Between January 1, 1959, and October 22, 1962, an estimated 248,070 Cubans entered the United States. Most chose to stay in South Florida and Miami. The Cuban Refugee Program of the U.S. Federal Division of Health, Education and Welfare worked closely with a range of ethnic and community organizations already in Miami to address the immediate needs of these new arrivals. Locating jobs was a top priority. Under U.S. immigration law, Cuban refugees were classified as "parolees," an ambiguous legal standing that granted them temporary residency status but limited their ability to enter many long-term or professional job fields.[57] Licensing requirements and new arrivals' inability to speak English further complicated the ability of many to enter the same types of middle-class and professional jobs they had left in Cuba. Miami's garment employers eagerly stepped in to offer training and work to Cuban migrants in need. As one middle-class Cuban woman who found a job in Miami's garment industry remarked, "Who could have imagined that those fine stitches I learned as a girl in convent school would become the bread and butter for my family?" As in Puerto Rico, the fact that Miami's most prevalent manufacturing jobs were considered "women's work" also meant that for the first time many Cuban woman became their family's primary breadwinner. By 1962, Miami labor leaders estimated that 90 percent of the city's garment workers were Cuban, compared with less than 50 percent a decade earlier.[58]

Industry owners were delighted. "The sky's the limit!" the head of Florida's Fashion Council proclaimed. "Thanks to a steady influx of Cuban seamstresses, Miami's industry is limited only the available labor."[59] Others compared the impact of the Cuban exiles on Miami's garment industries to the arrival of mass numbers of European immigrants in the late nineteenth and early twentieth centuries.[60] But for organizers, native-born, and Puerto Rican workers alike, the influx of Cubans was often viewed as increasing competition for jobs and potentially undermining their hard-won gains.

Gladnick returned to Miami in 1960 as the union focused its efforts on incorporating these newcomers. Again, Gladnick successfully recruited several new Hispanic organizers from New York, including Lolita Matamoros and Juan Lozano. His own knowledge of Latin American culture and history helped him avoid many of the pitfalls of a highly charged, exile political culture. As he frequently reminded members, "[T]he union cannot resolve their personal and political differences that so bitterly divides the Spanish colony here."[61] But the conditions in Miami also seemed to take a toll, challenging Gladnick's prevailing optimism about the union and workers alike. At times rather than intellectual understanding, he voiced prejudice of his own. "There is nothing that can be done when Latins have a difference of a personal or political nature," he told David Dubinsky during a moment of particularly high tension after a series of walkouts. Still, Hispanic workers and colleagues praised Gladnick's ability to understand their needs and appreciate their national, political, and ethnic diversity, even if he could not resolve their disputes.[62]

Gladnick also worked to apply his experience working in Puerto Rico and Miami to specific programs. In a series of appeals to U.S. Secretary of Labor Arthur Goldberg, Gladnick asked that the types of exchange and education programs they had successfully mounted in Puerto Rico be extended to foreign trade unionists living in Miami. "A large number of Cuban exiles are now living in Miami including many labor leaders," Gladnick wrote. "The time these men spend in the U.S.A. can serve to cement U.S.–Cuban relations through these grassroots leaders of opinion in free Cuba. If their exile is prolonged, these same men can be of invaluable service to us by spreading the message of freedom in Latin America."[63] Although his appeals failed to arouse much interest in Washington, Gladnick remained convinced that Miami and Puerto Rico were proving grounds for a new type of "American" unionizing and worker identity that would broadly encompass all of the Americas, not just the United States.

Yet few in the union's national leadership seemed to appreciate the impact of Cuban migration on local organizing efforts or to see any hope for unionizing beyond nation-state boundaries. "I disagree absolutely with the hysterical assertion by Manager Gladnick that 'when the season starts, these people will go to work in nonunion shops which will paralize [sic] our organization efforts in this area,'" E. T. Kehrer wrote in October 1960. "[Gladnick] apparently felt that he had been led to believe that he would be working as Manager with complete autonomy."[64]

Efforts by Gladnick to work more directly with organizations like the National Association for the Advancement of Colored People (NAACP) and the Southern Regional Council and with national leadership within the garment industry to open greater avenues of employment for African American workers also met with limited success.[65] Gladnick pushed the ILGWU to consider making a dedicated push to recruit black workers across the South and the West Indies in order to more fully racially integrate the rank and file. Instead, union leaders pointed to brassiere manufacturers like the Lovable Corporation in Atlanta where their attempts to organize black workers met with very limited results. "Again, I repeat, the reason for failure . . . is the fact the Negro worker got his job through the employer. . . . If, however, the union through use of the law forces the breach into the shops, then in spite of the inflated labor market, the union stands to gain," Gladnick argued. "[I]f the ILG ever appoints a Civil Rights director for the South,

I wouldn't mind tackling that job."[66] Still, his appeals fell on deaf ears. Increasingly the ILGWU's national and regional leadership felt Gladnick was moving too fast and that risk of isolating the few native-born, white workers who remained in the industry was just too high.

Instead, Gladnick's most successful efforts were mounted at a local level, building on individual and familial ties among workers in Miami that extended well beyond the confines of the city itself. In what proved to be one of the most protracted strikes in Miami's history, Gladnick successfully challenged local owners who sought to take advantage of Cuban newcomers by relocating their plants just outside of the Miami city limits, to the growing city of Hialeah. Beginning in 1960, numerous lingerie, dress, and sportswear manufacturers in Miami's Fashion District closed their doors without warning and reopened under new names within a matter of days in Hialeah. Workers returned from their lunch breaks to find all of the machines and materials packed up, with large trucks prepared to empty out the factory. As one longtime seamstress Espería Purón explained:

> I then left the factory to do some errands and told my forelady that I would be back in the afternoon to collect my pay. . . . When I came back in the afternoon, I noticed that no one was working and the equipment was packed getting ready to be moved. It was then that Ledya [Marroquín] told me that the plant was moving but she did not tell me where. I asked her where the plant was moving as I wanted to know where I could turn in my work tickets and collect my pay. She said she didn't know . . . and tole [sic] me not to worry about my pay as it would be mailed to me. Ledya tole me to give her my name and telephone and she would call me as soon as they started work. She did not call me.[67]

When the plant reopened, they hired back mostly new arrivals, charging a "learner's fee" to those who had not previously worked in the industry, and shifted whatever operations they could to "homework" where they paid by the piece rather than the hour.[68]

With the help of organizers Matamoros and Lozano, Gladnick quickly investigated the plants and filed a suit with the NLRB and the U.S. District Court.[69] He also organized pickets at the Hialeah factories, in the Fashion District in the heart of Miami's downtown, and in front of the major department stores that stocked their goods, including Sears Roebuck and Co. and J. C. Penney.[70] Press releases issued by the Miami locals emphasized the companies' attempts to take advantage of Cuban exiles and called for a boycott. The ads ran in both English and Spanish-language newspapers across the state and in nationally distributed publications like the *Chicago Tribune* and *New York Times*. They also appealed to all Latin workers in the city, underscoring their shared language and proud histories of their home countries. Miami's Spanish radio stations soon picked up the cause, interviewing striking workers' husbands and other family members. In an important show of international solidarity, the Confederation of Columbian Workers, along with representatives from more than twenty international unions across Latin and South America, issued a declaration in support of the strike.[71] Rather than raise wages, the companies moved once again. By 1965, four years after Gladnick had called for the initial work stoppages, all of the challenged plants had shut their doors and left Florida altogether. The union ensured that all of its members found work elsewhere in the city.

Epilogue: The Caribbean Basin Initiative and North American Free Trade Agreement, 1966–94

After nearly a half-century of work in the industry, Robert Gladnick resigned from the ILGWU in 1966. His last few years in Miami were decidedly mixed. As he wrote to ILGWU president Louis Stulberg, "[I]n Miami, I am in a blind alley."[72] Whatever tenuous alliances had been built between the city's Puerto Rican and Cuban seamstresses were often mitigated by anti-Semitic epithets flung at the industry's predominantly Jewish owners, even if Gladnick himself was largely excepted from such remarks. Gladnick was quick to point out that his disenchantment was with Miami, not the ILGWU. Nonetheless, the lack of responsiveness from the national office must certainly have proved frustrating. To organizers working in Florida, the lack of vision for dealing with the increasing movement of workers and corporations was troubling as was the steadfast refusal of others within the union's leadership to see the city, its immigrant laborers, and its industries as anything but exceptional within the Southeast Region. In January 1967, Gladnick accepted a position with the controversial American Institute for Free Labor Development's (AIFLD) Latin American Division, a joint initiative of the AFL and the U.S. Central Intelligence Agency. For Gladnick, joining the AIFLD seemed an ideal way to extend "American" unionism across national lines, offering the type of "good neighbor policy" that had developed over the World War II era. This was not an effort geared toward fostering the independent aims of Western Hemisphere nations, but rather a collapsing of national boundaries under the rubric of American industrialization, thereby extending the political and economic reach of the United States. Gladnick left after a few years. He ultimately returned to the United States and lived in Los Angeles before finally retiring to Miami Beach in the 1980s.

As successful as Gladnick's efforts may have been, they were ultimately hampered by the lack of support from the upper echelons of union leadership and directly undermined by international trade agreements sponsored by the U.S. government and the reactive tendency of the industry itself.[73] Two of Maidenform's biggest competitors, Lovable and Playtex, were sold to a Canadian conglomerate that became Sara Lee. Many more moved their production even farther offshore. In 1982, President Ronald Reagan announced plans for a new "Caribbean Basin Initiative." Modeled on Puerto Rico's "Operation Bootstrap," the program offered tax incentives on U.S. investments in the region, promised one-way, duty-free exports from the Caribbean for a period of 12 years, and provided an additional $350 million in emergency aid for some countries in the region.[74] Under the terms of this agreement, Maidenform moved several processing operations to the Dominican Republic. The company also opened up two factories along the border of Mexico and Texas in the developing "Free Trade Zone" spanning the U.S.–Mexico border. Unlike many garment corporations, Maidenform did not move off the U.S. mainland altogether, at least not initially. The same year that Maidenform opened its new Caribbean and Mexican plants, the company also opened a cutting facility and hired more than a hundred employees in Jacksonville, Florida.[75]

The North American Free Trade Agreement, signed in 1994, only seemed to accelerate this trend. Despite numerous attempts to revise its "I Dream . . ." campaign, it never seemed to reach the full market share it had in the 1950s and 1960s. Maidenform also faced growing competition from overseas manufacturers and a new generation of companies, like Victoria's Secret, whose innovative use of old and new media, including mail-order catalogs, cable television, and the Internet, soon replaced Maidenform as the leading manufacturers of lingerie for the American market.[76] In 1990, Maidenform closed its West Virginia operations, relocating all of its assembly operations to Central America. As one seamstress of thirty-three years remarked, "We are good workers and they have been here a long time. They should leave the plant here for the American people."[77] In 1997, Maidenform declared bankruptcy, closing its Puerto Rican plants altogether, and one of its two Jacksonville operations. Two years later the company reorganized under nonfamily leadership for the first time in its history. In 2005, Maidenform announced it would close its Jacksonville cutting facility, putting 111 people out of work. "We were lucky to be able to preserve this one for a number of years," Harris Raynor, director for the UNITE-HERE Southeast region, the successor union to the ILGWU, told the local press.[78] Today, Maidenform's manufacturing operations are entirely located outside of the United States.

Conclusion

Maidenform's history in many ways mirrors that of American industry and economic policy over the past half-century. As this family-owned company elevated the female form (both literally and figuratively) through one of the most successful advertising campaigns in world history, they not only took the intimate and made it public, but they reaped the benefits of midcentury federal policies that lowered the cost of doing business in some of the country's most vulnerable areas. As southern cities both on- and offshore clamored to attract these new industries, union representatives scrambled to meet the needs of a new generation of worker. These workers were more likely to speak Spanish than English. They were disproportionately female. They, like the companies who employed them, were also highly mobile. It rested on the shoulders of union leaders like Robert Gladnick who were fluent in Spanish and well versed in the politics and history of the Americas to fully recognize the implications of these international, interregional developments, for workers and industry alike.

Yet to many ILGWU leaders, Florida was still an aberration. Neither fully "southern" nor truly "northern," they did not understand why policies and approaches that had worked so well a decade earlier in New York and New Jersey failed to mobilize workers in Miami. Nor did they recognize the extent to which federal policies applied to Puerto Rico would pave the way for a growing number of trade initiatives across the region and around the globe.

*   *   *

The author gratefully acknowledges the helpful advice and assistance of the following scholars and archivists: David Haberstich, Reuben Jackson, and Kay Peterson at the Archives Center, National Museum of American History, Patrizia Sione and Melissa Holland at the Kheel Center, Cornell University, Lauren Kata, Special Collections at the Pullen Library, Georgia State University, Dawn Hugh at the George Tebeau Library, Historical Museum of Southern Florida, Gail Malmgreen at the Robert F. Wagner Labor Archives, Tamiment Library, New York University, and Ronald Bulatoff, Hoover Institution Archives. Without them, this project would not have been possible. Special thanks also go to David Prouty and UNITE-HERE for allowing the use of the ILGWU Archives. Alex Lichtenstein, Simone Caron, and the members of the Social Science Research Seminar at Wake Forest University all offered helpful comments and suggestions. This chapter is stronger for their guidance. Any shortcomings or errors are mine alone.

Notes

1. Pablo Ghigliani, "International Trade Unionism in a Globalizing World: A Case Study of New Labour Internationalism," *Economic and Industrial Democracy* 26, no. 3 (2005): 359–82; Michael P. Hanagan, "Labor Internationalism: An Introduction," *Social Science History* 27, no. 4 (Winter 2003): 485–99; Peter Waterman, *Space, Place, and the New Labour Internationalism* (London: Blackwell, 2001).

2. *Downes v. Bidwell*, 182 U.S. 244 (1901), Law Library, Library of Congress (hereafter cited as LOC).

3. 81st Cong., Ch. 446, 64 Stat. 319 (July 3, 1950), LOC.

4. The advertising concept was designed by Kitty D'Alessio of the Weintraub Agency, which assumed the Maidenform account after World War II. See "Market Survey" (1947), Maidenform Collection (hereafter cited as MC), box 23, folder 1, National Museum of American History, Smithsonian Institution (hereafter cited as NMAH); "Recommended Program for the Marketing Function" (1957), MC, box 23, folder 2, NMAH; "Interview with Kitty D'Alessio," August 8, 1990, MC, box 1, folder 21, NMAH.

5. "Foundation Style Book" and Advertisements, MC, box 71, folder 4, NMAH; "I Dreamed . . . ," MC, box 68, folder 4, NMAH.

6. Press release, "Maidenform Dreams for 20 Years" (October 1955), MC, box 69, folder 1, NMAH; Sales and Distribution, Spreadsheets (1949–60), MC, box 77, NMAH; Joe Sacco, "Dreams for Sale: How the One for Maidenform Came True," *Advertising Age*, September 12, 1977, 63–64; Erla Zwingle, "Maidenform," *American Photographer*, July 1981, 92–93.

7. "Maidenform's Mrs. R.," *Fortune Magazine*, July 1950, 76.

8. On the torpedo bra's place in history, see Jane Farrell-Beck and Colleen Gau, *Uplift: The Bra in America* (Philadelphia: University of Pennsylvania Press, 2002), 126–32. On the structure and construction of this model, see "Stiffening Ribs, Protection Thereof and Method of Making the Same," Serial No. 615781, June 14, 1952, MC, box 5, folder 3, NMAH; "Sewing instructions with pattern and sample operations," MC, boxes 59 and 60, NMAH. On the transformation of mid-twentieth-century women's fashion and idealized body type, see Carolyn Latteier, *Breasts: The Women's Perspective on an American Obsession* (New York: Harrington Park, 1998), 37–38; Elaine Tyler May, *Homeward Bound: American Families in the Cold War Era* (New York: Basic Books,

1988), 93–94; Maura Spiegel and Lithe Sebesta, *The Breast Book: An Intimate and Curious History* (New York: Workman, 2002), 279–82.

9. "Maidenform's Mrs. R.," 76, 130; "Market Survey" (1947), MC, box 23, folder 1, NMAH; *Women's Wear Daily*, June 3, 1954.

10. See "Maidenform, Inc.: A History of the Company, 1922–1972," MC, box 1, folder 12, NMAH. Quote from press release (March 1955), MC, box 69, folder 1, NMAH.

11. All of these companies operated factories in Puerto Rico. Other locations for lingerie cutting and assembly operations over this period included Maryland, Alabama, Georgia, and Tennessee. Some, like Peter Pan, also relocated plants to the Philippines, Taiwan, and Southeast Asia. See Southeast Regional Records, ILGWU Archives, Coll. #5780/058, Kheel Center, Cornell University (hereafter cited as KCCU); J. Farrell-Beck and C. Gau, *Uplift*, 134.

12. Harry L. Golden, "Garment Industry Goes South," *Congress Weekly: A Review of Jewish Interests* 21 (May 17, 1954): 10.

13. Merrill Johnson, "Postwar Industrial Development in the Southeast and the Pioneer Role of Labor-Intensive Industry," *Economic Geography* 61 (January 1985): 46–85. The right-to-work states at this time included Alabama, Arizona, Arkansas, Florida, Georgia, Iowa, Mississippi, Nebraska, Nevada, North Carolina, North Dakota, South Carolina, South Dakota, Tennessee, Texas, and Virginia. See Keith Lumsden and Craig Petersen, "The Effect of Right-to-Work Laws on Unionization in the United States," *Journal of Political Economy* 83 (December 1975): 1237–48; W. R. Brown, "State Experience in Defending the Right to Work," *Proceedings of the American Academy of Political Science* 26 (May 1954): 32–43. On Miami's industrial recruitment, see "Miami Industrial Survey," compiled by the Industrial Division of the Miami Chamber of Commerce (May 1941), Florida Collection, Miami-Dade Public Library.

14. "Industrial and Commercial Advantages of Miami, Dade County, Florida: An Analysis of Investment Opportunities Offered by the International Gateway to the Americas," comp. Industrial Department of the Miami Chamber of Commerce (April 1941), 5, Historical Museum of Southern Florida, Miami; Herbert Hill, "Recent Effects of Racial Conflict on Southern Industrial Development," *Phylon Quarterly* 20, no. 4 (1959): 319–26.

15. *Miami Herald* (hereafter cited as *MH*), June 26, 1955.

16. Palmira N. Rios, "Export-Oriented Industrialization and the Demand for Female Labor: Puerto Rican Women in the Manufacturing Sector, 1952–1980," *Gender and Society* 4 (September 1990): 322–23.

17. Robert Gladnick, manager, Dressmakers Local No. 420, ILGWU, Cleveland, to Angela Bombace, Upper South Department, ILGWU, Baltimore, June 7, 1949, ILGWU Archives, Coll. #5780/039, box 16, folder 12, KCCU; *Justice*, February 1, 1954; *Justice*, June 1, 1954, 3; Carlos Santiago, "The Migratory Impact of Minimum Wage Legislation, Puerto Rico, 1970–1987," *International Migration Review* 27 (Winter 1993): 772–95.

18. *El Sosten* (January/February 1967), MC, box 22, folder 16, NMAH; *El Sosten* (February 1968), MC, box 22, folder 17, NMAH; Henry Lee, "Maidenform's J. A. Coleman," *Madison Avenue*, November 1960? MC, box 2, folder 6, NMAH.

19. *Women's Wear Daily*, October 4, 1954.

20. Robert A. Pastor, "U.S. Immigration Policy and Latin America: In Search of the 'Special Relationship,'" *Latin American Research Review* 19, no. 3 (1984): 35–56.

21. Gladnick to Bombace, June 7, 1949.

22. This was an oft-quoted phrase by ILGWU leaders, including union president David Dubinsky. See David Dubinsky, "American by Choice," *Liberty Magazine* (July 1950), ILGWU Southeast Regional Office Records, Coll. #3046/4, Southern Labor Archives, Special Collections Department, Pullen Library, Georgia State University (hereafter cited as PLGSU); Mark Starr, "Why Union Education? Aims, History, and Philosophy of the Educational Work of the International Ladies' Garment Workers' Union," *Proceedings of the American Philosophical Society* 92 (July 1948): 194–202.

23. Robert Gladnick, Biographical Notes, ILGWU Archives, Coll. #5780/177, box 1, KCCU. On Gladnick's early union work, see Philip Taft, "Strife in the Maritime Industry," *Political Science Quarterly* 54 (June 1939): 216–36; "Union Hiring Hall Operated Discriminatorily Illegal under Taft-Hartley Act," *Columbia Law Review* 49 (March 1949): 422–24. On his work in the ILGWU and reflections on the labor movement, see Robert Gladnick, interviewed by John Gerassi, John Gerassi Papers, 1979–1983, series 1, Robert F. Wagner Labor Archives, Tamiment Library, New York University (hereafter cited as WLA-NYU). On Gladnick's reflections on serving in Spanish Civil War and how it influenced his later work with the ILGWU and AIFLD, see Robert Gladnick, West Palm Beach, Florida, to Jay Lovestone, International Affairs Dept., ILGWU, New York City, April 29, 1974, Jay Lovestone Papers, box 370, folder: Gladnick, Hoover Institution Archives, Stanford, Calif.; R. Gladnick, interviewed by Jonathan Solovy, Jonathan Solovy Papers (ALBA Audio 101), WLA-NYU; Peter N. Carroll, *The Odyssey of the Abraham Lincoln Brigade: Americans in the Spanish Civil War,* 120–22, 228–32, 296–306; William Herrick, *Jumping the Line: The Adventures and Misadventures of an American Radical,* 2d ed. (Oakland, Calif.: AK Press, 2001), 124–37, 150–58, 176–78. Journalist John Gerassi later used Gladnick, and Gladnick's political views, as the inspiration for one of his main characters in his novel *The Anachronists* (London: Black Apollo Press, 2006).

24. Robert Gladnick, ILGWU, Cleveland, Ohio, to Angela Bombace, Upper South Division, ILGWU, Baltimore, June 7, 1949, February 26, 1951, ILGWU Archives, Coll. #5780/039, box 16, folder 12, KCCU.

25. Nancy Green, *Ready-to-Wear, Ready-to-Work: A Century of Industry and Immigrants in Paris and New York* (Durham, N.C.: Duke University Press, 1997), 160–62; Abram J. Jaffe, "Demographic and Labor Forces Characteristics of the New York Puerto Rican Population," *Puerto Rican Population of New York City,* ed. Abram J. Jaffe (New York: Bureau of Applied Social Research, 1954); Clarence Senior, "Patterns of Puerto Rican Dispersion in the Continental United States," *Social Problems* 2 (October 1954): 98.

26. David Dubinsky, ILGWU, New York City to Samuel Macy, ILGWU, Miami, July 26, 1954, ILGWU Archives, Coll. #5780/002, box 293, folder 4C, KCCU; *MH,* February 21, 1954.

27. Francis Schaufenbil to Joseph Jacobs, Atlanta, November 23, 1955, ILGWU Southeast Regional Office Records, Coll. #414/828, Southern Labor Archives, Special

Collections Department, PLGSU; Samuel Macy, ILGWU, Miami, to Joseph Jacobs, southern director, United Textile Workers of America, Atlanta, October 17, 1955, Coll. #414/828, Southern Labor Archives, Special Collections Department, PLGSU.

28. Translated from Spanish. See "Notícias," Carlos J. Cintrón and Juan Pérez, Union Obrera de *Beatrice Needle Craft, Inc.*, November 1955, MC, box 58, folder 17, NMAH.

29. Miles Galvin, "The Early Development of the Organized Labor Movement in Puerto Rico," *Latin American Perspectives* 3 (Summer 1976): 31–35.

30. Ellis Rosenthal, assistant general manager, Maidenform, Bayonne, N.J., to Robert Gladnick, ILGWU, Huntington, W. Va., March 7, 1949, MC, box 57, folder 2, NMAH.

31. The gifts of brassieres were the subject of frequent exchanges and jokes between the company and ILGWU office staff, dating back to the mid-1940s. See MC, box 57, folders 1–4, NMAH. For the poem, see office memo, Upper South Dept, ILGWU, Baltimore, to Ellis Rosenthal, assistant general manager, Maidenform, Bayonne, N.J., December 17, 1952, MC, box 57, folder 1, NMAH.

32. National Labor Relations Board, case #24-CA-453, Beatrice Needle Craft, Inc., July 31, 1953, MC, box 57, folder 7, NMAH.

33. Notes and testimony, Ted Metzger, Maidenform, Poncé, Puerto Rico, July 7, 1953, MC, box 57, folder 5, NMAH.

34. Kurt A. Metzger, Maidenform, Bayonne, N.J., to Ellis Rosenthal, Asst. General Manager, Maidenform, Bayonne, N.J., November 18, 1953, MC, box 57, folder 6, NMAH.

35. See memos from Beatrice Needlecraft, Poncé and Mayagüez, to Maidenform, Bayonne, N.J., November/December 1953, MC, box 57, folder 6, NMAH.

36. *Justice*, February 1, 1954.

37. National Labor Relations Board, case No. 24-RC-719, June 3, 1954, MC, box 57, folder 5, NMAH.

38. Telegram, Hernán Franco, Cordova y González, San Juan, Puerto Rico, to Kurt Metzger and Ellis Rosenthal, Maidenform, Bayonne, N.J., May 26, 1954, MC, box 57, folder 6, NMAH.

39. *Miami Labor Citizen*, July 22, 1954; *MH*, July 25, 1954; Abraham Plotkin, ILGWU, Miami, to David Dubinsky, ILGWU, New York City, July 27, 1954, ILGWU Archives, Coll. #5780/002, box 293, folder 4C, KCCU.

40. *Miami Daily News* (hereafter cited as *MN*), November 4, 1954.

41. Quote from "Miami Class Erases Language Barriers," *Justice* 15 (November 1954): 10. See also Miami Joint Council, census figures, 1954–56, 1956–58, ILGWU Archives, Coll. #5780/002, box 293, folder 3B, KCCU; "'No Reason Miami's Garment Industry Should Not Be Organized'—Dubinsky," *Journal—North Dade Edition*, February 17, 1955, clippings file, Dade Industry–Garment, Florida Collection, Miami-Dade Public Library.

42. *MH*, December 18, 1955; "Lead Anti-Red Fight: Sam Macy Dies; Services Friday," News Clipping (1958), ILGWU Archives, Coll. #5780/058, box 53, folder 1, KCCU; J. S. Martin, ILGWU S.E. Regional Headquarters, Chattanooga, Tenn., to David Dubinsky, ILGWU, New York City, May 25, 1954, ILGWU Archives, Coll. #5780/058, box 17, folder 6, KCCU; Abraham Plotkin, ILGWU, Miami to Samuel Macy, ILGWU, Miami, June 24, 1955, ILGWU Archives, Coll. #5780/002, box 293, folder 4A, KCCU.

43. Robert Gladnick, ILGWU, Miami, to David Dubinsky, president, ILGWU, New York City, July 19, 1954, ILGWU Archives, Coll. #5780/002, box 63, folder 4B, KCCU; "Report on Conditions in Miami," Robert Gladnick, July 1955, ILGWU Archives, Coll. #5780/002, box 63, folder 4B, KCCU; "Final Report and Recommendations," Abraham Plotnik, International Organizer, ILGWU, Miami, June 28, 1955, ILGWU Archives, Coll. #5780/002, box 293, folder 4A, KCCU.

44. Fernando Sierra Berdecia, commissioner, Dept. of Labor, Migration Division, Commonwealth of Puerto Rico, New York City, to David Dubinsky, president, ILGWU, New York City, March 4; Abraham Plotkin, ILGWU, Miami, to David Dubinsky, ILGWU, New York City, February 23, 1954, ILGWU Archives, Coll. #5780/002, box 293, file 4D, KCCU; *MN*, February 15, 1954.

45. On depictions of Puerto Rico in the popular media, see "Tourist Card," *Time*, December 1, 1958. For public perception of Puerto Ricans in Miami, see *MH*, January 10, 1960. On crime and local police response, see *MH*, April 23, 1957, August 21 and December 1, 1958.

46. *MH*, August 27, 1958.

47. *MH*, May 2, 1960.

48. Abraham Plotkin, ILGWU, Miami, to David Dubinsky, ILGWU, New York City, February 23, 1954, ILGWU Archives, Coll. #5780/002, box 293, file 4D, KCCU. On moving the local's offices, see Samuel Macy, ILGWU, Miami, to David Dubinsky, president, ILGWU, New York City, September 23, 1954, ILGWU Archives, Coll. #5780/002, box 293, folder 4C, KCCU.

49. Local 339, a cloak makers' local, was disbanded in 1960, and its few remaining members joined Local 415. A third local, Local 475, was created in the early 1960s in response to the tremendous membership growth within the regional industry. See E. T. Kehrer, Southeast Region, ILGWU, Atlanta, to David Dubinsky, president, ILGWU, New York City, December 5, 1960, ILGWU Archives, Coll. #5780/058, box 33, folder 3, KCCU. On response to Gladnick's management, see Samuel Macy, Locals 339 and 415, ILGWU, Miami, to David Dubinsky, president, ILGWU, New York City, August 1, 1955, ILGWU Archives, Coll. #5780/002, box 293, folder 4A, KCCU; Lolita Cartagena, president, Local 600, Caguas to David Dubinsky, president, ILGWU, ILGWU Archives, Coll. #5780/058, box 14, folder 3, KCCU; E. T. Kehrer, director, Southeast Region, ILGWU, Atlanta, to Louis Stulberg, executive vice president, ILGWU, January 2, 1959, ILGWU Archives, Coll. #5780/058, box 33, folder 5, KCCU.

50. Robert Gladnick, manager, Local 600, ILGWU, San Juan, Puerto Rico, to Max Wexler, Florida state director, ILGWU, July 29, 1957, ILGWU Archives, Coll. #5780/003, box 15, folder 4, KCCU.

51. E. T. Kehrer, ILGWU, Atlanta, to Louis Stulberg, executive vice president, ILGWU, New York City, October 11, 1958, ILGWU Archives, Coll. #5780/003, box 17, folder 7, KCCU.

52. E. T. Kehrer, director, Southeast Region, ILGWU, Atlanta, to David Dubinsky, president, ILGWU, New York City, October 9, 1958, ILGWU Archives, Coll. #5780/058, box 17, folder 3, KCCU.

53. Central States Institute, ILGWU, School for Workers, University of Wisconsin, Madison, June 11–17, 1961, ILGWU Archives, Coll. #5780/058, box 11, folder 6, KCCU.

54. This effort also built on a renewed interest in Latin American theater on the island and the institution of a new theater festival by Governor Muñoz Marín. See Robert Gladnick, ILGWU Local 600, Puerto Rico, to Louis Stulberg, ILGWU, New York City, April 29, 1958, Coll. #5780/003, box 14, folder 6, ILGWU Archives, KCCU; José Juan Arrom, "Perfil del Teatro Contemporáneo en Hispanoamérica," *Hispanica* 36, no. 1 (February 1953): 26–27; Kirwin Shaffer, "Freedom Teaching: Anarchism and Education in Early Republican Cuba, 1898–1925," *Americas* 60 (October 2003): 151–83.

55. Martin Morand, director, Southeast Region, ILGWU, Atlanta, to Louis Rolnick, administrator, ILGWU National Retirement Fund, February 11, 1967, ILGWU Archives, Coll. #5780/058, box 33, folder 5, KCCU; *El Diario*, February 6, 1958. On sterilization and conflict over the ILGWU's leadership and approach, see Francis M. Beal, "Double Jeopardy: To Be Black and Female," (Third World Women's Alliance, 1969), published in *Sisterhood Is Powerful*, ed. Robin Morgan (New York: Vintage Press, 1970), 344.

56. Letters from members of Puerto Rican and Northeastern locals looking for work in Miami and Florida pepper the Southeast Regional Office reports of the ILGWU Archives in the 1950s and 1960s. See especially ILGWU Archives, Coll. #5780/058, box 53, folder 2, and box 14, folders 2–4, KCCU; Melvin Warshaw, Mel Warshaw, Inc., Miami, to E. T. Kehrer, director, Southeast Region, ILGWU, Atlanta, February 16, 1960, ILGWU Archives, Coll. #5780/058, folder 3, KCCU. On organizers, see Emília Rodríguez Maisonet, biography files, ILGWU Archives, Coll. #5780/177, box 1, KCCU. Quote from: Lolita Cartagena, president, Local 600, Caguas to David Dubinsky, president, ILGWU, ILGWU Archives, Coll. #5780/058, box 14, folder 3, KCCU.

57. On "fastest growing group," see *MH*, January 24, 1960. Officials in Cuba and the United States debate exactly how many Cuban nationals entered the United States during this time. But most scholars rely on the estimates of Juan M. Clark, who conducted one of the first and most comprehensive studies to be done on the migration of Cubans to the United States over this period. See J. M. Clark, "The Exodus from Revolutionary Cuba (1959–1974): A Sociological Analysis," PhD diss., University of Florida, 1975, 75. Some of these local aid agencies included the Florida State Department of Public Welfare, Catholic Welfare Bureau, Jewish Family and Children Services, Florida State Children's Bureau, and the United Hebrew Immigrant Aid Society. See María Cristína García, *Havana, U.S.A.: Cuban Exiles and Cuban Americans in South Florida* (Berkeley: University of California Press, 1996), 13; Dana Evan Kaplan, "Fleeing the Revolution: The Exodus of Cuban Jewry in the Early 1960s," *Cuban Studies* 36 (2005): 129–54; Richard Ferrée Smith, "Refugees," *Annals of the American Academy of Political and Social Science* 367 (September 1966): 43–52; Robert G. Wright, "Voluntary Agencies and the Resettlement of Refugees," *International Migration Review* 15 (Spring 1981): 157–74. On job placement, see Raymond F. Farrell, "The Role of the Immigration and Naturalization Service in the Administration of Current Immigration Law," *International Migration Review* 4 (Summer 1970): 16–30.

58. Quote from *MN*, December 2, 1960. See also Marie LaLiberté Richmond, *Immigrant Adaptation and Family Structure among Cubans in Miami, Florida* (New York: Arno Press, 1980), 102–3; María Patrícia Fernández-Kelly and Anna M. Garcia, "Power Surrendered, Power Restored: The Politics of Work and Family among Hispanic Garment Workers in California and Florida," *Women, Politics and Change*, ed. Louise A.

Tilly and Patricia Gurin (New York: Russell Sage, 1990), 130–48. On changing demographics within Miami's garment industry, see Robert Gladnick, Local 415, ILGWU, Miami, to David Dubinsky, president, ILGWU, New York City, June 14, 1961, ILGWU Archives, Coll. #5780/058, box 53, folder 3, KCCU.

59. *MH*, Associated Press article, June 12, 1969.

60. *New York Times*, November 19, 1967.

61. Robert Gladnick, ILGWU, Miami, to David Dubinsky, president, ILGWU, March 20, 1962, ILGWU Archives, Coll. #5780/058, box 17, folder 1, KCCU.

62. Ibid; Lolita Cartagena, president, Local 600, Caguas, to David Dubinsky, president, ILGWU, ILGWU Archives, Coll. #5780/058, box 14, folder 3, KCCU; E. T. Kehrer, director, Southeast Region, ILGWU, Atlanta, to Louis Stulberg, executive vice president, ILGWU, January 2, 1959, ILGWU Archives, Coll. #5780/058, box 33, folder 5, KCCU.

63. Robert Gladnick, ILGWU, Miami, to Arthur Goldberg, Secretary of Labor, Department of Labor, Washington, D.C., June 7, 1961, ILGWU Archives, Coll. #5780/058, box 53, folder 3, KCCU.

64. E.T. Kehrer, director, Southeast Region, ILGWU, Atlanta, to David Dubinsky, president, ILGWU, New York City, October 7, 1960, ILGWU Archives, Coll. #5780/058, box 53, folder 2, KCCU.

65. Emory Via, labor consultant, Southern Regional Council, Atlanta, to E. T. Kehrer, ILGWU, Atlanta, April 25, 1957, ILGWU Archives, Coll. #5780/058, box 17, folder 4, KCCU.

66. Robert Gladnick, ILGWU, Miami, to Martin Morand, director, Southeastern Region, ILGWU, Atlanta, March 29, 1965, and Morand to Gladnick, March 26, 1965, ILGWU Archives, Coll. #5780/008, box 53, folder 5, KCCU.

67. Testimony, Espería Purón, to National Labor Relations Board, June 5, 1961, Miami, 3146/13, Southern Labor Archives, Special Collections, PLGSU.

68. Robert Gladnick, business manager, Locals 415/475, ILGWU, Miami, to Ben Rosenberg, Bennett Fashions, Miami, June 16, 1961, 3062/6, Southern Labor Archives, Special Collections, PLGSU.

69. U.S. District Court, Southern District of Florida, Miami Division, No. 11,058–M-Civil9 (E.C.), Local 415, ILGWU, AFL-CIO, Plaintiff, vs. Bennett Fashions, Inc., Defendant, 3110/6, Southern Labor Archives, Special Collections, PLGSU; Official Report of Proceedings Before the National Labor Relations Board, Docket No. 12-CA-2027, in the matter of Lori-Ann of Miami, Inc., Rose Uniforms, Inc., Myron Warshaw and Rose Uniforms of Miami, Inc., and Local 415, ILGWU, AFL-CIO, Miami, Florida, November 13–16, 1961 (Washington, D.C.), 3146/10–12, Southern Labor Archives, Special Collections, PLGSU.

70. "Story for Justice," January 29, 1962, press release by the ILGWU, 3110/4, Southern Labor Archives, PLGSU.

71. "Be Fair: Buy Fair Union Made Garments," Local 415, ILGWU, AFL-CIO, Miami, 3110/4, Southern Labor Archives, PLGSU; Juan Amador Rodríguez, director, "El Periodico del Aire," Radio Station WMIE, September 17, 1963, 12:30 p.m. to 1:30 p.m., ILGWU SERO Records, 3157/1, Southern Labor Archives, Special Collections, PLGSU; *Diario Las Américas*, December 15, 1963.

72. Robert Gladnick, ILGWU, Miami to Louis Stulberg, president, ILGWU, New York City, September 23, 1966, ILGWU Archives, Coll. #5780/008, box 53, folder 5, KCCU.

73. J. Farrell-Beck and C. Gau, *Uplift*, 162–63.

74. Ronald Reagan, "America's Economic Strategy in the Caribbean," address to Organization of American States (1982), Recorded Sound Reference Center, LOC; U.S. Department of State, Bureau of Public Affairs, "Background on the Caribbean Basin Initiative," *Special Report* 97 (Washington, D.C.: Government Printing Office, 1982); U.S. Department of State, Bureau of Public Affairs, "Programs Underway for the Caribbean Basin Initiative," *Current Policy* 444 (Washington, D.C.: Government Printing Office, 1982); Emílio Pantojas-García, "The U.S. Caribbean Basin Initiative and the Puerto Rican Experience: Some Parallels and Lessons," *Latin American Perspectives* 12 (Fall 1985): 105–28.

75. *Women's Wear Daily*, April 20, 1998; "Jacksonville Employees Celebrate First Anniversary" (1983), MC, box 52, folder 23, NMAH.

76. *Wall Street Journal*, April 10, 2000, A1, A19; *Los Angeles Times*, August 11, 2000, E1, E4.

77. *Princeton Times*, September 17, 1990.

78. *Florida Times-Union*, March 9, 2005.

Epilogue

Florida and the Contemporary Labor Movement

ROBERT CASSANELLO AND MELANIE SHELL-WEISS

As we were editing this collection of essays about Florida's labor history, we were cognizant of the importance of labor activism as a contemporary force for change and were fortunate to find many dynamic examples in our own backyards, both literally and figuratively. Florida showcases some of the most exciting ways that activism is transforming the workplace and the national and international economic landscape. For this reason, we thought it important to provide a record of these events as a testament to the ongoing process of labor activism across the region and as an interpretive diary of what we have witnessed as we worked to bring this project to publication. This, then, is a structured review of how the labor movement has diversified its approach and adapted to the ever-changing set of challenges that workers encounter today. As such, these anecdotes provide a fitting end to this collection and suggest questions that we hope will inspire new works about Florida's labor past and present.

The New Labor Movement

The mid-1990s proved something of a watershed moment for organized labor in the United States. Locals from coast to coast had been bleeding members for two decades. Some of the disenchantment from members was due to long-standing problems in the structure of many AFL-CIO locals, including a leadership that often failed to represent the ethnicity, sex, and even the interests of the rank and file. The restructuring American economy presented other challenges. Deindustrialization, the proliferation of subcontracting, and a globalizing economy rendered the more reactive business model style of unionism that had prevailed throughout much of the twentieth century inadequate to address the problems faced by the nation's workers and effectively bargain on their behalf. Owners of many large employers were likely to be situated outside the United States or to have outsourced large segments of their operations. Workers, particularly in the country's most numerous and lowest paying service sector occupations, were likely to hail from across the globe. The most vulnerable were those without proper documentation or work permits. Whereas conflict between white and black workers divided the labor movement throughout the first half of the twentieth century, the current split between native and foreign-born workers has been every bit as acute.

Poverty has also remained. In cities like Miami, close to a quarter of residents lived at or below the federal poverty line in 1994, earning it the dubious honor of being the single poorest city in America. By 2004, the most recent data available at the time of this writing, the percentage of those living in poverty remained around 18.4 percent for the greater metropolitan area, with close to half living below the poverty level in several census tracts within the city. Several Florida counties also topped the list of places where close to half of all residents live at or below the poverty line, including Polk County, Lake County, and Pasco County.[1] Equally troubling, of the nation's impoverished families, close to a third were headed by women who were employed at least part-time.[2] Underemployment, it seems, has become as big a contributor to the nation's poverty rolls as unemployment. Hispanic and African American families have been particularly hard hit, showing poverty rates nearly double that of white families. Until the mid-1990s, organized labor seemed either unprepared or unable to respond.

This began to change, however, after 1995 as a result of two important developments. The first was a major transformation within the AFL-CIO. Emphasizing recruitment as a cornerstone, John Sweeney was elected president of the AFL-CIO on a platform of movement revitalization, urging locals to devote at least 30 percent of their resources to new organizing, focusing on what he called "the new face of labor": women, immigrants, young workers, nonwhite workers, and those in the growing service sector.[3] Given that Sweeney had served as president of the Service Employees International Union (SEIU) since 1980, this was an area where he had particular expertise. Sweeney immediately implemented new strategies for organizing modeled on efforts that had been enacted by individual locals but that had never been systematically used by the AFL-CIO on a national scale. In place of the staff-driven, reactive model that had characterized most labor activism for close to a century, Sweeney advocated a new "social movement style" of organizing. Promising that the new labor movement would be "at your doorstep, in your face, and on your conscience," Sweeney restructured the AFL-CIO, establishing a centralized Department of Organizing, merging the previously autonomous Organizing Institute run by the SEIU, Union of Needletrades, Industrial and Textile Employees (UNITE, formerly the International Ladies' Garment Workers Union), the United Food and Commercial Workers (UFCW), and the American Federation of State, County, and Municipal Employees (AFSCME). He increased their budget and emphasized new tactics modeled on the civil rights and anti-war movements of the 1960s: nonviolent direct action, a greater militancy, large-scale demonstrations, and partnerships with local social change organizations.[4] Sweeney was reelected three times, although conflict over other issues propelled UNITE, UFCW, and the SEIU to leave the AFL-CIO in 2005.

The second major development was an increasing desire for more direct forms of activism among the nation's workers. It was these members of the rank and file that elected Sweeney to the AFL-CIO presidency. But other groups of workers were also organizing outside of formal labor unions, forming new coalitions for change. There is probably nothing that more represents this type of social movements approach in Florida than the activism of the Coalition of Immokalee Workers (CIW). Located in Collier County in southwest Florida, Immokalee is currently the largest community of agricultural laborers in the state and one of the biggest nationwide. Roughly half of the workers are Mexican, one-third are Guatemalan, and 10 percent are Haitian. The remaining 10 percent are predominantly African American, with a smattering of workers from other nations or ethnic groups. During the winter months, they work long hours in Florida's citrus groves and tomato fields. For the rest of the year, they migrate up the East Coast, following the harvest season before returning to south Florida.

Immokalee is also an area known for some of the worst labor abuses in the nation. About 40 percent of the workers who come to Immokalee each season are new. Many are unsure of their rights. They fear being seized by immigration authorities or are especially vulnerable to exploitation because of high debts to loan sharks and collateral in the form of their homes or risks to family and friends. Located in a very rural area, far from towns or other resources, isolation puts these workers at additional risk for being abused by employers. As a former prosecutor for the U.S. Justice Department put it, south Florida has become "ground zero for modern slavery."[5] However problematic this rhetorical choice, the inhumane conditions experienced by workers are undeniable.

In 1993, a small group of Immokalee workers began meeting in a local church. Their numbers grew quickly. Today the CIW claims 2,500 members with a particularly active core of about 100 organizers.[6] One way the have attempted to improve the conditions of farmworkers is by integrating their vision of a better working environment with like-minded social and civil rights organizations. In this way CIW has nationalized, and in some ways internationalized, the social movements approach that seems to be reinvigorating the labor movement today.

After a four-year struggle, marked by a series of hunger strikes and other actions, in March 2005 the CIW won a significant victory in negotiations with the Taco Bell Company (owned by Yums! Brands). Taco Bell agreed to implement the CIW's demands, including consenting to buy only from tomato growers who paid workers a penny more per pound than they were currently receiving and who guaranteed their agricultural workers sanitary facilities and health and safety protections comparable to those enjoyed by workers in other industries, including protections not necessarily guaranteed to agricultural workers under federal or state law. Although Taco Bell's business makes up only a very small fraction of the total sales of tomatoes, it was the CIW's hope that if it could get this one fast-food company to agree to their demands, others in the industry would follow suit.

As Taco Bell's president, Emil Brolick, said in a press release issued at the close of the boycott, "As an industry leader, we are pleased to lend our support to and work with the CIW to improve working and pay conditions for farmworkers in the Florida tomato fields. We recognize that Florida tomato workers do not enjoy the same rights and conditions as employees in other industries. . . . We have indicated that any solution must be industry-wide, as our company simply does not have the clout to solve the issues raised by the CIW, but we are willing to play a leadership role within our industry to be part of the solution. . . . [H]uman rights are universal and we hope others will follow our company's lead."[7]

Counting on this pledge, the CIW then increased the pressure on other fast-food companies. In April 2007, with the help of former president Jimmy Carter and the Carter Center, an international human rights organization, McDonald's agreed to demand that its suppliers pay their workers an extra cent per pound of tomatoes. CIW has most recently targeted Burger King, the last of the fast-food triumvirate. It also has extended its *Un Centavo Mas* (One Cent More) campaign to coffee growers.[8]

What makes CIW's efforts so noteworthy is not just its success but its approach. CIW has succeeded in folding national, international, and local groups around the country into a working coalition. These partnerships usually come in the form of recognition of the workers' struggle, as well as an effort to coordinate protests in cities and farming communities across the state and the country. One of the most endearing partnerships has been with the Student Farmworker Alliance. SFA is a college-based community organization that was launched following the 2000 March for Dignity, Dialogue and a Fair Wage, a mass demonstration modeled on the civil rights era March on Washington. Organized by the CIW, the march led labor, living wage, human, and civil rights advocates on a 230-mile walk from Ft. Meyers to Orlando in February 2000.[9] The following year, the CIW and SFA marched from Quincy to the governor's mansion in Tallahassee with the goal of getting Governor Jeb Bush more directly involved in issues affecting the state's farmworkers. Later that year, the two organizations visited five major Florida universities, talking about the issues at stake and pressing student government to pass resolutions supporting the *Un Centavo Mas* campaign and calling for better legislation to protect farmworkers. Like the CIW, the SFA aims to raise consciousness about the conditions workers face, press consumers to take responsibility for those who harvest food, and ultimately ignite a larger rights-based movement on behalf of workers across the hemisphere.[10]

With a main office located in Immokalee, the SFA currently boasts more than thirty-five chapters on college campuses and in community centers across the country, including the University of Notre Dame, University of Minnesota, and Central Michigan University. Inspired by what she had learned through SFA-organized teach-ins, one student traveled from Michigan to Naples, Florida, for the SFA's *Encuentro* over the 2007 Labor Day weekend. Speaking to reporters later that day, she said that what struck her the most about the event was the sight of "very privileged people living next to very poor people and not taking an interest in their neighbors."[11] Since college students are one of the most important groups of consumers for the fast-food industry, their mobilization has played a significant role in forcing big corporations like Taco Bell and McDonald's to take notice.

Church groups such as Redlands Christian Migrant Association and the Catholic Campaign for Human Development also make a significant contribution to the coalition, giving money and time. Their involvement was sparked by what they see as an inextricable connection between the social gospel and the plight of international workers. As Catholic bishop John J. Nevins recently told members of the Immokalee parish, the *"mestiza* face" of their congregation testifies that Christ's message "cuts across all cultures." The tremendous achievements of groups like the CIW moved the AFL-CIO to formally join the coalition in September 2007, ultimately linking the struggle of more traditional labor unions with these community-based initiatives.[12]

CIW's mission not only resonates with groups within the United States but has also made critical strides toward internationalizing its movement, again drawing directly on issues of importance to the nation's agricultural workers. Nearly half of Immokalee workers hail from Mexico, mostly from impoverished southern Mexican states. These very rural regions, which often lack access to education and health care, have been historically marginalized ever since the period of Spanish colonialism. Drawing on the inspiration of early twentieth-century figures like Emiliano Zapata, a leading counterrevolutionary figure in the Mexican Revolution best known for his demand for *tierra y libertad* (land and liberty), a new group of revolutionaries was formed in the 1980s; since 1994, the Zapatistas have become an important political force in the region.[13] Drawing heavily on the philosophy of Zapatísmo, the CIW, like the Zapatistas, opposes the North American Free Trade Agreement and neoliberal policies that have adversely impacted the agricultural regions of southern Mexico.

Formal connections with other South American political groups have been important to the CIW as well. The organization recently recognized and exchanged flags with the Movimento dos Travalhadores Rurais Sem Terra (Landless Workers' Movement) (MST), a Brazilian organization devoted to improving living conditions and land rights for rural workers in that nation. Among their most publicized work have been efforts to reclaim unused rural land owned by wealthy landowners. MST then assumes control over the land, farming, establishing schools and clinics, and organizing a cooperative so that poor families can work the land. Many activists in the CIW see the struggle of Immokalee workers and the struggle for agricultural economic rights throughout Latin America as similar, linked in the same hemispheric social movement for economic change and indigenous workers' rights.[14]

CIW and its partners also involved themselves in the federal immigration debates, which reached a fever pitch in 2006. Working with the Farmworker Association of Florida, the CIW, SEIU, UNITE-HERE, and civil rights and community organizations like the Immigrant Solidarity Network held a series of rallies in connection with the national Day Without an Immigrant on May 1, 2006, and again in 2007. Thousands of children skipped school, men and women walked off the job, and businesses shut down for lack of patrons or employees as a national day of protest unfolded in cities from Pensacola, Orlando, Miami, Tampa, and Jacksonville to Washington,

D.C., New York, Chicago, and Los Angeles. Marches were also organized in more rural areas of Florida where immigrant labor was especially important to local economies, including Polk County.[15]

New Models of Labor Activism

These types of broad-based movements for social change have inspired new models of collaboration outside the ranks of more traditional labor unions as well. Among the most widely known examples is the Change to Win coalition. Launched in 2005, Change to Win represents a collaborative effort among seven former AFL-CIO member unions, including the International Brotherhood of Teamsters (IBT), Laborers' International Union of North America (LIUNA), the SEIU, United Brotherhood of Carpenters and Joiners of America (UBC), United Farm Workers of America (UFW), the UFCW, and UNITE-HERE (the joint union of UNITE and the Hotel Employees and Restaurant Employees International Union, who merged in 2004). United by the goal of restoring the American Dream in the twenty-first century, including "a paycheck that can support a family, affordable health care, a secure retirement, and dignity on the job," the coalition has used this kind of issue-based approach to partner with local organizations rather than organizing along trade or industrial lines as unions did in the past.[16]

With its large number of service jobs and a workforce that was ready and willing to organize, Florida became the site of several important actions by Change to Win almost immediately. Among the first was a well-publicized series of demonstrations at the University of Miami (UM) that began in March 2006 as part of the SEIU-led Justice for Janitors campaign.[17] Like many other large companies and universities, UM no longer directly employed most of its cleaning and maintenance staff, choosing instead to outsource these services to a contractor. In this case, UM hired a Boston-based company named UNICCO to perform these services. UNICCO employed mostly Latino and Haitian workers, paying them $6.40 an hour (the lowest rate allowed under Florida law) and providing no health insurance.[18] These wages were far below those paid for comparable work at other universities across the country. A study conducted by the Association of Higher Education Facilities Officers found that UM custodial workers were the second lowest paid out of more than 195 other universities surveyed across the country.[19]

Several other factors also made UM a particularly desirable wedge to attempt to force better wages and working conditions at universities nationwide. The university's president, Donna Shalala, had served as the U.S. secretary of health and human services under the Clinton administration for eight years before coming to UM. As negotiations commenced between members of the Change to Win coalition and UM officials, the *New York Times Magazine* ran a profile of Shalala that showcased her 9,000-square-foot waterfront mansion and her many amenities, including an antique 1790 French country cabinet, her dog's four beds, and a 29-foot motorboat she regretted barely using. Laid against the average $13,120 per year earned by university custodians, an amount well below the federal poverty threshold of $20,000 for a family of four, the disparity between what appeared to be the luxurious life of rich university officials and the impoverished existence of university service employees was particularly important in amassing public support for the coalition's efforts. Nor did the profile go unnoticed by the national and local press. One particularly tongue-in-cheek column penned by Amy Argetsinger and Roxanne Roberts in the *Washington Post* advised future university presidents to forgo any "lifestyles of the rich-and-famous" profiles while embroiled in heated contract negotiations with custodians.[20] Meanwhile, coalition members upped their efforts, staging a major hunger strike in March 2006 that extended for several weeks.

Shalala had hoped to stay above the fray by taking a laissez-faire approach to the dispute, arguing as other universities had that she bore no direct responsibility for the pay or labor conditions experienced by these workers because they were not UM employees. But with a highly publicized trip to Haiti fast approaching, designed to tout the efforts of a UM medical program to improve the health care system of the struggling island nation, Shalala did not want the janitors' strike to overshadow her efforts. Thus she quickly abandoned her refusal to engage directly in negotiations and helped to settle the strike in a few short weeks, securing a raise and better health care benefits for all of the university's service workers before any more bad publicity could negatively impact the university.[21]

Watched closely by other schools, both in Florida and across the nation, the action had an important effect. Actions followed at other universities, including a particularly well publicized hunger strike led by a student/worker alliance group at Harvard.[22] But perhaps the most important impact of these organizing efforts was the positive future it seems to indicate for organizing in the U.S. South. As Bruce Nissen, director of Florida International University's Center for Labor Research and Studies, recently told the *Herald Tribune:* "Previously national unions had pretty much written off Florida, thinking it was unwinnable. But now, Florida and a few other places are being used as a testing ground—to see if organizing can be done in the South."[23] In a state renowned for its right-to-work legislation, where labor organizing has traditionally been weaker than in other states because it has been tougher for unions to gain a toehold, this trend also represents an important reversal of long-standing union strategies. Rather than concentrating their organizing efforts in states where unions are already strong, labor activists are now focusing on national companies where unionized employees in other states are already better paid than unorganized Florida workers. So far, this approach seems to be enjoying a great deal of success.

Like the actions by the CIW, another part of what made the Change to Win action so effective was the way it melded action by organized labor with a broad base of community support. While hunger strikes were taking place at the university, organizers established a "Freedom Village" under the tracks of Miami's Metrorail, where strikers and their supporters met with the press and the public, becoming a visible presence in the city center as well as on UM's campus. Emphasizing the extent to which the janitors' case was a human rights issue also attracted social activists from across the Miami community. Tanya Aquino, who was a student at UM during the strikes and later joined SEIU Local 11 as communications director, explained that student activists like herself were conscious of the CIW's earlier actions and saw this as an excellent model for learning effective organizational and public relations strategies. Connections with campus groups like Students Toward a New Democracy as well as local pastors and civil rights organizations like the Southern Christian Leadership Conference also helped mobilize effective support for the action, both on and off campus.[24]

Not all of the Change to Win coalition's efforts have met with such sweeping success, however. While negotiations at UM were continuing, Change to Win expanded its efforts to Nova Southeastern University in Broward County, just north of Miami-Dade County. Protests were kicked off in November 2006 with a series of Janitors for a Day activities where local politicians, clergy, and activists took up brooms, mops, and landscaping tools, laboring alongside Nova's workers to raise awareness about the conditions workers faced. Like UM, Nova outsourced most of their cleaning and maintenance jobs to UNICCO. As at UM, Nova's cleaning staff also voted favorably to unionize. Rather than negotiate for higher wages and benefits for Nova workers, university president Ray Ferrero Jr. chose a much different path: he terminated Nova's contract with UNICCO and split the jobs among four companies, voiding the union election. Those who were employed with UNICCO had to reapply to whichever of the four new companies took over their positions just to maintain their existing jobs. Many who had voted in favor of unionizing were not rehired. In one case, a Haitian janitor who had lost her job in the course of the labor dispute at Nova was forced to take a job picking tomatoes. When she died of a heart attack on the job in Virginia six months later, her death prompted tremendous outcry from a range of organizations including Haitian Women of Miami, who raised money for her funeral.[25]

Soon after Ferrero implemented these new "cost-saving" measures, as he described them, Broward County's Urban League honored him as a "Diversity Champion" at a local event. As at UM, the bulk of the employees who were paid the least and had the greatest at stake in these efforts were Haitian and Latino.[26] Editorials in the *Miami Herald* and *Sun Sentinel* questioned the merits of the Urban League's choice for the award. Local clergy and civil rights activists held a demonstration in front of the ceremony while pastors invited to the event staged a walkout during Ferrero's speech. Ferrero continued undeterred, arguing that the "restructuring" which he instituted at Nova was in everyone's best interests.[27]

The demographics of Nova's students and faculty also differed in important ways from those at UM. Nova is a university that targets nontraditional students, most of whom are employed full-time while furthering their education. From the perspective of the SEIU, one of the lead unions in both the UM and Nova actions, this meant that the students spent less time on campus and thus did not have the same network of socially conscious organizations to tap into. Without these same networks, the Change to Win organizers had to rely on UM students who were able to travel north to Broward once they realized that local student protestors were unlikely. Aquino also noted that the administration at Nova successfully thwarted their efforts at informing and organizing Nova students by blocking e-mail that originated from the SEIU server and warning activists that they would be arrested if they protested on campus.[28]

Many community groups rallied to support the Nova workers, including the Haitian Women of Miami and the Haitian Emmanuel Baptist Church. But they did not receive the same attention from the national media as was afforded to the UM action. Timothy S. Smiley, pastor of the Plantation United Methodist Church, lamented that even though Ferrero and Nova's board of trustees were weary of bad publicity, protestors' actions could not seem to bring any national attention to the plight of the workers.[29] Nor did they garner the same sympathy from the local press as the UM actions. One *Miami Herald* article, for example, described organizers' strategy as "overcooked theatrics," arguing that the labor movement had become "as off-putting as its underpaid workers are sympathetic."[30] In other cases, the actions garnered little or no press coverage at all. Where the UM action brought results rather quickly, Nova administrators continued to thwart the coalition for well over a year.

Meanwhile, the SEIU took the lead in another series of demonstrations showcasing the disparity between rich and poor across the city of Miami. When the city hosted the Super Bowl in early 2007, the union partnered with the Miami Workers Center and Power U Center for Social Change, two Miami-based social justice organizations, to offer journalists the opportunity to take what they called a "reality bus tour" of the city's richest and poorest neighborhoods.[31] In addition to seeing the Umoja Village shantytown in Liberty City and meeting with displaced residents and low-wage service workers, the tour ended on Fisher Island, a small key in Biscayne Bay, located between the city of Miami and Miami Beach.

According to the U.S. Bureau of the Census—numbers published broadly by the SEIU Local 11's Research Department—Fisher Island boasts the highest per capita income of any community in the United States. The average net worth of each adult resident on the island is estimated at $10 million.[32] Equally striking, the island's motto, "Live like the Vanderbilts . . . only better," crafted by the island's primary real estate developer to inspire the very rich to move there, only underscored the posh excesses of this community's lifestyle.[33] Accessible only by ferry, private seaplane, or helicopter, Fisher Island's exclusivity contributes to this vision of wealth and inaccessibility to all but a fortunate few.

Maintaining this fantasy, however, requires a mass amount of labor. Thus the SEIU adopted a tactic both they and the Change to Win coalition had employed with great success in earlier demonstrations. Countering arguments that outsourcing made owners, managers, and CEOs immune from responsibility for their subcontractors' choices, labor activists pressed Fisher Island residents to take responsibility for the wages and living conditions of the maids, groundskeepers, maintenance workers, and security guards who make their luxurious lives possible. As Stephen Lerner, a member of the national SEIU staff and leader of the Justice for Janitors, told the *New York Times*, "This is the way the rich are protecting themselves against the unpleasantness growing just outside their walls. But in the end what they want is unsustainable."[34]

In June 2007, the *New York Times Magazine* published a full-length feature on the struggle to organize and gain better pay for Fisher Island's workers. Shortly after the feature was published, researchers for the SEIU publicized another fact about the island: despite having the highest concentration of wealth of any community in the nation, owners regularly used the Miami-Dade Value Adjustment Board to lower their property values. Using data obtained from the Board, the union published a report highlighting exactly how Fisher Island's owners obtained these exemptions, arguing that when owners used these exemptions they were essentially robbing the county's coffers of funds that could go to support schools, nursing homes, and essential services like the fire and police departments.[35] Although attorneys for the owners countered that the union had inflated the total cuts to these property values ($965 million from 2002 to 2005 according to the union versus $52 million according to the owners' attorney), the numbers were still staggering. Published via the Internet, the report was widely disseminated and picked up by news agencies across the country as well as internationally.[36] The union then brought similar pressure to bear upon Nova, publishing their sources of government funding and a list of companies providing student loans, pressing these public and private agencies to support the rights of workers at the university.

While Fisher Island showcased the glaring disparity between rich and poor, Disney World's meticulously projected public facade and the real-life faces of its low-level service employees provided another important opening for Florida labor activists. Disney's workers are represented by the Service Trades Council Union (STCU) of Orlando, a coalition of six unions including the International Alliance of Theatrical Stage Employees (IATSE), UFCW, HERE, IBT, and the Transportation Communications International Union. Together, they represent just about every level of service employee from the "cast members," who serve as the company's public face and dress up like the various cartoon characters who have made Disney famous, to custodians, valets, bellhops, and bus drivers. In late 2006, the Disney Corporation began to outsource some of its night-shift cleaning jobs, using contractors like Hotel Cleaning Services of Phoenix, who advertised that they could do the same work cheaper since their nonunionized workforce was paid less and did not receive any benefits.[37] Disney then shifted their in-house cleaners entirely to daytime work. Many workers were outraged because the change in shift forced them to quit. UNITE-HERE, who represented the bulk of the affected workers, argued that this decision was but one step in the direction of outsourcing, which many employees worried would soon affect the entire in-house workforce. In a play on Disney's motto, "Dreams Do Come True," UNITE-HERE launched its own "Dreams

Don't Come True" campaign to shed light on the low wages and benefits paid to Disney's predominantly immigrant and nonwhite cleaning and maintenance staff.[38]

Disney is, in many ways, the classic company town. As a result, it presented several challenges for organizers. Isolated from the larger community of Orlando, Disney's vast size and self-contained resources made it a different kind of organizing venture than others that were rooted in the middle of urban communities or even small towns.[39] Although UNITE-HERE raised issues of poverty, health care, and the human costs of outsourcing, it proved more difficult for organizers to partner with a broad spectrum of community activists and organizations as coalitions like Change to Win or the Justice for Janitors campaign had done elsewhere. And unlike the CIW, which faced even greater obstacles due to the extreme isolation of Immokalee's workforce, UNITE-HERE never managed to amass the same groundswell of public support or to play on social and political networks that united workers outside the workplace at Disney.[40]

By spring 2007, the STCU had negotiated a new contract with Disney. It was approved by all member unions with the exception of the IBT. For the Teamsters, wages proved the sticking point, and they wanted to hold out to secure better raises for those at the top of their pay scale as well as those at the bottom. The Teamsters also objected to increases in the cost of health care. Throughout the summer, talks remained at an impasse. The Teamsters accused Disney of contracting with a transportation company to drive employee shuttles to the union election site, thus preventing union drivers from influencing their colleagues in the SCTU. Despite ongoing advocacy by UNITE-HERE activists who argued that signing the contract was in the best interests of all concerned, particularly those most vulnerable employees at the lowest end of the company's pay scale, they could not bridge the divide with the Teamsters until September 2007, when a majority of union members finally approved the new contract.[41]

Exploring the Past to Learn for the Future

These are just a few of the important labor activities that have taken place across the state over the past several years. Florida has become the site of a major drive to organize health care workers. At Wal-Mart, one of the nation's most notoriously anti-union companies, over one hundred of its Florida workers walked off the job in 2006–2007, organized by a coalition called the Wal-Mart Workers Association. There are many more examples.

Where manufacturing jobs have increasingly moved offshore, there seems to be a growing recognition that service work is here to stay and that workers in these critical fields deserve a good wage, financial security, and the right to a high quality of life.

This sampling of recent events gives a taste of the type of broad-based social movement coalitions that seem to be breathing new life into the contemporary labor movement, as well as the limitations of organizations who are either unwilling or unable to bridge these divides. Social infrastructure is critical, too, as SEIU Florida Healthcare Union president Monica Russo and Bruce Nissen have argued. Without a well-developed infrastructure in the form of leadership development, civic participation, and research to uncover, verify, and validate the concerns raised by community groups, movements cannot proceed beyond consciousness-raising to real social change.[42]

It is at this intersection that academic institutions and scholars themselves are poised to play an important role. Today, Florida is a center of new labor activism not only because of the will of its working classes but also because of the growing appreciation that labor is a community concern. Florida has always been a working state. By uncovering the richness of the state's labor history, which has too often been ignored—that preserved in the archaeological record, new voices uncovered in texts not typically associated with more institutionally based studies, non-English-language sources, and smaller repositories as well as large, looking beyond the narrow boundaries of the state and nation-state to more fully capture the experience of its moving people—scholars begin to uncover the experiences of Florida's working classes, both past and present, and may help to shape its future.

*   *   *

The editors would like to thank Tanya Aquino, Renee Asher, and Eric Brakken of SEIU Local 11, Frank Kubicki of SEIU Local 362, Rev. Timothy S. Smiley of Plantation United Methodist Church, and Morty Miller of UNITE-HERE Local 362 for answering our questions and talking about their experiences.

Notes

1. National Urban League, Policy Institute, "Poverty Concentrated Poverty and Urban Areas," May 19, 2006; U.S. Bureau of the Census, Current Population Reports, series P60-189, *Income, Poverty, and Valuation of Non-Cash Benefits: 1994* (Washington,

D.C.: Government Printing Office, 1996); U.S. Census Bureau, American Community Survey: 2003, Miami PMSA, Table 3: Selected Economic Characteristics. Poverty estimates vary depending on how measure is set. In four of the tracts within Miami City, poverty rates are close to 50 percent. For the PMSA, however, the most recent estimates place 18.4 percent of individuals below the federal poverty statute.

2. On ranking of poorest big cities and counties in America, see U.S. Census Bureau. For current and historic poverty estimates by race and family type, see U.S. Bureau of the Census, Historical Poverty Tables, Table 4: Poverty Status, by Type of Family, Presence of Related Children, Race, and Hispanic Origin (Washington, D.C.: U.S. Census Bureau, Housing and Household Economic Statistics Division, 2006). On poverty and underemployment, see Gordon F. DeJong and Anna B. Madamba, "A Double Disadvantage? Minority Group, Immigrant Status, and Underemployment in the United States," *Social Science Quarterly* 82 (March 2001): 117–30; Leif Jensen and Tim Slack, "Underemployment in America: Measurement and Evidence," *American Journal of Community Psychology* 32 (September 2003): 21–31.

3. On the revitalization of the American labor movement, see Dan Clawson and Mary Ann Clawson, "What Has Happened to the U.S. Labor Movement?" *Annual Review of Sociology* 25 (August 1999): 95–119; Richard Hurd, Ruth Milkman, and Lowell Turner, "Reviving the American Labour Movement: Institutions and Mobilization," *European Journal of Industrial Relations* 9 (Winter 2003): 99–117; Kim Voss and Rachel Sherman, "Breaking the Iron Law of Oligarchy: Union Revitalization in the American Labor Movement," *American Journal of Sociology* 106 (2000): 303–49. This transformation has also been described as the need to change both the structure of unions and the need to reconstruct political institutions themselves. For a well-articulated argument on each, see Stephen Lerner, "Reviving Unions," *Boston Review* 21 (April/May 1996): 3–12; Adam Przeworski, "A Better Democracy, a Better Economy," *Boston Review* 21 (April/May 1996): 13–24.

4. The literature on the restructuring of the AFL-CIO and social movement strategy is vast. Selected works include Bruce Nissen, ed., *Unions in a Globalized Environment: Changing Borders, Organizational Boundaries, and Social Roles* (Armonk, N.Y.: M. E. Sharpe, 2002); Lowell Turner, Harry C. Katz, and Richard W. Hurd, eds., *Rekindling the Movement: Labor's Quest for Relevance in the Twenty-first Century* (Ithaca, N.Y.: Cornell University Press, 2001). For a more critical portrayal of this transformation, see Daisy Rooks, "The Cowboy Mentality: Organizers and Occupational Commitment in the New Labor Movement," *Labor Studies Journal* 28, no. 3 (2003): 33–62. UNITE-HERE and the SEIU left the AFL-CIO in 2005, followed by the UFWA in 2006.

5. John Bowe, *Nobodies: Modern American Slave Labor and the Dark Side of the New Global Economy* (New York: Random House, 2007), 12–13, 22–33, 43, 61–64.

6. "About CIW: Consciousness + Commitment = Change: How and Why We Are Organizing . . . ," Coalition of Immokalee Workers Online Headquarters, www.ciw-online.org/about.html.

7. Press release, "Coalition of Immokalee Workers, Taco Bell Reach Groundbreaking Agreement," March 8, 2005.

8. Nano Riley, *Florida's Farmworkers in the Twenty-first Century* (Gainesville: University Press of Florida, 2002), 60; Elly Leary, "Immokalee Workers Take Down Taco

Bell," *Monthly Review* 57 (October 2005): 11–25; *St. Petersburg Times*, March 5, 2006; *Guardian* (Manchester, U.K.), April 11, 2007; *New Standard* (New York), April 19, 2007; *Palm Beach Post* (West Palm Beach), September 5, 2007.

9. *Sarasota Herald-Tribune*, February 19, 2000; *Bradenton Herald*, February 25, 2000; *Miami Herald*, May 9, 2000; *Palm Beach Post*, March 21, 2000.

10. Student Farmworker Alliance, www.sfalliance.org/about.html; *Naples News*, September 1, 2007.

11. *Naples News*, September 1, 2007.

12. E. Leary, "Immokalee Workers," 11–25; Minnesota AFL-CIO, "Workday Minnesota," September 8, 2007, www.workdayminnesota.org; *St. Petersburg Times*, March 5, 2006; *Catholic News Service*, January 17, 2007; AFL-CIO Weblog, "AFL-CIO Union Movement and Farm Workers Fight Modern Day Slavery," April 24, 2006, http://blog.aflcio.org.

13. On the Zapatistas and *Zapatísmo*, see Mark T. Berger, "Romancing the Zapatistas: International Intellectuals and the Chiapas Rebellion," *Latin American Perspectives* 28 (March 2001): 149–70; George Allen Collier and Elizabeth Lowery Quaratiello, *Basta! Land and the Zapatista Rebellion in Chiapas*, 3d ed. (Oakland, Calif.: Food First Books, 2005); Neil Harvey, *The Chiapas Rebellion: The Struggle for Land and Democracy* (Durham, N.C.: Duke University Press, 1998); Bill Weinberg, *Homage to Chiapas* (New York: Verso, 2000). Like the CIW, the Zapatistas have become particularly adept at adapting new technologies to use in political organizing. See Harry M. Cleaver Jr., "The Zapatista Effect: The Internet and the Rise of an Alternative Political Fabric," *Journal of International Affairs* 51 (1998): 621–41; Oliver Froehling, "The Cyberspace 'War of Ink and Internet' in Chiapas, Mexico," *Geographical Review* 87 (April 1997): 291–307.

14. E. Leary, "Immokalee Workers," 11–25; Zapagringo, *Anarkismo*, "Zapatismo vs. McDonald's," February 21, 2007, www.anarkismo.net/index.php; Movimento dos Trabalhadores Rurais Sem Terra, www.mstbrazil.org.

15. "Hundreds of Thousands March for Immigrant Rights," *CNN News*, May 3, 2006; "May Day: The Fight behind the Protest," *Business Week*, May 1, 2006; *Sarasota Herald-Tribune*, May 1 and 3, 2006; *Orlando Sentinel*, April 30, 2006.

16. For a comprehensive review of the literature on labor-community coalitions and the strengths and limits of this organizing approach in Florida, see Bruce Nissen, "The Effectiveness and Limits of Labor-Community Coalitions: Evidence from South Florida," *Labor Studies Journal* 29 (Spring 2004): 67–89. On new directions in organizing more generally, see Bruce Nissen, "Alternative Strategic Directions for the U.S. Labor Movement: Recent Scholarship," *Labor Studies Journal* 28 (Spring 2003): 133–55.

17. On the Justice for Janitors campaign, see Preston Rudy, "'Justice for Janitors,' Not 'Compensation for Custodians': The Political Context and Organizing in San Jose and Sacramento," in *Rebuilding Labor: Organizing and Organizers*, ed. Ruth Milkman and Kim Voss (Ithaca, N.Y.: Cornell University Press, 2004), 133–49; Lydia Savage, "Justice for Janitors: Scales of Organizing and Representing Workers," *Antipode* 38, no. 3 (2006): 645–66.

18. Since 2006, Florida has maintained a separate minimum wage for all employees in the state. It was approved as a state constitutional amendment in November 2004,

and put into effect September 1, 2006, and was $.82 higher than the federal minimum of $5.85. See Florida Statutes, State Minimum Wage, 448.110 (Tallahassee: Florida State Senate, 2007).

19. Tennessee State University barely beat out UM for the bottom spot. See Martin Van Der Werf, "How Much Should Colleges Pay Their Janitors?" *Chronicle of Higher Education,* August 3, 2001, 8–12.

20. *Ft. Lauderdale Sun Sentinel*, March 1, 2006; *Washington Post*, February 22, 2006. On federal poverty guidelines, see *Federal Register* 71, no. 15 (January 2006): 3848–49. Original profile on Shalala in *New York Times Magazine*, February 12, 2006. On response to profile, see *New York Times Magazine*, February 26, 2006.

21. *Orlando Sentinel*, April 30, 2006; *Knight Ridder Tribune Business News* (Washington, D.C.), March 11, 17, 2006; Andrew Mytelka, "Janitor Strike at U. of Miami Ends in Deal between Union and Outside Company," *Chronicle of Higher Education*, May 2, 2006. Beginning janitor salaries went from $6.40 an hour (state minimum wage at the time) to $8.55 an hour, landscapers received $9.30 an hour, and food-service employees received $8 an hour. All contracted companies that UM employed had to offer health care to their employees, and the SEIU was recognized as the union of the employees through a card-check process.

22. Carlos Suárez-Boulangger, "Hunger Strike at Harvard," *Z Magazine*, July/August 2007; *Crimson*, May 10, 2007. In December 2006, students at Purdue University also staged a hunger strike to demand that the university no longer patronize vendors to force workers into sweatshop conditions.

23. *Herald Tribune*, January 15, 2007. Nissen's scholarship on organizing in Florida remains some of the most extensive work on the contemporary labor movement across the state. See especially Guillermo Grenier and Bruce Nissen, "Comparative Union Responses to Mass Immigration: Evidence from an Immigrant City," *Critical Sociology* 26 (Winter 2001): 82–105; Bruce Nissen and Guillermo Grenier, "Union Responses to Mass Immigration: The Case of Miami, USA," in *Place, Space, and the New Labour Internationalisms*, ed. Peter Waterman and Jane Wills (Malden, Mass.: Blackwell, 2001), 263–88; Bruce Nissen, "The Effectiveness and Limits of Labor-Community Coalitions: Evidence from South Florida," *Labor Studies Journal* 29 (Spring 2004): 67–89.

24. Tanya Aquino, telephone interview with Robert Cassanello, September 20, 2007; *Orlando Sentinel*, April 30, 2006; South Florida Interfaith Worker Justice, "About Us," www.sfiwj.org/SFIWJ_about_us.html. See also *Miami Herald*, October 21, 2006.

25. *Miami Herald*, September 19, 29, 2007; *Sun Sentinel*, September 21, 2007. See also *Miami Herald*, February 23, 2007; *Sun Sentinel*, October 3, 2007.

26. Membership demographics kindly provided by Eric Brakken, SEIU 11, correspondence with Melanie Shell-Weiss, September 24, 2007. The union estimates that its current membership is mostly Latino, with a minority being Haitian and a small number of African American workers as well. Within current organizing projects workers are roughly half Latino and half Haitian with a significant number of African American security guards at the various property sites.

27. *Knight Ridder Tribune Business News*, March 22, 2006; *Miami Herald*, October 21, 2006; *Sun Sentinel*, March 11, 2007.

28. T. Aquino, interview; Renee Asher, telephone interview with Robert Cassanello, September 20, 2007.

29. Timothy S. Smiley, telephone interview with Robert Cassanello, October 4, 2007.

30. "Civil Liberties Swept under Rug by NSU," *Miami Herald*, May 10, 2007.

31. *El Nuevo Herald*, January 16, 2007; *Forbes*, January 24, 2007; *Orlando Sentinel*, January 28, 2007; *New York Times*, February 1, 2007.

32. According to the U.S. Census, average per capita income was $236,238 in 1999 compared to $21,587 nationwide. See U.S. Census, *Fact Sheet: 2000 Census of Population*, Fisher Island CDP, Fla.

33. Advertisement, Fisher Island Reality Corp., 2006.

34. *New York Times Magazine*, June 10, 2007. See also *Miami Herald*, May 10, 2007.

35. SEIU Local 11, "Fisher Island: Rich Play, Poor Pay: How Rich Fisher Island Residents Challenge Property Tax Assessments for Big Breaks, While Miami-Dade's Poor Can't Afford to Pay to Play," June 12, 2007, www.seiu11.org/docUploads/FisherIsland. pdf.

36. On response to the SEIU report, see *Miami Herald*, August 8, 2007.

37. Hotel Cleaning Services of Phoenix, "About Us," www.hotelcleaningservices. com. Shortly after the UNITE-HERE protest, the company removed this information from their Web site.

38. Mike Budd and Max H. Kirsch, *Rethinking Disney: Private Control, Public Dimensions* (Lebanon, N.H.: Wesleyan University Press, 2005), 2–13; Robert J. Liubicic, "Corporate Codes of Conduct and Product Labeling Schemes: The Limits and Possibilities of Promoting International Labor Rights through Private Initiatives," *Law and Policy in International Business* 30 (Fall 1998): 111–58.

39. Organizing at Disney World has a long history, dating back to its building in the mid-twentieth century. On Disney's development and political economy, see Stephen M. Fjellman, *Vinyl Leaves: Walt Disney World and America* (Boulder: Westview Press, 1992); Richard Fogelsong, *Married to the Mouse: Walt Disney World and Orlando* (New Haven: Yale University Press, 2001); Peter Schweizer and Rochelle Schweizer, *Disney: The Mouse Betrayed: Greed, Corruption, and Children at Risk* (Washington, D.C.: Regnery, 1998).

40. On the current demonstrations and protests, see *Orlando Sentinel*, December 8, 2006; UNITE HERE Local 362, "We Are Disney: An Exposé on the Condition of Service Workers at Walt Disney World," http://wearedisney.info.

41. *Orlando Business Journal*, March 19, 2007; *Orlando Sentinel*, May 18, 19, 2007; Morty Miller, telephone interview with Robert Cassanello, October 12, 2007.

42. Bruce Nissen and Monica Russo, "Building a Movement: Revitalizing Labor in Miami," *WorkingUSA: The Journal of Labor and Society* 9 (March 2006): 135–37.

Editors

Robert Cassanello is an assistant professor of history at the University of Central Florida and specializes in American social history.

Melanie Shell-Weiss is a visiting assistant professor of history at the Johns Hopkins University and specializes in labor, immigration, and race relations in the United States and the Caribbean.

Contributors

Edward E. Baptist, winner of the 2003 Rembert Patrick Best Book in Florida History Award, is an associate professor of history at Cornell University.

Thomas A. Castillo is the 2004 winner of the Thompson Award for best article in Florida history published in the *Florida Historical Quarterly* and is a PhD candidate in the Department of History at the University of Maryland, College Park.

Cindy Hahamovitch teaches labor and immigration history at the College of William and Mary, where she is an associate professor.

Alex Lichtenstein is an associate professor of history at Florida International University and specializes in the history of the U.S. South, labor, and comparative race relations.

Mark Long is an instructor of history at the University of Central Florida where he teaches courses in modern U.S. history, the American South, and American frontier history.

Tamara Spike is an assistant professor of history at North Georgia College and State University. She specializes in colonial Latin American and Native American history.

Brent R. Weisman received the 2006 Rembert Patrick Best Book in Florida History award. He is a professor of anthropology and associate dean of the Graduate School at the University of South Florida.

Index

Page numbers in italic type indicate illustrations.